The Wars of Truth

THE
WARS *of* TRUTH

STUDIES IN THE DECAY OF CHRISTIAN
HUMANISM IN THE EARLIER
SEVENTEENTH CENTURY

HERSCHEL BAKER

Wipf & Stock
PUBLISHERS
Eugene, Oregon

Wipf and Stock Publishers
199 W 8th Ave, Suite 3
Eugene, OR 97401

The Wars of Truth
Studies in the Decay of Christian Humanism in the Earlier
Seventeenth Century
By Baker, Herschel C.
ISBN: 1-59752-890-0
Publication date 9/22/2006
Previously published by Harvard University Press, 1952

For Barbara

When a man hath been laboring the hardest labor in the deep mines of knowledge, hath furnished out his findings in all their equipage, drawn forth his reasons as it were a battle ranged, scattered and defeated all objections in his way, calls out his adversary into the plain, offers him the advantage of wind and sun, if he please; only that he may try the matter by dint of argument, for his opponents then to skulk, to lay ambushments, to keep a narrow bridge of licensing where the challenger should pass, though it be valor enough in soldiership, is but weakness and cowardice in the wars of Truth.

JOHN MILTON, *Areopagitica*

PREFACE

WITH THIS BOOK I bring to a close the studies begun in *The Dignity of Man*. Since the present work is a thematic and chronological extension of, if not precisely a sequel to, its predecessor, a common title might have served for both; however, here my subject is the deterioration, or at least the radical mutation, of the idea whose development I earlier tried to trace. More specifically, I am here concerned with the traditional and the emerging concepts of 'truth' – theological, scientific, political, and other – whose collision generated such heat and even such light in the age of Milton. I have tried to describe, at least in broad terms, the meshing of those inherited and newly formulated values which in my judgment gives the period its peculiar poignancy and relevance for the modern world. Between the birth and death of Milton English thought underwent a transformation whose consequences we perhaps do not fully understand even now. Yet in attempting to seek out the origins of this transformation in the early Renaissance and to sketch its progress through the earlier seventeenth century I have sought to indicate the intellectual and emotional pressures which shaped men's conception of 'truth' and of their capacity to attain it, and to suggest some of the consequences for literature.

In an effort to keep the bibliographical apparatus at a minimum I have, except in rare instances, confined my references to the primary sources. To anyone who has worked in the period, however, my debts to many scholars will be sufficiently plain. The quality of much of the scholarship relating to the late Renaissance is uncommonly high, and from much of it I have learned more than I could adequately acknowledge in footnotes. Douglas Bush has put us all in his debt with his recent survey (and bibliography) of the period, and his researches, together with those of Messrs Haller, Willey, Jordan, Clark, Woodhouse, Miller, Jones, Davies, and many others – to say nothing of such of their predecessors as Tulloch and the estimable Gardiner – have in various ways shaped my thinking about the earlier seventeenth century. I hope that this general acknowledgment will serve to record my large debt to their work. A grant from the Administrative Committee of the Harvard Foundation for Advanced Study and Research greatly facilitated the final stages of this work. As always, my colleagues Hyder Rollins and Douglas Bush have been generous beyond the call of duty with erudition and encouragement, and their patient, learned scrutiny of my manuscript has saved me from many blunders; those that remain are, of course, my own. Finally, the dedication can only record, but not express, my gratitude to one who for many years has sustained my labors and mopped my brow.

H. B.

DUNSTER HOUSE
HARVARD UNIVERSITY
June 15th, 1951

CONTENTS

I. THE STRENGTH OF TRADITION
 I. *The Habit of Authority*   Page   1
 II. *The Axiom of Knowledge*   4
 III. *The Anthropomorphic God*   6
 IV. *The Doctrine of Providence*   12
 V. *Heights and Declensions: the Estate of Man*   25

II. DEATH AND TIME
 I. *De contemptu mundi*   43
 II. *The Literature of Disenchantment*   50
 III. *The Great Threnodists*   56
 IV. *Corroding Time*   65
 V. *The Idea of Progress*   78

III. THE USES OF REASON
 I. *The General and Perpetual Voice of Men*   90
 II. *Ramean Logic*   98
 III. *Neo-Stoicism*   110
 IV. *Natural Theology*   116
 V. *The Cambridge Platonists*   124
 VI. *Milton*   131

IV. THE ATTACK ON AUTHORITY
 I. *Ockham*   135
 II. *Renaissance Skepticism*   144
 III. *Custom and Error*   154
 IV. *Nature and Grace*   162
 V. *Bacon*   169
 VI. *Anti-scholasticism*   173

CONTENTS

V. ANGLICAN AND PURITAN

I. 'The Bible Only'	Page 187
II. The via media	194
III. The Puritan Dissent	203
IV. Disputandi pruritus ecclesiarum scabies	215
V. Anglican Rationalism	220
VI. The Flight from Reason	226
VII. Hobbes: The Secular Argument	238

VI. CHURCH AND STATE

I. Jus Divinum	246
II. Civil Disobedience	259
III. Natural Sanctions	267
IV. Puritanism and Liberty	276
V. The Two Covenants	291

VII. THE CONQUEST OF NATURE

I. The Reconstruction of Knowledge	303
II. The Knowledge of Nature	309
III. The Baconian Legacy	323
IV. Nature as Mechanism	331
V. The Restoration Dilemma	347
VI. Mechanism vs. Experiment	354

BIBLIOGRAPHY	367
INDEX	373

A BIBLIOGRAPHICAL NOTE

The following abbreviations and short titles have been used throughout the notes:

AL	Francis Bacon, *The Advancement of Learning*
Anatomy	Robert Burton, *The Anatomy of Melancholy*
ELH	*English Literary History*
Essay	John Locke, *An Essay Concerning Human Understanding*
Fuller	Thomas Fuller, *The Church History of Britain*
Haller	William Haller (ed.), *Tracts on Liberty in the Puritan Revolution 1638–47*
History	Sir Walter Ralegh, *The History of the World*
JHI	*Journal of the History of Ideas*
Laws	Richard Hooker, *Of the Laws of Ecclesiastical Polity*
Migne, PL	*Patrologiae cursus completus, series Latina*
Miller-Johnson	Perry Miller and Thomas Johnson (edd.), *The Puritans*
MP	*Modern Philology*
NO	Francis Bacon, *Novum Organum*
PL	John Milton, *Paradise Lost*
PMLA	*Publications of the Modern Language Association of America*
PR	John Milton, *Paradise Regained*
PW	John Milton, *The Prose Works*
RP	Ernst Cassirer, Paul Oskar Kristeller, John Herman Randall, Jr. (edd.), *The Renaissance Philosophy of Man*
SP	*Studies in Philology*
ST	St Thomas Aquinas, *Summa Theologica*
Wild	John Wild (ed.), *Spinoza Selections*
Woodhouse	A. S. P. Woodhouse (ed.), *Puritanism and Liberty: Being the Army Debates (1647–9) from the Clarke Manuscripts with Supplementary Documents*

In the interest of readability, titles mentioned in the text have been modernized (e.g. Hakewill's *Apology*) even though the original spelling has been retained in the notes (e.g. Hakewill's *Apologie*). Quotations have been transcribed as accurately as human frailty permits, with the exception that italics have been eliminated and the orthography of *i, j, u,* and *vv* have been brought into conformity with modern usage.

Foreign titles have been rendered in the conventional form (e.g. Althusius' *Politica methodice digesta,* Busson's *Les Sources et le développement du rationalisme*) except when they serve for English works (e.g. Browne's *Religio Medici,* Taylor's *Ductor Dubitantium*).

I

THE STRENGTH OF TRADITION

1. THE HABIT OF AUTHORITY

The more we study the Renaissance the more we come to understand its fundamental conservatism. For all its vitality and its impatience with this or that vested authority, it was never willing or able to push its exuberant discontent to the limits of iconoclasm. In the long view of intellectual history it was an age bent on exploiting and refining its inherited values, but curiously unproductive of new ideas. Almost in spite of itself it was compelled to deal practically with urgent political and social developments which it seemed unable to accept intellectually. In the age of the Tudors and the Valois and the Hapsburgs, Sir Thomas Elyot and Erasmus could still prescribe wistfully the proper education for Christian princes. Machiavelli so outraged men of all political persuasions that not until the Renaissance was nearly over did Bodin dare to defend the sovereign state which had been a *fait accompli* for generations. In an age of ruthlessly competitive capitalism Thomas Wilson and many others were repeating the medieval strictures on 'usury'. In an age when the fissure between faith and reason was growing ominously wide the Catholic Church – grown sleek, soft, and worldly – at the Council of Trent barricaded itself behind the wall of Thomism, while the Augustinian reformers launched a frontal attack on the most advanced elements of contemporary thought.

Yet for all this, the centuries between Petrarch and Hooker demonstrate a passion for scrutiny and revaluation that, though never eventuating in any genuine reconstructions, was an indispensable legacy for the age of Bacon, Hobbes, and Descartes. They were centuries of an incessant intellectual effort that reveals itself everywhere: in the cordial vilification of scholasticism, in the anticlericalism of Erasmus and Rabelais, in the prodigious antiquarian efforts of the humanists ferreting out relics of *bonae literae*. But for the most part this activity was contained within the limits of inherited thought and values. For all their mighty efforts the men of the Renaissance were cautious and reverent of authority. They initiated those lines of critical, skeptical, and secular thought which converged in the seventeenth century to make possible a revaluation of man and his place in nature; but they could never quite disengage themselves from their inherited assumptions. Indeed, they rarely even examined them. Although the habit of authority was too strong to permit them the kind of audacity endemic in the seventeenth century, it was not strong enough to check the spirit of quest and enterprise. It is the note we hear so often in the din of Gabriel Harvey's *Marginalia*, where novelty and activity seem to enchant even a second-string pedant (and literary authoritarian).

> Statim properandum a potentia in actum; et semper ab actu in actum incessanter. . . . The praesent tense only in effect to be regardid. . . . Industry, is ye fift Element: & Confidence, ye life & vigour of all five. . . . Il pensare non importa, ma il fare. Resolutely for intent: lustily for act; mightily for effect.[1]

This almost boyish vitality informs some of the most characteristic products of the Renaissance – the incredible exploits of Jenkinson and Hawkins, the bewildering fertility of Ariosto and Spenser, the rich but untidy prose of Nashe and Greene – but only toward the turn of the seventeenth century does it become conscious and purposeful; for then it begins to find a goal, or several goals, in reform and reconstruction.

Although a tonic critical impulse was one of the glories of Renaissance thought, its main effort was to strengthen and purify rather than break with tradition. In spite of its yeasty ferment, the Renaissance generally sought to preserve inherited values rather than formulate new ones. Erasmus, a conservative if one ever lived, bent his critical and exegetical labors toward a purified language no less than a purified religion. Luther stumbled into the Reformation, and on to the stage of history, through his zeal for reforming ecclesiastical abuses; but for his theology he resuscitated Augustine, and he hysterically denounced the social leveling that he had unwittingly fostered. Copernicus contrived his hypothesis in order to correct some of the inconsistencies of Ptolemaic astronomy. Pomponazzi skirted the fringes of heresy through his efforts to restore a purer reading of Aristotle – only to retreat behind the doctrine of the double truth. Agrippa and

[1] *Marginalia*, pp. 149, 151, 153, 193.

THE HABIT OF AUTHORITY

Montaigne had raised skepticism to something like an epistemological absolute, yet in one it led to the mumbo-jumbo of occultism and in the other to a fideism that even the Catholic Church was compelled to reject. The endless citations from Hippocrates and Celsus, Galen and Dioscorides and Pliny, show that even in medicine such conservatives as Linacre, Elyot, Boorde, and Wright lacked Paracelsus' courage to burn their Galen.

It is ironical, in view of the iconoclasm which posterity has attributed to these movers and shakers, that they were all united by a desire not to strike off into strange seas of thought alone, but to restore a primal purity lost in the accretions and distortions of time. They were, in their own way, primitivists who tried to shore up tradition by purifying it. They sought neither new objects nor new methods of knowledge; their main effort was in restoration rather than creation. To attack the impious naturalism of the Averroists, Petrarch advanced under the banners of Cicero and Augustine; to check the barbarous Latin and the conceptual aridities of the Schoolmen, Erasmus, a century and a half later, urbanely and endlessly prescribed *bonae literae* and the simple virtues of a primitive Christianity; to chasten the pretensions of Thomistic rationalism, Luther and Calvin exhumed Augustine. The various intellectual vogues of the Renaissance – for example, Ficino's Neo-Platonism and Lipsius' Neo-Stoicism – had generally employed the same strategy: a critical scrutiny of prevailing corruptions leading to reform through the rediscovery of an earlier and somehow purer authority. The Renaissance was not antiauthoritarian; its most strenuous labors led to substituting one authority for another, all safely within the framework of the Christian tradition without which nothing had meaning. As Spenser and Hooker so brilliantly reveal, the genius of the Renaissance was for synthesis and compromise. But when the synthesis at last dissolved and the compromise inevitably shattered, the Renaissance was over, and the advent of the modern world was at hand.

That is not to say that promptly in 1601 thinking men said with one voice, 'Come, let us take thought how to destroy the past and build the future.' Movements of thought are never precipitate, and inertia is a necessary principle in intellectual history as well as in Newtonian dynamics. But as the seventeenth century wore on, the expressions of discontent and the projected measures of reform take on a new intensity and a new daring. What had once been a fashionable skepticism – Donne's youthful *Paradoxes and Problems* is a very fair specimen – could become the starting point of Bacon's methodology, of Descartes' metaphysics, of Hobbes's political juggernaut. We cannot properly say that the seventeenth century was ignorant or unmindful of its immense intellectual legacy – *quod Seldenus nescit, nemo scit* – but its antiauthoritarian impatience was so powerful, its hopes for a great instauration so pervasive, that it could not, like the Renaissance, be content merely to rediscover the past; it had to push on. The frontispiece of the *Instauratio magna* – the gallant ship straining under full sail through the pillars of the known into the limitless beyond – takes on a larger meaning than even Bacon could have dreamed. But Bacon's muscular attack on the habits of indolence and authority, which he denounced as impediments to man's well-being, rested on a tradition of Renaissance skepticism which was of inestimable importance for the seventeenth century. Though often inchoate, ill-articulated, and misdirected, this skepticism, which waxed as the Renaissance waned, was basically a protest against scholastic rationalism. And though that protest was destined to have a formative influence on the thought of the seventeenth century, we must not forget how powerful for the Renaissance itself were the uses of tradition.

II. THE AXIOM OF KNOWLEDGE

From the very beginning the Renaissance found itself saddled with a first-rate epistemological problem. For the most part it was ignored – as such abstruse problems usually are – but by the end of the sixteenth century it had become so compelling as to jeopardize the great rationalistic assumption that had made scholastic and Renaissance optimism possible. That assumption we shall call the axiom of knowledge. It was the conviction that an essentially rational God, who created and sustains the universe for His own benevolent ends, is the legitimate object of man's supreme knowledge, and that this knowledge, attained through the discourse of reason and confirmed by revelation, constitutes his ultimate well-being.

The great effort of scholasticism had been to achieve a rational theology, and in the work of St Thomas, as in its poetic redaction by Dante, we have the monument to what some have wistfully called the medieval synthesis. By this synthesis the great forces of pagan and Christian, secular and religious, philosophical and theological thought were brought into some sort of equilibrium. This means, I suppose, that for a brief moment in the intellectual history of Europe all aspects of experience – religious, political, economic, esthetic – could be regarded as parts of a whole which could be described as the glory of God. In the contemplation of this glory man attained the fulfillment of his natural function, which was intellection. Peter Lombard had established the canon of topics legitimate for speculation – God and His attributes, God in relation to the world, God in relation to man, and the Church and its institutions – and St Thomas had demonstrated the immense resources of thought organized under such rubrics.

For our purposes, the significance of the great *summae* of the twelfth and thirteenth centuries lies not in their marshaling of thousands of details, authorities, and conjectures toward the supreme end of the knowledge of God, but rather in the assumption that made such an effort possible. For by the axiom of knowledge every element in man's experience – all the data of sensation from which he derives both the 'images' and the capacity for drawing inferences from them which constitute natural knowledge[2] – becomes an object of cognition that in its hierarchical upward sweep leads ultimately to God. Thus every fact takes on, as it were, a sacramental function of attesting the glory of God. The book of nature, as the Renaissance delighted to call it, provided a ready approach to the comprehension of a theocratic universe – for man's 'proper form' in Aristotelian terms is the 'intellectual principle'[3] – and the inference is clear that man's 'ultimate beatitude' consists in exploiting his highest function of intellection to arrive at a knowledge of God. God is both the cause and 'supremely the end of all things' to which the whole creation inexorably and teleologically strives. Man, uniquely blessed through his intellectual faculty,

> attains to Him in a special way, namely through its proper operation, by understanding Him. Consequently this must be the end of the intellectual creature, namely, to understand God.[4]

In thus regarding the realm of nature as through and through knowable, in regarding the knowledge of it as fulfilling man's

[2] *ST*, I.xii.13.   [3] *ST*, I.lxxvi.1.
[4] *Summa contra Gentiles*, III.xvii.

natural desire to attain 'the contemplation of truth', and in identifying this apogee of wisdom with God Himself, St Thomas construed man's dignity in the highest possible terms. For even when human reason wavers and falls – as it must – before such awful mysteries as the Trinity, the creation of the world *ex nihilo*, and the Incarnation, God comes to his aid with the divine gift of grace and His revealed word in the Scripture.

> Hoc quoque vera ac pia fide tenendum est, quod Trinitas unus sit et solus verus Deus . . . ; et haec trinitas unius ejusdemque substantiae vel essentiae dicitur, creditur et intelligitur; quae est summum bonum, quod purgatissimis mentibus cernitur. Mentis enim humanae acies invalida, in tam excellenti luce non figitur, nisi per justitiam fidei emundetur.[5]

In God the 'act of understanding [is] the same as His very Being', whereas in lesser creatures it is merely a power of the soul that has been corrupted in the Fall.[6] But, though fallen, man retains that freedom of choice which makes intellectually valid and morally responsible conduct possible ('in that man is rational, it is necessary that he have free choice');[7] to this is added the ineffable grace of God which supplements natural truth by the 'light of faith or of prophecy'.[8] And so his natural knowledge with his supernatural knowledge leads him at last to that 'ultimate happiness [which] consists solely in the contemplation of God'.[9] For this purpose he was created, and in God's divine economy the benevolent end is attained by means that are as benevolent as they are rational.

III. THE ANTHROPOMORPHIC GOD

In a famous passage Whitehead has described as the end-product of seventeenth-century scientific thought a concept of nature as 'soundless, scentless, colourless; merely the hurrying of material, endlessly, meaninglessly'.[10] If we trace the dehumanization of nature from Galileo through Descartes to Locke and Newton such a view is justified; but in the seventeenth century, as in any period, the vast majority of men were either unable or unwilling to adopt the advanced and abstruse thought of their age: they found it easier (and safer) to cling to the assumptions they had inherited. Although their traditional values were perhaps not

---

[5] *De Mysterio Trinitatis*, I.ii.
[6] *ST*, I.lxxxix.1.
[7] *ST*, I.lxxxiii.1.
[8] *ST*, I-II. cix.1.
[9] *Summa contra Gentiles*, III.xxxvii.
[10] *Science and the Modern World*, p. 80.

THE ANTHROPOMORPHIC GOD

'true', they were – after a fashion – workable; we must not commit the fallacy of attributing to the average seventeenth-century thinker and writer more originality than he would claim for himself. As we have learned from the Renaissance (in spite of Burckhardt's flattering distortions), even in the most energetic periods the elements of tradition and conservation are potent. The seventeenth century represents to an extraordinary degree the meshing of new and old attitudes, and before we can hope to understand the significances of the new, we must remind ourselves of the persistence of the old.

One of the most persistent of traditional attitudes was what we may call the habit of anthropomorphism. The inclination to project both history and theology in human terms, and to construe God and nature as the coördinates of man's struggle for salvation, was not a habit to be sloughed off as soon as the new science jeopardized the old cosmology. What has been termed the Christian epic – that massive Augustinian complex of a paternalistic but inscrutable God, *natura naturata* and *natura naturans*, the whole course of divine and human history as focused on the human drama of salvation – was seriously challenged in the seventeenth century; but it by no means lost its power to shape the very nature of man's speculations regarding himself and the universe he inhabited. Spinoza, a heretic even if he was *ein Gottbetrunkener Mensch*, was to argue that nature does not have either 'beauty or ugliness, order or confusion' except with reference to man's distorting imagination;[11] but for most of his contemporaries, as for their ancestors, nature remained a more or less animistic projection of human attitudes: it was a meaningful array of things and forces, good and bad, manipulated by God as the backdrop of the human drama. The traditional view of God and nature provided, as it were, a containing vessel which gave shape and limits to the play of the human intellect. Nothing, in fact, is more relevant to the concept of human dignity than the truism that man has always, and not least in the seventeenth century, unconsciously construed the whole universe as the stage for his activities and has built his theologies and his philosophic systems on his own hopes and fears; he has drawn his gods after his own image, and to the motives and operations of those gods he has given an essentially human orientation.

[11] *Letters*, no. XXXII (Wild, p. 440).

Although the habit of anthropomorphism has obvious optimistic implications – to regard the whole creation as intimately concerned with man's chances for well-being is sufficiently anthropocentric – the Renaissance and seventeenth century were not content with mere implications; the optimism had to be formulated in theological and cosmological and mythopoeic terms. To suggest the density and power of such formulations in the Renaissance is not necessary here, but we should try to sketch some of the lines of continuity which carried Renaissance optimism into the seventeenth century. The main anchor of such an optimism was a God whose attributes could be inferred from the universe which He created in time and sustains by His providence, even though His essence be unknowable. Both in the book of nature (whose theocratic lesson is available to anyone who runs and reads) and in His divinely revealed Scriptures He makes His purposes clear. Some of these purposes are hidden in His secret will – hence the audacity of man's lamenting apparent and transitory evils – but the whole evidence points clearly to His overruling purpose: the enhancement of His own glory. Though all His works are manipulated inexorably toward this end, man is the preëminent object of His care and vehicle of His will. For man, though now fallen and corrupt, was made in God's own image and is uniquely distinguished by his immortal soul and rational intellect. A regard for the good of his soul and a proper use of his intellect will ensure him a life of piety and an eternity of bliss. By his soul linked to God, by his body to nature, man crowns the hierarchy of created things; the intricately ordered rankings of all created things beneath him, no less than the intricately ordered rankings of the starry heavens above him, point to his unique importance. Even in his sinful fallen state, by which he is alienated from God, his importance is revealed; for God has left man some spark of the divine reason which, properly used, will lead him to a knowledge of his creator, and to this natural distinction he has added the incalculable gift of grace, which permits him to embrace by faith those mysteries (not available to reason) essential to eternal beatitude.

Within this great complex of myth, knowledge, and wish-projection most men of the late Renaissance exercised their thoughts and emotions. It formed the very matrix of their mental operations, and its 'truth' seemed too evident to require demon-

THE ANTHROPOMORPHIC GOD

strations. 'The worlde is made for man, and man for God,' said Thomas Wilson, 'to the ende that man may have all pleasure, and God may have all honour.'[12] Although the variations possible within this framework of truisms were very great, merely to state the central proposition was to command assent from men of the most different persuasions. By emphasizing one rather than another of its components St Thomas could construct his massive theology of reason, Calvin his of will – but both the Angelic Doctor and the Tyrant of Geneva were securely within the limits of the Christian epic. Their views of man were radically different, yet both derived from the central tradition of western thought. They appeared to be primarily concerned with the nature of God, and to adjust all the facts of the physical, spiritual, and moral universe to God; yet at the hidden center of both their systems was man – essentially good or essentially bad – and the whole universe took its meaning with reference to him, his nature, and his needs. Their systems were of course theistic, but the main lines of those systems radiated from an anthropocentric hub. Not only did they both assent to the Ptolemaic cosmology; they subconsciously followed its pattern in erecting their own theologies on a securely geocentric and anthropocentric base.

This radical anthropomorphism reveals itself at once in the traditional doctrine of God's attributes which the seventeenth century inherited and found indispensable. Ralegh (the alleged atheist) might define God as an 'infinite power and every-where-presence (compassing, embracing, and piercing all things)'[13] or Browne as the 'Omneity [which] informed Nullity into an Essence',[14] yet they and their contemporaries could actually think of this infinite, and ultimately unknowable, power only in terms of His attributes – which they at least partially shared and thus could comprehend. In God such attributes were projected on an infinite plane, and they all focused in His perfection, but they did humanize the concept of deity and brought Him, as it were, down to earth, where He could be handled in familiar fashion. The negative attributes of simplicity, eternity, and immutability could be inferred from God's infinite perfection; the positive attributes of wisdom, holiness, and liberty from His infinite goodness; and the relative attributes of providence, sovereignty, mercy, and

---

[12] *A Discourse upon Usury*, 'Preface' (ed. Tawney, p. 175).
[13] *History*, I.i.10.   [14] *Religio Medici*, p. 40.

justice from His intimate relationship with the realm of space and time which He created and transcends.[15]

This doctrine of attributes – there were of course many variations – not only served as a ground for theological and scientific speculation; it also enabled the man of the seventeenth century to enjoy a sense of God's intimacy and immediacy; the result is an animistic density and richness that shoots through the period like spun gold in a rich brocade. Sometimes, as in Hobbes, the inherited notion of a personal God is used with glassy irony; sometimes, as in Donne, it is teased into wonderfully intricate paradoxes and problems; sometimes, as in Milton and Taylor and Browne, it is the stimulus of great art; sometimes, as in Crashaw, it induces sensual – almost erotic – excitement; but always it is present to give a fourth dimension to experience. Before the concept of an anthropomorphic God was dehumanized and sterilized and finally abandoned, it provided for all kinds of thought and emotion – aesthetic and political as well as theological and moral – a set of coördinates in infinity.

Although a satisfactory history of seventeenth-century thought could be written in terms of the doctrine of attributes, we must be content merely to remind ourselves of its vitality. It provided a hallowed and indispensable orientation for most men's speculations; it gave color and metaphor to literature, holiness to politics, majesty to morality. When Hieronimo, in *The Spanish Tragedy*, is wronged in this world, he can invoke the aid of a stern but righteous despot who spans the gulf between the infinite to the temporal:

> God hath engrossed all his justice in his hands,
> And there is none but what comes from him.[16]

Bacon, even though his eyes were fixed on a very secular 'commodity' resulting from man's exploitation of nature, could not dispense with God; he merely barricaded Him behind a string of second causes. For Donne, He is many things – now a psychoanalyst, now a sovereign, now a tender friend – but always on the main axis of his thought. Jeremy Taylor brings to his con-

---

[15] Virtually every seventeenth-century work on theology contains a treatment of the attributes of God. A couple of examples, from an Anglican and a Puritan, will perhaps be useful: Andrewes, *A Pattern of Catechistical Doctrine*, p. 94; Milton, *De doctrina*, I.ii (*PW*, IV, 21–9).
[16] *The Spanish Tragedy*, IV.vi.

THE ANTHROPOMORPHIC GOD

ception of God all the subtle, intimate insights of a great literary artist: the subject seems to fascinate him because it exists for him on so many planes, doctrinal, metaphysical, and personal; but he reverts most often to his supple and warmly human portrait of a God of love and social amity. God is, of course, a sum of all attributes, wrath and justice as well as mercy and benignity, but Taylor prefers to write of Him as 'gentle and easy, chaste and pure, righteous and peaceable'.[17] His very language irradiates into metaphors of light and glory when he tries to persuade men to regard God not as an enemy but a friend: as we come to know God we should pass from fear

> to carefulness, from carefulness to love, from love to diligence, and from diligence to perfection; and the enemies shall become servants, and the servants shall become adopted sons, and pass into the society and the participation of the inheritance of Jesus: for this fear is also reverence, and then our God, instead of being 'a consuming fire', shall become to us the circle of a glorious crown, and a globe of eternal light.[18]

The same sense of intimacy, of immediate sensuous apprehension, is seen in Taylor's rapt visions of beatitude. Heaven for him is a very real place, just as God is a very real being, and when he writes of them his language quickens into a vibrant intensity.

> Men shall be like angels, and angels shall be comprehended in the lap of spiritual and eternal felicities; the soul shall not understand by material phantasms, neither be served by the provisions of the body, but the body itself shall become spiritual, and the eye shall see intellectual objects, and the mouth shall feed upon hymns and glorifications of God; the belly shall be then satisfied by the fulness of righteousness, and the tongue shall speak nothing but praises, and the propositions of a celestial wisdom; the motion shall be the swiftness of an angel, and it shall be clothed with white as with a garment; holiness is the sun and righteousness is the moon in that region; our society shall be choirs of singers, and our conversation wonder; contemplation shall be our food, and love shall be 'the wine of elect souls'.[19]

Even though an increasing secularization would inevitably weaken the traditional sense of God's immediacy, few contemporaries of Milton could free themselves of the habit of anthropomorphism. Thanks to the doctrine of attributes, there was no need to; for by emphasizing one rather than another of God's attributes a man could accommodate God under whichever of His infinite aspects were most convenient to his system. Not the

---

[17] *Sermons*, p. 63. [18] *Ibid.*, p. 65. [19] *Ibid.*, p. 87.

least of the advantages of the doctrine, in fact, was its flexibility. It had a certain baroque glory in unifying unity and multiplicity: though Laud might construe God as uncommonly like a Stuart king in His paternal despotism, and Richard Sibbes construe Him as a Puritan minister in His intimate concern with the soul of man struggling for salvation, it was the same God – the sum of all attributes and the obliging, protean deity who made Himself known by many signs and under many guises. Though he despised the belittling anthropomorphic theology of his age, Spinoza most compendiously (and traditionally) defined God as 'a being of whom all attributes are predicated.'[20] If, as Mr Willey has said, God for Hobbes was merely a symbol of the philosopher's fatigue, He was useful in bridging Descartes' divided nature of thought and extension; and when Henry More tried to exhaust all His attributes with a catalogue of twenty units he had to accommodate the spirit of his Cartesian age by including that of infinite extension in space and time.[21] Robert Boyle (to whom 'atheist' meant 'monster') was appalled by Descartes' implicitly mechanistic view of God, because to relegate Him to the role of a removed spectator, or to deprive man and nature of His constant surveillance and intervention, was in his view impious. Newton shared this view. When we remember that the author of the *Principia* regarded the Book of Daniel as the height of theology we should not be surprised at the importance of a traditional God in his 'General Scolium':

> The true God is a living, intelligent, and powerful Being; and, from his other perfections, [it follows] that he is supreme, or most perfect. He is eternal and infinite, omnipotent and omniscient; that is, his duration reaches from eternity to eternity; his presence from infinity to infinity; he governs all things, and knows all things that are or can be done.[22]

IV. THE DOCTRINE OF PROVIDENCE

The habit of anthropomorphism, then, was one wide channel which carried the stream of tradition into the seventeenth century. Closely related to it was the doctrine of providence, God's 'ser-

---

[20] *Short Treatise*, ch. iii; cf. *Ethics*, I.xv; *Letters*, no. XXXV (where the attributes of God are given as eternity, simplicity, illimitableness, indivisibility, and perfection.
[21] Burtt, *Metaphysical Foundations*, p. 140.
[22] *Principia*, 'General Scolium' (p. 545). For Hobbes's angry attack on the common – and, as he thought, vulgar – doctrine of attributes, see *Philosophical Rudiments*, XV.14 (*English Works*, II, 213-6).

THE DOCTRINE OF PROVIDENCE

pentine and crooked line', as Browne calls it, 'whereby He draws those actions His wisdom intends, in a more unknown and secret way'.[23] Since it implied His sovereignty and demonstrated His watchful care, the providence of God seemed to the orthodox the surest sign of His intimate connection with His creation. Watching its workings, the very pious could with folded hands marvel at God's inscrutable ways; those brought under Bacon's spell could talk glibly of second causes, for all practical purposes ignoring God while seeking to usurp His power over nature; wayfaring Christians striving to achieve the reign of the saints could sanctify their efforts by viewing themselves as God's instruments; and, as the century wore on, men who thought they understood Galileo and Newton could identify providence with mechanism – even after God was well on His way to becoming an unnecessary hypothesis.

Like most cornerstones of the Christian tradition, the doctrine of providence derived from Augustine's version of the Christian epic. The theme of *The City of God* stamped itself deeply upon the medieval mind; and Augustine's view of history as God's direct manipulation of all events for His ultimate glory was strengthened rather than weakened by the Stoic, Thomistic, and Calvinistic accretions it picked up in the course of time. For the doctrine of providence has always served to justify the apparent evils of a world that, though sunk in sin and temporality, must somehow be adjusted to the hypothesis of a theocratic universe. Boethius, whether Stoic or Christian or both, could argue even in the face of disaster that though God's ways are mysterious they must be good; Aquinas's theology and philosophy alike led him inexorably to the conviction that the whole creation was designed to exemplify the fact of God's sovereign reason; the doctrine of providence was a necessary ingredient of Calvin's theological voluntarism. Compatible with both the new science and the new emphasis on natural law, the doctrine had obvious utility for the seventeenth century; and although it was to be jeopardized by the Cartesian dualism which dug a chasm between God and nature, it was restored when Descartes invoked the ancient *concursus Dei* to hold his dualistic universe together. The appearance,

---

[23] *Religio Medici*, p. 19. St Thomas (*ST*, I.xxii.2) defines providence as the 'notion of the order of things towards an end'; therefore, he infers, in so far as a thing exists at all it must be 'subject to divine providence'.

at the end of the century, of Bossuet's *Discourse on Universal History* and of Newton's 'General Scolium' in the *Principia* should remind us that for archbishops as for experimental philosophers the doctrine of providence remained a potent force in European thought.

Like the doctrine of attributes, the doctrine of providence was very flexible. Men of the most unlike interests and convictions could shape it to their purposes. Moreover, it fully protected that complex of theocratic and humanistic values which constituted the intellectual legacy of the Renaissance. While it permitted men to refer every event in the realm of nature to God, it also underscored God's transcendence to the realm of nature. Like the mystery of the Incarnation it brought God and man into an intimate relation with no jeopardy to God's sovereignty but with the prodigious increase of man's dignity. If everything that happens – the traffickings of daily life no less than the great movements of history – can be referred to God for causality and therefore justification, then everything assumes a dimension in infinity. The dignity of man and the patterned significance of all temporal affairs were immediate corollaries of the conviction that God manipulates all events to the consummation of His great design. At whatever expense to metaphysics, the timeless and the temporal were brought into the most organic relationship. For as Calvin warns, we should conceive of God not as idly glancing now and again at His creation from heaven, but 'as holding the helm of the universe and regulating all events'. We must not mistake this regulation for either (Stoic) fate or mere chance, since what we call fortune is God's secret ordering of all events, and what we call chance is that 'with the reason and cause of which we are not acquainted'. If one is set upon by robbers, or meets with wild beasts, or is shipwrecked, or is killed by a falling tree, 'carnal reason will ascribe all these occurrences, both prosperous and adverse, to fortune. But whoever has been taught from the mouth of Christ that the hairs of his head are all numbered, will seek further for a cause, and conclude that all events are governed by the secret counsel of God. By His providence God blesses the pious and chastises the wicked, a fact that must be obvious even to sinful man (that 'worm five feet long') by 'evident and daily indication'.[24]

[24] *Institutes*, I.xvi.4; I.xvi.8; I.xvi.2; I.v.7.

THE DOCTRINE OF PROVIDENCE

Though among the most zealous devotees of the doctrine of providence, the Puritans were not unsympathetic to science or to a Baconian scrutiny of natural processes. None the less, they insisted that providence be acknowledged as the surest sign of God's sovereignty, for unless they could keep inviolate the heart of God's sovereignty and mystery from the claims of rationalism and natural philosophy, they would gut their theology and forfeit their title as Puritans. They never honestly met the philosophical difficulties of their Augustinian-Baconian position; but men who could believe simultaneously in predestination and Ramean logic would certainly have no trouble in assuming that, though God ordinarily permits nature to act by second causes, He can at any moment disrupt them for His own inscrutable purposes. As Urian Oakes put it in a classical statement of the Puritan position, fire generates (i.e. is the second cause of) heat, but it is God who controls and sustains both the fire and the heat; and without this *concursus Dei* we could by no means be certain that the causal sequence would occur. God

> can stop the Sun in its course, and cause it to withdraw its shining; He can give check to the Fire, that it shall not burn; & to the hungry Lions, that they shall not devour. . . . In a word: the Lord being the Absolute First Cause, and supream Governour of all his Creatures, and all their Actions; though He hath set an Order among his Creatures, this shall be the cause of that effect, &c. yet He himself is not tied to that Order; but Interrupts the course of it, when He pleases.[25]

Since, in a favorite metaphor of the seventeenth century, the course of events is the handwriting of God, man has only to read the book of nature to recognize the power of His providence. Perhaps, as has been suggested, Prospero is Shakespeare's version of the power that shapes all events for good ends, but in less subtle art the theme is made painfully explicit. Though its didactic crudities are on a par with those of Lodge and Greene's *A Looking-Glass for London and England*, Cyril Tourneur's *Atheist's Tragedy* is a typical Jacobean survival of the ancient morality erected on the theme of providence. D'Amville is a monster who, refusing to see God's hand in the course of events, denies the fact of moral causality. His victims, however, calmly await the inevitable.

---

[25] *The Sovereign Efficacy of Divine Providence*, Miller-Johnson, pp. 360-1.

> How can earth endure
> The burden of this wickedness without
> An earthquake? Or the angry face of Heaven
> Be not inflamed with lightning?[26]

What is inevitable is D'Amville's destruction – achieved when he 'strikes out his own brains' – and the meaning is clear. As the judge says to D'Amville's intended victims,

> The power of that eternal providence
> Which overthrew his projects in their pride
> Hath made your griefs the instruments to raise
> Your blessings to a higher height than ever.[27]

Putting the matter in rather different terms, William Perkins, the great Puritan casuist, concluded that an 'evill Conscience, Hell, and Death are good, because they are ordained of God, for the execution of his justice, howsoever in themselves and to us they be evill'.[28] Long before Marlowe wrote *Tamburlaine*, the notion of the tyrant as the scourge of God was a commonplace.[29]

The very embarrassing problem of evil makes something like a doctrine of providence imperative in any theism. Milton, taking the most cheerful view, speaks of the ways of providence as 'equal, easy, and not burdensome';[30] but many others saw them as tokens of God's displeasure with the erring. When Jeremy Taylor attributes social and economic inequalities to God's providence, he echoes Paul's figure of the body and its members and repeats one of the political commonplaces of the Middle Ages.[31] When he urges the pious to thank God for 'every weakness, deformity, and imperfection' as providential aids to the virtue of humility,[32] he gives the Christian version of the argument from design: in the totality of God's design for a world fallen away from goodness, apparent evils must be accepted as leading to an ultimate good. The tone is optimistic, for the doctrine of providence sanctified optimism. Not to believe that the affairs of daily life, no less than the rise and fall of dynasties or the paths of the stars in their courses, are sustained and directed by God for His own good purposes is to blaspheme God's sovereignty. Naturally, the ways of providence are not always clear to sinful man. A

---

[26] IV.iii. [27] V.ii.
[28] *Cases of Conscience*, I.i.2.
[29] In the *Institutes* (I.xviii) Calvin devotes a whole chapter to this topic.
[30] *The Doctrine and Discipline of Divorce*, II.xx (*PW*, III, 262).
[31] *Holy Living*, I.i. [32] *Ibid.*, II.iv.

THE DOCTRINE OF PROVIDENCE

mighty worker for the Lord like Baxter might permit himself to wonder at the dispensations of God – 'It is the most astonishing part of all God's providence to me, that he so far forsaketh almost all the world, and confineth his special favour to so few'[33] – but he would never presume to complain. To try to penetrate such deific mysteries by means of reason, said Dryden, 'is to take away the pillars from our faith, and to prop it only with a twig'.[34] Henry More, also speaking of the disproportionate number of the unsaved to the saved, advances the orthodox opinion:

> It is an outrageous Presumption, to expect that he [God] should not act according to his own Mind and Will, but according to the groundless enlargments and expansions of our wanton and busie Phancies. So long as we see that the things that are well and rightly administered, and according to the Laws of Goodness and Justice, it is a marvellous piece of Capriciousness to complain, that such things with the unexceptionable Oeconomie of them began no sooner, nor reach no farther.[35]

Though metaphysically shaky the doctrine of providence posits in intimate relation the antithetical elements of permanence and change, the absolute and the relative, God and man. Hooker projects this theistic optimism on a typically large scale.

> God's own eternity is the hand which leadeth Angels in the course of their perpetuity; their perpetuity the hand that draweth out celestial motion, the line of which motion and the thread of time are spun together.[36]

But whether viewed in Hooker's terms of Dantesque sublimity or Browne's of cozy acquiescence ('Guide not the Hand of God ... but sit quiet in the soft showers of Providence'),[37] a confidence in God's unceasing supervision of His creation was one of the axioms of traditional optimism.

The doctrine of providence was also a basic component of seventeenth-century historiography. Neither Ralegh's universal history at one end of the century nor Bossuet's at the other would have been possible without the conviction that in the fall of the sparrow, as in larger events, God's purposes are made manifest: history is the record of the ways in which He directs events for His own ends, and providence is what we call this deific marshaling of events to presumably good ends. It is, as Ralegh says, 'an

---

[33] *Autobiography*, p. 117.
[34] *Religio Laici*, 'Preface' (*Poetical Works*, p. 158).
[35] *Divine Dialogues*, pp. 264–5.
[36] *Laws*, V.lxix.2.   [37] *Christian Morals*, III.v.

intellectual knowledge, both foreseeing, caring for, and ordaining all things, and doth not only behold all past, all present, and all to come, but is the cause of their so being.³⁸ In such a view it is obvious that fortune, that wanton with whom the Renaissance had sometimes dared to dally, is a meaningless principle of explanation. When foolish men attribute their good or bad luck to fortune, they ignore the inexorable moral workings of all events under providence. Things do not just happen; they follow causal patterns. The Anglican Browne and the Puritan Bradford were agreed that events occur because God wills them, and He wills them because the occurrence somehow – in ways not always apparent to man – furthers His purposes.

> Let not Fortune, which hath no name in Scripture, have any in thy Divinity. Let Providence, not Chance, have the honour of thy acknowledgments, and be thy Oedipus in Contingencies. Mark well the Paths and winding Ways thereof; but be not too wise in the Construction, or sudden in the Application. The Hand of Providence writes often by Abbreviatures, Hieroglyphics or short Characters, which, like the Laconism on the Wall, are not to be made out but by a Hint or Key from that Spirit which indicted them.³⁹

The great Puritan experiments in dissidence and reform gave a special urgency to the view of history as providence. Young Milton, as well as many others, was convinced that God had ordained the civil broils of the 'forties so that the Reformation (sadly hindered by the prelates) might be speedily completed, and his contemporaries who had fled the Laudian terror construed the transatlantic experiment in similar terms: 'God creates a New England to muster up the first of his Forces in.'⁴⁰ William Bradford's incomparable *History of the Plymoth Plantation* throbs with the certainty that God's particular providence may be traced in every detail of the taxing but triumphant adventure. The whole undertaking was a major part of His plan for reformation with no tarrying, but even the most casual incidents, projected through Bradford's view of history, take on meaning. For example, there is the sad but edifying tale of a 'very profane yonge man', a

---

³⁸ *History*, I.i.10. Note Ralegh's witty and cynical perversion of this principle of causality (*History*, I.i.15): 'For whosoever shall tell any great man or magistrate, that he is not just; the general of an army, that he is not valiant; and great ladies, that they are not fair; shall never be made a counsellor, a captain, or a courtier.'
³⁹ Browne, *Christian Morals*, I.xxv.
⁴⁰ Edward Johnson, *Wonder-Working Providence of Sions Saviour*, Miller-Johnson, pp. 143–62, and esp. 159–62.

THE DOCTRINE OF PROVIDENCE

mariner on the ship bearing the saints to New England, who had nothing but curses and contempt for the passengers.

> But it plased God before they came halfe seas over, to smite this yong man with a greevous disease, of which he dyed in a desperate maner, and so was him selfe the first that was throwne overbord. Thus his curses light on his owne head; and it was an astonishmente to all his fellows, for they noted it to be the just hand of God upon him.[41]

Clearly, however, the doctrine of providence was not the exclusive property of the Puritans. Opening his great work, Clarendon locates the events he was to record directly along a moral axis. Though the 'finger and wrath of God' were everywhere discernible, yet the miseries of the Great Rebellion were generated by 'the same natural causes and means, which have usually attended kingdoms swoln with long plenty, pride, and excess, towards some signal mortification, and castigation of Heaven'.[42] The Presbyterian Baxter could rejoice in Charles's restoration – 'without one bloody nose' – as proof 'there is a God that governeth the world and disposeth of the Powers of the world according to his Will';[43] an Anglican bishop, reflecting on the same event, could infer that the 'circles of the divine providence turn themselves upon the affairs of the world so, that every spondel of the wheels may mark out those virtues which we are then to exercise; and every new event in the economy of God is God's finger to point out to us by what instances He will be served'.[44]

When the doctrine of providence is used to explain and sanctify the great upheavals of the seventeenth century it takes on a majestic force. But in other contexts it is less majestic, if no less convenient. Izaak Walton, a devout Christian if emphatically no Puritan, invokes the doctrine to justify God's apparent hard dealing with Richard Hooker in permitting him to be trapped in matrimony. The unfortunate lady (happily exonerated by modern scholarship) assumes a role not unlike the serpent's in Eden – but let the pious be instructed:

> The Prophet Ezekiel says, 'There is a wheel within a wheel'; a secret sacred wheel of Providence, – most visible in marriages . . . and let the Reader cease to wonder, for affliction is a divine diet; which though it be

[41] pp. 92–3.   [42] *History*, I, 36–7.
[43] *Autobiography*, p. 92.
[44] Taylor, *Ductor Dubitantium*, 'Epistle Dedicatory' (*Works*, IX, 1).

not pleasing to mankind, yet Almighty God hath often, very often, imposed it as good, though bitter physic to those children whose souls are dearest to him.[45].

There is a charming picture of Samuel Sewall and Cotton Mather dining together and speculating on the 'awfull Providence' of hailstones as 'bigg as pistoll and Musquet Bullets' which had that day damaged a number of ministers' houses. But Mather, characteristically, came up with a pat explanation: God had broken the 'brittle part' of our houses so that we 'might be ready for the time when our Clay-Tabernacles should be broken.[46] Richard Baxter was another on whom the lessons of God's most trivial workings were not lost. There was the time, for example, when God preserved him from a whole shelf of falling books in his library – a providential escape,

> whereas the place, the weight and greatness of the books was such, and my head just under them, that it was a wonder they had not beaten out my brains, one of the shelves right over my head having the six volumes of Dr Walton's *Oriental Bible* and all Austin's Works, and the *Bibliotheca Patrum* and *Marlorate*, etc.[47]

Cromwell was sure that God had covered his retreat from Dunbar by putting the moon under a cloud; the Dean of Windsor explained the unseasonable heat of January 1662 as a sign of God's anger at the unpunished regicides; John Evelyn – who has not come down to us as a superstitious zealot – was alarmed at several recent comets which, though explainable in scientific terms, might very well be a 'warning from God, as they are commonly forerunners of his animadversions'.[48] We perhaps smile at such credulity, but it shows the persistence and the utility of the doctrine of providence.

Long before the rise of science and the triumph of mechanism jeopardized the doctrine, however, there were signs of danger. In the Renaissance and early seventeenth century the danger was that foolish men might regard God and nature as synonymous: they might confuse the workings of providence with the 'natural' course of events as determined by fate, or mechanistic causality, or natural law; and they might think this law operative on

---

[45] *Lives*, II, 30.
[46] Sewall, *Diary*, April 29th, 1695 (Miller-Johnson, p. 512).
[47] *Autobiography*, p. 77. For a more systematic statement of Baxter's views on providence, see *The Catechizing of Families*, ch. iv (*Works*, XIX, 20 f.).
[48] Smith, *A History of Modern Culture*, pp. 429, 433.

THE DOCTRINE OF PROVIDENCE

mechanical lines describable by mathematics rather than on moral lines made clear by revelation and the discourse of reason. To do so was to permit God's sovereignty to be swallowed up in second causes and to commit a blasphemy which the orthodox cried out against as one man. For this meant both a denial of the attribute of sovereignty by confining God within the limits of mechanical causation and a desecration and pollution of the Divine Essence by equating it with the realm of nature.

If Bruno's anthropomorphic pantheism was enough to bring him to the stake, what could be said of the heresies of Gassendi, Hobbes, and Spinoza? Or even of Cartesian dualism? For the threat posed by Descartes (even though he tried to skirt the alternatives of materialism and pantheism) was the most sinister because it was the most subtle. As a good Christian and a good mathematician, he was faced with the basic dilemma of his age – that of accepting simultaneously the theism of tradition and the emerging mechanism of natural philosophy. Driving a fatal wedge into the organic theism of the medieval (and Renaissance) synthesis, his dualism of *res extensa* and *res cogitans* signalized the collapse of the cardinal axiom of Christendom. When he achieved the metaphysical segregation of God and nature, thought and matter, which Bacon had called for, he alienated morality from the processes of nature; by subjugating nature to mechanism he made the doctrine of providence superfluous. Whether, like Spinoza, one evaded the dualism by reducing all to *res cogitans*, or, like Hobbes, to *res extensa*, the harm was done; and by his lights Dr Sacheverell was justified in denouncing both as atheistical monsters. 'Je ne puis pardonner à Descartes', said Pascal with his customary acuteness; he would like to dispense with God, but since he needs Him 'de lui faire donner une chiquenaude, pour mettre le monde en mouvement' he in effect used Him as a generator and then exiled Him from His creation.[49]

The *Principles of Philosophy* undertakes to account for the universe 'as if it were simply a machine in which there was nothing to consider but [the] figure and movements [of its parts]',[50] but, as Gassendi quickly pointed out, this procedure makes it impossible to account for God. He put his finger on the crucial difficulty which has plagued every dualism since Plato's: 'how the

---
[49] *Pensées*, no. 194 (*Œuvres*, p. 874).
[50] IV.clxxxviii (*Works*, I, 289).

corporeal can have anything in common with the incorporeal, or what relationship may be established between the one and the other.'[51] It was a difficulty that the Renaissance had chosen to ignore, but when Descartes had shown it could no longer be ignored the doctrine of providence was in real danger. When Descartes could define providence as 'fatality or an immutable necessity'[52] and Spinoza as 'nothing else than the striving which we find in the whole of Nature and in individual things to maintain and preserve their own existence',[53] it was clear that the rich theistic color was fading from European thought. Thomas Sprat, urbanely ridiculing the fear of witches and apparitions that the progress of experimental philosophy had demolished, rejoices to reduce nature to a formula: 'The cours of things goes quietly along, in its own true channel of Natural Causes and Effects.'[54]

Hence the repeated and urgent warnings not to confine God within the limits of His instruments. The first step toward atheism, warned Fuller, is the denying God's 'ordering of sublunarie matters . . . making him a maimed Deity, without an eye of Providence or an arm of Power, and at most restraining him onely to matters above the clouds'.[55] An extreme rationalist like Cudworth, in defending the ways of providence, could speak of rewards and punishments being 'measured out in geometrical proportions',[56] but neither he nor any of the Cambridge Platonists would deny God's transcendence to the processes of nature. Second causes are the marvelously useful means of implementing His will, but they are only agencies whose principle is God; in Milton's view we must not doubt that God can, when He wills, produce those effects 'out of the usual order of nature' which we call miracles.[57] As the very influential William Perkins said, following the Calvinistic line, although everything is ultimately dependent on God's eternal decrees, such decrees do not jeopardize the 'nature and property of second causes but only brings them into a certaine order, that is, it directeth them to the determinate end'.[58]

---

[51] *Objections V* (*Works*, II, 202).
[52] *The Passions of the Soul*, II.cxlv (*Works*, I, 396).
[53] *Short Treatise*, ch. v.
[54] *The History of the Royal Society*, p. 340.
[55] *The Holy State*, V.6.
[56] *The True Intellectual System of the Universe*, IV. 173.
[57] *De doctrina*, I.viii (*PW*, IV, 212).
[58] *A Golden Chaine*, p. 31.

THE DOCTRINE OF PROVIDENCE 23

Even without the support of Cartesian dualism, however, there was a good deal of urbane skepticism concerning the more flamboyant operations of providence. Ralegh, cautiously comparing second causes to pipes and conduits which lead away from 'the head and fountain of the universal', thought they have no more 'self ability, than a clock, after it is wound up by a man's hand'.[59] The mechanistic metaphor is revealing; it suggests Selden's sophisticated contempt for the effort to read moral significance into the events of nature: 'Wee cannott tell what is a Judgmt. of God, 'tes p[re]sumpcion to take upon us to knowe. . . . Comonly wee say a Judgmt. falls upon a Man for something in him wee cannott abide.'[60] But most of their contemporaries were by no means convinced of God's absenting Himself from the daily business of the world. Lancelot Andrewes' statement of the orthodox view would recommend itself to Anglican and Puritan alike. There are some, he says, who believe there is no providence at all, so that a 'curtain' is drawn between God and man; others subscribe to a providence of only 'general things not of particular'; others, admitting a providence of both general and particular things, think 'it is idle and not rewarding'; and still others, the the majority for whom Andrewes speaks, are convinced by both revelation and natural reason of a general and particular providence 'which rewardeth good to the good and evil to the evil; and this is the truth which we hold'.[61]

The Baconian program to isolate the apparently orderly processes of nature from the reach of God's providence was widely decried. Taylor repeatedly insists that His sovereignty does not pause at the threshold of second causes – 'whatsoever is disposed to happen by the order of natural causes, or civil counsels, may be rescinded by a peculiar decree of Providence'[62] – and his opinion was one of the Renaissance commonplaces echoed everywhere. John Swan, a traditionalist if one ever lived, thought that only 'foolish naturalists' would 'presume to bind Gods mighty hand in natures bands, and tie him so to second causes, as if he were no free or voluntary agent, but must always be bound to work

---

[59] *History*, I.i.10.   [60] *Table Talk*, p. 59.
[61] *A Pattern of Catechistical Doctrine*, p. 32. George Herbert's attitude toward the complexities of God's providence is typical: see his quaint use of unnatural natural history in 'Providence' (*Works*, p. 124) and his more synoptic treatment in *A Priest to the Temple*, ch. xxx (*Works*, pp. 276–7).
[62] *Holy Dying*, I. ii.

by means'.⁶³ Although Donne at the beginning of his ministry yields rather grudging assent to miracles – 'Nature is the Common law by which God governs us, and Miracle is his Prerogative'⁶⁴ – in his later sermons he makes providence one of his great themes. Since every event is under the direct control of God – calamities and deliverances are His handwriting in the book of nature – 'to ascribe things wholy to nature, to fortune, to power, to second causes, this is to mistake the hand, not to know God's hand'. God speaks to man everywhere and in all ways, but only atheists refuse to hear His voice: in their insane presumption they construe 'naturall accidents, causall occurrencies, emergent contingencies' as events which 'would fall out though there were no God'. Beyond this, folly cannot go. For the 'world is the theatre that represents God, and everywhere every man may, nay must see him'.⁶⁵

It is well and good to seek a systematic knowledge of those processes by which God usually permits nature to work, says the Puritan John Goodwin, but we remember that God is still God, and 'reserves a liberty' to disrupt these processes 'against all advantages and likelihoods of second causes, when and where and as oft as he pleaseth'.⁶⁶ But as Pascal admits in the fourth Provinciale, it is hard for a lewd modern naturalist to humble himself before God's sovereignty.

> Qui pourra croire que les épicuriens, qui niaient la Providence divine, eussent des mouvements de prier Dieu? eux qui disaient, que c'était lui faire injure de l'implorer dans nos besoins, comme s'il eût été capable de s'amuser à penser à nous?⁶⁷

Who would know more poignantly than Pascal the shock of the collision between theism and mechanism? Under its impact he recoiled into fideism, but for most of his contemporaries the doctrine of providence – for all its imperfections – could still justify the ways of God to men. By that doctrine, Milton was convinced, man could know that in the essentially moral structure

---

⁶³ *Speculum Mundi*, VII.i.
⁶⁴ *Essays in Divinity*, pp. 179 f. What we would call miracles, says Donne, were planned from the beginning and 'inserted into the body of the whole History of Nature (though they seem to us to be but interlineary and Marginall)'. They are, therefore, natural, for 'nothing can be done against the Order of Nature'. If we could know all of nature and all of God's purposes, then 'nothing would be *Miraculum*'.
⁶⁵ *Works*, I, 120; *LXXX Sermons*, p. 465; *Works*, I, 415.
⁶⁶ *The Danger of Fighting against God*, Haller, III, 50.
⁶⁷ *Œuvres*, p. 466.

of the universe good would ultimately conquer evil.

> If this fail,
> The pillar'd firmament is rott'ness
> And earth's base built on stubble.[68]

George Herbert could only concur. Whatever the reach of human knowledge, it was a paltry, hollow thing without those truths that gave it moral dimensions, and those were the truths laid up in the bosom of God.

> Philosophers have measured mountains,
> Fathom'd the depths of seas, of states, and kings,
> Walk'd with a staffe to heav'n, and traced fountains:
> But there are two vast, spacious things,
> The which to measure it doth those behove:
> Yet few there are that found them: Sinne and Love.[69]

V. HEIGHTS AND DECLENSIONS: THE ESTATE OF MAN

If anthropomorphism made possible the doctrines of attributes and providence, it also made possible a broadly optimistic view of man's nature and status in a theocratic universe. That status comprised the widest extremes of dignity and infamy. In the main stream of Christian humanism man's prestige was immense; in the theology which Calvin had revived primarily to combat such optimism man's degradation was made the pivotal fact of history. The seventeenth century, inheriting both views, spent its best efforts, as we shall see, in trying to resolve the antinomy. 'Thou art a man', intones Jeremy Taylor, 'than whom there is not in the world any greater instance of heights and declensions, of lights and shadows, or misery and folly, of laughter and tears, of groans and death.'[70]

But in the tradition of Renaissance optimism, which carried over powerfully into the seventeenth century, man's dignity was assured. Even though a sinful, fallen creature he still retained two inestimable advantages: for comprehending the realm of nature God had endowed him with a divinely rational faculty which, though impaired by the Fall, set him at the apex of the creation; for believing those mysteries essential to salvation God had showered on him the unmerited gift of grace which made faith

[68] *Comus*, ll. 597-9.   [69] 'The Agonie', *Works*, p. 30.
[70] *Holy Dying*, I.i; cf. II.iv; Browne, *Religio Medici*, p. 77; Ralegh, *History*, I.i.14.

possible. Thus, if he used his advantages properly, he was assured of dominion in this life and of eternal bliss in the one to follow. In that philosophically confusing but emotionally comfortable cosmology inherited from the Renaissance, the universe was regarded as comprising the realms of the seen and the unseen – of nature and grace, matter and form, *natura naturata* and *natura naturans*, earth and heaven – and these two realms of God's creation were by His providence linked in a crude parallelism permitting the most intimate correspondence and interaction. 'How good, how fair,' exclaims Milton, 'answering his great Idea.' The realm of the unseen or the spiritual included a Trinitarian God, the nine orders of angels, the minor spirits, and the immortal soul of man; the realm of the seen included the high heavens, the geocentric solar system, the earth, corporeal man, animals, plants, metals, and minerals. And over all brooded a benevolent God who directed every event in His creation toward the aggrandizement of His own glory.

Linking the two realms of matter and spirit, man occupied a central position in this hierarchy. The *scala naturae* stretched from the minerals in the bowels of the earth up through all the ranks of animate and inanimate creation, the starry skies, and the celestial orders to a sovereign God continually sustaining His creation through His divine providence. And in the very center, of both the physical and the spiritual orders, was placed man – 'that amphibious piece between a corporal and spiritual Essence, that middle form that links those two together, and makes good the Method of GOD and Nature, that jumps not from extreams, but unites the incompatible distances by some middle and participating natures'.[71] Physically, man was a composition of the four elements common to all material things; spiritually, he possessed a soul comprising vegetative, sensitive, and rational faculties; and this very ambivalence, as Pico had pointed out in his famous *Oratio*, made him the nodus of the universe. When God the great artificer tells Adam that he is placed at the center of all created things, He underscores his unique importance: 'Thou shalt have the power to degenerate into the lower forms of life, which are brutish. Thou shalt have the power, out of thy soul's judgment, to be reborn into the higher forms, which are divine.' Since his creation on the sixth day crowned God's efforts, he was, said

[71] Browne, *Religio Medici*, pp. 38–9.

John Swan in echoing Pico from afar, 'the Map, Epitome, and Compendium of what was made before him'.[72]

> There wanted yet the Master work, the end
> Of all yet done; a Creature who not prone
> And brute as other Creatures, but endu'd
> With Sanctity of Reason, might erect
> His Stature, and upright with Front serene
> Govern the rest, self-knowing, and from thence
> Magnanimous to correspond with Heav'n.[73]

Man was, then, the microcosm to the macrocosm, the little world comprising all the elements and all the cohesive principles of order and symmetry that point inexorably to God the artificer. 'The world is a great volume', said Donne, 'and man the index of that book; even in the body of man, you may turn to the whole world; this body is an illustration of all nature.'[74] As a mortal creature, he crowned the realm of nature which lay spread before him for his commodity and his instruction; as the heir of God's grace and the possessor of an immortal soul he could, through faith, aspire to eternal bliss when he had ascended to the realm of spirit. Thus, as Hooker argued from the doctrine of the Incarnation, man's prestige is immense: since God deified his nature by making it His 'own inseparable habitation, we cannot conceive how God should without man either exercise divine power, or receive the glory of divine praise. For man is in both an associate of Deity'.[75] With the earth as his throne, the skies his 'well wrought canopie',[76] man as made in the image of God is the focus of the whole creation.

> Terrestrial Heav'n, danc't round by other Heav'ns
> That shine, yet bear thir bright officious Lamps,
> Light above Light, for thee alone, as seems,
> In thee concentring all thir precious beams
> Of sacred influence: As God in Heav'n
> Is Centre, yet extends to all, so thou
> Centring receiv'st from all those Orbs; in thee,
> Not in themselves, all thir known virtue appears
> Productive in Herb, Plant, and nobler birth
> Of Creatures animate with gradual life
> Of Growth, Sense, Reason, all summ'd up in Man.[77]

[72] Swan, *Speculum Mundi*, IX.ii. For Pico, see *RP*, p. 225.
[73] *PL*, VII.505-12.   [74] *Works*, III, 484.
[75] *Laws*, V.liv.5.   [76] Swan, *Speculum Mundi*, VII.i.
[77] *PL*, IX.103-13.

'An associate of Deity' – Hooker's phrase suggests the central prop of traditional optimism and the essentially anthropomorphic quality of Renaissance thought. For in that philosophically ill-formulated but deeply felt set of values which constituted the intellectual legacy of the seventeenth century all experience was located along an axis of which the co-ordinates were God and man. This means that not only theology but also 'science' (the study of the book of nature), politics, literature, even economics, are grounded in morality. Like everything in the realm of nature, they have analogues and correspondences in the realm of spirit, and they are all brought ultimately to bear upon the grand strategy of creation: the glory of God. Since the main outlines of this plan are made doubly certain to man – in the book of nature and in the book of revelation – everything becomes explicable as part of God's design. It follows that man has the moral duty of comprehending this design and adjusting himself to it. 'The World was made to be inhabited by Beasts, but studied and contemplated by Man: 'tis the Debt of our Reason we owe unto God, and the homage we pay for not being Beasts.'[78] Andrewes and Laud, Donne and Herbert, would channelize this homage through the Anglican discipline:

> Now, as for the sight of God here, our theatre was the world, our medium and glass was the creature, and our light was reason, and then for our knowledge of God here, our academy was the church, our medium the ordinances of the church, and our light the light of faith.[79]

Calvin and Cartwright, Perkins and Sibbes, would channelize it through another discipline. But as the Thirty-Nine Articles and the Westminster Confessional make clear, beneath the exfoliations of sects and disciplines lay the broad base of the Christian epic to which all parties subscribed.

In the Christian epic, then, man is the protagonist. His creation, his fall, his regeneration are the central facts of that drama which Dante had called a comedy. Every fact of history, like every detail in God's miraculously sustained universe, points to his central importance. The world exists for moral purposes, and the transaction between God and man is the fundamental moral relationship which informs the whole creation. The object of knowledge is moral truth (which even the data of 'scientific' ob-

---

[78] Browne, *Religio Medici*, p. 15.   [79] Donne, *Works*, I, 422.

HEIGHTS AND DECLENSIONS

servation confirm), and the pursuit of this knowledge, through the exercise of either reason or faith, sanctifies man's lot in this world and insures his felicity in the next. For as Hooker argued, if to be a man is to desire 'evermore to know the truth according to the most infallible certainty which the nature of things can yield', then the moral compulsion to seek the highest knowledge in God sanctifies man's efforts and confirms his dignity.[80]

The great Thomistic assumption of a rational God revealed in a rational universe and comprehensible by rational man found repeated restatement in the seventeenth century – mainly from those Anglican apologists for the *via media* between paths of faith and knowledge, but also from Puritans trying to mitigate the harsh voluntarism of Calvinism. Its optimistic implications are clear. In such a universe, created for such purposes, the goal of all endeavor becomes, as Hooker put it, the striving for higher perfections. 'All which perfections are contained under the general name of Goodness. And because there is not in the world any thing whereby another may not some way be made the perfecter, therefore all things that are, are good.'[81] The direction of events was inexorably toward God, the principle of movement was orderly under law, the end was God's glory. Hence Raphael's words to Adam:

> O Adam, one Almighty is, from whom
> All things proceed, and up to him return,
> If not deprav'd from good, created all
> Such to perfection, one first matter all,
> Indu'd with various forms, various degrees
> Of substance, and in things that live, of life.[82]

Although every part of God's creation was meaningful, and related meaningfully to every other part, man through his unique position in the great design merited and gained the closest study. Cornwallis, a commonplace man, states the commonplace neatly:

> Man hath the superioritie of al and is the worthiest of all; for he consisteth of a soule by his father's side, divinely descended and capable of a devine inheritance, and of a body, the most perfect and full of mysteries that it is possible for earth to put on. Whether can knowledge bend her force more excellently then, then man to look upon man?[83]

---

[80] *Laws*, II.vii.5.   [81] *Ibid.*, I.v.1.   [82] *PL*, V.469–74.
[83] 'Of Knowledge', *Essayes*, no. 36 (ed. Allen, pt. II, p. 131).

When the focus shifted and the scrutiny of nature supplanted the scrutiny of man, the Renaissance had finally spent itself. Mechanism replaced morality; the dense anthropomorphic coloring of all nature faded away into the cold light of science; *how* rather than *why* became the beginning of every question; and man ultimately created by his efforts a glittering, inhuman mechanism which, paradoxically, could not accommodate man himself.

In the Renaissance tradition, however, man looked upon man, as Cornwallis urged, with unceasing zeal. The rich and free variations on the great themes of moral philosophy received both in systematic exposition and in literature their fullest development. These themes were, briefly, the fall and the regeneration of man – a pair of moral facts from which, in the Renaissance view, fanned out in all directions the systems of theology, cosmology, psychology, and political theory. The Christian epic, with the embellishments and accretions of centuries, provided an incomparably rich mythopoeic ground for Renaissance thought. From the main fact of this tradition, sanctified by Scripture and domesticated in the consciousness of Europe, radiated all the lines of seventeenth-century thought and emotion. It served both as the generator and the receptacle of imaginative literature, and to think of Spenser and Milton, Donne and Browne, Chapman and Herbert is to be reminded of its vitality.

In thus sketching the grounds of Renaissance optimism we must not forget that the Christian epic made a large allowance for sin and error. Although Roger Ascham states as a commonplace that where the will is inclined to goodness the mind is bent to truth, Sir Philip Sidney reminds us that our erected wit makes us know what perfection is while our infected will keeps us from attaining it. Always available to check the pretensions of the aggressive intellect or to combat the secularism to which Renaissance optimism was so liable was the dark doctrine of the Fall. Its main points commanded assent from all Christians, and it received emphatic statement in all credal pronouncements, Catholic, Anglican, and Puritan. Providing a necessary polarity for Christian optimism, it levied responsibility for all those imperfections otherwise so hard to explain in a benevolent theism. Moreover, in the broad Augustinian view that had shaped Western theology, it could serve also as the most dramatic evidence

HEIGHTS AND DECLENSIONS 31

of that design, or providence, with which God sustains and would eventually redeem His creation.

Characteristically, Robert Burton sets forth the consequences of the Fall with copious unoriginality:

> Man, the most excellent and noble creature of the World, the principal and mighty work of God, wonder of Nature, as Zoroaster calls him; *audacis naturae miraculum*, the marvel of marvels, as Plato; the Abridgement and Epitome of the World, as Pliny; *Microcosmos*, a little world, Sovereign Lord of the Earth, Viceroy of the World, sole Commander and Governor of all the Creatures in it; to whose Empire they are subject in particular, and yield obedience; far surpassing all the rest, not in body only, but in soul; *Imaginis Imago*, created to Gods own Image, to that immortal and incorporeal substance, with all the faculties and powers belonging unto it; was at first pure, divine, perfect, happy, created after God in true holiness and righteousness; *Deo congruens*, free from all manner of infirmities, and put in Paradise, to know God, to praise and glorify him, to do his will:
>
> *Ut dis consimiles parturiat deos,*
>
> (as an old Poet saith) to propagate the Church.
>
> But this most noble creature, *Heu tristis & lacrimosa commutatio* (one exclaims) O pitiful change! is fallen from that he was, and forfeited his estate, become *miserabilis homuncio*, a castaway, a caitiff, one of the most miserable creatures of the world, if he be considered in his own nature, an unregenerate man, and so much obscured by his fall (that some few reliques excepted) he is inferior to a beast.[84]

Burton's summary of that cardinal ambivalence of the traditional view of man would command at least nominal assent from every Christian. Since Luther and Calvin had so emphatically restated the Augustinian account of the Fall, and since this account had been given canonical status by the Elizabethan settlement, we must expect to find Englishmen, of whatever doctrinal persuasion, lugubriously repeating the stock strictures on the sin of pride. For through pride fell Adam ('from whom we derive our Being, and the several wounds of constitution')[85] and Adam's legacy to the race is, in the words of William Perkins, that 'corruption ingendered in our first conception, whereby every facultie of our soule and bodie is prone and disposed to evill'.[86] In spite of the modifications and evasions of his followers, Calvin's thundering emphasis on the Fall and on the supra-rational workings of grace

---

[84] *Anatomy*, I, 149-50. [85] Browne, *Pseudodoxia Epidemica*, I.i.
[86] *A Golden Chaine*, p. 55.

as the only means of salvation became commonplace in late Renaissance thought. Perhaps in reaction to steady secularization of the sacramental view of nature bequeathed the Renaissance by the Middle Ages,[87] it was thought necessary to preserve doctrinally those attitudes made meaningless by the new idols of progress and utility and science. Hence the fervor of Calvin's adoration of God and grace, his contempt of fallen man and nature.

> For as long as our views are bounded by the earth, perfectly content with our own righteousness, wisdom, and strength, we fondly flatter ourselves, and fancy we are little less than demigods. But, if we once elevate our thoughts to God, and consider his nature, and the consummate perfection of his righteousness, wisdom, and strength to which we ought to be conformed, – what before charmed us in ourselves under the false pretext of righteousness, will soon be loathed as the greatest iniquity; what strangely deceived us under the title of wisdom, will be despised as extreme folly; and what wore the appearance of strength, will be proved to be most wretched impotence. So very remote from the divine purity is what seems in us the highest perfection.[88]

Such studied derogation of man's natural faculties, especially as it was repeated by humanists like Milton, sounds odd amid the din of paeans to man's dignity, but it was traditionally one of the anchors of Christian thought – one that had nearly slipped away in the onrushing currents of Thomistic rationalism and scientific naturalism. Since for those of Calvin's temper it was absolutely essential to shore up the almost forgotten virtue of humility, the handiest weapon for doing so was to remind man – proud man – of the Fall. To do so was, of course, to draw on the arsenal of Augustine. Hooker, a prince among rational theologians, joins the refrain with Donne and Taylor, and they with Milton and Burton, the clinical psychologist, in attributing to that catastrophe the innate proclivity to evil which serves to define man. For the Fall meant, as Augustine had taught Christendom, the perversion of man's originally noble faculties, the falling away from a state of grace to a state of nature, the *privatio boni* which must be charged to the evil will. 'For the corruption of the body, which weighs down the soul, is not the cause but the punishment of the first sin; and it was not the corruptible flesh that made the soul sinful, but the sinful soul that made the flesh corruptible.'[89] Adam's perverted will, whence all our woe, was

---

[87] See Calvin, *Institutes*, I.v.14; I.xiii.21; I.xiv.4; III.vii.1.
[88] *Ibid.*, I.i.2.   [89] *The City of God*, XIV.iii.

the result of his sinful pride; when he set his will against God's commandment it established the pattern of man's iniquity for all time.

> Our first parents fell into open disobedience because already they were secretly corrupted; for the evil act had never been done had not an evil will preceded it. And what is the origin of our evil will but pride? For 'pride is the beginning of sin'. And what is pride but the craving for undue exaltation?[90]

On the passionately held and tenaciously argued conviction of the cleavage between God and man, nature and grace, Calvin built his theology. It was his answer to all varieties of Renaissance naturalism and rationalism. To those optimists who would derive man's dignity from his natural condition or from his natural faculties Calvin had a ready answer: man in his natural state is a worm alienated from God and incapable of good. Owing to the Adamic curse that corrodes his moral and physical being, his condition is hopeless and helpless without the aid of God's unmerited grace; therefore his only faint chance for redemption lies not in the cultivation of his natural assets but in imploring the supernatural help of God. The guilt of Adam

> being the origin of that curse which extends to every part of the world, it is reasonable to conclude its propagation to all his offspring. Therefore, when the Divine image in him was obliterated, and he was punished with the loss of wisdom, strength, sanctity, truth, and righteousness, with which he had been adorned, but which were succeeded by the dreadful pests of ignorance, impotence, impurity, vanity, and iniquity, he suffered not alone, but involved all his posterity with him, and plunged them into the same miseries. This is that hereditary corruption which the fathers called original sin; meaning by sin, the depravation of a nature previously good and pure.[91]

Such a doctrine of despair, developed with all the tenacity and subtlety that the Puritans could summon, posed a formidable threat to the tradition of Renaissance optimism. For its corollaries were even more shattering: since man by his evil will and pride had flung himself into the abomination of sin he has lost every faculty for regeneration. Like 'the heroes of the field' he is a creature of will, not reason, and his will 'is so bound by the slavery of sin, that it cannot excite itself, much less devote itself

[90] Ibid., XIV.xiii; cf. Milton's comparable version, *De doctrina*, I.x (*PW*, IV, 221).
[91] *Institutes*, II.i.5.

to any thing good'.[92] Thus man retains no capacity for pleasing God; moreover, through imputed guilt every member of the human race is quite literally doomed to the fiery torments of hell. But among His other attributes God has infinite mercy, which leads Him to elect – arbitrarily, since He is not restricted by the limits of man's puny reason – certain sinners for the 'justification' which can assure redemption. This justification is of crucial significance as 'an acceptance, by which God receives us into his favour'. It means that our unspeakable sins are absolved by the 'imputation of the righteousness of Christ',[93] itself the most dramatic manifestation of that providence by which God redeems a universe inexorably doomed to destruction.

Such redemption cannot be merited; no number of good works can serve to obliterate the stain of original sin; indeed, good works are impossible without justification, for

> according to the constitution of our nature, oil might be extracted from a stone sooner than we could perform a good work. It is wonderful, indeed, that man, condemned to such ignominy, dares to pretend to have anything left.[94]

Therefore if a man is saved he is saved only by an infusion of divine grace that enables him to have faith, and such grace is solely the gift of God. Likewise, some – obviously a vast majority – are doomed by God to reprobation, against which eternal decree they are powerless. This election, either for salvation or reprobation, is the conclusive mark of God's sovereignty: *Quos deus praeterit reprobat*. It signalizes that awful doctrine of predestination by which man is subjected to a theological determinism that makes the horrors of a later, mechanistic determinism seem warm and comfortable.

> In conformity, therefore, to the clear doctrine of the Scripture, we assert, that by an eternal and immutable counsel, God has once for all determined, both whom he would admit to salvation, and whom he would condemn to destruction. We affirm that this counsel, as far as concerns the elect, is founded on his gratuitous mercy, totally irrespective of human merit; but that to those whom he devotes to condemnation, the gate of life is closed by a just and irreprehensible, but incomprehensible, judgment. In the elect, we consider calling as an evidence of election, and justification as another token of its manifestation, till they arrive in glory, which constitutes its completion. As God seals his elect by vocation and justification,

---

[92] *Ibid.*, II.ii.26; II.iii.5.   [93] *Ibid.*, III.xi.2.   [94] *Ibid.*, III.xiv.5.

so by excluding the reprobate from the knowledge of his name and the sanctification of his Spirit, he affords an indication of the judgment that awaits them.[95]

Thus even infants, as William Perkins explains, may obtain eternal salvation, being 'after a secret & unspeakable manner by Gods spirit engraffed unto Christ'.[96] Since this divine strategy of redemption and destruction is hopelessly beyond man's power to understand, it is impious to scrutinize God's secret counsels.

> If, therefore, we can assign no reason why he grants mercy to his people but because such is his pleasure, neither shall we find any other cause but his will for the reprobation of others. For when God is said to harden or show mercy to whom he pleases, men are taught by this declaration to seek no cause beside his will.[97]

As Augustine had asked, if God could, by willing it, convert the depraved will of the wicked to good, then why does He not? 'Because he would not. Why he would not, remains with himself.'[98] The whole cosmic drama, then, is immutably determined by God. From the beginning He had laid down the lines along which the human race would be created, would fall, would be regenerated: Adam's will was bound, not free, and he had to fall so that God might exploit such an apparent disaster for His own ultimate glory. In the secret will of God are decreed those mechanics of sin and regeneration which, defying any test of reason and mocking all efforts at comprehension, confirm His glory and sovereignty, man's guilt and impotence. With dreadful logic Calvin works out the details of the appalling plot against the dignity of man: he flouts human pretensions to free will;[99] denying any element of contingency in the Fall, he hammers the inference that by willing it God *caused* the catastrophe;[100] he flings man into an abysm of predetermined sin and guilt. All this he does for one purpose: to declare the glory of God. For that, the infamy of man is a small price. Obsessed with the impious claim of man's natural faculties for achieving a life of rational well-being, Calvin made the whole realm of nature the sink of corruption, alien from the

---

[95] Ibid., III.xxi.7. For Milton's view of the doctrine of election, see *PL*, II.1032-3; III.136, 183-4; IV.618-9; *De doctrina*, I.iv.
[96] *A Golden Chaine*, p. 361.
[97] *Institutes*, III.xxii.11.
[98] Ibid., III.xxiv.13.
[99] Ibid., II.v.
[100] Ibid., III.xxiii.7-8; cf. William W. Fenn, 'The Marrow of Calvin's Theology', *Harvard Theological Review*, II (1909), 337-8. Men who 'assert that God is himself the cause and origin of sin', says Milton (*De doctrina*, I.iii [*PW*, IV, 42]), are, if not merely misguided, 'among the most abandoned of all blasphemers'.

realm of grace. Theologically, he fractured the medieval synthesis as sharply as Descartes would fracture it philosophically. Resuscitating those dark Pauline and Augustinian elements almost obscured by the rational theology of the Schoolmen, he dramatically contravened the whole movement of Renaissance optimism.

But if Calvin contributed importantly to the decline of Renaissance optimism, he gave a powerful impetus to a typically Protestant individualism – religious, economic, political – which flatters man's dignity in ways largely unknown before the sixteenth century. Although he ruthlessly demolished the traditional sense of corporate dignity by convicting the whole race of Adam's guilt, he reserved for the elect of God a status truly sublime. Like Plato, whom he so often recalls, he provided for an elite – spiritual rather than rational – whose prerogatives were unassailable on earth or in heaven. Moreover, he based his strategy for attaining and distinguishing such special status on an essentially personal and subjective transaction with God. The real strength (and the real weakness) of Protestantism lay in its inwardness. Although the Calvinistic emphasis on the individual sinner and the individual saint was directly counter to the medieval sense of status and of community, it did articulate one of the most powerful drives of the late Renaissance – that individualism which has largely informed modern thought.

Thus Calvin's impact was a major event of late Renaissance intellectual history. It not only checked the rampant rationalism but served as well to transform political and economic conduct, and before the first great tidal wave of Reformation theology had spent itself, it had changed the course of European history. There is no doubt that Calvin's intentions were more modest. As he explained in dedicating the *Institutes* to François I, he wished only to reduce man to a proper humility before God by challenging, out of the Scripture, the impious errors of Thomistic rationalism – the 'blind light of nature, pretended preparations, free will and works meritorious of eternal salvation' – which flatter man's vanity and lead him to hell. But the Reformation unleashed forces that went far beyond theology. The vitality of the Lutheran church was soon spent: although its doctrinal rigidities have left a permanent mark on German thought, it ceased to be an aggressive and expanding church after the Formula of Concord (1577) had reconciled its warring sects, and instead slipped into that sterile Erastianism implicit in Luther's own timid views of secular authority.

The history of Calvinism is more exciting. Steadily refusing the Erastian gambit to secure its safety, it upset the political economy of western Europe to claim its rights. Under the Edict of Nantes the Calvinists achieved a state within a state; in 1613 the Lutheran house of Brandenburg – for reasons not unrelated to expediency – turned the whole Palatinate over to the Calvinistic camp; in Scotland, John Knox played with Mary Stuart as with a tennis ball; in England the Puritans, declining to come to terms with the established church, unleashed the hounds of war to win their brief ascendancy; in New England the Calvinists, fleeing from the Laudian terror, failed to achieve the reign of the saints but they did shape a dominant strain in American thought.[101] And although by the close of the seventeenth century both the theological and the political impetus of Calvinism was waning, it had by then generated – or shown itself compatible with – certain habits of political and economic conduct upon which western culture has been built.

Apart from these extra-theological successes, however, Calvinist doctrine worked itself into the very heart of the Anglican church. The Marian exiles who flocked back at the accession of Elizabeth not unnaturally expected to help shape ecclesiastical policy, and the Elizabethan settlement testifies to their success, at least doctrinally. We must presently attempt to trace in more detail the history of this influence; for the purposes of this chapter it is perhaps enough to remind ourselves that for England Calvin was the dominant Reformation figure, and that Calvin's assessment of the natural man was so low that it is possible to write the intellectual history of seventeenth-century England in terms of the efforts to mitigate and modify his strictures on human dignity.

Although Spenser and Milton, the twin peaks of Christian humanism in England, may be described as essentially Augustinian in their theology, both sought to evade the desperate implications of a strict Calvinism. In the third 'Hymne' Spenser treats the Fall soberly enough:

[101] See Clark, *The Seventeenth Century*, pp. 309–10.

> But man, forgetfull of his Makers grace,
> No lesse then angels, whom he did ensew,
> Fell from the hope of promist heavenly place,
> Into the mouth of death, to sinners dew,
> And all his off-spring into thraldome threw.

But his main concern is with the Atonement and with that 'great Lord of Love' who for 'mans deare sake' became a man. Love is the key to the 'Hymne': almost like the Platonic *eros* it is the compelling motive of all creation, the mystery of man's Atonement, the stimulus to social amity and spiritual truth.

> O blessed Well of Love! O Floure of Grace!
> O glorious Morning Starre! O Lampe of Light!
> Most lively image of thy Fathers face,
> Eternall King of Glorie, Lord of Might,
> Meeke Lambe of God, before all worlds behight,
> How can we thee requite for all this good?
> Or what can prize that thy most precious blood?[102]

Spenser was far too good a humanist to accept Calvin's evaluation of human dignity. The Red Cross Knight may be a blundering fool, but his is also a very human and very sympathetically drawn portrait of a man seeking holiness. Of course he cannot achieve holiness alone: without the intervention of Arthur (or grace) he would have perished in Orgoglio's dungeon, but with it he rises to sanctity, and when he descends from the Mount of Contemplation it is to go forth and wage victorious battle against the enemies of truth and holiness. Sir Guyon, in the second book, is even more remote from the Calvinistic ethos. If the Red Cross Knight is the warfaring Christian fighting the good fight with a fair hope of victory, Sir Guyon is the Aristotelian hero for whom reason, moderation, and self-discipline are the cardinal ethical principles. Arthur saves him, too, but we feel that his help is not absolutely necessary for so self-sufficient a machine as Guyon. The villain of the second book is unreason, and for this psychological disorder Guyon (and his prosy Palmer) have a certain remedy in temperance, the faculty intrinsic to man's nature that needs nothing but itself. 'Old syre', says Sir Guyon to the Palmer when they look on the corpses of Sir Mortdant and Amavia,

---

[102] 'An Hymne of Heavenly Love', ll.120–4; 169–75.

> Behold the ymage of mortalitie,
> And feeble nature cloth'd with fleshly tyre.
> When raging passion with fierce tyranny
> Robs reason of her dew regalitie, . . .
> The strong it weakens with infirmitie. . . .
>
> But Temperaunce, said he, with golden squire
> Betwixt them both can measure out a meane,
> Nether to melt in pleasures whott desyre,
> Nor frye in hartlesse griefe and dolefull tene.
> Thrise happy man, who fares them both atweene![103]

As a better poet and a more systematic thinker, Milton brings to his estimate of human dignity a plastic fullness impossible in Spenser's unwieldy allegory. It is not that he refuses to face the brutal fact of evil, or that he relapses into a glib Neo-Platonic optimism to escape from Augustine and Calvin. But he does try to salvage human dignity by fixing the responsibility for evil on man's perverted will, and he infers that if man is free to sin he is also free to cease from sinning. In the great art of *Paradise Lost* and *Samson Agonistes*, as in the tortuous mental gymnastic of the *De doctrina Christiana*, he hammers out his theme: since, through the defection of the will, passion had usurped the throne of reason and thus radically disrupted the economy of man's moral being, he is reduced to the level of the beasts, and – 'some few reliques' alone remaining of his primal virtue – he is morally obligated to use all his resources, natural and supernatural, to attain again that wisdom and self-knowledge which means dignity in this life and salvation in the next.

In Milton's most systematic statement the consequences of man's falling away from God were immense:

> It comprehended at once distrust in the divine veracity, and a proportionate credulity in the assurances of Satan; unbelief; ingratitude; disobedience; gluttony; in the man excessive uxoriousness, in the woman a want of proper regard for her husband, in both an insensibility to the welfare of their offspring, and that offspring the whole human race; parricide, theft, invasion of the rights of others, sacrilege, deceit, presumption in aspiring to divine attributes, fraud in the means employed to attain the object, pride, and arrogance.[104]

---

[103] *FQ*, II.i.57–8. For an admirable discussion of Spenser's role as a Christian humanist see A. S. P. Woodhouse, 'Nature and Grace in The Faerie Queene', *ELH*, XVI (1949), 194–228.
[104] *De doctrina*, I. xi (*PW*, IV, 254).

As for *Paradise Lost*, that study in the conflict of human and divine wills is the noblest statement in our language of the Augustinian view of man. Just as Satan fell through pride – 'O foul descent', he soliloquizes[105] – so he tempts the foolish Eve with the dream that the forbidden fruit, once eaten, may make 'Gods of Men'.[106] The importance of that one prohibition, however, was incalculable: 'It was necessary that something should be forbidden or commanded as a test of fidelity, and that an act in its own nature indifferent, in order that man's obedience might be thereby manifested.'[107] But Eve's desire for independence and self-sufficiency (miscalled liberty)[108] can only mean irrational turning away from God; the conquest of reason by will denies this symbolic subordination of man to God, just as Adam's submitting to the blandishments of the fallen Eve meant the conquest of his reason by his passion,

> Against his better knowledge, not deceiv'd,
> But fondly overcome with Female charm.[109]

Eve, then, had sinned because her reason was deceived, but Adam – more heinously – sins 'against his better knowledge, not deceiv'd'. His is clearly a transgression of the will, which, left free by God, is at liberty to follow or ignore the advice of reason.[110] Nothing, in Milton's un-Calvinistic view, is more crucial in fixing responsibility for the Fall than this freedom. As Adam himself tells Eve, God created man so that when tempted

> within himself
> The danger lies, yet lies within his power:
> Against his will he can receive no harm.
> But God left free the will, for what obeys
> Reason, is free, and Reason he made right.[111]

And to this testimony God adds His own:

---

[105] IX.163; cf. I.35; IV.503; V.662.
[106] V.70; cf. IX.703–12.
[107] *De doctrina*, I.x (*PW*, IV, 221).
[108] *PL*, IX.335–41; cf. IX.1175–7; and, for Gabriel's denunciation of similar motives in Satan's fall, IV.957–61.
[109] IX.998–1000; cf. VIII.530–9, 551–3, 588–94; IX.906–10; X.888–95.
[110] Milton's psychology is, of course, generally Elizabethan. See *PL*, IV.801–9; V.100–13. For its differences from Calvin's, see the *Institutes*, I.xv.6–7.
[111] IX.348–52.

> No Decree of mine
> Concurring to necessitate his Fall,
> Or touch with lightest moment of impulse
> His free Will, to her own inclining left
> In even scale.[112]

And so the sinister motifs of pride and sensuality wind through the cosmic calamity. In the first anguish of his guilt Adam – or Milton? – seems almost to blame God for the whole sorry business,[113] but he at last attains that acquiescence and humility that, in terms of the Christian epic, constitute wisdom.

> What better can we do, than to the place
> Repairing where he judg'd us, prostrate fall
> Before him reverent, and there confess
> Humbly our faults, and pardon beg, with tears
> Watering the ground, and with our sighs the Air
> Frequenting, sent from hearts contrite, in sign
> Of sorrow unfeign'd, and humiliation meek.[114]

In *Paradise Lost*, as in *Samson Agonistes*, error leads to truth, defeat to victory, and the erring human will, by a 'new acquist Of true experience', is disciplined to piety. Seeking to preserve both human responsibility and divine sovereignty, Milton celebrates this consummation of God's great design with an art that ennobles his language and enriches his religion.

> Nothing is here for tears, nothing to wail
> Or knock the breast, no weakness, no contempt,
> Dispraise or blame, nothing but well and fair,
> And what may quiet us in a death so noble.[115]

Such a vision of erring man wrestling with the infinite justice of God not only places Milton securely within the central tradition of Christian humanism; it also reminds us that even in the age of Hobbes and Newton the Renaissance view of man, in both his strength and weakness, retained immense reserves of power.

Milton's is only one voice, though powerful, that swells the testimony. To him Calvin's theology came to present a moral affront, but others found other reasons for modifying it. However the creeds might memorialize the infamy of a worm five

---

[112] X.43–7; cf. III.96–128; V.235–7, 520–40; also the thorny discussion in *De doctrina* I.iv.
[113] X.743 ff.   [114] X.1086–92.
[115] *Samson Agonistes*, ll.1721–4.

feet long, the Calvinist theology was intolerable for the conduct of daily life. It simply could not be accommodated in men's business and bosoms. Hence the efforts, direct or oblique, to escape the implications of Calvin's steely logic. In Puritan thought proper the result was such un-Calvinistic developments as Ramean dialectic and covenantal theology, both of which conferred upon man a freedom and a capacity for moral action that contravened the most fundamental points of Genevan theology. Another result was that series of internal tensions and paradoxes between the express theological convictions of the Puritans and their actual conduct in the bustle of politics and business. Among the Anglicans, who subscribed at least in part to Calvin's theology but challenged his views of church discipline, there was a steady desire, as we learn from Hooker and Laud and Chillingworth, to salvage the best parts of rational theology, to mollify Reformed theology with the aid of tradition, and reason, and moderation. Meanwhile, the broad stream of Renaissance optimism had by no means dried up: Spenser was an Anglican with apparent Puritan sympathies, Milton an outright Puritan; yet they both proclaimed, in the teeth of Calvinistic theology, the humanistic values of the Renaissance. Finally, there were those like Bacon who, accepting Calvin's alienation of faith from reason, grace from nature, addressed themselves to reconstructing man's knowledge of nature: in doing so, they pointed to the rise of science, the most momentous development of seventeenth-century thought.

II

DEATH AND TIME

1. *DE CONTEMPTU MUNDI*

In his great symbol of the two cities Augustine unforgettably enunciated that basic Christian dualism which gives meaning to all its dichotomies of earth and heaven, nature and grace, man and God, the relative and the absolute, time and eternity. Even though the earthly city has, in certain periods, been assigned a prestige that would have grieved Augustine (to say nothing of St Paul), the Christian tradition which he so profoundly shaped could never quite forget its essential other-worldliness. Indeed, it never should, as St Thomas, *facile princeps* among rational theologians, reminds us repeatedly. Man's mortality and the inevitable deficiencies of his knowledge alike teach him that he is born to trouble as sparks fly upward.

> But man cannot be wholly free from evils in this state of life; and not only from evils of the body, such as hunger, thirst, heat, cold and the like, but also from evils of the soul. For there is no one who at times is not disturbed by inordinate passions; who sometimes does not go beyond the mean, wherein virtue consists, either in excess or in deficiency; who is not deceived in some thing or another; or who at least is not ignorant of what he would wish to know, or does not feel doubtful about an opinion of which he would like to be certain. Therefore no man is happy in this life.[1]

In this passage, as in many others like it, St Thomas restates that central motif of Christian pessimism which the Middle Ages had stylized as *contemptus mundi*.

Ironically enough, it was in the Renaissance largely made possible by St Thomas's attempted synthesis of reason and faith that the motif was most eagerly exploited. In the centuries between Petrarch and Milton, when the main current of European thought seemed to be so optimistic, we find, as if in subconscious reaction to a too bland and secular complacency, persistent mutterings against proud man – who, for all his pretensions, is the sinful spawn of Adam, the heir of affliction, the food for worms. This reaction runs with a steady crescendo through the Renais-

[1] *Summa contra Gentiles*, III.xlviii.

sance until it reaches a climax at the turn of the seventeenth century. Then it at last became clear that the Renaissance, for all its glory, had failed. Confronted by this failure, men could either succumb into the pessimism made canonical by the Christian tradition (and powerfully reinforced by the Reformers) or they could set themselves to the task of restudying and reconstructing human felicity. Montaigne and Ralegh and Godfrey Goodman illustrate one alternative, Bacon and Descartes the other – while of course the vast majority (for whom Milton is a noble spokesman) were convinced that the claims of man's dignity and of God's sovereignty could still be accommodated within the limits of the Christian epic.

Having surveyed the broad outlines of Renaissance optimism, we must now examine the ways in which the traditional *contemptus mundi* was given new urgency by the pressures generated in a crucial period. The *contemptus mundi* of the Christian tradition comprises the great themes of death and time. Although death, with its corollary of sex, and time or mutability were of obsessive concern to a period of such unsteady values as the late Renaissance, both themes had been stock for centuries, and we must sketch their development if we are to put an alleged Jacobean melancholy in its proper context.

When Lotario de' Conti di Segni, shortly before his elevation as Innocent III in 1196, wrote his *De contemptu mundi* he transmitted an ancient Christian attitude to the Renaissance. Behind Innocent's diatribe lay a long line of ascetics: the *De contemptu mundi* of the pseudo-St Bernard, the very popular *Meditationes piissimae de cognitione humanae conditionis* ('Nihil aliud est homo quam sperma fetidum, saccus stercorum, cibus vermium'),[2] the famous *De contemptu mundi* of Bernard of Cluny, even the Old English *Address of the Lost Soul to the Body*.[3] But we may take Innocent's statement of the thesis as central to the whole tradition:

> Formatus est homo de pulvere, de luto, de cinere: quoque vilius est, de spurcissimo spermate: conceptus in pruritu carnis, in fervore libidinis, in fetore luxuriae: quodque deterius est, in labe peccati; natus ad laborem, dolorem, timorem: quodque miserius est, ad mortem.[4]

[2] See Benjamin P. Kurtz, 'Gifer the Worm: An Essay toward the History of an Idea', *University of California Publications in English*, II (1928–29), 238. For the *Meditationes*, see Migne, *PL*, CLXXXIV, 485 ff.
[3] For the literary milieu of this famous invective, see Rudolf Willard, 'The Address of the Soul to the Body', *PMLA*, L (1935), 937–83.
[4] I.i (Migne, *PL*, CCXVII, 702).

There follow two books of particulars – all bitter, some obscene – on such topics as the conception of infants, the ills of old age, the brevity of man's pleasures, and sexual perversion. But in the third book Innocent warms to his subject in developing the dread refrain, *natus ad mortem*; death, decay, hell fire, and judgment are his topics, and he treats them with formidable enthusiasm.

> Conceptus est enim homo de sanguine per adorem libidinis putrefacto, cujus tandem libidinis cadaveri quasi funebres vermes assistent. Vivus generavit pediculos et lumbricos, mortuus generabit vermes et muscas; vivus produxit stercus et vomitum, mortuus producet putredinem et fetorem; vivus hominem unicum impinguavit, mortuus vermes plurimos impinguabit. Quid ergo foetidius humano cadavere?[5]

To trace the progress of this attitude in the Renaissance is a useful corrective to the fallacy that the period was distinguished mainly by its *joie de vivre*. Even though Giannozzo Manetti wrote his influential *On the Excellency and Dignity of Man* in rebuttal of Innocent's slanders, and though Ficino and Pico and many others insisted on man's unique glory in a theocratic universe, there were those who could not forget the skeleton and the grave, and the hopeless terror that they inspired. As M. Mâle has shown by his exciting studies,[6] a macabre and mangled Christ as exemplifying the primary facts of suffering and death was the favorite subject of fifteenth-century religious art; it could lead, by a perversion of 'la tendresse humaine' which St Bernard and St Francis had injected into the conceptual aridities of scholasticism, to the most vulgar excesses. These excesses, in turn, remind us of the intense Renaissance concern with man's mortality, and connect us thematically with the magnificent threnodies of Ralegh and Browne and Jeremy Taylor – to say nothing of those countless Puritan tracts and sermons which under the impact of a revived Augustinianism had given a new poignancy to the latent pessimism of the Renaissance.

In spite of his almost mystical exaltation of the freedom of the Christian man regenerated by God's grace, Luther preached an Augustinian contempt for his natural faculties and felicities. 'Tantum orietur stercoris, mucoris, et sudoris.'[7] Calvin's assault on

---

[5] III.i (*PL*, CCXVII, 738).
[6] *L'art religieux de la fin du moyen âge en France*, pp. 85, 145 f. See Theodore Spencer, *Death and Elizabethan Tragedy*, pp. 15 f.; J. Huizinga, *The Waning of the Middle Ages*, ch. xi ('The Vision of Death').
[7] *Tischreden*, no. 6097 (V, 487).

man's pride generated the demonic energy of this theology; he relentlessly exploits the theme in the second book of the *Institutes* that 'man is corrupted by a natural depravity . . . which did not originate from nature'.

> We therefore truly derive advantage from the discipline of the cross, only when we learn that this life, considered in itself, is unquiet, turbulent, miserable and [sic] numberless instances, and in no respect altogether happy; and that all its reputed blessings are uncertain, transient, vain, and adulterated with a mixture of many evils; and in consequence of this at once conclude, that nothing can be sought or expected on earth by conflict, and that when we think of a crown we must raise our eyes towards heaven.[8]

The embellishments of this theme, which informs so many thousands of Puritan sermons and tracts, have been compelling enough to obscure some of the more hopeful elements in Puritan doctrine. The diarist Richard Rogers, a stout Elizabethan Calvinist, noting the recent death of a friend, rejoices to confirm by it 'a sensible contempt of this world and joyfull expectation of the departure from hence. And the contrary is an estat full of uncomfortableness and anguish'.[9] Richard Sibbes, author of the immensely popular *Bruised Reed and Smoking Flax*, compares man's miseries with a widening and deepening river that 'till it be overpowered by grace, swelleth bigger and bigger'.[10] The chief result of his religious education, records Baxter, was to view the world as a 'carkass that had neither Life nor Loveliness'.[11] And so on; testimony on this point could be endless.

The systematic development of the *contemptus mundi* by the great Reformers was an arsenal for countless Puritan obscurantists, of course, but even a bare catalogue of lay writers confirms the obvious fact that such pessimism occurs everywhere in the Renaissance. The early and very popular *Dit des trois morts et des trois vifs* is a verbalization of the loathsome fact of death that appears pictorially in the *danse macabre*; and the same obsession with mortality is seen in Villon's acid realism, in Skelton's elegies,[12] in Sir Thomas More's *Four Last Things*, in the realistic

---

[8] *Institutes*, III.ix.1.
[9] Knappen, *Two Elizabethan Puritan Diaries*, p. 54.
[10] *The Soul's Conflict*, ch. xii (*Works*, I, 173).
[11] Cited by Grierson, *Cross Currents*, p. 30.
[12] It is not surprising that 'Of the Death of the Noble Prince, Kynge Edward the Fourth' should have provided lines for tombstones, or that the whole piece should have found its way into *A Mirror for Magistrates*. But 'Uppon a Deedmans Hed' – recom-

horrors of the Campo Santo at Pisa, in the apocalyptic visions of Dürer, in *A Mirror for Magistrates*, in Spenser's jejune *Ruins of Time*, in the Elizabethan lyric cry, in the metaphysical shudder, in dozens of dull if moral treatises. When William Baldwin, in his very popular *Treatise of Morall Philosophy* (1547), had pointed out that 'Life is a bridle and miserable fetter, which chaineth the pure and everlasting soule, to the vile, sinfull, and corruptible body', he was adorning the same commonplace as George Chapman a half-century later:

> Kneele then with me, fall worm-like on the ground,
> And from th' infectious dunghill of this Round,
> From mens brasse wits, and golden foolerie
> Weepe, weepe your soules, into felicitie.[13]

From Jonson's incomparable gallery of fools and knaves we can only infer a radical disenchantment with the humanistic ethos he professed to hold, and when he speaks off the cuff he seems to reveal a soul grown gray with sadness. 'What a deale of cold busines doth a man mis-spend the better part of his life in! in scattering compliments, tendring visits, gathering and venting newes, following Feasts and Playes, making a little winter-love in a darke corner.'[14] This statement reminds us of another Christian humanist deploring the decay of those virtues which should dignify a good man's life.

> This Isle is a meere Bedlam, and therein,
> We all lye raving, mad in every sinne.[15]

Indeed, Chapman's contention that men are merely 'huge impolisht heapes of filthinesse' could stand as the rubric for a vast body of Elizabethan literature.

Even a little book like *The Paradise of Dainty Devices* – which went through ten editions between 1576 and 1606 – makes us realize how indispensable the *contemptus mundi* theme was to the mended by its author as 'lamentable, lacrymable, profytable for the soule' – strikes a more grimly realistic note:

> Oure eyen synkyng,
> Oure bodys stynkyng,
> Oure gummys grynnyng,
> Oure soulys brynnyng.

[13] *Hymnus in Noctem*, ll.324–7.   [14] *Discoveries*, p. 7.
[15] Michael Drayton, 'To my noble friend Master William Browne, of the evill time', *Minor Poems*, p. 94.

Renaissance. *The Paradise* is distinguished neither intellectually nor literarily, but it does show what the fun-loving Elizabethans liked in their popular verse. We should not be surprised to find the usual amorous ditties, but the many pieces lamenting man's depravity, his painful life, and his sorry end do perhaps jar some of our misconceptions. Significantly, the collection opens with a paraphrase of the popular medieval hymn that begins 'Cur mundus militat, sub vana gloria, cuius prosperitas est transitoria?' and that tells us just as Solomon, Caesar, and Tully are now dust – 'O foode of filthy woorme, or lumpe of loathsome clay' – we shall all be shortly. This depressing truism gives the tone to dozens of pieces in the *Paradise*. They urge that 'Our pleasures are vanities', that when man's body sickens he should think of heaven, that human misery cries aloud for death, that change is the law of nature, that man is 'dust, slime, a puffe of wynde', that life is a sickness.[16] Unless we attribute to writers like Edwards, Churchyard, Heywood, and Kinwelmersh a special awareness of man's desolation, we must infer that they were gracefully developing platitudes – platitudes which appear in an even grimmer guise in *A Gorgeous Gallery of Gallant Inventions* (1578).

Although it is often hard to disengage the competently handled formula from the sincere utterance in Elizabethan literature, it is sufficiently clear that toward the end of the sixteenth century the *contemptus mundi* motif had become both very popular and very stereotyped. The stream whose course we are tracing is what Browne called 'the incessant Mortality of Mankind', and when it reached the delta of the late Elizabethan period it fanned off in many sinuous channels. But the rather silly fad for melancholic humors (amorous, religious, or political), the Calvinists' obsession with human frailty, the Jacobeans' with lust, the swelling rhetoric of Ralegh's world-weariness, the charnel-house realism of Dekker's *Wonderful Year* are all fed by the tradition that surges with a steady power throughout the age until it reaches a capacious ocean in *The Anatomy of Melancholy*: 'You may as soon separate weight from lead, heat from fire, moistness from water, brightness from the sun, as misery, discontent, care, calamity, danger, from a man.'[17]

---

[16] To note how pervasive this tritely stylized pessimism is in the *Paradise*, see, *inter alia*, nos. 1, 5, 8, 13, 20, 24, 27, 32, 39, 40, 45, 118.
[17] *Anatomy*, I, 317.

In spite of its lapses into literary affectation, we may everywhere see the persistence of the pessimism which Burton so remorselessly develops. Its vitality is obviously sapped (or parodied) in the amorously melancholic inanities of the Elizabethan sonnet sequences, as in Berowne's puns and the discontent of the repulsed stallion of *Venus and Adonis*. Even in the midst of the witty obscenities of *The Metamorphosis of Ajax* Sir John Harington can conventionally – ironically? – lament that man's life is an 'Ocean of miseries'.[18] But Nashe, the hack turned penitent worldling, gets genuine fervor into such a palinode as *Christ's Tears over Jerusalem*, and Dekker's plaints in *The Bellman of London* – like his ironical advice to the would-be melancholic in *The Gull's Horn Book* – show the edge that good writing could give to platitudes.[19] Even in such a hack-work as *A Looking-Glass for London and England* Greene (or Lodge) sounds sincere in denouncing – well before the Jacobeans grew melancholic – the iniquities of contemporary London:

> Contempt of God, despite of reverend age,
> Neglect of law, desire to wrong the poor,
> Corruption, whoredom, drunkenness, and pride.[20]

Shakespeare knew sin and death, of course, and with ineffable poignancy. Romeo in the Capulets' tomb, the dirge in *Cymbeline*, Claudio's terror in *Measure for Measure*, Troilus' revulsion from unclean love lose nothing by being constructed on a bed of commonplaces. Moreover, Sonnet CXXIX stands always as the consummate statement of a theme worn thin by repetition. But even descending from the peaks of literature we may find in the broad plateau of the contemporary moral philosophy the intensity of the tradition. Thomas Beard – one day to be Oliver Cromwell's schoolmaster – brings a typical Puritan ardor to his survey of the world's iniquities in the often-reprinted *Theater of God's Judgments*. 'Every affection of the flesh is deadly,' chants La Primaudaye after St Paul, 'and . . . the workes thereof are uncleannesse, pride, fornication, enmitie, debate.' Although he could take the customary solace in reflecting on the providence that rules a

---

[18] pp. 3–4.
[19] For example, see *The Bellman*, pp. 71 f., 109.
[20] V.v. Note the interesting, if dramaturgically inept, scene (V.iv) in *James the Fourth*, where Greene has a lawyer, a merchant, and a divine intone a litany on the evils of the body politic.

theocratic universe, La Primaudaye was painfully aware of man's brief and sinful career on this planet. All parts of a sheep are useful – the flesh for food, the wool for clothing, 'the guts to make strings for musicall Instruments' – but

> in man it is cleane contrary, for all things in him are naught, and serve to doe evill, his reason to decline, his libertie to disordered lust, his eies to see and behold vanitie, his heart to covet the same, his hands to fight and steale, his feet to runne unto evill, and his tongue to slander, lye, and blaspheme: In such manner . . . there is not member in man, that serveth not for an instruement of some iniquitie, (As S. Paul saith).[21]

This sort of invective – so common as an antidote to Renaissance secularism – leads us straight back to the second chapter of the Epistle to the Romans.

II. THE LITERATURE OF DISENCHANTMENT

The misanthropy of certain late sixteenth-century satirists was another vent for the traditional *contemptus mundi*. Like the sonnet, satire was a literary fad at the end of the century, but a fad with a most respectable lineage. Not only had the classical tradition of Horace, Martial, Juvenal, and Persius been kept alive during the humanistic revival in new editions and in translations,[22] but there had been the indigenous satire of social classes – the old categorical satire which had flourished in England ever since Barclay translated Brant's *Narrenschiff* in 1509. Chaucer, Langland, and Skelton had often written satirically, of course, but formal satire (the ridicule of individuals or classes under assumed names in non-narrative verse) became the norm after the middle of the sixteenth century. There is such satire in Wyatt's quasi-Horatian

---

[21] *The French Academie*, p. 913.
[22] Horace, of course, was always popular. In 1567 Thomas Drant had published *Horace his arte of Poetrie, pistles, and Satyrs Englished*; even earlier (1564–65) *The Fyrste twoo Satars or poyses of H[orace]* had been licensed to T. Colwell; in 1566 Thomas Drant had published his *Medicinable Morall, that is, the two Bookes of Horace his Satyres*.
Thomas Kendall had included a sheaf of 'Epigrammes out of Martial' in his *Flowres of Epigrammes out of sundrie the most singular authors* (1577), and in 1629 there appeared *Selected Epigrams of Martial. Englished by Thomas May Esquire*.
Persius and Juvenal apparently had to wait until the seventeenth century for translators. In 1614 Thomas Bond published an elaborate edition, in Latin, of Persius; two years later Barten Holyday published his translation, *Aulus Persius Flaccus his Satires translated into English* (which went into a second printing the same year, and into new editions in 1617 and 1635). Juvenal was translated by W. B[arksted?] in 1617, by George Chapman (in his *Justification of A strange action of Nero*) in 1629, and by J. Beaumont (in his *Bosworth-field*) in 1629.

THE LITERATURE OF DISENCHANTMENT 51

pieces and in Edward Hake's *News out of Paul's Churchyard* (1567), as well as in the 'epigrams' and assorted social commentaries of Heywood, Turberville, and Gascoigne. Spenser opened no new paths, then, in *Colin Clout's Come Home Again*, when he interpolated into an essentially narrative poem his attack on the intrigues of court.[23]

It was in the 'nineties, however, that the astonishing development of more or less consciously classical satire occurred. Young Jack Donne seems to have led the pack, but he was quickly followed by Lodge and Hall and in 1598 by Marston with his *Metamorphosis of Pygmalion's Image*. When *The Scourge of Villainy* appeared a year later, the vogue was so well established that apparently every poetaster in London was turning his hand to scurrility,[24] and Archbishop Whitgift arranged a public bonfire for the offending works. Most of this satire was framed on ostensibly classical models. In the wit and bite of his satires Donne spared no affectation, from the piety of the sullen Calvinists and the erudition of the savants to the jargon of the law courts and the sexual habits of the gallants and whores infesting the streets of London. But it is clear that Donne had read his Juvenal and Persius, as had Lodge and Hall. Their derivation accounts for a good deal of their willful obscurity, but it also accounts for their implicit view of the function of satire. These men, and Ben Jonson in his dramatic satire, stood ready to expose the foolish and the wicked to ridicule, and thus to reform them. Accepting the humanistic doctrine of man's essential goodness, they could flay his follies on the cheerful assumption that they were corrigible. To them an aberration was actually an aberration, and not inherent depravity. When exposing obscenity they often wrote obscenely, but their motives – at least in theory – were impeccably moral.

Marston, however, seems to cut through such theory to a bedrock of misanthropy. Perhaps in revulsion from the glib eroticism of his *Pygmalion's Image* and perhaps in an effort to achieve fame by a strategy of shock he became the 'barking satirist' of *The Scourge of Villainy*, one of the most atrabiliar books in the

[23] See especially ll. 698 ff.
[24] A selective list will show the extent of the fad: Edward Guilpin, *Skialetheia* (1599); William Rankins, *Seaven Satyres applyed to the weeke* (1598); Thomas Bastard, *Chrestoleros: Seven bookes of Epigrammes* (1598); T. M[iddleton?], *Microcynicon. Sixe Snarling Satyres* (1599); William Goddard, *A Mastif Whelp* (1599).

language. What had been a literary fad based on a classical tradition was twisted into a savage renunciation of humanity itself. In his view the erring were not educable, for error was the condition of their being; his aim was not to ridicule them back into their primal virtue, but to 'snarl, rail, bark, bite' at their vileness. As Mr Allen has said, Marston speaks not in admonition, but in shrill abhorrence. Although in some respects he imitates his contemporary satirists,[25] he is set apart by his pathological concern with the loathsome marks of man's degeneration. He, like Swift, is horribly fascinated by the ordure of sex. 'Lust hath confounded all', he wails:

> The bright gloss of our intellectual
> Is foully soil'd. The wanton wallowing
> In fond delights, and amorous dallying,
> Hath dusk'd the fairest splendour of our soul;
> Nothing now left but carcass, loathsome, foul.[26]

And like Innocent III he grimly wades through all degrees of lust: adultery, fornication, incest, perversion.

For Marston's announced purpose was to 'plow the hidden entrails of rank villainy' and to 'purge the snottery of our slimy time'. The proudest monuments of the human intellect had merely proved the folly of concealing our native canker. Aristotle and 'Old crabb'd Scotus' were obsolete, Zeno was presumptuous, Seneca belched blasphemy.[27] The accumulated moral values of two thousand years are buried in sin and crime, and the humanistic claims for human dignity are exposed as a colossal lie. The average man is a swine, and the best man

> hath no soul the which the Stagyrite
> Term'd rational: for beastly appetite,
> Base dunghill thoughts, and sensual action,
> Hath made him lose that fair creation.
> And now no man, since Circe's magic charm
> Hath turn'd him to a maggot that doth swarm
> In tainted flesh, whose foul corruption
> Is his fair food: whose generation
> Another's ruin.[28]

[25] For example, the *Scourge* is conventionally divided into books embracing such standard topics as general satire, class satire, humours, manners, literature. Like the detested Hall, Marston ridicules courtiers, 'dunghill peasants', and social affectations.
[26] *Scourge*, VIII.165–9.   [27] *Ibid.*, II.71; IV.129 ff.
[28] *Ibid.*, VII.66–74.

THE LITERATURE OF DISENCHANTMENT 53

'Preach not the Stoic's patience to me', yelps Marston;

> I hate no man, but man's impiety.
> My soul is vexed.[29]

It should not surprise us that the misanthrope who was obviously his own model for Malevole and Lampatho should turn at last to the church to sublimate his sense of sin. Men with Marston's intelligence, and with his savage indignation, must either seek such vicarious atonement or, like Swift, die staring with idiot horror at the blackness of life.

Marston's obsession with sex at once suggests one of the most conspicuous aspects of the *contemptus mundi* theme in Jacobean drama. Perhaps we tend to think that before Hamlet confronts his mother with her adulterous guilt or the mad Lear raves obscenely of the darkness, scalding, and stench of copulation no one had conceived of human frailties in quite those terms; but we must remember that Shakespeare was treating a theme made canonical by St Paul and Augustine and sustained by centuries of Christian ascetics. In the Garden of Adonis, Spenser had achieved a genuinely humanistic symbol of *natura naturans* where sex is the healthy, vitalistic center of life itself.

> For here all plenty and all pleasure flowes,
> And sweete Love gentle fitts emongst them throwes,
> Without fell rancor or fond gealosy:
> Franckly each paramor his leman knowes,
> Each bird his mate, ne any does envy
> Their goodly meriment and gay felicity.[30]

But in the drama a dozen years or so later we find sex abhorred as sterile lust, at once the symptom and the symbol of man's mortality. This was a point of view not unknown to Spenser, but Acrasia's Bower is speedily and allegorically demolished.[31]

---

[29] *Ibid.*, II.5–7.   [30] *FQ*, III.vi.41.
[31] See C. S. Lewis, *The Allegory of Love*, p. 337. Spenser's humanistic ethos had presumably lost its appeal for John Ford, a generation later. Perhaps Mr Craig is right (*The Enchanted Glass*, p. 137) in seeing Chapman and his immediate successors as sympathizing with the passionate sinner against the moral law: although Bussy is given the proper therapy for his transgressions, he is not an unattractive malcontent, and the passionate individualism that destroys him is far from the stark evil of Webster's Bosola or Tourneur's D'Amville. But Ford, as Mr Sensabaugh has pointed out, seems to be frankly sympathetic to the passion-driven wretches that populate his plays. Like Burton, he seems to regard moral aberrations with a new 'scientific' objectivity which refuses to pass moral judgments on crimes against society – and yet he permits the inexorable moral pressure of social convention to exact its retribution. His Bassanes is virtually a comic inversion of Tourneur's jealous monsters (*The Broken Heart*, II.i, for instance), and yet his chief charac-

It is quite otherwise in *The Dutch Courtesan, The Honest Whore, The White Devil, The Revenger's Tragedy*. With them we are hurled into a world loosed from moral value, including humanistic moderation and rational self-control, to be confronted by the leering masks of sex and death. Dekker's Hippolito, believing his Infelice to be dead, once each week indulges in an orgy of morbid platitudes. Fondling a skull he reflects on the condition of man:

> What fools are men to build a garish tomb,
> Only to save the carcase whilst it rots,
> To maintain't long in stinking, made good carrion,
> But leave no good deeds to preserve them sound!
> For good deeds keep men sweet, long above ground.
> And must all come to this? fools, wife, all hither?
> Must all heads then at last be laid together?[32]

Webster wryly asks why it is that man refuses to admit his monstrosity. When he sees a colt or lamb with human features he foolishly shudders, amazed 'to see his deformity In any other creature but himself'.[33] For Webster, the indignity of death is the only possible complement for the evil of life.

> But in our own flesh, though we bear diseases
> Which have their true names only ta'en from beasts, —
> As the most ulcerous wolf and swinish measle, —
> Though we are eaten up of lice and worms,
> And though continually we bear about us
> A rotten and dead body, we delight
> To hide it in rich tissue: all our fear,
> Nay, all our terror, is lest our physician
> Should put us in the ground to be made sweet.[34]

Significantly, in Jacobean drama evil is commonly projected in terms of sexuality. We are repeatedly reminded of the fourteenth book of *The City of God*. Marston's Malevole almost goes

ters – Penthea and Orgilus, Biancha and Fernando, Giovanni and Annabella – are essentially studies in frustrated sexuality. Their sin is not in loving, but in challenging the (obsolete?) conventions of society. They are as far removed from Spenser's genuine humanistic decorum as from the facile nonsense of *A King and no King*.

Donne significantly challenges the psychological determinism which Burton and Ford use to rationalize sin. 'Let no man therefore think to present his complexion to God for an excuse, and say, my choler with which my constitution abounded, and which I could not remedy, inclined me to wrath, and so to blood; my melancholy inclined me to sadness, and so to desperation, as though thy sins were medicinal sins, sins to vent humours' (*Works*, II, 158).

[32] *The Honest Whore*, pt. I, IV.i.
[33] *The Duchess of Malfi*, II.i.   [34] *Ibid.*, II.i.

THE LITERATURE OF DISENCHANTMENT 55

mad in contemplating the fact of sex,[35] and Malheureux comes to regard it as man's distinguishing iniquity. He envies the nightingales, for

> They have no bawds, no mercenary beds,
> No polite restraints, no artificial heats,
> No faint dissemblings; no custom makes them blush,
> No shame afflicts their name....
> That I should love a strumpet! I, a man of snow!
> Now, shame forsake me – whither am I fallen![36]

Sex in early Jacobean drama was ordinarily sterile, burning lust unrelieved by generative love. The primal itch leading to the grave-like bed whence no life sprang inevitably suggests the paradox of death as the goal of life, and so the cognate themes of sex and death entwine themselves into the recurrent symbol of lust as man's death in life. As Middleton's Anselmero says in horror, 'The bed's itself a charnel, the sheets shrouds For murdered carcasses'.[37] Similarly, Tourneur's Vendice recoils at the sight of the old duke impotently fondling his unfaithful wife:

> O that marrowless age
> Should stuff the hollow bones with damned desires!
> And, 'stead of heat, kindle infernal fires
> Within the spendthrift veins of a dry duke,
> A parched and juiceless luxur.[38]

The fact that this morbid eroticism is often wrenched toward didactic ends gives it another link to tradition. Drama had begun in religion, and the didactic element, though steadily waning, was persistent in the work of Shakespeare's contemporaries.[39] The idea that in a moral universe disaster must follow wrongdoing was a commonplace that the increasing secularism of Elizabethan tragedy never quite obliterated. Basically, tragedy was construed as a cause and effect sequence in morality, if not in religion. In the melodramas of Tourneur and Marston, however, this didactic element is attenuated, while Webster's characters

---

[35] Note the parody of Hamlet's encomium of man, *The Malcontent*, I.i.
[36] *The Dutch Courtesan*, II.i.   [37] *The Changeling*, V.iii.
[38] *The Revenger's Tragedy*, I.i.
[39] This is made sufficiently clear in Nashe's famous defense of plays and players (*Pierce Pennilesse, Works*, I, 213): 'In Playes, all coosenages, all cunning drifts over-guylded with outward holinesse, all stratagems of warre, all the cankerwormes that breede on the rust of peace, are most lively anatomiz'd: they shew the ill successe of treason, the fall of hastie climbers, the wretched end of usurpers, the miserie of civill dissention, and how just God is evermore in punishing of murther.'

inhabit a terrible world where evil, not good, seems to be the ultimate truth. With Webster we are at least dealing with an artist who had a searing vision of evil, but when the heavy-handed Tourneur tries to be didactic we can only wish he had Webster's integrity. Levidulcia is a sexual monster who announces candidly that she could 'clasp with any man', yet she and Sebastian seem to sin that they might repent and, repenting, instruct us.[40] The readiest dramatic projection of evil was sex; to this was added death, and in their favorite paradox of man's being doomed to both the Jacobean playwrights are very near the mortuary horrors of the late Middle Ages. Tourneur's duke is poisoned by kissing the skull of a lady whom he had poisoned for resisting his improper advances, and as he lies in his death agonies he is compelled to witness the coupling of his wife and bastard son.[41] Middleton has a dreadful scene in *The Changeling*,[42] where Antonio poses as a madman to get at Isabella, and while the two are parleying the idiots within make their awful noises, 'some as birds, some as beasts'. Marston's Erichtho obscenely fondles corpses:

> she bursts up tombs,
> From half-rot sear-cloths then she scrapes dry gums
> For her black rites; but when she finds a corpse
> But newly graved, whose entrails are not turn'd
> To slimy filth, with greedy havock then
> She makes fierce spoil, and swells with wicked triumph
> To bury her lean knuckles in his eyes;
> Then doth she gnaw the pale and o'ergrown nails
> From his dry hand.[43]

This is grotesque and vulgar nonsense, but it is very close indeed to the realistic horrors of the *danse macabre* of the Chaise-Dieu.

III. THE GREAT THRENODISTS

Although his perversions of the theme of death had precedents and analogues, Marston was in any event a case for a psychiatrist. Passing from his vulgarities to artists of the caliber of Browne, Donne, and Taylor we are in saner company; for when they used

---

[40] *The Atheist's Tragedy*, act V. Shirley seems to be parodying this sort of hollow didacticism in *The Witty Fair One* (V.iii) when Penelope redeems Fowler from his carnal ways: 'Now you begin to live.' On another level, the last act of *The Cardinal* subtly mocks the convention of the repentant Machiavellian.
[41] *The Revenger's Tragedy*, III.v.
[42] III.iii.   [43] *The Tragedy of Sophonisba*, IV.i.

THE GREAT THRENODISTS

the *contemptus mundi* motif it was for other than scatological purposes. Never has the ancient theme been invested with such gorgeous raiment. The doctor, the dean, and the bishop conspire, as it were, to give a last majestic statement to those truisms which had been uttered by generations of the pious – and which would presently lose their power to stir the heirs of Bacon and the champions of progress. Browne lived a long life of cheerful zeal, Donne consorted with the peers of the realm, Taylor attained the dignity of a bishop's miter; yet as religious men they would all agree that, as Taylor said with one of his favorite adverbs, 'a delicate and prosperous life is hugely contrary to the hopes of a blessed eternity',[44] and when the occasion demanded they could weave a rich fabric of such ancient truisms. 'Certainly there is no happiness within this circle of flesh, nor is it in the Opticks of these eyes to behold felicity.'[45] To say that Ralegh, the last Elizabethan, Dr Browne, the amateur of Baconian science, Donne, the sporadic skeptic, and Taylor, the exponent of the Anglican *via media*, could draw at will on the venerable tradition of pessimism is not to charge them with insincerity; it is to suggest that in the early seventeenth century men were still close to their medieval heritage, and that the inherited patterns of thought and emotion were still powerful.[46]

Glory is the only vanity, chants Ralegh. It leads inexorably to that point where men

> by the workmanship of death, finish the sorrowful business of a wretched life; towards which we always travel both sleeping and waking; neither have those beloved companions of honour and riches any power to hold us any one day by the glorious promise of entertainments; but by what crooked path soever we walk, the same leadeth on directly to the house of death, whose doors lie open at all hours, and to all persons. For this tide of man's life, after it once turneth and declineth, ever runneth with a perpetual ebb and falling stream, but never floweth again; our leaf once fallen, springeth no more; neither doth the sun or the summer adorn us again, with the garment of new leaves or flowers.[47]

[44] *Holy Dying*, II.i.   [45] Browne, *Religio Medici*, p. 49.
[46] Many lesser men showed the same tendency to oscillate between a typically seventeenth-century vitality and traditional pessimism. Thus in Thomas James' narrative of his fabulous pursuit of the Northwest Passage we learn that in a particularly violent storm he despaired of his life, his crew, and his ship – and so wrote some 'ragged and teared Rimes' expressing his hope of heaven. He had hitherto trusted on his charts and compass, but now his soul could rest only on the gales of saving grace to escape its 'dunghill dungeon: A meere sinke of sinne' (*The Strange and Dangerous Voyage of Captain Thomas James*, p. 39).
[47] *History*, I.ii.5.

Although there is a certain irony in the thought of the disgraced
courtier, a victim of his monarch's desperate Spanish policy, ending his days with a work to be cherished by generations of Puritans, pessimism must have come easily to the grizzled worldling
awaiting the executioner's ax. He could project his own futility
in a hypothesis of man's generic futility; his blasted career confirmed for him the Adamic curse and the world's decay. But there
was always God's overruling providence that gave meaning and
direction to each man's life just as to the large movements of history. In Ralegh we hear little of the physical horrors of the four
last things, but much of the serenity which is the gift of eloquent,
just, and mighty death. His awareness of decay – like Taylor's of
'gray hairs, rotten teeth, dim eyes, trembling joints, short breath,
stiff limbs, wrinkled skin, short memory, decayed appetite'[48] –
is absorbed by the justice of God's strategy for saving a sinful
world. Like Webster's Bosola, Ralegh finds solace in reflecting
that death is the compensation for life.

> A long war disturbed your mind;
> Here your perfect peace is signed.
> Of what is't fools make such vain keeping?
> Sin their conception, their birth weeping,
> Their life a general mist of error,
> Their death a hideous storm of terror.[49]

Like Ralegh's, Browne's pessimism had an essentially religious
orientation. His proudest boast was that he always followed the
great wheel of the church, and his view of the world as not an
inn but a hospital, 'a place not to live, but to dye in',[50] suggests
how traditional his occasional melancholy was. This attitude crops
out in the work of the intermittent Baconian whose *Pseudodoxia*
calls for the demolition of all four idols, but in his age we must
expect to find divided allegiances. Such a bifurcation between
the new and the old, it has been argued, vastly expanded the
Jacobeans' spectrum of experience and helped to make metaphysical poetry possible. At any rate, Browne, like Pascal though
less acutely, could oscillate between divided and distinguishable
worlds. Although he could hardly write a sentence without
beauty, his theology, like Donne's, was essentially commonplace,
even uninteresting; and in a man who could simultaneously em-

---

[48] *Holy Dying*, I.i. [49] *The Duchess of Malfi*, IV.ii.
[50] *Religio Medici*, p. 83.

THE GREAT THRENODISTS

brace something very like fideism and philosophical skepticism, we are not surprised to find pessimism sanctified by tradition and made operative by faith. When Browne the literary artist – as distinguished from Browne the breezy empiricist – speaks, it is almost always on those great themes of death and eternity that had informed so much Renaissance literature – or more specifically on those Christian doctrines that stylized man's depravity and impotence. The incessant mortality of mankind dominates the *Letter to a Friend*, and it is woven into the very fabric of that mighty fifth chapter of *Hydriotaphia* which quotation can never stale.

> But to subsist in bones, and be but Pyramidally extant, is a fallacy in duration. Vain ashes, which in the oblivion of names, persons, times, and sexes, have found unto themselves, a fruitless continuation, and only arise unto late posterity, as Emblemes of mortall vanities; Antidotes against pride, vain-glory, and madding vices.[51]

When Browne thought on eternity, he did so in terms most readily available, and his thought was patterned by those ancient dogmas dramatizing man's impotence before the facts of death and judgment. ' 'Tis that unruly regiment within me, that will destroy me; 'tis I that do infect myself; the man without a Navel yet lives in me; I feel that original canker and corrode and devour me.'[52]

In his jarring opposites of naturalism and mysticism Browne suggests Donne, whose progress from Jack to Dr John has so fascinated our generation. It now seems likely that his alleged revulsion from the implications of the new science to a characteristically Jacobean pessimism has been exaggerated. When Donne is discussing scientific innovations, even in so late a work as the funeral sermon on Sir William Cokayne, he reveals a typical seventeenth-century flexibility of mind; and when he is reworking the hallowed formulas of pessimism he stays pretty closely within his ecclesiastical tradition. His distinction, in fact, would seem to be not a uniquely searing conviction of death and judgment, but an almost secular objectivity in exercising his intelligence on the old themes. We must beware of confusing the workings of his very subtle mind with the cry of his heart, for he teases all the implications of man's fallen state just as he relent-

[51] p. 133.   [52] *Religio Medici*, p. 82.

lessly pursues the linked metaphors of the globe in 'A Valediction: Forbidding Mourning'.

> But what had I for Heaven? Adam sinnd, and I suffer; I forfeited before I had any Possession, or could claime any Interest: I had a Punishment, before I had a being, And God was displeased with me before I was I; I was built up scarse 50. years agoe, in my Mothers womb, and I was cast down, almost 6000. years ago, in Adams loynes; I was borne in this last Age of the world, and dyed in the first.[53]

With good reason could he pray in *The Litany*,

> When we are mov'd to seeme religious
> Only to vent wit, Lord deliver us.[54]

When Donne exercised this kind of wit on the themes of death and decay, he was splendidly baroque. 'This is Natures nest of Boxes; The Heavens contains the Earth, the Earth, Cities, Cities, Men. And all these are Concentrique; the common center to them all, is decay, ruine.'[55] The *locus classicus* of this attitude in Donne is the *Devotions*, an occasional piece of which the occasion was sickness and death: 'O perplex'd discomposition, O ridling distemper, O miserable condition of Man.'[56] In these somberly brilliant meditations the theme is conventional, but the riot of metaphors makes it seem new. Man is the tenant of happiness, but the freeholder of misery; he is dust 'coagulated and kneaded' into earth by tears; 'his matter is earth, his forme, misery'.[57] For a man to 'anatomize' his soul is to admit that

> there is no veine in mee, that is not full of the bloud of thy Son, whom I have crucified, and Crucified againe, by multiplying many, and often repeating the same sinnes: that there is no Artery in me, that hath not the spirit of error, the spirit of lust, the spirit of giddiness in it; no bone that is not hardned with the custome of sin, and nourished, and soupled with the marrow of sinn; no sinews, no ligaments, that do not tie, and chain sin and sin together.[58]

All of which is thematically linked with the great sermons on death, the *Anniversaries*, and such pieces as 'A Valediction: of my name, in the window' and 'A Nocturnall upon S. Lucies day'. In them all are many passages that take us back to the

---

[53] *Complete Poetry and Selected Prose*, p. 556. For an example of the way Donne wittily tortures a text, see his baroque development of the metaphor of the world as a sea, *LXXX Sermons*, pp. 735–7.
[54] *Poems*, p. 315.
[55] *Devotions upon Emergent Occasions*, p. 54.
[56] *Ibid.*, p. 2.   [57] *Ibid.*, p. 42.   [58] *Ibid.*, pp. 51–2.

THE GREAT THRENODISTS

exacerbated medieval sense of man's indignity in death. 'Between that execremental jelly that thy body is made of at first, and that jelly which thy body dissolves to at last; there is not so noisome, so putrid a thing in nature.'[59]

But in spite of this sometimes sickly concern with death and corruption, the main stream of Donne's theological thinking is Neo-Platonic and optimistic. As the great Trinity sermons show, at the core of his belief is a Christ of love and a God of benevolent plenitude.[60] Even much of his morality, as distinguished from his theology, is marked by a typical Anglican regard for the good things of life. Like his friend and colleague Herbert, he had not reached the serenity of his office easily, and, having reached it, he was often afflicted by a sense of vanity, emptiness, and error.

> My stock lies dead, and no increase
> Doth my dull husbandrie improve.[61]

But they both used their pulpits to preach an essentially optimistic view of God and man's relation to God. Donne was painfully aware of man's capacity for evil: to purge his own sins he prays for the purifying fire of zeal which is a sign of regeneration,[62] yet he never doubts that such regeneration is possible, and he abhors Calvin's doctrine of reprobation. It is God's greatest mercy and man's greatest good that He is willing 'to erect and settle a tottering, a dejected soul, an overthrowne, a bruised, a broken, a trodden, a ground, a battered, an evaporated, an annihilated spirit'.[63] It is as 'detestable' to believe that God made man for damnation as that He tempts him with 'temporall' pleasures only to ensnare him deeper in his predetermined depravity. Man was made to know and love God, and to despise His good gifts is to scorn His commandment, *Gaudete semper*.[64]

Donne's mental ambivalence could fuse the most formidable pessimism with the most radiant sense of universal benevolence. The beautiful sermons on the conversion of Paul must be read as his own spiritual autobiography.[65] Like Pascal, he was haunted by the sin of pride, yet fully aware of man's claim to pride on

---

[59] *Works*, IV, 231.
[60] For example, see *LXXX Sermons*, pp. 400 ff.
[61] George Herbert, 'Grace', *Works*, p. 55.
[62] 'Holy Sonnets', no. V, *Poems*, p. 295.
[63] *LXXX Sermons*, p. 382.   [64] *Fifty Sermons*, pp. 469–70.
[65] *LXXX Sermons*, nos. xlvi–xlix.

both traditional Renaissance and new Baconian grounds. But neither Donne nor Pascal could forget the paradox of man's pride and man's infamy. The intolerable irony that this paradox involves is explicit in them and implicit in almost every thoughtful man of their age.

> Quelle chimère est-ce donc que l'homme? Quelle nouveauté, quel monstre, quel chaos, quel sujet de contradition, quel prodige! Juge de toutes choses, imbécile ver de terre; dépositaire du vrai, cloaque d'incertitude et d'erreur; gloire et rebut de l'univers.[66]

Burton's thesis that 'Folly, melancholy, madness, are but one disease, *delirium* is a common name to all' could find no support in Donne's iridescent view of man as the object, splendid though fallen, of God's regenerative love.[67] As a young iconoclast he could flirt with the disquieting implications of the new astronomy as learnedly as with Burton's brand of abnormal psychology; as a divine he could gorgeously embellish the themes of death and time with his own blend of grandeur and subtlety; but he moved steadily toward that final position of quasi-mystic optimism by which he could regard all man's natural infirmities as obliterated in the rapturous love of God.

> For though through many streights, and lands I roame
> I launch at paradise, and I saile towards home.[68]

Jeremy Taylor will be the last of the Jacobeans whose pessimism we shall examine, and in many ways he is the most interesting of them all. An exquisite artist, the Shakespeare of divines, he splendidly shows the uses of *contemptus mundi* for Christian morals – never, like Marston or Tourneur, for sensationalism, or, like Donne, as a ground for the gymnastics of wit. This perhaps dulls our interest, but it places Taylor in an ancient and distinguished tradition. No one any longer reads the *Ductor Dubitantium* or *The Worthy Communicant*, yet a little manual like *Holy Dying* has led

---

[66] *Pensées*, no. 438 (*Œuvres*, p. 947).
[67] In one of his greatest sermons (*LXXX Sermons*, no. xxvii) Donne yearns (p. 274) for that *mortem raptus* which St Gregory spoke of. 'The contemplation of God, and heaven, is a kinde of buriall, and Sepulchre, and rest of the soule; and in this death of rapture, and extasie, in this death of the Contemplation of my interest in my Saviour, I shall finde my self, and all my sins enterred, and entombed in his wounds, and like a Lily in Paradise, out of red earth, I shall see my soule rise out of his blade, in a candor, and in an innocence, contracted there, acceptable in the sight of his Father.' The peroration of this remarkable sermon attains an intensity rare even in Donne.
[68] 'The Progresse of the Soule', *Poems*, p. 271.

some to see Taylor as the last of those Caroline divines for whom to exist was to be melancholy. And although Taylor himself would have been the first to resist such an inference, no one has ever written with more beauty on the themes of death and time. Owing to the happy accident of Taylor's literary intelligence, there is a temptation to quote 'hugely' from the devotional manuals and the sermons, but their whole meaning can be reduced to a truism: the condition of man is misery; therefore he should fix his hope on heaven. 'As our life is very short, so it is very miserable, and therefore it is well it is short.'[69] The use of mortality is to teach us morality, and it becomes 'hugely necessary' to meditate on our frailties if we are to transcend them.[70] One cannot walk without treading on dead men's bones, a fact which should teach us wisdom. 'Learn to despise the world', runs one of the sermons, for it is merely 'an image and a noise, with a hyena's lip and a serpent's tale'.[71] Revel in your sensuous joys; feel the wines 'distilling through the limbeck of thy tongue and larynx, and suck the delicious juice of fishes, the marrow of the laborious ox' – but lose no time, for the sun drives hard, and the 'number of thy days of darkness and the grave cannot be told'.[72] We are always running to our graves; the years slip by like water, and finally 'nothing is to be seen but like a shower of tears upon a spot of ground'.[73]

> Here is no place to sit down in, but you must rise as soon as you are set; for we have gnats in our chambers, and worms in our gardens, and spiders and flies in the palaces of the greatest kings. How few men in the world are prosperous! What an infinite number of slaves and beggars, of persecuted and oppressed people fill all corners of the earth with groans, and heaven itself with weeping prayers and sad remembrances! how many provinces and kingdoms are afflicted by a violent war, or made desolate by popular diseases![74]

Is there any wonder, then, that man never has one day of entire peace, but that 'his very fullness swells him and makes him breathe short upon his bed'?[75] For here we long for perishing meats to fill our stomachs with corruption; we yearn for the weaker beauties of the night; 'we are passionate after rings and seals, and enraged at the breaking of a crystal'. Is it any wonder

---

[69] *Holy Dying*, I.iv.
[70] *Ibid.*, 'Epistle Dedicatory'.
[71] *Sermons*, p. 86.
[72] *Ibid.*, p. 110.
[73] *Ibid.*, p. 491.
[74] *Holy Dying*, I.iv.
[75] *Ibid.*, I.iv.

that in our sin and misery we are 'a huge way off from the kingdom of God'?[76] And at the end of life there ever looms the fact of death. Sometimes Taylor sees it as the saint's everlasting rest and writes of it caressingly as 'the same harmless thing that a poor shepherd suffered yesterday, or a maid-servant to-day'.[77] But his customary tone is one of horror, in the *danse macabre* manner. Then his prose becomes as sharp and jagged as a Dürer etching. 'Reckon but from the sprightfulness of youth and the fair cheeks and the full eyes of childhood, from the vigorousness and strong flexure of the joints of five and twenty, to the hollowness and dead paleness, to the loathsomeness and horror of a three days' burial, and we shall perceive the distance to be very great and very strange.'[78] When he treats the last judgment he takes us back to the plangent heavings of the *Dies irae*:

> That shriek must needs be terrible, when millions of men and women, at the same instant, shall fearfully cry out, and the noise shall mingle with the trumpet of the archangel, with the thunders of the dying and groaning heavens, and the crack of the dissolving world, when the whole fabric of nature shall shake into dissolution and eternal ashes.[79]

However magnificent this strain in Taylor's work, it should not obscure the main lines of his thought. To a Calvinist his theology would seem intolerably optimistic and latitudinarian. For any Anglican clergyman contemporary with Abbot and Laud to write *The Liberty of Prophesying*, to hold that Adam's fall did not 'introduce a natural necessity of sinning',[80] and to make a defense of free will central in his theology was to align himself with the most liberal wing of a prevailingly liberal theology. Indeed, the fact that he could hold such views and also write *Holy Dying* suggests the thesis we have been advancing: since the *contemptus mundi* motif, a persistent if sometimes submerged element in Renaissance thought, was perennially available for writers of the most varied beliefs and intentions, it should not be regarded as peculiar to the early seventeenth century. In Taylor's great doctrinal passages we hear the same tone of majesty as in his treat-

[76] *Sermons*, p. 88.   [77] *Holy Dying*, III.vii.
[78] *Ibid.*, I.ii. This passage continues with one of Taylor's most celebrated similes: 'But so I have seen a rose newly springing from the clefts of its hood, etc.' It is one of those common lyrical splendors in Taylor that gives point to Hazlitt's characteristically acute comment: 'In his writings, the frail stalk of human life reclines on the bosom of eternity. His Holy Living and Dying is a divine pastoral.'
[79] *Sermons*, p. 7.
[80] *Unum Necessarium*, VIII.v.18 (*Works*, VII, 320).

ment of death and judgment, but here the implications would make a genuine pessimist wince. To deny free will – that is, man's moral and rational responsibility for conduct – meant, in Taylor's view,

> a destruction of all laws, it takes away reward and punishment, and we have nothing whereby we can serve God. And precepts of holiness might as well be preached to a wolf as to a man, if man were naturally and inevitably wicked.
> *Improbitas nullo flectitur obsequio.*
> There would be no use of reason or of discourse, no deliberation or counsel: and it were impossible for the wit of man to make sense of thousands of places of scripture, which speak to us as if we could hear and obey, or could refuse. Why are promises made, and threatenings recorded? Why are God's judgments registered? to what purpose is our reason above, and our affections below, if they were not to minister to and attend upon the will?[81]

As the overwhelming catalogue of man's infirmities in *Unum Necessarium*[82] makes clear, Taylor knew that we all 'have reason to lie down flat on our faces, and confess God's glory and our own shame'. His main effort, however, was not to repeat the immemorial counsels of despair, but to salvage man's dignity from all detractors, whether Presbyterians or Hobbesians. Although, as we shall see, he could not subscribe to the principles of universal reason so unquestioningly as Aquinas and Hooker, in his labors to adjust traditional values to new facts he, like Chillingworth, ennobled his church and enriched our literature.

IV. CORRODING TIME

If the Jacobean and Caroline moralists, then, brought a baroque splendor to the theme of death, the theme itself was encrusted with tradition. Their treatment of the cognate theme of time, or mutability, also suggests one of the primal literary and religious motifs of Christendom. It is true that in the early seventeenth century there were certain grounds for believing, as Burton said, that nothing is 'firm and sure'; but as we shall see when we come to examine the course of scientific thought, the disturbing implications of the Copernican hypothesis were generally absorbed

---

[81] *Ibid.*, VI.v.72 (*Works*, VII, 279). See Taylor's analysis of sin as merely the absence of reason, *Sermons*, p. 149.
[82] *Unum Necessarium* VI.vii.82–5 (*Works*, VII, 284–9).

into an optimistic deism. Meanwhile, the perennial fact of change that generations had inferred, without the aid of science, from the processes of life itself was persistently restated until it, too, came to find a new sanction in the idea of progress. Although the poignant Elizabethan theme of mutability was congenial to the doctrine of universal decay after the Fall of Adam, decay itself was a notion incompatible with the tone of seventeenth-century thought: it could not long withstand the pressures of the pervasive optimism dominating the period. Godfrey Goodman's *Fall of Man* actually marks the end of a line, but George Hakewill's *Apology* proved to be one of the most admired (and plagiarized) books of a century whose vitality could not be reconciled with any notion of universal degradation.

Although Sir Thomas Browne advanced the proposition that no one could speak of eternity without a solecism or think of it without an ecstasy, his predecessors had no such sophisticated reservations. They had learned from both classical antiquity and medieval Christianity the stock attitudes toward time and change, and they developed these attitudes tirelessly. Renaissance speculation about mutability was dominated by the doctrine of degeneration. The myth of the primal perfection of a golden age from which the race had steadily declined was, as Plato's *Timaeus* shows, a commonplace in Greek thought. The Greeks were so obsessed with the sanctity of the immutable and the timeless that they construed any change as change for the worse. Parmenides and Plato made this conviction the basis of their metaphysics, but the interlocking assumptions that permanence is good and change is bad appear in every department of Greek thought. The most wanly optimistic explanation of change that they could contrive was the Stoic cyclic theory of history, which itself implied periodic degeneration.

The doctrine of degeneration was obviously congenial to Christian theology. It is true that there was some mild inconvenience in explaining the long-delayed Incarnation and consequent promulgation of the Gospel, but from Tertullian through Aquinas the explanation was that the Old Law had to appear first and fructify in the New. As Augustine put it, 'Recta creditio per quosdam articulos temporum tanquam aetatum profecit'.[83] This

---

[83] See R. S. Crane, 'Anglican Apologetics and the Idea of Progress, 1699–1745', *MP* XXXI (1933–34), 374–9.

CORRODING TIME

rationalization was somehow adjusted to the main plank in Augustine's theology: the notion that the universe and all it contained had pursued a course of sinful deterioration since the Adamic fall. Inevitably, the Middle Ages viewed history in the Augustinian terms of *The City of God*, and regarded man's sorry lot in this world as merely a prelude for the eternity of heaven or hell in the next. The doctrine of providence, made necessary by that of original sin and powerfully supported by the tradition of Stoic determinism, was obviously inimical to any hope of man's gradual improvement. As the Nicene disputants had determined once and for all, the world had a creation in time, no matter what Aristotle had said, and it would have an ending in time; between those terminal points it was sustained, even in its sinful state, by the continual direction of God. Under His inscrutable control the whole creation, sunk in sin and temporality, was inexorably moving toward the holocaust of the last judgment.

Working out its variations on the theme of time, the Renaissance accepted the medieval view without question. The scandalous corruption of the Catholic church on the eve of the Reformation seemed to confirm the fact of decay. 'It is with religions as with other things subject to generation and corruption', said the arch-naturalist Pomponazzi:

> We observe that they and their miracles are weak at first, then they increase, come to a climax, then decline, until they return to nothing. Whence now too in our own faith all things are growing frigid, and miracles are ceasing, except those counterfeit and simulated, for it seems to be near its end.[84]

When Calvin, dedicating the *Institutes* to François I, groaned that the 'world is unundated with more than an ocean of evils, that it is overrun with numerous destructive pests, that everything is fast verging to ruin', he was trying to make political capital of the shameless Roman curia, but he was also echoing a belief largely responsible for the early successes of the church he sought to destroy. Milton's account of the consequences embodies the central – indeed the indispensable – theme in Christian thought.[85]

The theme could also be supported with copious pagan testimony. Seneca's faintly optimistic theory of time[86] was more than

---

[84] Quoted from *De fato, libero aribitrio, et de praedestinatione* in *RP*, p. 278.
[85] *PL*, X.641 ff.　　　　[86] *Epistolae*, XIV.ii.

counterbalanced: the fifteenth book of the *Metamorphoses* became a standard reference for the Stoic theme of circular change as a possible mitigation of the dreaful doctrine of decay; and even the unspeakable atheist Lucretius was occasionally cited[87] in support of a basic substance which endures through various mutations. From such virtually canonical sources as Cyprian and the apocryphal Esdras – to say nothing of the Psalm cii – it was clear that the earth waxed old like a garment, and most men agreed that mutability, however domesticated or rationalized as providence or fickle fortune or atomistic determinism, was the inescapable fact of life. As the Renaissance came to an end the accumulated intellectual capital of both pagan and Christian Europe was variously used by men like Bodin, Lipsius, Spenser, Le Roy, Norden, Goodman, and Hakewill either to acknowledge the fact of change or to find some sort of pattern in it. And once the seventeenth century had achieved its most signal success in establishing the uniformity of nature, the fact of superficial change could be subordinated to the more important fact of fundamental permanence. The next step, of course, came when the eighteenth century reversed the Augustinian hypothesis to construe mutation not as decay but progress – a comfortable assumption anticipated more than once by Bacon's immediate posterity.

Yeats has recorded how, as a boy, he became ecstatic at the contemplation of ruin. So did the late Elizabethans, for whom such a contemplation served both æsthetic and moral purposes. Gabriel Harvey could jauntily acknowledge the fact of mutability – 'Ecce leges, mores, verba, facta, human omnia, varia, fluxa, caduca postremo mortalia'[88] – but most of his contemporaries assumed a more conventional and properly somber demeanor before the fact. The lyricists employed the ageless themes of the passing of love and youth and beauty for merely poetical purposes; Spenser tried to elevate the Elizabethan sense of corroding time into at least a hope for some sort of underlying permanence; and, of course, the moralists and theologians had merely to refer all change to God's inscrutable final purposes and wait patiently for the oblivion that would soon swallow all. Time, 'under the deathful shade of whose wings all things decay and wither', had almost done its work, thought Ralegh: history was approaching

[87] *De rerum natura*, V.1448 ff.   [88] *Marginalia*, p. 207.

its final end, since age 'hath wasted and worn out that lively virtue of nature in man, and beasts, and plants, yea the heavens themselves, being of a most pure and cleansed matter, shall wax old as a garment'.[89]

This doctrine of deterioration was widely held both before and after the turn of the century.[90] Sackville's beautiful 'Induction' in *A Mirror for Magistrates* projects those 'sundry chaunges that in earth we finde' as the theme of the subsequent histories. Sorrow laments that it is her

> drearie destinie
> And luckeles lot for to bemone of those,
> Whom Fortune in this maze of miserie
> Of wretched chaunce most wofull myrrours chose
> Than when thou seest how lightly they did lose
> Theyre pompe, theyre power, & that they thought most sure,
> Thou mayest soone deeme no earthly joye may dure.[91]

Rather than the medieval *de casibus virorum illustrium* motif (which Lydgate had labored so indefatigably) Spenser chose to treat mutability in terms of elementary, seasonal, and planetary inconstancy. In projecting his philosophical views mythologically as a contest between Mutabilitie and Jove, Spenser seems almost in spite of himself to sympathize with her claims of universal sovereignty. Skilfully arguing her case before Nature (the mysterious and majestic arbiter whose head is veiled) she concludes by posing the perennial question:

> Since within this wide great universe
> Nothing doth firme and permanent appeare,
> But all things tost and turned by transverse:
> What then should let, but I aloft should reare
> My trophee, and from all the triumph beare?[92]

But Spenser was too good a Christian to surrender the universe to chance and change. Great Nature, her 'firme eyes' fixed medi-

---

[89] *History*, I.v.5.
[90] One of its most persistent corollaries was that of literary authoritarianism. The doctrine of imitation was indispensable for critical theorists of the Renaissance: since the first writers were the best, subsequent literature has represented a steady decline, and a modern's safest strategy is to imitate the mighty dead. Dryden's critical relativism was a powerful challenge a century later, but Johnson could advance it as a 'commonly observed' truth that 'early writers are in possession of nature, and their followers of art'. The fact that Edward Young's *Conjectures on Original Composition* (1759) was the last important attack on the theory of imitation suggests, however, that by Johnson's time its strength was nearly spent.
[91] Lines 113-9.   [92] *Two Cantos of Mutabilitie*, VII.lvi.

tatively on the ground, ponders long before passing judgment, but the 'chearefull view' with which she finally speaks her 'doome' bodes ill for Mutabilitie, good for Jove and the concept of order:

> I well consider all that ye have sayd,
> And judge that all things stedfastnes doe hate
> And changed be: yet being rightly wayd,
> They are not changed from their first estate;
> But by their change their being doe dilate:
> And turning to themselves at length againe,
> Do worke their owne perfection so by fate:
> Then over them Change doth not rule and raigne;
> But they raigne over Change, and doe their states maintaine.[93]

Spenser's pastiche of pagan and medieval commonplaces is significant because it adumbrates a typical Renaissance attitude: a poignant awareness of change and also a reluctance to assess that change as without meaning or direction. It is striking that in a poem of nearly a thousand lines, only twenty or so are given to affirming order and design, and yet Nature's short 'doome' is about the best rationalization for stability that the Renaissance could contrive with the old formulas. Change is obviously basic and cosmic – but perhaps after all we may hope that the change is meaningful, that the universe is orderly, rational, and moral.[94]

A more systematic statement of a similarly optimistic view of change is Louis le Roy's *La Vicissitude de choses* (1577),[95] which takes the melioristic position that any change must be for the better. Even by pre-Baconian standards it is a remarkable defense of the idea of progress – based, of course, on traditionally theistic grounds. Le Roy's opinion, developed copiously and eruditely, is that both sensation and reflection lead us to recognize the fact of change, and that faith leads us to believe it operates for either

---

[93] *Ibid.*, VII.lviii.
[94] The indefatigable Spenserians have not been idle, of course. Mr Greenlaw ('Spenser and Lucretius', *SP*, XVII [1920], 439–64) interprets the poem as a fall from Renaissance optimism to the despair of Lucretian determinism. Miss Albright ('Spenser's Cosmic Philosophy', *PMLA*, XLIV [1929], 715–59) denies this by finding its origins in Empedocles rather than Lucretius and by dating it early (certainly before the Garden of Adonis episode in *FQ*). Ronald B. Levinson ('Spenser and Bruno', *PMLA*, XLIII [1928], 675–81) argues for the influence of Giordano Bruno's heretical new cosmology – a view sharply challenged by Mr Greenlaw ('Spenser's Mutabilitie', *PMLA*, XLV [1930], 684–703). But yet others have joined the fray: Brents Stirling ('The Concluding Stanzas of Mutabilitie', *SP*, XXX [1933], 193–204) has found traces of Boethius; and W. P. Cumming ('The Influence of Ovid's *Metamorphoses* on Spenser's "Mutabilitie" Cantos', *SP*, XXVIII [1931], 241–56) thinks he has ferreted out another classical source.
[95] Translated in 1594 by R[obert] A[shley] as *Of the Interchangeable Course, or Variety of Things in the Whole World*.

an immediate or an ultimate good.⁹⁶ Opposition is a condition of life itself; 'the Earth, and every other thing in the world [are] tempered and conserved by things of dislike and contrarie qualitie'⁹⁷ – planet against planet, water against water, man against man, nation against nation. To know history is to realize this, and because in Le Roy's significantly novel view the present age is in all ways superior to its predecessors, the inference is clear that melioration through continual change is part of God's providence.⁹⁸

Though he does considerable violence to the Augustinian view of history, Le Roy anchors his meliorism on a theistic base. John Norden, arguing from a similarly theistic position, can see no meliorism in the awful fact of change, but only degeneration. With his 'slender verse'⁹⁹ he lugubriously describes the symptoms of universal decay in his translation of Le Roy. The stars in their spheres are reeling, the elements and 'elementall things' decay by slow degrees, and man himself, like a 'waving Twig', is either bent or broken with the wind. To Norden it is obvious that mutability rules all, and all we may hope for is eventual extinction.¹⁰⁰ Political, astronomical, and cultural conflicts have thus far been kept in some sort of equilibrium by God's providence,¹⁰¹ but the worm of doubt intrudes itself: perhaps the delicate balance is being destroyed; perhaps God is permitting His creation to be engulfed again in chaos; perhaps the universe, like an old man, will sicken and die. At any rate, the recent course of events suggests that time, which consumes all, will swallow man and all his works in deserved oblivion:

> Heav'd up, hurl'd downe, dismay'd, or in aspire:
> Grac'd now, then in distaine, now in the sunne
> Of sweetest favour: then eclips'd, undonne.¹⁰²

With which dismal prophecy Norden closes his limping verses, so that his muse 'may mourne and pause a while, Sad and in silence'.

Spenser and Le Roy suggest the most favorable interpretations of mutability possible in the late Renaissance; Norden the most

---

⁹⁶ pp. 1–17. ⁹⁷ p. 5ᵛ.
⁹⁸ pp. 126ʳ–126ᵛ. ⁹⁹ *Vicissitudo Rerum*, sig. A2ʳ.
¹⁰⁰ On the contrast between Le Roy and Norden, see Kathrine Koller, 'Two Elizabethan Expressions of the Idea of Mutability', SP, XXXV (1938), 228–37.
¹⁰¹ Sig. C1ᵛ f. ¹⁰² Sig. F3ʳ.

pessimistic, for he wrote when the current unrest at alleged astronomical irregularities was rife. Copernicus, a half-century earlier, had dared advance the heretical hypothesis of a heliocentric universe, and by the end of the century his implications were percolating down to the layman. Moreover, he suggested that the eighth, or tightly enveloping outer, sphere of the old Ptolemaic universe was not, as virtually everyone since Aristotle had agreed, closed and finite but perhaps infinite and capable of infinite alteration.[103] When, in the late sixteenth century certain disturbing facts concerning the eternal stars in their courses seemed to confirm the Copernican hypothesis, it was for the first time viewed as a threat to the one permanent fact in a world of flux and decay. In 1572 a new star appeared in the constellation of Cassiopeia; in 1577 Tycho Brahe traced a comet's orbit around the sun and outside the orbit of Venus (thus jeopardizing the notion that comets, not being made of 'celestial' substance, could not go above the sphere of the moon as the limit of the elementary world); in 1604 a second new star was seen in the constellation of Serpentarius; in 1610 Galileo's *Siderius nuncius* announced that Jupiter had four satellites and that there was an infinity of stars in the Milky Way.

Such astronomical scandals seemed, in the judgment of many conservatives, to confirm the suspicion that the universe was entering its penultimate period of disorder before its collapse. Le Roy, characteristically, tried to adjust such disturbances to his meliorism: since heaven itself 'can not wholly warrant or preserve it selfe from alteration & change', and since on earth the constant warring of the four elements makes conflict and change functions of life, it is a 'mervaile, that being so vexed in all its parts' created matter has not long since been consumed. Since it has not, however, it will obviously endure until God's (benevolent) purposes have been fulfilled.[104] Like Le Roy, John Swan – whose *Speculum Mundi* is a tissue of pious commonplaces that continued popular

[103] See *De revolutionibus*, VI.i; VIII.x. See Grant McColley, 'The Seventeenth-Century Doctrine of a Plurality of Worlds', *Annals of Science*, I (1936), 406 f. and also his 'The Eighth Sphere of *De revolutionibus*', *Annals of Science*, II (1937), 354 f. For a discussion of the importance of this infinite eighth sphere in *Paradise Lost*, see Marjorie Nicholson, 'Milton and the Telescope', *ELH*, II (1935), 1–32, and also her 'The Telescope and Imagination', *MP*, XXXII (1934–35), 233–60; 'The "New Astronomy" and English Literary Imagination', *SP*, XXXII (1935), 428–62. The fullest work on the subject is Francis R. Johnson, *Astronomical Thought in Renaissance England* (1937).

[104] pp. 1r, 5v. See Spenser, *Colin Clouts Come Home Againe*, ll. 839 ff.; 'An Hymne in Honour of Love', ll. 57 ff.

CORRODING TIME 73

throughout the early seventeenth century – was determined not to be disheartened by apparent irregularities in a deifically ordered universe. Swan can quote Tycho Brahe and Kepler glibly enough, but his own scientific conjectures are appealingly naive: stars, after all, are merely elemental compounds 'glewed together, and firmly concreted into a durable lump', and we must attribute any apparent instability to faulty composition; at any rate, it is impious to infer that the universe is out of God's control.[105]

There were a few of Shakespeare's contemporaries – very few indeed, in all probability – who could both understand and welcome the implications of the new astronomy. Thomas Digges, that extraordinary Elizabethan disciple of Copernicus, was quite prepared to advocate the notion of an infinite universe (even though he deplored the 'continual mutabilitye' of all earthly things);[106] Giordano Bruno, who visited England in the 'eighties, exploited the Copernican hypothesis because it was so congenial to his pantheistic (and heretical) metaphysics;[107] Edward Wright, in his preface to Gilbert's *De magnete*, cautiously suggested that it might be possible to reconcile the diurnal motion of the earth with contrary Scriptural testimony (e.g. Psalms xciv: 5).[108] But a little later, John Wilkins (who lived to rejoice in the Royal Society) not only accepted the hypothesis of an infinite universe; he notoriously and audaciously declared that it was compatible with Scripture, flouted Aristotle's opinion,[109] and even went so far as to suggest that 'our posteritie' would one day visit familiarly back and forth with their friends living on the moon.[110] To mention Wilkins is to anticipate, however; the *Tractatus de sphaera* of Johannes de Sacro Bosco – an elementary redaction of

---

[105] *Speculum Mundi*, VII.ii. Swan soberly reviews the current conjectures that the world will end catastrophically in 1657, only to reject the evidence (I.iii). Indeed, he refuses to believe that God will destroy the world at all; rather, He will purge away its dross and impurities, so that 'all things shall be renewed, and each thing brought into a perfect state' for all eternity (I.ii).

[106] See Francis R. Johnson and Sanford V. Larkey, 'Thomas Digges, the Copernican System and the Idea of the Infinity of the Universe in 1576', *The Huntington Library Bulletin*, no. 5 (1934), pp. 69–117.

[107] 'Ideo perfectum simpliciter et per se et absolute est unum infinitum, quod et quo neque majus esse potest quippiam, neque melius. Hoc est unum ubique totum, Deus, naturaque universalis: cujus perfecta imago et simulacrum nullum esse potest, nisi infinitum' (*De Immenso*, II.xii [*Opera*, I, 307]).

[108] *On the Loadstone*, 'Laudatory Address', p. xliii.

[109] *The First Book. The Discovery of a New World*, p. 26.

[110] The mechanics of this intercourse may be difficult, Wilkins admits (p. 206), 'yet why may not succeeding times, rayse up some spirits as eminent for new attempts and strange inventions, as any that were before them?'

the Ptolemaic system – long sustained its prestige among solid citizens in spite of enthusiasm in certain quarters for the *De revolutionibus*.

Of course, there must have been many who, like old Gloucester and Sir Politick Would-Be, were genuinely disturbed by current astronomical developments. In the somber prologue to the fifth book of *The Faery Queen* Spenser saw the decay in morals and manners as analogous to the disorders in the heavens; and men of Norden's temper could only infer universal dissolution from the new stars, the comets, and the eclipses. The whole creation seemed to stagger to its end:

> Such are the changes of this earthes estate,
> It may be sayd, Times wings beginne to frie,
> Now crouching low, that erst did soare so hie.[111]

To a Stoic like Justus Lipsius these modern instances merely confirmed old saws, for history can only mean cyclic decay and we are caught at the end of a cycle – a thesis which Browne, characteristically, works into literature:

> For the lives, not only of men, but of Commonwealths, and the whole World, run not upon an Helix that still enlargeth, but on a Circle, where, arriving to their Meridian, they decline in obscurity, and fall under the Horizon again.[112]

As the new star of 1572 demonstrates, argued Lipsius, the heavens are flying apart, thus confounding 'both the rules and wittes of the Mathematicians' and portending the end of a cycle.[113] For just as iron rusts and wood rots,

> so to all living creatures, citties and kingdomes, there be certaine inward causes of their own decay. Looke upon all things high and lowe, great and small, made with hand, or composed by the minde, they always have decayed, and ever shal. And as the rivers with a continual swift course runne into the sea: So all humane thinges through this conduit of wastings and calamities slyde to the marke of their desolation.[114]

Richard Hooker, to whom order is reason and reason is God, would not permit himself to believe that chaos could come again, but he does speculate on the terrifying consequences of a lawless universe – and recoils in horror. If 'nature should intermit her

---
[111] Sig. B4r.   [112] *Religio Medici*, p. 21.
[113] *Two Bookes of Constancie*, I.xxi. See Andreas Laurentius, *A Discourse of the Preservation of the Sight*, p. 168; Bacon, 'Of Vicissitudes of Things', *Essays* (*Works*, VII, 274).
[114] *Two Bookes of Constancie*, I.xv; cf. I.xvi.

course', if things should lose their qualities, if the overarching heaven should loosen and dissolve itself, if the 'celestial spheres should forget their wonted motions' and the moon wander from her beaten path, then 'what would become of man himself, whom these things now do all serve? See we not plainly that obedience of creatures unto the law of nature is the stay of the whole world?'[115]

Although Milton's contemporaries eagerly reworked the theme of mutability, they could scarcely add to the poignant Elizabethan obsession with corroding time. When we hear Browne say that it is too late to be ambitious because the 'great mutations of the world are acted, or time may be too short for our designes',[116] we are reminded of the commonplaces of William Cornwallis.[117] Jeremy Taylor enriched Lady Carbery's funeral sermon with his musings on the world's vanity and instability, but he drew on two thousand years of Stoic and Christian thought for his thesis:

> The whole temple and the religion, the ceremonies ordained by God, and the nation beloved by God, and the fabric erected for the service of God, shall run to their own period, and lie down in their several graves.[118]

In Donne's *Anniversaries* we find the most notorious Jacobean statement of the old doubts and fears. Man's life is a sickness, and he lives scarcely long enough to know whether his clocks are right or wrong. If he were ever anything, 'he's nothing now', and his decay suggests the universal ruin whose signs may be read in the disordered heavens no less than in the chaos of man's moral and intellectual systems. Donne's great threnody is unique in the quality and complexity of its emotion, yet thematically it suggests dozens of Renaissance moralists.[119] Indeed, Donne himself elsewhere states the obvious fact that a sense of the world's fragility and of man's decline to death is inevitable even without the disquieting data of the new science.

> I need not call in new philosophy, that denies a settledness, an acquiescence in the very body of the earth, but makes the earth to move in that place, where we thought the sun had moved; I need not that help, that the earth itself is in motion, to prove this, that nothing upon earth is permanent: the assertion will stand of itself, till some man assign me some instance, something that a man may rely upon and find permanent.

[115] *Laws*, I.iii.2; cf. I.ix.1.
[116] *Hydriotaphia*, ch. v (*Religio Medici & Other Writings*, p. 133).
[117] For example, see 'Of Fame', *Essayes*, pt. I, p. 76.
[118] *Sermons*, p. 489.
[119] For example, see Pedro Mexio, *Treasurie of Auncient and Moderne Times*, I.viii.

The 'vicissitudinary transmution' of all things is a truth that no one can escape: a monarchy 'will ruin' just as hair will grow gray, for it is in the nature of all sublunary things to change.[120]

The same kind of ironical acquiescence dominates Burton's account of contemporary science.[121] Like a 'long-winged Hawk', as he says, he roves through past and present theories of the heavens – summarizing, weighing, doubting, mocking. Why, if there be *'justae dimensiones, et prudens partium dispositio'* throughout all nature's other works, 'are the heavens so irregular, *neque paribus molibus, neque paribus intervallis*. Whence is this difference?' Copernicus ('Atlas his successor') and his crew tell us that the earth is a planet that moves and shines to others just as the moon does to us; if the earth is a moon, then no wonder we are 'giddy, vertiginous and lunatick'. The vexing implications of the earth's diurnal motion, 'now so much in question', are enough to drive us mad.

> For if the Earth be the Center of the World, stand still, and the Heavens move, as the most received opinion is, which they call *inordinatam coeli dispositionem*, though stiffly maintained by Tycho, Ptolemaeus, and their adherents, *quis ille furor?* &c. what fury is that, saith Dr. Gilbert, *satis animose*, as Cabeus notes, that shall drive the Heavens about with such incomprehensible celerity in 24 hours, when as every point of the Firmament, and in the Aequator, must needs move (so Clavius calculates) 176,660 times in one 246th part of an hour: and an arrow shot out of a bow must go seven times about the earth whilst a man can say an *Ave Maria*, if it keep the same space, or compass the earth 1,884 times in an hour, which is *supra humanam cogitationem*, beyond human conceit: *Ocior et jaculo, et ventos aequante sagitta*.[122]

The hypothesis of an infinite universe as argued by the 'Copernican Giants' is profoundly unsettling to all received opinion, and yet – who knows? At any rate, our world has a warm and cozy place 'nearest the heart of the Sun', and that is some small comfort. The fact is, that clashing authorities – or alleged authorities – cancel each other out: as a tinker 'stops one hole and makes two', the defenders of the old astronomy try to patch up their system to accommodate new facts. 'In the mean time the World is tossed in a blanket amongst them, they hoise the Earth up and down like a ball, make it stand and go at their pleasure.'

[120] *Works*, III, 483-4.
[121] 'Air Rectified. With a digression of the Air', *Anatomy*, II, 40-70.
[122] II, 60-1.

CORRODING TIME

Godfrey Goodman's *Fall of Man* is the most elaborate Jacobean lament on the theme of time. At once traditional and theological, its argument is rooted not in the current unrest over astronomical irregularities, but in Augustinian theology. The decay it celebrates is moral and cultural, and so it is in a sense the capstone of Renaissance pessimism. The new signs of heavenly decay become for Goodman merely the most recent data to be added to the evidence of all history that man's path since Adam's Fall has been irretrievably downward. For that primal catastrophe resulted not only in man's generic pollution, but in the infection of the whole realm of nature. Since age implies debility, the world grows weaker as it grows older: from man's steadily declining morals and learning and institutions we can only infer that the physical universe, too, is hastening to its extinction.

> Reason and all humane learning shall backe me, for certaine it is, that the Sunne hath descended much lower by many degrees, then he was in the time of King Ptolemie; the same Mathematicall instruments, which agree together in all other dimentions doe undoubtedly prove the diversity; by vertue of perspective glasses, we have lately discerned spots and shadowes in the Moone; and within our memorie, in the yeere 1572, a true Comet did appeare in the eighth Heaven, which as it had a time of beginning, so had it a period, and time of dissolving. And thus being mortall of our selves, wee dwell in houses of clay, the roofe of this world, as well as the foundations shall together be mooved; for wherefore serves the diversitie of seasons, the day and night succeeding each other, Summer and Winter, the rising and setting of Starres, the different and contrarie motions, the various aspects and oppositions? but that in some sort they partake of our nature, and shall have their part and portion with ours?[123]

Goodman's jeremiad is the most sustained essay in that pessimism which has been miscalled Jacobean. And since it provoked Hakewill's great *Apology* – which served both as an answer to the prophets of disaster and an arsenal for subsequent optimists – it makes a fitting terminus for this sketch of Renaissance pessimism. Although that pessimism, usually generated by the contemplation of time and change, found new support even in modern astronomy, it was still contained within Augustinian terms and adapted to Augustinian purposes. Augustine's view of man and history had served western Europe for a thousand years, and its efflores-

---

[123] *The Fall of Man* is an extremely rare book. I quote from Jones, *Ancients and Moderns*, pp. 29-30. See George Williamson, 'Mutability, Decay, and Seventeenth-Century Melancholy', *ELH*, II (1935), 121-50. A more extended and more recent treatment is Victor Harris' *All Cohaerence Gone* (1949).

cence at the end of the Renaissance was one of its most emphatic restatements. But if we realize that the melancholy of Ralegh and Goodman, like the funerary horrors of Tourneur and Marston, was a reprise rather than a prologue, we shall be in a sounder position to understand the temper of the seventeenth century.

V. THE IDEA OF PROGRESS

In his famous essay on Bacon, Macaulay remarks with considerable satisfaction that the accumulated interest of modern thought exceeded the principal inherited from antiquity. Few would have used his mercantile jargon, or have subscribed unquestioningly to his chesty confidence; yet in the early seventeenth century in many quarters there was a discernible reaction to the Augustinian theory of degeneration, and a felt need to find new sanctions for new pursuits. Viewed in its largest terms, this reaction must be accounted a part of the great revolt against scholasticism – a revolt whose course we must presently sketch – but it also marked a development of those optimistic theories of mutability that occasionally crop out in the late Renaissance. Without ascribing to the Renaissance a genuine theory of progress, that shibboleth of the modern world, we can see that the conception, birth, and baptism of the idea awaited only the secularization of knowledge which was to be the work of the seventeenth century; and that, even before its necessary assumptions had been secured, the idea itself was germinating in the minds of certain men like Le Roy and Bodin and Bacon.

As I have tried to point out elsewhere, the Christian humanism of the Renaissance – which included the rhapsodies of the Neo-Platonists – had been built on a generally optimistic view of human possibilities, both secular and religious. But, since it was a tradition that canonized authority, it could hardly achieve a real theory of progress. In spite of its high evaluation of human reason, it lacked the necessary view of nature as everywhere and always the same. By and large, the Renaissance still conceived of nature in terms of the Christian epic, which identified change with deterioration and progress with man's translation to a celestial realm of eternity. The optimism made familiar by the Christian humanists was predicated on the possibilities for reform – usually moral and literary reform – within rigidly prescribed limits laid down by the Bible and ancient classics. Thus Erasmus, writing to Leo X on the golden age he hoped to see, looked forward to the restoration of the three chief blessings of the human race (*tria quaedam praecipua generis humani bona restitutum iri videam*): piety, letters, and Christian concord.[124] Though Erasmus' hopes were doomed, we presently find Hooker, owning allegiance to the same tradition but to a different church, prescribing moderation and reason to cure all ills: though the times are bad, they are vastly better than when 'there were not above eight persons righteous living upon the face of the earth'.[125] For both Erasmus and Hooker the terminus to which this world was moving under the providence of God was the final conflagration and the last judgment.

Before the idea of progress could take shape it was obviously necessary that men come to regard nature in other than Augustinian terms. This gigantic change in the intellectual habits of Europe was to take a long time, beginning early in the Renaissance and extending far beyond the seventeenth century. But it was in the seventeenth century that its results first became apparent on a large scale. Without tracing the change in detail we may see certain obvious stages. Perhaps the first was the Thomistic defense of natural reason – that is, the forging of an instrument of knowledge which operated through man's natural faculties and afforded truth about natural objects. Another important step was the emancipation of nature from its theological anchors. Ironically enough, it was taken by the nominalists and voluntarists like Ockham and Calvin who, seeking to preserve religion from natural theology, emphatically if inadvertently segregated nature and grace, natural knowledge and divine revelation. Nature having thus been isolated as the sole proper object of man's natural intellection, the split between the truths of theology and all other forms of truth at once became apparent in the work of such Renaissance naturalists as Pomponazzi and Telesio. The doctrine of the double truth – in which Pomponazzi took refuge – signalized an ominous fracture in the medieval synthesis. And so at the opening of the seventeenth century we find Bacon, a great propagandist if a very bad scientist, demanding that men focus their intellectual efforts on the realm of nature – not to

[124] Quoted by Grierson, *Cross Currents*, p. 284.
[125] *Laws*, I.x.3.

attain goodness but to attain power. Bacon inaugurates the seventeenth-century quest for a proper methodology of knowledge to supplant the discredited 'notional' epistemology of the Schoolmen. In mathematics the titans of the century thought they had at last found the instrument for both exploring and explaining the processes of nature. With this development we enter the history of science, by then regarded, in spite of the pious disclaimers of Bacon and Galileo and Descartes and Hobbes, as separate from (perhaps antagonistic to) the supernatural 'truths' of theology.[126]

It is clear that the Augustinian view of God, nature, man, and history could not long survive in such a climate of ideas. The emergence of the doctrine of uniformity, the most fundamental axiom of pre-atomic science, was inevitable, and it meant the death of religious anthropomorphism. Nature, said Spinoza,

> is always the same and everywhere one. Her virtue is the same, and her power of acting; that is to say, her laws and rules, according to which all things are and are changed from form to form, and everywhere and always the same; so that there must also be one and the same method of understanding the nature of all things whatsoever, that is to say, by the universal laws and rules of nature.[127]

Nature, reduced to law and formula, was seen to be not a vehicle for articulating moral and teleological purposes but an apparently mechanistic complex of matter and motion where a given cause inevitably produced a certain effect. Before Hume's attack on this concept of mechanical causality it was thought that man had at last established the axioms and found the tools for attaining natural knowledge. This development, the most momentous in the history of modern thought, struck a lethal blow at the doctrine of providence (unless that doctrine was to be attenuated into a pallid deism), and it made necessary a radical revision in the traditional attitude toward time and mutability.

Even though not secured empirically, the uniformity of nature lies as an assumption behind a good deal of Renaissance optimism. In his *Methodus ad facilem historiarum cognitionem* (1566) Bodin had advanced it as a principle for explaining the course of human

---

[126] Citation here could be endless, but the point is trenchantly made by Pascal, 'Préface pour le Traité du Vide', *Œuvres*, p. 307.
[127] *Ethics*, bk. III, introduction (Wild, p. 206).

THE IDEA OF PROGRESS

events. Assuming that the capacities of nature are constant, then the differences between one historical epoch and another may be attributed not to cosmic deterioration but to the will of man. The assumption behind Bodin's cyclic theory of cultures – Eastern (religious), Mediterranean (moralistic), Northern (military and inventive) – disqualifies the notion of degeneration and anticipates the anti-authoritarianism of the next century. Even Ben Jonson, securely within the tradition of Christian humanism, challenges the notion of decay:

> I cannot thinke Nature is so spent, and decay'd, that she can bring forth nothing worth her former yeares. She is always the same, like her selfe: And when she collects her strength, is abler still. Men are decay'd, and studies: She is not.[128]

In the early seventeenth century this assumption of uniformity usually appears as a protest against obsolete authority – scholastic, papal, or literary. 'The mortallest enemy unto knowledge, and that which hath done the greatest execution upon truth,' says Browne, 'hath been a peremptory adhesion unto Authority.'[129] And when he goes on to check such authority by 'common and Country observation' he is operating on the notion that man has still the faculties for attaining truth. Certain technological advances of the Renaissance seemed to support such a view: the compass, gunpowder, and printing – cited by Cardan, Bodin, Bacon, Campanella, Le Roy, and many others – seemed to offer clear proof that in certain respects, at least, the modern age had improved upon the past, and that man might properly hope for further gains.

It is the promise of such a hope that generates so much enthusiasm in Bacon. Like most of his contemporaries, he could only believe as a Christian that he was living in the old age of the world (*antiquitas seculi iuventus mundi*), and that no indefinite advance in the future was possible; yet he shared the Renaissance concern with man and his life on this sinful planet, and he ceaselessly preached the necessity of improving that life through an augmented knowledge of nature. The whole of *The Advancement of Learning* – significant title – is informed with confidence in the future as better than the past, and better not in terms of a Stoic, cyclic progress and regression but in terms of continual progress

[128] *Discoveries*, p. 9.   [129] *Pseudodoxia*, I.vi.

by incrementation directed by the providence of God and accelerated by a proper (Baconian) methodology.

> There is therefore much ground for hoping that there are still laid up in the womb of nature many secrets of excellent use, having no affinity or parallelism with any thing that is now known, but lying entirely out of the beat of the imagination, which have not yet been found out. They too no doubt will some time or other, in the course and revolution of many ages, come to light of themselves, just as the others [i.e. gunpowder, the discovery of silk, the magnet] did; only by the method of which we are now treating they can be speedily and suddenly and simultaneously presented and anticipated.[130]

It was George Hakewill, an Anglican clergyman, who most emphatically challenged the doctrine of decay and thus bequeathed to the seventeenth century an arsenal of arguments and proofs for the idea of progress. His massive monument, *An Apology or Declaration of the Power and Providence of God in the Government of the World*, first published in 1627 to refute Goodman and reaching a third edition by 1635, sought to locate within the Christian epic a defensible theory of progress. It marks a significant transition from Christian meliorism to the thoroughly secular optimism of Fontenelle and Saint-Pierre of the next century. Hakewill returns to Goodman's lugubrious argument for universal decay the answer that Spenser had advanced in the *Two Cantos of Mutability*: time and mutation are obvious facts, but under all change a pattern is discernible – 'as a Wheele, at every turne, bringeth about all his Spoakes to the same places, observing a constancy even in turning'.[131] In his six-hundred-page folio Hakewill surveys many fields – morals, natural history, literature, science[132] – and in each he finds a notable advance from ancient to modern times. Although he thinks that he is living in the world's old age, and that the overthrow of the Roman antiChrist and the conversion of the Jews will lead directly to the last judgment, he views the course of universal history as a *continuata productio* under the providence of God. As the metaphor of the wheel demonstrates, change for Hakewill means circular

---

[130] NO, I.cix (*Works*, VIII, 142).
[131] See *Two Cantos*, VII.lviii.
[132] The *Apologie* is arranged in four books: the first a general statement refuting the doctrine of decay; the second refuting the 'pretended decay of the Heavens and Elements'; the third concerning the age, strength, stature, and capacities of man; and the fourth refuting the 'pretended decay' of manners and morals and closing with a proof of the 'future consummation' of the world in the last judgment.

THE IDEA OF PROGRESS 83

change, and circular change refutes the notion of decay.

> There is (it seemes) both in wits and Arts, as in all things besides, a kinde of circular progresse: they have their birth, their growth, their flourishing, their fayling, their fading, and within a while after their resurrection, and refloureshing againe.[133]

Hakewill does not ignore the new stars and the threatening implications of the new science – in the second edition he inserts an essay on the new astronomy by his friend Henry Briggs, Savilian professor at Oxford – but he refuses to subscribe to the 'pretended decay of the Heavens and Elements'.[134] He argues that men have uniform capacities at all times. If we find our productions in learning and knowledge less than the ancients', we must not conclude that they were giants and we are dwarfs, but that our want of 'studiousnesse, watchfulnesse and love of truth' makes us men 'of a competent stature groveling on the earth'.[135] The implication of a necessary reform is sufficiently clear. And yet, as all evidence shows, the moderns have in many ways advanced significantly beyond their predecessors. The futilities of the Schoolmen teach us ('not to conceale a truth') that theirs were 'lightsome times in regard of those succeeding ages that followed after, when Divinity was woven into distinctions, which like Cobwebs were fine and curious in working but not much usefull'.[136] Thanks to the 'generally received' opinion of the world's decay we tend to venerate the ancients unduly, so that 'if wee meete with any thing which excells, wee thinke it must be ancient, or if with any thing that is ancient, it cannot but excell'.[137] Yet a larger view refutes this blasphemy against God's providence and establishes His great principle of compensation. If men look only at their own lives, or at their own family or country or age, they may erroneously conclude

> that all things decay and goe backwards, which makes men murmure and repine against God, under the name of Fortune and Destinie; whereas he that as a part of mankinde in generall, takes a view of the universall, compares person with person, family with family, corporation with corporation, nation with nation, age with age; suspends his judgement, and upon examination clearely findes, that all things worke toegether for the best to them that love God: and that though some numbers suffer, yet

[133] p. 230. [134] pp. 70 ff., 127 ff.
[135] 'The Preface', sig. C3ᵛ. [136] p. 236.
[137] p. 27.

the whole is no way thereby indammaged at any time; and at other times those same members are againe relieved, as the Sunne when it sets to us, it rises to our Antipodes, and when it remooves from the Northerne parts of the world, it cherishes the Southerne, yet stayes not there, but returnes againe with his comfortable beames to those very parts which for a time it seemed to have forsaken: O that men would therefore praise the Lord for his goodnesse, and declare the wonders that he hath done for the children of men![138]

Arguing, then, from the principles of circular mutation and of compensation, Hakewill sought to prove, as one of his disciples put it, that by the doctrine of degeneration 'the Majesty of God is dishonoured, the commendable indeavours of Men are hindered'.[139] The words suggest the two main lines that coalesced into an incipient theory of progress for seventeenth century England. These lines we may call the providential and the Baconian. One adapted the ancient doctrine of providence to the events of the Puritan revolution and the details of Puritan theology; the other looked to the fulfillment of man's dream of at long last conquering nature for his own commodity. Both worked on the assumption that change is always for the better. The specter of cormorant time was thus gradually domesticated to the facts of life as they were understood in the seventeenth century.

Hakewill's became one of the most widely read books of the century, for in it optimists of all persuasions could find arguments to their purpose. John Milton's 'Naturam non pati senium', a Hakewillian little poem written for a Cambridge disputation, says nothing about men and morals but comes out strongly for the constancy of natural forces.

> At pater omnipotens, fundatis fortius astris,
> Consuluit rerum summae, certoque peregit
> Pondere fatorum lances, atque ordine summo
> Singula perpetuum iussit servare tenorum.[140]

In his later career as a Puritan publicist, however, Milton had a great deal to say about the prospects for moral improvement once men had cast off the shackles of custom and error. Milton is a notable spokesman for the concept of providential progress, and he sees history as the slow but inexorable spread of true religion, culminating in the perfected Reformation of his own

---
[138] 'The Preface', sig. C2r.
[139] John Jonston, *An History of the Constancy of Nature*, p. 2.
[140] Lines 33–6.

age.¹⁴¹ His imagination takes fire at the thought of how the 'blissful Reformation (by Divine Power) struck through the black and settled Night of Ignorance and Antichristian Tyranny'; and he sees it as the mighty work of his own day and of his own party to consummate what was then begun.¹⁴² This note is common in Puritan thought, deriving as much from the Puritan view of history as from the Puritan ethos of an inward, struggling quest for personal salvation. Lord Brooke, tracing the Reformation from the Albigensians ('Holy Good men') to the 'more glorious Light among these Northerne Isles', calls for the speedy fulfillment, under God's providence, of the work unfinished.

> Thus Light dilating, and enlarging it selfe, seemeth to become more pure, more Light, more Glorious: and yet it seemes not to be Noone. The Light, still, will, must, cannot but encrease; why then doe wee shut our eyes?¹⁴³

Likewise from the Independents fighting for toleration rose an insistent demand for the unchecked development of grace; theirs was a program for personal progress which could only construe human possibilities in the most cheerful terms:

> though a Christian live never so long, yet he both may, and ought still to grow from grace to grace, and from knowledge to knowledge, continually ayming, and endeavouring, untill he arrive to a perfect man according to the measure of stature and fulnesse of Christ.¹⁴⁴

The extremest form of this Puritan optimism is revealed in the Utopian rhapsodies of those – like Hanserd Knollys – who fully expected the reign of the saints within their own lifetime. But Puritans of virtually every shade and sect could join in celebrating the progress of piety under the providence of God.

Although the Savoy Conference and the ludicrous disasters of the Fifth Monarchy Men dampened this kind of millenarian thinking, the stream of Baconian optimism deepened and strengthened as the century advanced. It represented the secular version of the triumph of time. In 1632 John Jonston published his *Naturae constantia* (translated in 1657 as *An History of the Constancy of Nature*) which restated Hakewill's main points with a good deal of technological evidence. Jonston not only argues for the 'con-

---

¹⁴¹ *The Doctrine and Discipline of Divorce*, PW, III, 171-2.
¹⁴² *Of Reformation in England*, bk. I (PW, II, 366-7).
¹⁴³ *A Discourse Opening the Nature of Episcopacy*, II.vii (Haller, II, 160).
¹⁴⁴ *Liberty of Conscience*, Haller, III, 166.

stancy' of nature, however; he urges its general improvement,[145] and concludes that from the general advance in arts and sciences 'It is very probable that the notable ruine of Antichrist is hard at hand'.[146] The progress of the new science has demolished the old fears of nature's imminent destruction, and the spectacular gains of modern learning have made that of the ancients contemptible. Witness the great Scaliger: as Casaubon reported, 'he had read nothing, (and what had he not read?) but he presently remembered it'.[147] One can only agree with Ramus, that in modern times we have seen a 'greater increase' of learned men than 'our Ancestours saw before in fourteen ages that are past'.[148]

The same note is struck in John Hall's Utopian vision of industrialism in 1649. Urging Parliament to cast its watchful eye on the arts and crafts of England – now that political and ecclesiastical iniquities have been purged – Hall prophesies 'an happy inversion of that common saying, that our Ancients were Gyants, and we are Dwarfs'.[149] Granted his fallen state, man need only use 'that little knowledge which chance, or the dark Axiomes of his owne reason can helpe him with' to attain undreamed control over his environment.[150] Henry Power, writing just after the Restoration and the establishment of the Royal Society, dispenses with Hall's Calvinism but elaborates his optimism. No one who has witnessed the gigantic strides of sciences and technology within a man's lifetime can doubt that an infinite future lies ahead. The only possible deterrents to continued advance is a deference to those 'Notional Speculators' whose now discredited follies disgraced both theology and philosophy in the Middle Ages, and a belief in the absurd 'Universal Exclamation of the World's decay and approximation to its period'.[151]

---

[145] pp. 115 f.   [146] p. 177.
[147] p. 70.   [148] p. 72.
[149] *An Humble Motion to the Parliament*, p. 6.
[150] *Ibid.*, pp. 6–7.
[151] *Experimental Philosophy*, pp. 186–8. How may we properly speak of deterioration when we, with our microscopes and telescopes, can see more things more clearly than Adam even before the fall, asks Power (sig. A4ᵛ). We live in a fresh and heady season, and the great men now walking the corridors of Gresham College and directing the pursuits of the Royal Society will put all posterity in their debt. 'You are the enlarged and Elastical Souls of the world, who, removing all former rubbish, and prejudicial resistances, do make way for the Springy Intellect to flye out into its desired Expansion. When I seriously contemplate the freedom of your Spirits, the excellency of your Principles, the vast reach of your Designs, to unriddle all Nature; me-thinks you have done more than men already, and may be well placed in a rank Specifically different from the rest of grovelling Humanity' (pp. 191–2).

THE IDEA OF PROGRESS

After the Restoration this distrust of the past and hope for the future is cast in increasingly secular terms. We hear virtually nothing of the forthcoming reign of the saints, but a great deal about the benefits to be conferred by the spread of natural knowledge through the gains of experimental philosophy. As a wit of the town and a member of the Royal Society young Dryden was writing almost *de rigueur* in making Crites say that 'almost a new Nature has been revealed to us' within the past century. Is it not true, he continues,

> that more errors of the school have been detected, more useful experiments in philosophy have been made, more noble secrets in optics, medicine, anatomy, astronomy, discovered, than in all those credulous and doting ages from Aristotle to us? – so true it is, that nothing spreads more fast than science, when rightly and generally cultivated.[152]

The same conviction propels Dryden's poem to Dr Charleton, which in less than a hundred lines runs over all the stock themes: contempt for the long 'tyranny' of Aristotle, praise for the advances (many of them made by Englishmen) of the modern world, hope for a glorious future.

> The world to Bacon does not only owe
> Its present knowledge, but its future too.
> Gilbert shall live, till loadstones cease to draw,
> Or British fleets the boundless oceans awe.[153]

In more sober terms Hooke's preface to his *Micrographia* develops the theme that man's liabilities may be redeemed by his technological advances. Hooke is nothing if not practical: he is concerned less with philosophical programs than with the actual ways in which man may control nature for his purposes, and he blandly assumes that such control is inevitable if observation and experimentation are properly conducted. Who knows? Just as 'optical glasses' have opened up new areas to man's naturally limited vision, so may future discoveries sharpen and improve his deficiencies of smell and taste. And there always remains, as a monument to the temper of his age, Bishop Sprat's *History of the Royal Society*, with its vision of a future bliss to be secured less by the offices of the Anglican church than by the spread of 'mechanic genius'.

[152] *An Essay of Dramatic Poesy, Essays,* I, 36–7.
[153] *Poetical Works,* p. 18.

The most graceful statement of this new hope, however, is Joseph Glanvill's. His *Plus Ultra* (1668) is largely indebted to Hakewill even for its plan, but all his work is informed with the secular dream of the new millenarians. Like his idol Bacon, Glanvill was a propagandist; but rather than a rosy dream to announce, he had the Royal Society to celebrate; and he knew, as Bacon had not known, that the future of science depended on the powerful methodological aid of mathematics. Against all opponents – notably Henry Stubbe – he urbanely argued the case for experimental philosophy, not as a possible avenue of progress but as a *fait accompli*. Like Sprat an Anglican clergyman, he has the same facile answer to those who saw revealed religion being swallowed up by secular knowledge: render unto faith the things that belong to faith, but be sure not to confuse them with the empirical data of the new philosophy. We shall examine his work more closely later; here it is enough to point out that he was inevitably and emphatically a disciple of progress. The *Plus Ultra* is a paean of modern times. The future of man's natural knowledge, hitherto limited only by his foolish reliance on discredited authority, opens gloriously before him in this age in which 'it hath pleased God to excite a very vigorous and active Spirit for the advancement of real and useful Learning'.[154] Whatever the sad condition of Adam's faculties after the Fall, his posterity is now rebuilding them apace. Indeed, the first chapter of *The Vanity of Dogmatizing* – ostensibly an essay in skepticism – seems to mean little more than that before the Fall Adam was equipped to be a first-rate experimental philosopher; the rest of the book makes it clear that with the aid of modern technology the race can retain his happy condition. Adam knew without experiment 'whether the Lodestone doth attract by Atomical Effluviums'; he was a better anatomist than Harvey, a better astronomer than Kelper. 'Causes are hid in night and obscurity from us, which were all Sun to him.'[155] As a result of Adam's sin, however, the race had to 'go on its belly, and lick the dust' – that is, before God, in His own good time, vouchsafed the method of experimental philosophy for restoring fallen humanity.[156]

Now that the golden age is opening before him, man need

---

[154] 'Of the Modern Improvements of Useful Knowledge', *Essays*, p. 2.
[155] *The Vanity of Dogmatizing*, pp. 5–7.
[156] *Ibid.*, p. 12.

THE IDEA OF PROGRESS

only set his eyes to the future. Bacon and Galileo and Descartes are the 'illustrious Heroes' who have filled the world with new wonders and shown it the 'way to be happy'.[157] Far from decaying, the universe is spinning merrily towards new acquisitions of knowledge. Each generation will leave its earthly habitation better and happier than they found it, and the notable champions of the new philosophy – 'Cartes, Gassendus, Galilaeo, Tycho, Harvey, More, Digby' – unite to tell us that truth is the daughter of time. They 'strike dead the opinion of the worlds decay, and conclude it, in its Prime'.[158]

With Glanvill we are getting beyond the limits of this study. He seems to anticipate Peacock's Mr Foster who, in *Headlong Hall*, argued against Mr Escot, the atrabiliar 'deteriorationist', that 'the various arts of life . . ., in their rapid and interminable progress, will finally conduct every individual of the race to the philosophic pinnacle of pure and perfect felicity'. Even so, as a man more conspicuous for his style than for his originality, Glanvill shows us how drastically the champions of the new philosophy had revised the Elizabethan fear of corroding time. This is not the place to treat Malebranche's and Leibnitz' redactions of this new optimism, or to follow it to its full flowering in the next century. But we have perhaps gone far enough to suggest, if not to trace fully, a crucial modification of the ancient Christian attitude toward time and change. Men like Glanvill teach us that under the benevolent aegis of experimental philosophy even if death retained its mystery, time had lost its terrors.

[157] *Ibid.*, pp. 181–2.   [158] *Ibid.*, p. 240.

III

THE USES OF REASON

1. THE GENERAL AND PERPETUAL VOICE OF MEN

The tradition of human dignity lay at the heart of Renaissance optimism. Since it was a tradition that could encompass both the heights and declensions of human possibilities it could – until the success of science seemed to make it obsolete – reserve even for fallen man an honorable role in the Christian epic. Not even Calvin could permanently dislodge those ancient assumptions from which the dignity of man was derived; for if Calvin was content to degrade man so that he would have to throw himself on the unmerited mercy of God even to hope for salvation, the heirs of Renaissance humanism were not. Fallen though he is, the relics of his primal virtue are still in him, and offer glorious possibilities for reconstruction. For if we strengthen these relics by discipline, education, and piety, as Milton urges, we may 'repair the ruins of our first parents by regaining to know God aright, and out of that knowledge to love him, to imitate him, to be like him'.[1] The proper use of man's tarnished rational faculty, then, is one broad path to God, and it opens into another – that of revelation. Man, made in the image of God, has fallen, but he is capable of raising himself again. And thus the wheel comes full circle under the providence of God.

This is Hooker's great theme, and it informed the traditional optimism of the seventeenth century.

> Wherefore seeing that God hath endued us with sense, to the end that we might perceive such things as this present life doth need; and with reason, lest that which sense cannot reach unto, being both now and also in regard of a future estate hereafter necessary to be known, should lie obscure; finally, with the heavenly support of prophetical revelation, which doth open those hidden mysteries that reason could never have been able to find out, or to have known the necessity of them unto our everlasting good: use we the precious gifts of God unto his glory and honour that gave them, seeking by all means to know what the will of our God is.[2]

---

[1] *On Education*, PW, III, 464.   [2] *Laws*, I.xv.4; cf. II.i.5.

From the axiom of knowledge it is clear, I think, that the traditional dignity of man rested upon an epistemological base. Certainly, most statements of that dignity are cast in epistemological terms. And since an epistemology always involves a metaphysic, it is clear that for men like Hooker and Milton the kinds of knowledge available to man are securely anchored in the kinds of reality which are the objects of knowledge. Those kinds of knowledge may be compendiously described under the rubrics established by Augustine as *ratio scientiae* and *ratio sapientiae*. In the broadest view we may associate the first with classicism, with nature, with man, with reason, with truth; the second with Christianity, with grace, with God, with faith, with goodness; and we may say that it was the great achievement of Aquinas (and of the Schoolmen in general) to attempt a workable synthesis of the two, allocating to reason the things proper to reason, to faith the things proper to faith, and reconciling the two under the providence of God. For if Augustine upset the equilibrium sharply in favour of *ratio sapientiae*,[3] Aquinas tried, at least, to restore the balance.

At the very opening of the great *Summa* he distinguishes the knowledge that comes by faith and that constructed by the processes of reason working on the data of sensory cognition,[4] and his main effort is to effect a synthesis of goodness-truth from the thesis goodness and the antithesis truth. That is to say, in terms of human psychology he seeks to identify goodness, the object of will, with truth, the object of reason, and thus to adjust the claims of God and man, grace and nature, revelation and reason, heaven and earth. 'Truth and good include one another; for truth is something good, or otherwise it would not be desirable; and good is something true, or otherwise it could not be intelligible.'[5] This does not mean that Aquinas – as his later antagonists charged – ignored the primacy of the supra-rational, the intuitive, and the revealed,[6] but that he asserted the uses of human reason in arriving at an intelligible view of God's creation. Hence his supreme importance for the Renaissance, and for that tradition of Christian humanism which found its last strong statement in Milton.

[3] See *The Confessions*, VII.xvii; *De Trinitate*, XII.xiv; cf. Cochrane, *Christianity and Classical Culture*, pp. 435 f.
[4] I.i.1.   [5] *ST*, I.lxxix.11.
[6] For example, see his discussion of the vexed question of the Eucharist (a mystery 'wholly supernatural, effected solely by the power of God'), *ST*, III.lxxx.4.

Aquinas' thought is theocratic, teleological, and rational. The universe described by the *Summa* is one in which every element of human experience is referred ultimately to God, in which every event is intelligible – either by the intellect (speculative or practical) or by faith – as conducting to an eventual good.[7] The practical intellect has as its object truth in relation to other things or to conduct; the speculative intellect, truth as having reference to things outside the intellect; but subsuming both modes of mental activity is man's rational and immortal soul, and both coincide in the moral duty of reaching an intelligible notion of God's workings.[8] Similarly, the intellectual and moral virtues (relating to reason and will)[9] are subsumed by the indispensable virtue of prudence, which Aquinas equates quite simply with right reason. This *recta ratio* (whose complicated Aristotelian and Stoic sources we cannot explore here) is that immutable coalescence of truth and goodness whose source is God and whose formative cosmic role is manifested in all the workings of nature.[10]

Even this inadequate sketch is enough, perhaps, to suggest the importance of Aquinas for Renaissance optimism. Whatever the vicissitudes of ecclesiastical history – and after the Reformation it became *de rigueur* for the Hot Gospelers to vilify Aquinas as the chief of Schoolmen – his significance for the thought of the Renaissance is incalculable. Whether or not men plowed through his interminable *Summa*, he had made it possible for them to assume the axiom of knowledge; and this meant that between Petrarch and Milton Christian humanists could justify both secular and religious activity as deriving from the great principle of *recta ratio*. Although he stimulated the nominalistic reaction of Ockham and the subsequent voluntarism of Calvin, he also established a concord of faith and reason *sub specie aeternitatis*. Thanks to him, it was possible for men as late as Milton to ground truth in morality, and to believe that to think right is to do right, both truth and goodness being intelligible to the faculties of knowledge which belong to man *qua* man.

The impact of this rationalism is felt everywhere in the Renaissance. Petrarch, for example, most frequently quotes Augustine and shows strong traces of nominalistic skepticism, yet he worships Cicero as the exponent of natural reason. Petrarch's theology

[7] *Summa contra Gentiles*, I.xvi.
[8] *ST*, I.lxxix.11.
[9] *ST*, I-II.lviii.2–3.
[10] *ST*, I-II.lvii.5.

is essentially Augustinian: on Mont Ventoux he is torn between a life of sense and one of religious dedication, and (in reaction to the impious naturalism of the Averroists) he ignores the claims of natural knowledge in a way that would not have pleased Aquinas;[11] but he follows the main line of Thomistic rationalism in regarding learning as an adjunct of piety: 'Whenever I have made a sober use of learning, I have sought in it nothing but to become good.'[12] Although he anticipates the widening abyss between reason and will which would lead Calvin to his attack on the Thomistic synthesis,[13] yet he could only agree with Erasmus, and with Christian humanists in general, that ideally all man's faculties may be fused in the pursuit of that goodness which constitutes the highest truth.

The most systematic exposition of this fusion in English is Hooker's. In reaffirming the legitimate claims of reason and tradition against the rebellious voluntarism of the Puritans he not only set the course of Anglican thought but he also gave a definitive statement of that Renaissance humanism which would presently crumble before the advent of science and a secularized natural knowledge. To refute the arguments of Cartwright and Travers against the Elizabethan settlement might have been his immediate object, but ultimately he was marshaling all the artillery of history, reason, and tradition against the heresy of Calvin. For Calvin had alienated nature from God, truth from goodness, piety from conduct, reason from theology; and the result, in Hooker's view, was a universe rendered unintelligible and therefore meaningless. The main lines of Hooker's rebuttal are those laid down by Aquinas; and although they reach beyond Aquinas to Aristotle and the Stoics, the tone and accent are his own.

In this ancient tradition the universe was construed as essentially rational, and consequently as at least partially intelligible by man's rational faculties. Hence the significant role of law, as both a metaphysical and an ethical principle. 'That which doth assign

---

[11] 'What is the use – I beseech you – of knowing the nature of quadrupeds, fowls, fishes, and serpents and not knowing or even neglecting man's nature, the purpose for which we are born, and whence and whereto we travel' (*On his own Ignorance* in *RP*, pp. 58–9)? For the comparable position of a Puritan rationalist, see Baxter, *Knowledge and Love Compared*, I.vi (*Works*, XV, 47–67).

[12] *On his own Ignorance*, p. 62; cf. p. 117.

[13] 'It is safer to strive for a good and pious will than for a capable and clear intellect. The object of the will, as it pleases the wise, is to be good; that of the intellect is truth. It is better to will the good than to know the truth' (*ibid.*, p. 105).

unto each thing the kind,' says Hooker in opening his great defense of reason, 'that which doth moderate the force and power, that which doth appoint the form and measure, of working, the same we term a Law.'[14] The Greeks had elevated *nous* into a metaphysical absolute to which all the fluctuations of matter (and sensation) could be referred for meaning. The Roman lawyers – eclectic Stoics as well as hard-headed administrators of an empire – had applied this principle to the ends of government and conduct; they were convinced that a cosmic rationality, expressible in terms of law, governed all transformations and patterned all changes. It was inevitable that the Middle Ages, instructed by Augustine and Gratian, should identify this principle of order and moral causality with the will of God and call it providence.[15] Its utility for Thomistic thought is too obvious to be labored, but more important for our survey is its utility for the late Renaissance. When in the sixteenth century the Roman church finally lost its status as the divinely sanctioned agent for interpreting and articulating God's will, the result seemed to be a moral vacuum. Aquinas' majestic hierarchy of laws descending from the reason of God to the law of nature and then centering in the divine mandate of the Church[16] inevitably lost its prestige in the age of the Tudors and the Valois. Broadly speaking, the vacuum was filled in two ways: by the postulation of a law of nature which, though independent of any particular ecclesiastical authority, none the less represented those moral absolutes binding on human conduct; and by the private moral judgment of the Protestant who, fortified by the Scripture and the grace of God, substituted inner conviction for Aquinas' universally valid moral principles.

At this moment in the history of Protestant thought – a moment of intense reaction to natural and rational theology – Hooker came forward to defend the axiom of knowledge, and to restate, in a different context, the Thomistic claims for human reason. We need not describe his elaborate hierarchy of laws, from that Eternal Law laid up in the bosom of God to the human laws by which the body politic is sustained, or to point its similarity to Aquinas';[17] but to understand the nature of Renaissance optimism we should remember that in Hooker's view law is the

---

[14] *Laws*, I.ii.1.
[15] See Sir Frederick Pollock, *Essays in the Law*, pp. 31–79.
[16] *ST*, I.ii.90 f.
[17] *Laws*, I.ii.1; cf. Ralegh's analysis of law, *History*, I.ix.106.

symbol for those essentially rational principles by which God created and preserves His universe, and through which His workings are made intelligible to man. 'The general and perpetual voice of men is as the sentence of God himself. For that which all men have at all times learned, Nature herself must needs have taught; and God being the author of Nature, her voice is but his instrument.'[18]

The assumptions felt as facts which underlie systems are always more important than the details of those systems; and it is Hooker's assumption that 'the mind of man desireth evermore to know the truth according to the most infallible certainty which the nature of things can yield'.[19] Since God had given man this desire for knowledge, He had given him a capacity for knowledge – knowledge beginning with sensibles, rising to the inferred rational principles subsuming those sensibles, and finally, having crossed the threshold of human reason, attaining the celestial truths of revelation. But in Hooker's theocratic universe all forms of knowledge are modes of goodness, in that they derive from the wisdom of God. Thus sin itself – 'the singular disgrace of Nature' – is merely a form of error, or ignorance; for in doing evil 'we prefer a less good before a greater, the greatness whereof is by reason investigable and may be known'.[20] For Hooker as for Socrates knowledge is virtue, and his restatement of the cardinal principle of European humanism takes on urgency and poignancy when juxtaposed against Bacon's pregnant assertion that knowledge is power. 'Goodness is seen with the eye of the understanding. . . . For the Laws of well-doing are the dictates of right Reason.'[21] With such a pronouncement Hooker reaches the very heart of Christian humanism.

However, this identification of truth with virtue concealed a threat to revealed religion which Hooker, like all other Christian humanists, was careful to guard against. It was all too easy, as the seventeenth century was to learn, to slip down the path of rational theology to deism, or even worse. Once the delicate equilibrium between reason and faith was dislocated, or the claims of natural knowledge permitted to usurp the prerogatives of revelation, then there was real danger to the sovereignty of God.

[18] *Laws*, I.viii.3.   [19] *Laws*, I.vii.5.   [20] *Laws*, I.vii.7.
[21] *Laws*, I.vi.1–4. The whole section, embodying Hooker's psychology of will as articulating the dictates of reason, is a *locus classicus* of Renaissance humanism .

THE USES OF REASON

With the steady secularization of knowledge, powerfully accelerated by the methodology of science, the seventeenth century was to win its most dazzling triumphs, but in the tradition we are trying to describe every effort was made to preserve the dignity of man without impairing the sovereignty of God. Hence the insistent warnings, from Hooker and Chapman and Milton and many others, that God has set limits to the reaches of human reason.

> Dangerous it were for the feeble brain of man to wade far into the doings of the Most High; . . . our soundest knowledge is to know that we know him not as indeed he is, neither can know him: and our safest eloquence concerning him is our silence, when we confess without confession that his glory is inexplicable, his greatness above our capacity and reach. He is above, and we upon earth; therefore it behoveth our words to be wary and few.[22]

There is, obviously, a legitimate area for human speculation, that is, for natural knowledge derived from 'the bare contemplation of heaven and earth'; but it does not extend to 'the very principal mysteries of our faith; and whatsoever we may learn by them, the same we can only attain to know according to the manner of natural sciences, which mere discourse of wit and reason findeth out'.[23] The fact is that both reason and faith have their proper spheres, that man is richly equipped with faculties to attain the truth about both, and that since in the divine order governing the universe the truth of faith is higher than the truth of reason he must not presume to explore the mysteries of one with the instruments of the other.

> Some things she [i.e. wisdom] openeth by the sacred books of Scripture; some things by the glorious works of Nature: with some things she inspireth them from above by spiritual influence; in some things she leadeth and traineth them only by worldly experience and practice. We may not so in any one special kind admire her, that we disgrace her in any other; but let all her ways be according unto their place and degree adored.[24]

Hooker's discrimination of natural and revealed truth became a tedious commonplace in the following century. Lancelot Andrewes' strictures against a merely natural religion[25] tritely sum-

[22] *Laws*, I.ii.2. [23] *Laws*, V.xxii.5.
[24] *Laws*, II.i.iv. [25] *A Pattern of Catechistical Doctrine*, pp. 19–20.

marize the orthodox position[26] which is more poignantly stated by Browne, fascinated as he was by the *O altitudo* of faith and also by Bacon's program for the secular conquest of nature. We cannot hope to think we know God, Browne warns: our ignorance of the 'back-parts or lower side of His Divinity' should show us the folly of prying into His mysteries.[27] Though sore perplexed at the widening gulf between the truths of faith and natural knowledge, Browne is traditionalist enough to hope that the fissure can be somehow bridged. Just as reason and passion can be psychologically adjusted in a well-tempered personality, all antinomies should, by a 'moderate and peaceable discretion', be so ordered that 'they may all be Kings, and yet make but one Monarchy, every one exercising his Sovereignty and Prerogative in a due time and place, according to the restraint and limit of circumstance'.[28]

After the turn of the century many seemed to concur in Browne's pious and futile hope, for it was clear that secular knowledge was cutting deeper and deeper into the domain of revealed and supernatural truth. Opening his interminable *Ductor Dubitantium*, Taylor sees God not only in His providence but in those laws engraved on our hearts. 'He rules in us by His substitute our conscience. God sits there and gives us laws',[29] for conscience is 'nothing but right reason reduced to practice, and conducting moral actions'.[30] At least superficially this dictum would be compatible with Ralegh's that it is 'a true effect of true reason (there being no authority more binding than reason,) to acknowledge and adore the first and most sublime power'[31] – or even with the deistic 'common notions' to which Lord Herbert ascribed divine sanction, to Descartes' 'clear and distinct ideas', to Milton's inexorable moral sense, to the *recta ratio* of the Cambridge

---

[26] A few random examples will suggest its obvious importance in Elizabethan literature. Gabriel Harvey, writing to Spenser about the earthquake of 1580, attacks the audacious fools who pry into God's mysteries 'as if they had a key for all the lockes in Heaven'; Radagon, the evil counsellor in *A Looking-Glass for London and England*, seeks natural explanations for the calamities which an angry God pours on King Rasni – and of course he is grievously punished; Chapman interpolates into the Circe episode of his Odyssey some very un-Homeric remarks about the limits of human reason. But such examples could be multiplied without number.
[27] *Religio Medici*, pp. 14–5.
[28] *Ibid.*, p. 23; cf. pp. 10, 12, 53; *Christian Morals*, I.xvii, III.xxi.
[29] I.i.2.
[30] I.ii.1; cf. *Holy Dying*, IV.vi, on 'true natural religion', and *Holy Living*, II.i: 'Christian religion in all its moral parts is nothing but the law of nature.'
[31] *History*, 'Preface', p. liii.

Platonists.³² But even this bare catalogue suggests how steadily the uses of natural reason were encroaching upon that domain where mystery and adoration constituted wisdom.

II. RAMEAN LOGIC

The massive but flexible tradition of Christian humanism was the most powerful cohesive force in Renaissance thought. Especially after the emergence of the national state and the decline of Rome, it cut across national boundaries and party lines to give unity, of a sort, to the thinking of men otherwise as unlike as Erasmus and Spenser, Hooker and Milton, Elyot and Browne. A more specifically Protestant and Platonic (and, in England, Puritan) manifestation of the ancient conviction that God's creation is essentially rational and that man has the instruments for comprehending it was Ramean logic.³³

In the vanguard of the reaction to Aristotle and the Schoolmen, Peter Ramus (Pierre de la Ramée) had in 1536 proposed for his degree of Master of Arts the thesis 'all that Aristotle has said is forged'. His subsequent career as a logician, a teacher, a humanist, and a Protestant was shaped by his belief that the whole bulky accumulation of that methodology which was Aristotelian, Catholic, and scholastic was wrong. Consequently he put together a system that, though essentially Platonic, seemed to many of his coreligionists a new and invincible weapon for cutting through the jungle of custom, error, and authority to arrive at certain truth. Significantly, Ramus made no break with the axiom of

---

³² Two famous statements of this sense of the certainty of natural knowledge – both in the high tradition of Continental rationalism – are Descartes' and Spinoza's. See Descartes, *Principles*, I.xlv; Spinoza, *On the Improvement of the Understanding*, Wild, pp. 12–3.

³³ A definitive study of Ramean logic is yet to be written. By far the best account in English is Perry Miller's in *The New England Mind*, ch. v and appendix A. See also Miller-Johnson, pp. 27 ff.; Hardin Craig, *The Enchanted Glass*, pp. 142 ff.; Charles Waddington, *Ramus, sa vie, ses écrits, et ses opinions*; Frank P. Graves, *Peter Ramus and the Educational Reformation of the Sixteenth Century*. Ramus' chief textbook, *Dialecticae libri duo* (1556) was published in England with a commentary by William Temple in 1584, but the *Commentariis* of George Downame (delivered as lectures in 1590) became the most popular exposition of the system. Before Milton wrote his Ramean *Artis logicae* in 1672 there was a whole string of works which urged the merits of the system, among them Abraham Fraunce's *Lawiers Logike* (1588) and Alexander Richardson's *Logicians School-Master* (1657), which I have drawn on heavily. With Temple of King's, Downame of Christ's, and Richardson of Queens', Cambridge became the seat of Ramean logic in England. It was also, of course, the seedbed of Puritanism. *Technologia sive technometrie*, the manuscript summary of the system which Samuel Johnson wrote as an undergraduate at Yale, is translated by Herbert and Carol Schneider in *Samuel Johnson* (1929), II, 57–95.

knowledge; rather, he confirmed it. His initial Platonic assumption was that the universe reveals a simple order and rationality which is comprehensible – by the proper logic – even to the decayed faculties of fallen man. On the sound Renaissance principle of analogy and correspondence, he argued that the whole creation is patterned after that hierarchy of ideas which preëxisted in the mind of God. If man would attain truth, then, he has merely to understand the order and relationship of things in nature, and thence to derive the order and relationship in that realm which Plato called the Ideal and which a Christian would call God. Needless to say, there is nothing new in all this. Ramean logic, the instrument for seizing these immutable ideas which subsume and inform the created universe, was a dramatic example of the Renaissance compulsion to pour old wine into new casks. It would have been impossible without Plato and without the commonplace assumption that the universe yields a rational pattern to the questing mind of man; but because it was generated by antischolastic irritation and because Ramus died a Protestant martyr on St Bartholomew's Eve, it came to enjoy a prestige out of all proportion to its merits.

The reasons for its popularity are sufficiently clear. It carried on the axiom of knowledge, and yet it satisfied the demand for novelty. Ramus believed, and persuaded many others to believe, that the concepts and abstractions of the human mind are firmly fixed *sub specie aeternitatis*, that they draw their validity not from merely temporary or expedient constructs of experience but from the great eternal reservoir of truth laid up in the mind of God, that man can develop a methodology for inferring such universals from his experience of sensibles and then relating them to infinity. Absolute truth thus becomes available through the disciplined analysis of human perception. Man has buried within his mind the copies of divine truth, and if he will he can dredge them up. The consequences for religion, for morality, and for art are prodigious.

As all its advocates agreed, Ramean logic was wonderfully simple and utilitarian. Its patent weaknesses were swallowed up in its advantages as a quick and easy road to certainty. For the heavy machinery of predicaments and categories and syllogisms which all good antischolastics despised, Ramus offered his 'invention' and 'argument' and 'judgment' – tools by which any man could discipline his swarming perceptions, words, and concepts in the interests of knowledge and piety. Until Locke's lethal attack on innate ideas undermined its popularity, Ramus' *a priori* assumption served the late Renaissance very well. In constructing his logic on the Platonic conviction of the preëxistence of ideas as the informing principle of the created universe and the model of human intellection Ramus became one of the heroes of antischolasticism. Also he provided a most welcome tool to those seventeenth-century Puritans who were steadily revising Calvinism to accommodate the traditional values of reason, order, and humanism which Calvin had sought to destroy. As an English Ramean said, the new logic becomes a 'glasse' by which natural reason, 'seeing and viewing herselfe, may worke out those spottes and blemishes of natural imperfection'.[34]

The system itself was constructed on a principle of disjunction. Upon analysis, every fact of mental experience yields a dichotomy, and, when these dichotomies are properly arranged, knowledge becomes possible merely by a process of accepting the true and rejecting the false. Thus all dialectic falls into two parts, invention and judgment (or arrangement). The task of invention is to formulate (or literally to find) arguments; an argument is any word or concept that has a relation – causal, affective, subjective, adjunctive, opposed, etc. – with another word or concept: thus cause suggests effect, good suggests evil, long suggests short. As Ramus himself put it – and his own exposition in the *Dialecticae* is shorter and clearer than those of his disciples – 'Inventio est pars Dialecticae de inveniendis argumentis. Argumentum est quod ad aliquid arguendum affectum est: quales sunt singulae rationes solae & per se consideratus'.[35] Inevitably, all arguments fall into two classes: one whereby a man 'may see by himself, the other whereby he may see by another mans eye'.[36] Artificial arguments are obvious and natural, implicit in the very nature of man's intellection, and requiring nothing but themselves for demonstration; inartificial arguments must rely upon testimony or even authority (for example, the coronation of Charlemagne or the resurrection of Jesus Christ).

Although there are of course many refinements and sub-

[34] Fraunce, sig. B2r.
[35] I.ii. Thus Fraunce (sig. B4v): 'An argument is any severall conceipt apt to argue that whereunto in reason it is referred.'
[36] Richardson, p. 69.

RAMEAN LOGIC

divisions of these two basic kinds of arguments which depend on invention, they are less significant for the system than judgment, or the arrangement of arguments. As Abraham Fraunce explained, judgment is nothing 'but a Disposition, ordering or placing and settling of these severall argumentes already invented, to the intent, that a man may the better judge of them'.[37] Judgment is the process by which the fruits of invention are arranged in a meaningful sequence to yield truth. As George Downame, a celebrated English commentator on the *Dialecticae*, said, invention alone is like matter without form or a body without soul, 'ita inventio sine dispositione inanis, quasique mortus est'.[38] Just as there are, in Ramus' disjunctive analysis, two basic kinds of arguments, so there are two basic kinds of judgments – axiomatic and dianoetic, each of which, of course, yields further paired divisions on further analysis. By means of these the process of classifying or laying out the judgment of invention is wonderfully expedited. If difficulty arises, one can resort to the syllogism (a part of dianoetic judgment), but the axiomatic method is preferred because it proves that the arrangement, and choice between opposites, is self-evident. Thus, in briefest summary, a man seeking truth must first invent arguments, then relate these arguments into what the Ramean called axioms or self-evident propositions (which if 'perceived and graunted they bee straightway judged as true or false'),[39] then if necessary clarify the dubious axioms in a syllogism,[40] and thus reach his conclusion. To any good Ramean, then, Downame's succinct summary of the nature of logic would be invulnerable: 'Bene invenire, disponere, judicare.'[41]

Since the strength of Ramus' system lay in this facile logic, the immense vogue that it enjoyed among the heirs of Calvin strongly confirms the fact that seventeenth-century Puritans would not willingly let die the axiom of knowledge, no matter what their theology told them of man's impotence and depravity. Man's understanding is his chief glory, said Baxter, not because it can embrace only mundane and secular truth, but because it can lead him to God. 'O the wisdom and goodness of our blessed

---

[37] Sig. C2r.
[38] *Commentariis*, pp. 299–300.
[39] Fraunce, sig. C3r.
[40] Fraunce (sig. Dd2v) defines syllogism as a 'disposition of three axiomes, whereby or wherein a doubtfull question disposed with an argument invented, and the antecedent or former part beeing put and graunted, is necessarily concluded and determined'.
For footnote 41 see page 102.

Lord! He hath created the understanding with a natural bias and inclination to truth, as its object; and to the prime truth, as its prime object.'[42] In this matter as in all others, the Puritans occupied a mediate and paradoxical position. In spite of the studied derogation of man's natural cognitive faculties that Calvin had made compulsory for them, they sought out a middle ground between the natural, rational, and optimistic theology of Anglicans and Arminians on the one side and the mystic fideism or mere visionaries on the other. They wished to preserve untainted the sovereignty of God, yet they were reluctant to leave man and nature in the hopeless iniquity described by the early Reformers. In Ramean logic they seeemd to find a rationale for a universe of order and design, created by a God of reason, and at least partially available to man's imperfect tools of knowledge. As Alexander Richardson said in commenting on the uses of Ramean invention, it 'teacheth man thus much, that he is to seek out, and

---

[41] *Commentariis*, p. 14. In the seventeenth century every Ramean textbook contained a table in which the component bifurcations of logic were laid out for all to see at a glance. Thus our brief description of the system would be schematized, in part, as follows:

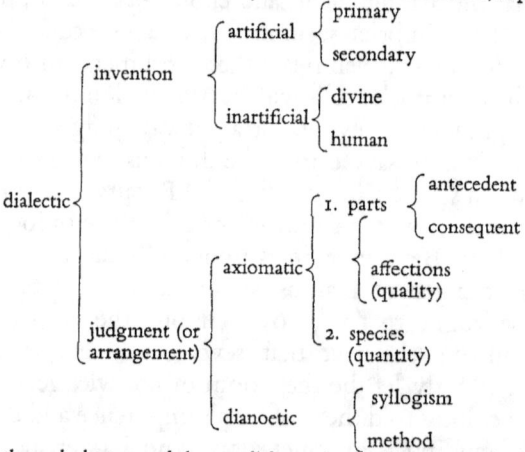

And so on, through sharper and sharper dichotomies, until at last on the right-hand side of the page would be listed the irreducible categories of human thought.

[42] *The Saints' Everlasting Rest*, I.10. As a Presbyterian, Baxter's insistence on the uses of reason is typical, as is his discrimination of three sorts of certainty (*Knowledge and Love Compared*, I.v [*Works*, XV, 44]): 'present objects of sense', 'our own internal acts of intellective cognition and volition', and 'the being of God'. He elaborately refutes the Sectarians' claim that the Spirit makes human learning unnecessary (*The Unreasonableness of Infidelity*, II.xxiii [*Works*, XX, 183–98]); and he draws up a terrifying list of books necessary for a minister: one group for the 'poorest library that is tolerable', one for 'the poorer (though not the poorest)', and one for the 'poor man's library' (*Christian Directory*, III. clxxiv [*Works*, V, 584–602]; cf. II.xxi [IV, 266–270]).

find the wisdom of God in the world, and not to be idle; for the world, and the creatures therein are like a book wherein Gods wisdom is written, and there must we seek it out'.[43] Even though logic 'yeeldeth no divinitie', explained Fraunce, it will teach a divine how to make sacred truth obvious – ' & not onely that, but also how to learne himselfe, to defend, to confute, to instruct, to reprehend'.[44] Short of revelation, what more could man need?

Inevitably, the glib and *a priori* expediencies of Ramean logic marked it for ridicule. 'Of marvellous quick dispatch it is', said Hooker drily, 'and doth shew them that have it as much almost in three days, as if it dwell threescore years with them.'[45] Godfrey Goodman, who hated all things modern and optimistic, of course hated the newfangled system: in undermining the authority of Aristotle, Ramus had merely reduced logic to his 'own fond invention, and barbarous innovation'.[46] But the Ramean's answer to such attacks was easy. As Fraunce remarked in defending the uses of the new logic in common law, the reactionary critics object merely to its claims of making logical propriety and therefore truth available to all men without the tedious verbiage of Aristotle. The denunciations of the angry snob whom Fraunce creates of course imply their own rebuttal:

> Good God, what a world is this? . . . New fangled, youngheaded, harebrayne boyes will needes be Maysters that never were Schollers; prate of methode, who never knew order; rayle against Aristotle as soone as they are crept out of the shell. Hereby it comes to passe that every Cobler can cogge a Syllogisme, every Carter crake of Propositions. Hereby is Logike prophaned, and lyeth prostitute, removoed out of her Sanctuary, robbed of her honour, left of her lovers, ravyshed of straungers, and made common to all, which before was proper to Schoolmen, and only consecrated to Philosophers.[47]

But 'Coblers bee men', retorts Fraunce, 'why therefore not Logicians? and Carters have reason, why therefore not Logike?'[48]

A more insidious attack on the new logic came not from the disgruntled Aristotelians but from the extreme Puritan left. Whether reason was regarded (in the Aristotelian, scholastic, and

---

[43] *The Logicians School-Master*, pp. 48–9.
[44] *The Lawiers Logike*, sig. B4ʳ.
[45] *Laws*, I.vi.4.
[46] Quoted by Jones, *Ancients and Moderns*, p. 30.
[47] *The Lawiers Logike*, sig. 2ᵛ.
[48] *Ibid.*, sig. 3ʳ.

Thomistic sense) as a strategy for deriving general notions of truth from the data of sensation or (in the Platonic, Augustinian, and generally Protestant sense) as that intuitive and subjective process by which we grasp the eternal verities, it was held in the deepest suspicion by those 'fanatick' Puritans who abhorred it as impotent and impious before the truths of revelation. Although the subjective element in Puritan theology was necessarily strong, those extremists who argued that the private illumination of grace made odious and futile any exertion of man's natural faculties of course constituted a real threat to Puritan rationalism. Until the end of the seventeenth century the orthodox Puritan held fast by those fundamentally rational and hierarchical values which had carried over from the Renaissance. He believed in a stratified society, in a fusion of natural intellect and 'spirit', in a learned clergy, and in education. Consequently, he had little patience with those visionaries who ruthlessly subordinated all the fruits of training, erudition, and tradition to the rapturous influx of divine grace. It was the Puritan left, and not its Presbyterian center, that initiated the most serious attack on pedagogical, political, and theological tradition; and this attack, as we shall see, gave rise to the most serious alarm among the orthodox.[49]

In the 'forties of the seventeenth century the Sectarian onslaught on tradition and rationalism became a real danger to the hard-pressed Presbyterians in Parliament and in the Westminster Assembly. The sputterings of anti-intellectualism could scarcely gather strength enough to sustain an organized movement, but they did have a very great nuisance value. As it happened, such enthusiasts as John Webster and William Dell were on firm

---

[49] A famous statement of this split is Butler's in *Hudibras*. The knight himself was a monster of intellection and erudition: he could speak Greek 'As naturally as pigs squeak'; he was steeped in Latin literature; he was
> in logic a great critic,
> Profoundly skilled in analytic;
> He could distinguish, and divide
> A hair 'twixt south and south-west side;

he was a rhetorician; and he could by geometric scale 'take the size of pots of ale' (I.i.51–122). His squire Ralph, on the other hand, had nothing but contempt for such Presbyterian and sophistical learning. He sought spiritual illumination, compared to which all secular knowledge is 'profane, erroneous, and vain' (I.iii.1340).
> His knowledge was not far behind
> The Knight's, but of another kind,
> And he another way came by't,
> Some call it Gifts, and some New-light;
> A lib'ral art, that costs no pains
> Of study, industry, or brains (I.i.479–84).

ground when they inferred from the primary doctrine of regeneration by grace that to God's elect such accomplishments as learning, logic, and systematic theology were superfluous. Without grace they are nothing; with grace they are unnecessary. 'Must that word be secured by Aristotle, which delivers all the Elect from sin, death and hell for ever? Are Grammer, Rhetoric, Logick, Ethicks, Physicks, Metaphysicks, Mathematicks, the weapons whereby we must defend the Gospel?'[50] All that believers need to know, insisted Dell (who at various times was a secretary to Laud, a chaplain to General Fairfax, and a master of Gonville and Caius College), is 'the gift of the spirit only, without all human learning'. Only thus can they discriminate truth and error, and 'so a poor, plain countryman, by the spirit which he hath received, is better able to judge of truth and error, touching the things of God, than the greatest philosopher, scholar, or doctor in the world, that is destitute of it'.[51]

Men like Dell posed in the sharpest terms the antithesis between an inward, searching, and intensely subjective as opposed to an outward, formal, and communal quality of religious emotion. It was, *au fond*, the antithesis between Puritan and Anglican; and, as we shall see, it had portentous consequences not only for Church discipline, but even for political theory. 'I joy, deare Mother', sang George Herbert to his church,

> when I view,
> Thy perfect lineaments and hue
> Both sweet and bright.[52]

This suggests an approach to religion radically incompatible with Puritan subjectivism: 'In the true Kingdome of Christ all things are inward and spirituall; and all the true Religion of Christ is written in the Soul and Spirit of man, by the Spirit of God.'[53] For the saints burning with the grace of God and sealed by His spirit, what need for stained glass and rituals, or for the sophistries and sham wisdom of the reprobate?

> The strength and might of their weapons is not Academick and Scholastical Learning (the rotten rubbish of Ethnical and Babylonish ruines) nor Fathers, Modern Writers, Expositors, Commentators (the ayery bubbles that ignorance, corrupt custom and humane Tradition hath blow up, and

[50] See Miller, *The New England Mind*, p. 78.
[51] *The Way of True Peace and Unity*, Woodhouse, p. 313.
[52] 'The British Church', *Works*, p. 111.   [53] Dell, *The Tryal of Spirits*, p. 20.

gilded over with the unsuitable and Heterogeneous title of Orthodoxal Authours) nor their wit, reason, nor collected notes (the rotten Crutches to support lameness) no nor any of these, or whatsoever can arise from the flesh, but onely that Spirit of Truth, that lends [sic] into all truth.[54]

This antagonism between the knowledge that comes through grace and the knowledge that comes through intellection – one of the most significant of those dualisms that split asunder the religious and the secular at the end of the Renaissance – led certain Separatists to a most cordial vilification of 'humane learning'. Dell groans in incredulous horror at the thought of universities conferring degrees in divinity, as if any human agency could create 'Masters in that Mystery, which none can teach but God himself; and which none can learn, but true believers who are borne of God, and are his true Disciples'.[55] Jerusalem is the only alma mater, and all the knowledge taught by the reprobate is abominable in the sight of God, a stench in the nostrils of the elect.[56] Webster puts the issue squarely: since 'no humane learning sanctified the mind', man's natural faculties are 'carnal' and set in 'enmity against God'.[57] For the universities to pose their puny knowledge against the illumination of the spirit constitutes 'horrible Envy, Enmity, and Opposition to the truth of the Gospel' – a sin beyond comprehension and expiation, thought Dell.[58]

Although the English advocates of this anti-intellectualism never became so ominous and powerful as Mrs Anne Hutchinson in New England, they did form a vigilant opposition to the rationalistic and sophistical tendencies of some Puritans. For example, Richard Overton's vivid *Arraignment of Mr Persecution* allegorizes the conflict in a way that suggests Bunyan. The young, university-bred Presbyterian Martin vehemently denounces the Sectarians:

> O these cursed Anabaptists, these wicked Brownists, these Heretickes, these Schismatickes, these Sectaries; O MARTIN hath it at his fingers end, he's an University man, skild in the Tongues and Sciences, and can sophisticate any Text, O he is excellent at false Glosses, and Scholasticke Interpretations, he can wrest the Scriptures most neatly, tell the people it is thus and thus in the Originall, an excellent man to make a Presbyter![59]

Similarly, Walwyn attacks the learned ministry. Why cannot we

---

[54] Webster, *The Saints Guide*, p. 15.
[55] *A Testimony from the Word Against Divinity-Degrees in the University*, p. 2.
[56] Ibid., pp. 10–1. [57] *The Saints Guide*, p. 3.
[58] *The Stumbling-Stone*, p. 30. [59] 'The Epistle Dedicatorie', Haller, III, 207.

read the Scriptures for ourselves? If they are improperly translated 'why have wee not beene told so all this while? why have wee beene cheated into errours? If they are rightly Translated, why should not Englishmen understand them?'[60] The baggage of languages, logic, and university training speeds no man's progress to heaven, and when ministers commend learning 'it is not for Learning's sake, but their owne; her esteeme gets them their Livings and preferments; and therefore she is to be kept up, or their Trade will go down'.[61] The great literary statement of this anti-intellectualism is Bunyan's. His Talkative is a glib and hollow Christian who professes 'great knowledge of gospel mysteries' but has no real sense of sin and no impulse to evangelical action. 'Indeed', says Faithful to him, 'to know is a thing that pleaseth talkers and boasters; but to do is that which pleaseth God.' There is more than one kind of knowledge – 'Knowledge that resteth in the bare speculation of things; and knowledge that is accompanied with the grace of faith and love; which puts a man upon doing even the will of God from the heart. The first of these will serve the talker; but without the other the true Christian is not content.' Talkative's house is as empty of religion, concludes Faithful, 'as the white of an egg is of savour'.[62]

The intense inwardness and subjectivism of certain Puritans, then, made them skeptical of all forms of rational theology. There was another side, moreover, to this anti-intellectualism which was ultimately to prove a graver threat to traditional rationalism than the fanaticism of the Sectarians. This was utilitarianism. Although Dell denied the efficacy of human intellection 'touching the things of God', he advanced the strongest claims for its secular utility. He shrilly denounced human learning 'as it is made another John Baptist, to prepare the way of Christ into the world, or to prepare the worlds way to Christ'; but in its 'own place and sphear' he praised it as man's greatest secular advantage.[63] Once religious truth is segregated from the aggressive human intellect, the whole realm of natural truth lies open for his legitimate scrutiny. If speculation about God is impious, a practical knowledge of His creation in the interests of man's secular well-being is not; and 'humane learning', thus conceived, is made synonymous with the

---

[60] *The Compassionate Samaritane*, Haller, III, 79.
[61] *Ibid.*, III, 83.
[62] *The Pilgrim's Progress*, pp. 96–7.
[63] *A Plain and Necessary Confutation*, 'An Apologie to the Reader', sig. A2ᵛ.

most empirical and utilitarian strain of 'experimental philosophy'. The end of such proper knowledge, said Webster, is 'not onely to know natures power in the causes and effects, but further to make use of them for the general good and benefit of mankind, especially for the conservation and restauration of the health of man, and of those creatures that are usefull to him'.[64] Mere speculative knowledge, then, is not only impious as applied to the mysteries of grace, but it is futile and unproductive as applied to nature. 'Is the admirable knowledge that Arethmetick afords [sic] worthy of nothing but a supine and silent speculation? Let the Merchant, Astronomer, Mariner, Mechanick and all speak whether its greatest glory stand not principally in the practick part.'[65]

Thus these men advanced their antirational thesis with a doublepronged argument. 'It is true, I am a yong man and noe Scholler, according to that which the world counts Schollership', boasted John Lilburne – and yet he became a demagogue whom kings and generals had to reckon with,[66] and his career, like Webster's *Academiarum Examen*, constituted a declaration of independence from the intellectual traditions of Europe. Lilburne and Webster, and many others, urged that segregation of nature and grace, learning and revealed truth, speculation and action which contravened the whole drift of Christian humanism. The tradition which they attacked was intimately associated with the universities, and the universities perpetuated that tradition of rhetoric and logic and letters which men of Webster's stripe professed to despise as conducive to neither piety nor utility. Seth Ward, Savilian professor at Oxford and a notable spokesman for that tradition, complained that lately there had risen up three 'severall kinds of Adversaries': the atheist and mechanist (like Hobbes), the 'angry fanatick man' (like Dell), and the utilitarian (like Webster). All were ominous, for all had denied the traditional uses of human reason and learning.[67]

---

[64] *Academiarum Examen*, p. 19.   [65] *Ibid.*, pp. 19–20.
[66] *A Worke of the Beast*, Haller, II, 21.
[67] *Vindiciae Academiarum*, pp. 6–7. To Webster's charge that the universities were ossified in their blind devotion to Aristotle Ward replied that they were vigorously liberal – so much so that 'scarce any Hypothesis, which has been formerly or lately entertained by Judicious men', lacks advocates at Oxford. He cites the 'Atomicall and Magneticall in Philosophy, the Copernican in Astronomy, &c.'. There follows a chapter by chapter refutation of Webster, and then a long appendix countering the attacks of Hobbes and Dell. Ward's style is pedantically jocose and ironical, yet parts of his book are very effective – for example, his defense of logic and his exposé of Webster's egregious errors about mathematics and his credulities about astrology.

This glance at Puritan antirationalism will perhaps help us to understand the wide appeal of Ramean logic. As antischolastic, it could not offend some of the deepest prejudices of men like Dell and Webster; as allegedly clear enough for all to comprehend, it put no premium on mere book learning and university training; as constructed on the assumption that man is able, through a proper methodology, to tap the eternal reservoir of truth, it counteracted the fideistic arguments of angry fanatic men. For all these reasons it was supremely useful to the orthodox Puritan.

That Puritan would not knowingly jeopardize the absolute sovereignty of God – the great design laid up in His 'secret will' mocked any effort at rational comprehension – and yet he was unwilling and unable to sink into the skepticism, irrationalism, fideism, and nominalism that posed the dreadful alternatives to Renaissance rationalism. For him, therefore, the advantages of Ramean logic were obvious. Through it he could believe, without impiety, that the created universe is essentially good not only as the embodiment of God's will, but also as the 'platform' for the orderly working-out of His great design and as the material projection of His divine ideas. Nature could thus acquire uses for both secular and religious truth, and the fruits of intellection be employed in the service of piety. Ramean logic was to the Puritan a device for making invisible ink visible, for revealing in all their splendor the innately rational principles or ideas that lie at the foundations of the created universe and that inform the mental processes of man. Properly employed, logic can discipline man's mind 'to the view and contemplation of that, which of it selfe it might perceave, if it were turned and framed thereunto'.[68]

Of course, there was always the mystery of grace necessary for justification and salvation; but apart from that the warfaring Christian had a powerful weapon of natural truth against all varieties of sin and error. Such commonplaces – virtually indistinguishable from those of traditional Renaissance optimism – concealed a justification for deism, even for a Baconian and utilitarian scrutiny of nature for man's secular commodity; and both incipient deism and a drift toward a wiry, utilitarian natural science are conspicuous developments of seventeenth-century Puritanism. The softening and decline of Puritan theology in New England

[68] *The Lawiers Logike*, sig. B4ᵛ.

in the following century, and the dramatic reversal of Jonathan Edwards to *echt* Calvinism, show how real these dangers were to become. Yet in the age of Milton all such ultimately incompatible elements could be somehow fused, and under the aegis of Ramus the Puritan could align the uses of reason with the quest for salvation.

III. NEO-STOICISM

If Hooker's influential version of Christian humanism and the Puritans' of Ramean logic tended to perpetuate the intimate correspondence of reason and piety, there were other forces tending to divorce reason from faith and to apply it to the uses of mere natural morality. Both the popularity of Neo-Stoicism as a moral discipline and the growth of deism suggest the increasing secularization of the axiom of knowledge. Concurrent with the steady pressure to reduce natural truth to its axioms – geometric or moral – there was also the effort to strip doctrine from religion, mystery from morality. Both movements represent the search for those absolutes – metaphysical, epistemological, moral – which the accretions of time and error had obscured. Both derived from the axiom of knowledge, and yet both strengthened the growing conviction that knowledge should be construed in natural terms.

Originally one of the neo-paganisms spawned by Renaissance humanists as a moral discipline, Neo-Stoicism soon came to be viewed with alarm by the orthodox. Indeed, this alarm had had a long history in Christian thought, for ancient Stoicism had been one of the important rivals of the primitive church in the days of the Empire. Its suppression of all passion jeopardized such Christian virtues as love and compassion and also accredited a thoroughly unwholesome self-sufficiency based on reason; and its deterministic materialism impugned the sovereignty of God no less than the freedom of man. None the less, Stoicism very early worked itself into the very fabric of Christian thought. As early as the fourth century there appeared a fabricated correspondence between St Paul and Seneca, so congenial were their values thought to be; and the facile assimilation of Christian providence and Stoic law was a commonplace from Boethius through the seventeenth century.

In so syncretistic an age as the Renaissance it was inevitable that the humanists should welcome Neo-Stoicism, like Neo-

NEO-STOICISM

Platonism, as a discipline with both classical authority and Christian coloring. Cicero's prestige as a moralist in the Renaissance was immense, and Cicero's morals, like his political theory, were largely Stoic. Thanks to the missionary zeal and scholarly reputation of Justus Lipsius, Seneca also emerged as one of those pagans who lacked merely the Gospels to be a noble Christian; and Epictetus and Marcus Aurelius were soon to be widely translated and adapted, after a fashion, to quasi-Christian purposes.[69]

As we learn from Marlowe, Chapman, and Marston, Neo-Stoicism was also extremely useful for other reasons. Such popular dramatists borrowed heavily from its secular morality and its sanction of individualism without, however, permitting their supermen – Tamburlaine, Faustus, Bussy, Biron, Andrugio – the sweet fruition of an earthly crown.

As a Platonist, a Stoic, and a Christian, Chapman was fond of urging 'learning' as the cure of all human ills, and reason as the divine faculty which reduces the chaos of nature and passion to human control.

> So when the Soule is to the body given,
> (Being substance, of Gods Image sent from heaven)
> It is not his true Image, till it take
> Into the Substance, those fit forms that make
> His perfect Image; which are then imprest
> By Learning and impulsion; that invest
> Man with Gods forme in living Holinesse,
> By cutting from his Body the excesse
> Of Humours, perturbations, and Affects;
> Which Nature (without Art) no more ejects,
> Then without tooles, a naked Artizan
> Can, in rude stone, cut th' Image of a man.[70]

The 'impulsion' to make 'learning' a formative moral principle comes, it seems, from man's identifying his will with God's,[71] but it leads to a glorious mastery of both psychological disorders and external misfortunes. The man thus refined is almost like God. His soul

---

[69] There were some notable translations of the Stoic classics around the turn of the sixteenth century. Nicholas Grimald had early (1553) published *Marcus Tullus Ciceroes Three bookes of duties*; John Stradling translated Lipsius' very influential *Two Bookes of Constancie* in 1595; George Stanhope and John Healy translated Epictetus (1594, 1610); Thomas Lodge's noble *Workes* of Seneca achieved its final form in 1620; Méric Casaubon translated Marcus Aurelius in 1634.
[70] *Euthymiæ Raptus*, ll. 373–84.
[71] See *Eugenia*, esp. ll. 273 ff.

>   the Scepter swaies
> Th' admired Fabricke of her world survaies,
> And as it hath a magnitude confinde,
> So all the powers therein, she sees combinde
> In fit Acts for one end, which is t'obay
> Reason, her Regent; Nature giving way:
> Peace, Concord, Order, Stay proclaim'd, and Law
> Are none commanding, if not all in Awe,
> Passion, and Anger, made to under lie,
> And heere concludes, mans mortall Monarchie.[72]

It is this bumptious state of self-sufficiency – presumably achieved without proper religious motivation – that leads Chapman's dramatic heroes to their downfall. The conflict in these titans represents various things: the angry outcry of an individualist against his hostile environment, the struggle of passion against reason, the collision between iniquitous human laws and the invincible natural law. In terms of both Christian and Stoic morality Bussy and Biron are, for all their flamboyant individualism, reprehensible, and they are destroyed; but Clermont, Chabot, and Cato – Senecal men all – are victims of a social system that jars with the eternal law a good man must follow. Whatever their differences, however, they are studies in the difficult art of moral self-sufficiency, and from their careers it is possible to infer Chapman's ideal of the Stoic sage. He is the man whose discipline of reason not only extirpates his passions, but also induces a deific understanding of and *rapport* with the workings of the universe.

> There is no danger to a man that knows
> What life and death is; there's not any law
> Exceeds his knowledge; neither is it lawful
> That he should stoop to any other law.
> He goes before them, and commands them all,
> That to himself is a law rational.[73]

---

[72] *Andromeda Liberata*, Epistle Dedicatory, ll. 139–48. One of the most majestic statements of this ethical principle – and Chapman is more often opaque than majestic – is the passage that Coleridge so much admired from 'The Epistle Dedicatory' to *The Iliads of Homer* (ll. 29–36). There, writing about Homer and to Prince Henry, Chapman says:
> O! 'tis wond'rous much,
> Though nothing prized, that the right virtuous touch
> Of a well written soul to virtue moves;
> Nor have we souls to purpose, if their loves
> Of fitting objects be not so inflamed.
> How much then were this kingdom's main soul maim'd,
> To want this great inflamer of all powers
> That move in human souls!

[73] *The Conspiracy and Tragedy of Byron*, III.iii.140–5.

NEO-STOICISM

Chapman's Neo-Stoicism is conscious and sustained, but by no means unique. It is true that Spenser[74] and many others inveigh against the Stoic resort to suicide; but Gabriel Harvey, a scholar if not quite a gentleman, admiringly recorded the moral precepts of the Stoics,[75] while many dramatists condoned, and even commended, self-slaughter. We think not only of Chapman's Clermont, but also of Shakespeare's Antony and Cleopatra, and, most notably, Brutus – all noble suicides. Marlowe's Guise, in *The Massacre at Paris*, is Catholic, Machiavellian, and villainous; and yet we cannot despise his Stoic individualism, for in his death he rises to something like grandeur.

> Thus Caesar did goe foorth, and thus he dyed.[76]

Marston's Andrugio, in *Antonio and Mellida*, is obviously a sort of Stoic sage,[77] and in the sequel, *Antonio's Revenge*, Pandulfo carries on the strain:[78] even though he seems on the point of cropping his Stoic mask ('Why, all this while I ha' but played a part'),[79] he quickly recovers his poise and ends the Senecal man. Tourneur's Charlemont is the *reductio ad absurdum* of the Stoic hero: he accepts the universe, but his acquiescence is indistinguishable from a tearful Christian sentimentality; his resignation reflects less of a philosophic policy than an incapacity for action, and he seems to be the death-wish made articulate.[80] Yet he mouths the Stoic formularies glibly enough. 'No, sir', he tells Sebastian,

> I have a heart above the reach
> Of thy most violent maliciousness;
> A fortitude in scorn of thy contempt
> (Since Fate is pleased to have me suffer it)
> That can bear more than thou hast power t' inflict. ...
> But now I am an emperor of a world,
> This little world of man. My passions are
> My subjects, and I can command them laugh,
> Whilst thou dost tickle 'em to death with misery.[81]

In a drama that was growing steadily more secular there was, then, a good deal of Stoic morality. It offered the easiest formulas

---

[74] See the orthodox attack on suicide, *FQ*, I.ix.33 ff.
[75] For example: 'sustine et abstine: sustine dura fortiter: abstine a mollibus temperanter, sustine viriles labores: abstine ab effæminatis voluptatibus' (*Marginalia*, p. 106; cf. p. 198).
[76] Line 1026.   [77] III.i.59–62; IV.i.53–66.
[78] I.i *passim*.   [79] IV.ii.70.
[80] *The Atheist's Tragedy*, V.ii.
[81] III.iii. The same sort of facile Neo-Stoicism appears in Tourneur's 'Funeral Poem upon the Death of ... Sir Francis Vere'.

for those virtues – fortitude, temperance, and the like – thought to be necessary in the face of disaster; and though they were not the Christian virtues of faith, hope, and charity, they were obviously more expedient for dramatic characterization. Besides, Stoic doctrine was easily convertible to Christian uses. As George Stanhope glibly put it at the end of the seventeenth century, 'by a light Change of Philosophy into Religion, and Plurality of Divine Beings into the one only True God ... any considering Christian may here find a Scheme of what Himself ought to be'.[82]

Nowhere is the truth of this remark better exemplified than in Jacobean and Caroline moral discourses. The name that immediately leaps to mind is, of course, Bishop Hall's. His *Meditations and Vows* and the six decades of *Epistles* clearly show the compatibility between Stoic and Christian morals, even if – significantly – they have little to say about matters of doctrine. In Hall's redaction, resignation telescopes into fortitude, a trust in providence into resolution and constancy, Christian asceticism into the rational contempt for sensual pleasures. Hall, the Christian Seneca, makes no effort to conceal his obligation to the Roman moralist. As a philosopher he finds him wholly admirable; as a Christian he can only deplore Seneca's ignorance of doctrine; and yet he finds in him almost everything a good man needs for living virtuously and rationally. It is the greatest pity, says Hall, that the Stoics (and especially Seneca) should not have had the incalculable gift of grace to sweeten their 'wit' and their morals.[83] And yet what outside the Scripture can tell us more of virtue than the great Stoic treatises? 'Never any heathen wrote more divinely, never any philosopher more probably' than Seneca.[84]

> I have wondered oft, and blushed for shame, to read in mere philosophers, which had no other mistress but nature, such strange resolution in the contempt of both fortunes, as they call them; such notable precepts for a constant settledness and tranquillity of mind: and to compare it with my own disposition and practice, whom I have found too much drooping and dejected under small crosses, and easily again carried away with a little prosperity. . . . O the dulness and blindness of us unworthy Christians, that suffer heathens, by the dim candlelight of nature, to go farther than we by the clear sun of the gospel, that an indifferent man could not tell by our practice whether were the pagan![85]

[82] *Epictetus his Morals*, sig. A7ʳ-A8ʳ.
[83] *Characters of Virtues and Vices*, Works, VI, 89–90; cf. *Heaven upon Earth*, Works, VI, 1.
[84] *Heaven upon Earth*, Works, VI, 3.   [85] *Meditations and Vows*, Works, VII, 475.

NEO-STOICISM

Jeremy Taylor is not so frank, but his incomparably beautiful moral treatises are similarly informed with Stoicism. In his sermons – perhaps written with Lord Carbery's gluttonous habits in mind? – he repeatedly urges rational self-control as the antidote to self-indulgence: 'all violence is an enemy to reason and counsel'.[86] Like Hall, he tacitly identifies a good life with Stoic virtue. Fate becomes providence, constancy becomes resignation. Where the Stoic would urge man to follow nature, Taylor urges him to acquiesce in the workings of God's great design; but they would both accept the universe and thread their way through error by the light of reason.

> The old Stoics, when you told them of a sad story, would still answer, ... What is that to me? Yes, for the tyrant hath sentenced you also unto prison. Well, what is that? He will put a chain upon my leg, but he cannot bind my soul. No, but he will kill you. Then I'll die. If presently, let me go, that I may presently be freer than himself; but if not till anon or tomorrow, I will dine first, or sleep, or do what reason and nature call for, as at other times. This in Gentile philosophy is the same with the discourse of St. Paul, I have learned in whatsoever state I am, therewith to be content. I know both how to be abased, and I know how to abound: everywhere and in all things I am instructed, both how to be full and to be hungry, both to abound and to suffer need.[87]

In both *Holy Living* and *Holy Dying* Taylor is concerned with morality, not doctrine, and there, of course, his latent Neo-Stoicism is most apparent. As a theologian and a metaphysician he falls far short of rationalism; but as a moralist, for whom the uses of reason need not be so sharply discriminated, he is quite content to repeat the ancient Stoic precepts of fortitude, temperance, and constancy. The third chapter of *Holy Dying* is a tissue of Senecan commonplaces, and all the precepts of *Holy Living* are focused on a life of reason and a trust in providence as the keys to virtue and dignity. Since God is the 'master of the scenes, we must not choose which part we shall act; it concerns us only to be careful that we do it well, always saying If this please God, let it be as it is'. Having thus by acquiescence ordered his relations with the universe, man has only by reason to order his internal economy. What is lacking – faith in those mysteries which defy reason – is supplied through grace. 'No man can make another man to be his slave, unless he hath first enslaved himself

---

[86] *Sermons*, p. 85.   [87] *Holy Living*, II.vi.

to life and death, to pleasure or pain, to hope or fear: command these passions, and you are freer than the Parthian kings.'[88] The path to virtue and grace is open to all, made plain by natural reason and illumined by God. 'Let the grounds of our actions be noble, beginning upon reason, proceeding with prudence, measured by the common lines of men, and confident upon the expectation of a usual providence.' If we go from cause to effect, 'from natural means to ordinary events', and believe felicity not to be a chance but a choice, then all will be well. Exacerbating doubts and the conviction of our own depravity will 'be cured only by reason and good company, a wise guide and a plain rule, a cheerful spirit and a contented mind, by joy in God according to the commandments, that is "a rejoicing evermore"'.[89]

IV. NATURAL THEOLOGY

The sporadic Neo-Stoicism which turns up so frequently in the drama and the moral philosophy of the seventeenth century may be viewed as one aspect of the larger growth of deism. Both developments could be accommodated under the rubric of religious rationalism, and are thus obviously related to the axiom of knowledge. For neither would be possible without the hypothesis – Stoic in origin – of a universal reason which orders the processes of nature and informs the mind of man. The Neo-Stoicism of Chapman and Hall was mainly a moral regimen: it emphasized the uses of man's innate rational faculty in attaining secular morality; it was concerned with conduct, and had almost nothing to say about Christian doctrine for the very good reason that such doctrine – erected on the great mysteries of the Trinity, the Incarnation, and the Atonement – was by definition supra-rational. But the incipient deism of the seventeenth century went further than to urge the discipline of reason for ordering man's psychological economy; it suggested that the very foundations of religion, not merely of morality, rested on the principles of reason, and that these principles were available to man's comprehension as *a priori* truths. Deism was, then, a significant development of that natural religion which Aquinas had bequeathed to the Renaissance. However shaky its scientific support, the argument from design was irresistible to men of the Renaissance;

[88] *Ibid.*, II.vi.   [89] *Sermons*, p. 70.

when, in the seventeenth century, it gathered new strength from the spectacular advances of natural science it came to be one of the most compelling forces of the century.

As we have seen, it was a matter of extreme importance to discriminate the areas of natural and supernatural truth. Though he had notably enlarged the former, Aquinas himself drew a sharp line between the two, and he never committed the heresy of reducing the mystery-content of Christianity to the level of natural reason. Of course, Calvin made natural religion synonymous with atheism. He confesses that even in his fallen state man retains some innate idea of God 'by natural instinct' – a dim, vitalistic urge to worship which alone 'renders men superior to brutes, and makes them aspire to immortality'.[90] But he is careful not to fall into the trap of deism: man can never come to God merely through natural agencies, nor can he hope to know Him by the feeble inferences of natural reason working on the data of observation. Hence the unspeakable blasphemy of those who bury God in nature. 'They will not say that they are distinguished from the brutes by chance; but they ascribe it to nature, which they consider as the author of all things, and remove God out of sight.'[91]

Hooker did as much as one man could to assert the claims of natural reason, and it is, I suppose, possible to isolate in the *Laws* passages which might be called deistic;[92] yet he, too, scrupulously distinguished grace from nature and faith from reason. Lancelot Andrewes was certain that no man could come to God by natural means alone, and Donne and Laud continued to hold this central Anglican conviction. Moreover, Hooker had established a strong tradition of tolerance: throughout the seventeenth century men of his persuasion sought to unite the factions of Protestantism against the real threat – political no less than theological – of Rome, and this effort resulted in a characteristic Anglican tendency to submerge doctrinal differences in the few essential truths necessary for salvation. Hooker's *Laws*, Laud's *Relation of the Conference*, Chillingworth's *Religion of Protestants*, Taylor's *Liberty of Prophesying* – all monuments to one of the most appealing elements in Anglican thought – may be regarded as efforts to elevate the compulsory truths of religion above the incessant forays and

[90] *Institutes*, I.iii.3. [91] *Ibid.*, I.v.4.
[92] For example, see I.viii.

rebuttals of petty sectarian zealots. In this regard, at least, they have strong deistic implications, for the appeal of each is to man's divine mandate for seeking truth through the processes of his natural reason.

Thus Donne, a very questionable rationalist at best, is constantly concerned with ending the guerilla warfare that threatened to rend Christ's seamless garment into shreds. In the third satire, in the eighteenth holy sonnet, in the *Essays in Divinity*[93] he repeatedly urges a *sensus communis* to make possible religious unity, or at least toleration for unessential doctrinal differences. In the *Pseudo-Martyr* he makes tediously clear the political threat of Rome, but at the same time wistfully yearns for reconciliation: synagogue and church, Rome and Geneva, sects and divisions are, after all, seeking the same goal. They make 'but one Church, journeying to one Jerusalem, and directed by one guide, Jesus Christ'.[94] Even so, there must be no confusion between the common truths of nature and those of grace. It is plain that every man is equipped with a 'Naturall Logique' and a 'Naturall Religion', but, as pagan polytheism shows, they lead to superstition and error. For religious truth we must fall back on the mysteries of grace and regeneration.[95] Those who seek to come to God only through nature are like the mariners who challenged the terrors of the deep before the invention of the compass.[96] From our 'ratiocination and discourse, our probabilities and verisimilitudes', we can infer the existence of a God whom we must worship, but we can never penetrate the mysteries which we must believe through grace and faith. The discourse of reason will never persuade us of a virgin's bearing a son, or of a God becoming man to die and then to rise again.[97]

> The atheist and all his philosophy, helper and he that is holpen, horse and man, nature and art, reason mounted and advanced upon learning, shall never be able to leap over, or break through this wall, no man, no natural man can do anything towards a supernatural work.[98]

For all such disclaimers (and they were common to the point

---

[93] pp. 104 f.
[94] See *Fifty Sermons*, nos. xxiv and xxx, *LXXX Sermons*, no. v, for Donne's defense of the *via media* against both Papists and Presbyterians.
[95] *LXXX Sermons*, pp. 477 f.
[96] *Essays in Divinity*, p. 37; cf. pp. 7 f. on the natural theology of Raymond Sebond; cf. *Fifty Sermons*, p. 327.
[97] *Works*, III, 22–3; cf. III, 366; IV, 270.   [98] *Ibid.*, II, 7.

of tedium) many lines of seventeenth-century thought were converging on deism. It was the price of keeping religion rational in an age when natural knowledge, powerfully buttressed by science, was entering the period of its greatest prestige. The ever-present danger that rational theology should become so rational that it would cease to be religious was widely recognized, but the danger persisted and even increased. In both major branches of seventeenth-century philosophy it is possible to isolate factors making for deism. Both the rationalism of Lord Herbert and Descartes (with its heavy if unacknowledged obligations to scholasticism) and the English empiricism announced by Bacon and climaxed by Locke could lead to a view of God and nature radically at variance with religion as such Christian humanists as Hooker and Milton understood it. Philosophical rationalists tended to derive religious truth, reduced to almost geometrically simple axioms, from the processes of the unaided human mind; empiricists, focusing their total intellectual effort on drawing proper inferences from the observed facts of experience, tended to isolate God, first causes, and related matters far behind the mechanistic second causes which alone were regarded as the proper objects of knowledge. Both, of course, did great violence to the traditional view of God as transcendent to but intimately concerned with the workings of His creation. When Ralegh speaks of nature as 'nothing else but the strength and faculty which God hath infused into every creature, having no other self-ability than a clock, after it is wound up by a hand', he (though neither a Baconian nor a Cartesian) suggests both the jargon and the basic attitude of later deists. If Ralegh's view of man and history fits comfortably enough into the Augustinian doctrine of providence, that doctrine itself could easily be absorbed into a corrosive theory of second causes, and such a theory lies at the very threshold of deism.

That is why English empiricism progressed so inexorably toward deism. Bacon had rigorously insisted on the supra-rational nature of religion, but having accepted the data of revelation he proceeded to direct man's intellectual efforts solely toward the realm of nature. As the arguments from design from the ancient Stoics through the paeans of Renaissance Neo-Platonists make clear, to mistake the creation for its creator is the tendency of every natural religion. Browne and many others warned against this error: the effects of nature are the works of God, but nature is only His hand and instrument, 'and therefore to ascribe His actions unto her, is to devolve the honour of the principal agent upon the instrument'.[99] A rampant naturalism, groans Burton, cannot protect itself against irreligion, whatever its pious disclaimers. Our modern empiricists and materialists insist that in 'spiritual things God must demonstrate all to sense, leave a pawn with them, or else seek some other creditor. They will acknowledge nature and fortune, yet not God'.[100]

Whatever we might call those whom Burton attacked – secularists, naturalists, deists – they presented a common threat to revealed religion in their appeal to nature, an appeal given urgency by the very facts of political life in the seventeenth century. In the age of Milton the pressure of events forced men to find new sanctions for their political and economic conduct in a so-called law of nature that depended on revelation for nothing. When both Hobbes and Lilburne could derive their antipodal political theories from such a 'law' obviously it had lost all ecclesiastical or theological meaning. When the Schoolmen invoke *recta ratio*, says Selden cynically, they understand by reason either a divine commandment or else they mean no more than a woman 'when shee sayes a thing is soe, because it is soe, that is, her reason p[er]swades her it is soe'. As for him, he prefers law to have legal status, be the morality what it may.[101]

However unlike in other ways, Lord Herbert of Cherbury shares with such secularists as Bacon and Selden and Hobbes the tendency to locate the necessary instruments of moral well-being within the scope of man's natural faculties. More concerned with fixing the nature and limits of religious truth than with exploring the realm of second causes, he was an unreconstructed rationalist who sought to identify religious truth with the principles of universal reason. His interest was epistemology rather than theology, and his low regard for the validity of mere sensory perception immediately alienated him from the main current of English empiricism. None the less, his labors contributed significantly to the discrediting of traditional theology.

Like so many others appalled by the credal conflicts that seemed to make religious certainty impossible, Lord Herbert sought to

---

[99] Browne, *Religio Medici*, p. 18.   [100] *Anatomy*, III, 440.
[101] *Table Talk*, p. 116.

NATURAL THEOLOGY

reconstruct religious truth on foundations that no man could destroy. He published *De veritate*, as he said, not to stir controversy but to make it unnecessary. Of man's four levels of knowledge – natural instinct, internal and external sense, and discursive reason[102] – only that which commands universal assent is certain; moreover, it is certain precisely because it does command such assent. Although he rejects Stoic sensationalism, Lord Herbert bases his epistemological test on a Stoic *consensus gentium*: man has an inner faculty for ascertaining truth, and the truths so ascertained are true always and everywhere. They are the principles that satisfy his natural demands of reason, the 'common notions' that are man's chief glory. Like Descartes' 'clear and distinct ideas' of the Cambridge Platonists' 'principles of truth and light' they are the irreducible elements of certainty, subsuming not only secular but also religious verity. By using them we can steer safely between skepticism and superstition, one of which slanders man's capacity for truth, the other the rationality of religion. They make unnecessary the interminable and degrading disputes of competing theologians, and they lead safely to that 'Eternal Blessedness' which is 'man's particular object and the general object of nature'.[103] No one who studies religions comparatively and who seeks within himself for those verities implanted by God can fail to realize that religious truth, at least in its elements, is the birthright of all men. By the mere exercise of natural reason, then, all men at all times and in all places may arrive at those common notions that constitute truth: a supreme deity exists, he must be worshiped, a good life is one of virtue and piety (resulting from 'the right formation of the faculties'), sin is expiated by repentance, and reward or punishment are our lot after death.[104] In these five articles are summed up the 'only Catholic and uniform Church'.

These common notions are *a priori*, independent, universal, certain, necessary, and in conformity with their objects in nature.[105] 'Derived from universal wisdom and imprinted on the soul by the dictates of nature itself',[106] they are the necessary ingredients of both piety and truth, and thus they support the additional truths of revelation just as a house supports its roof.[107] Revelation

---

[102] *De veritate*, p. 132.
[103] *Ibid.*, p. 143.
[104] *Ibid.*, pp. 291–303.
[105] *Ibid.*, pp. 139–41.
[106] *Ibid.*, p. 106; cf. pp. 120–1.
[107] *Ibid.*, p. 290.

is obviously truth of a very special kind: in it 'the breath of the Divine Spirit must be immediately felt',[108] but in the five common notions of religious certainty we have the basis of all religions. 'If we set aside superstitions and legends, the mind takes its stand on my five articles, and upon nothing else. To deny this would be to allow less sense to men than to sheep; for they at least when they are let into the pastures avoid those herbs which are harmful and only eat those which are good for them.'[109]

In his rationalism Lord Herbert is something of an oddity in English thought, but across the Channel Descartes and then Spinoza were presently to launch, with the utmost philosophical sophistication and (at least as far as Descartes was concerned) with immense influence, a comparable deistic view of religious truth. Descartes' ontological proof for the existence of God is one of the purple passages of European philosophy. Arguing that the innate idea of God which inexorably establishes the existence of God is 'like the mark of the workman imprinted on his work', Descartes goes on to locate the rudiments of religious truth inside the workings of the human mind.

> It only remains to me to examine into the manner in which I have acquired this idea from God; for I have not received it through the senses, and it is never presented to me unexpectedly, as is usual with the ideas of sensible things when these things present themselves, or seem to present themselves, to the external organs of my senses; nor is it likewise a fiction of my mind, for it is not in my power to take from or to add anything to it; and consequently the only alternative is that it is innate in me, just as the idea of myself is innate in me.[110]

The idea of God is thus 'implied' in the human mind in quite the same manner 'in which the equality of its three angles to two right angles is implied in the idea of a triangle; or in the idea of a sphere, that all the points on its surface are equidistant from its centre, or even more evidently still'.[111] Beginning with the two invincible perceptions of his own mind – that of his own existence and of the existence of God – and proceeding deductively from these *a priori* data, Descartes erected his entire philosophical system. Both its inception and development are uncompromisingly rationalistic. For all its important steps, as outlined in the four

---

[108] *Ibid.*, p. 308.
[109] *Ibid.*, p. 305.
[110] *Meditation III* (*Works*, I, 170).
[111] *Discourse*, pt. IV (*Works*, I, 104).

points of the *Discours*, man has only to rely on his own properly disciplined faculties. When he does, he has access to truth. The kind of ideas we may entertain about things in nature (or of our 'affections' of those things) may be false; our fantasies of the imagination (for example, of mermaids) are even further removed from reality; but our 'clear and distinct ideas' uncovered in our own minds and known only through the intellect are absolutely true.[112] Thus if we begin with such *a priori* truths we may derive the structure and operation of the whole universe. Since it is these ideas, belonging to the realm of *res cogitans*, that (somehow) activate the passive objects of *res extensa*, we may start from God the first mover and proceed to construe the universe mechanistically, even to describe it geometrically.

Such a system is based on the assumption of reality as determinate and immutable, and truth as resulting when our mental processes correspond to this static reality. Actually there is no room for revelation in such an epistemology, but as a true son of the Church Descartes makes the customary qualifications.[113] In terms of his system, however, he requires God not as the first member of the Trinity, not as the watchful and jealous Father whose Son atones for our sins, not as the Judge who decrees our rewards and punishments; he requires Him only as a philosophic principle, the generator of movement in a universe in which movement, described mathematically, is the highest object of knowledge. As the first mover God is the cause which, on sound scholastic principle, must be greater than its effects; but since existence is inexplicable in either origin or continuation God is also the eternal causal principle linking the operations of mind and matter. The *concursus Dei* is the necessary hypothesis for sustaining a dualistic universe, and, of course, occasionalism is the result.

> It is as a matter of fact perfectly clear and evident to all those who consider with attention the nature of time, that, in order to be conserved in each moment in which it endures, a substance has need of the same power and action as would be necessary to produce and create it anew, supposing it did not yet exist; so that the light of nature shows us clearly that the distinction between creation and conservation is solely a distinction of the reason.[114]

[112] *Principles*, I.xlviii. [113] *Ibid.*, III.ii.
[114] *Meditation III* (*Works*, I, 168).

God is, then, both the first cause and the principle of continuous recreation describable in terms of geometric regularity. He is not immanent in the universe, but His law is imposed upon it. Deism demands such impositional theology, and such theology is impossible except in deism.

We cannot follow further the complex development of Continental rationalism. But when we recall Spinoza's attitude toward religion, an anthropomorphic God, providence, and free will,[115] we can realize the irreparable injury to traditional theology. 'All things which come to pass, come to pass according to the eternal order and fixed laws of nature.'[116] Such a pronouncement is necessary to Spinoza's geometrically derived system, but it destroys, at one blow, the sovereignty of God and the freedom of man. Such fictions, however, appeared to Spinoza to belong to the myth of theology rather than the truth of philosophy, and between the two no reconciliation was possible. As he wrote to William van Blyenbergh, who had objected to his irreligious views, a philosopher must be concerned with truth, not anthropomorphic fantasies: he can have 'no other touchstone for truth than the natural understanding, and not theology'.[117] To act virtuously is to follow reason, to follow reason is to know God, and to know God is to be one with the order of the universe.[118] As Spinoza thought, a metaphysic and ethic based on this conviction, and arrived at by the operations of the unaided human intellect, have no need of that rich but erroneous complex of myth, morals, revelation, and self-deception which constitutes traditional theology. 'He who clearly and distinctly understands himself and his affects loves God, and loves Him better the better he understands himself and his affects.'[119]

V. THE CAMBRIDGE PLATONISTS

By the middle of the seventeenth century the sacramental view of nature was under attack, overt or concealed, from many quarters. Baconian empiricists, Cartesian rationalists, Puritan sectarians, Hobbesian mechanists were steadily alienating God and nature; and consequently the traditional organic epistemology fusing

---

[115] See *Ethics*, pt. I, appendix; II.xlviii.
[116] *On the Improvement of the Understanding*, Wild, pp. 4–5; cf. *Ethics*, II.iii.
[117] *Letters*, no. XXII (*Wild*, p. 435).
[118] *Ethics*, bk. IV, demonstration.   [119] *Ibid.*, V.xv.

THE CAMBRIDGE PLATONISTS

truth and goodness was everywhere being challenged for a wide variety of reasons. Nowhere is the impact of this threat to the theistic tradition recorded more sensitively than in the work of that heterogeneous group we have come to call the Cambridge Platonists.

In the broadest terms we may describe their efforts – carried on with only the loosest coöperation – as designed to interpret nature in sacramental rather than mechanistic ways. Apart from their academic connection with Emmanuel College, Cambridge, and their common desire to save the tradition of Christian humanism, they were a varied set of men. Although their spiritual father, Benjamin Whichcote, published nothing during his uneven career as a college tutor and preacher, after his death in 1683 his disciples put together the posthumous sermons and the beautiful *Aphorisms* (1703). John Smith's short life resulted in the posthumous *Select Discourses*, informed with a burning conviction of the soul's immortality. Nathanael Culverwel's strain of harsh Calvinism rather sets him apart from the others, yet his influential *Discourse of the Light of Nature* (1652) is a tediously learned defense of Christian rationalism. Few now read Henry More's unreadable poetry, and the defects of his prolix prose tend to obscure his importance as a bulwark of all things spiritual; yet his mind was well stocked and subtle, his correspondents were men of parts, and his influence was very wide. Ralph Cudworth is memorable for two things: his beautiful sermon on Christian love, delivered before Parliament in 1647, and his *True Intellectual System of the Universe* (1678), an important attack on atheism and materialism which few except his editors have ever read through.

For all their differences, this group of men – and such peripheral figures as Peter Sterry and John Worthington – shared a set of values that permits us to consider them together. Though variously 'Platonic' (Culverwel was an Aristotelian and More, before he realized its dangers, espoused Cartesianism), they were unanimously convinced of the claims of traditional Christianity against the new materialism, and they tried to accommodate both systems so as to close the widening gap between revealed and natural religion. That is to say, they sought to reëstablish human reason as a valid epistemological instrument and to subordinate the doctrinal struggles of their age to a Christian morality of charity and toleration. Like Lord Herbert, Lord Brooke, Chillingworth, and many others, they were opposed to Calvin's voluntarism and to the bitter party strife threatening to destroy all religions; credal subtleties, scholastic or other, interested them less than practical morality and virtuous conduct; and morality, they insisted, was the first fruit of man's rational intellection. 'Virtue is the health, true state, natural complexion of the Soul: he, that is Vicious in his practice, is diseased in his mind.'[120] Taking as their text the proposition that 'the spirit of man is the candle of the Lord', they ceaselessly urged the uses of both revelation and reason in attaining that fusion of goodness and truth which constitutes the dignity of man. 'Reason discovers, what is Natural; and Reason receives, what is Supernatural.'[121]

As Whichcote told his old tutor Anthony Tuckney, in answer to his charges of Arminianism, *recta ratio* and *vera fides* always go together.

> To go against Reason, is to go against God: it is the self same thing, to do that which the Reason of the Case doth require; and that which God Himself doth appoint: Reason is the Divine Governor of Man's Life; it is the very Voice of God.[122]

Or, more succinctly: 'He knows most, who Does best.'[123] Similarly, Cudworth could only lump together with the atheists those theologians (like Ockham and Calvin) who minimize God's reason to magnify His will. It would be better to live under the terrors of mechanistic determinism than under 'a will altogether undetermined by goodness, justice, and wisdom, armed with omnipotence; because the former could harbour no hurtful or mischievous designs against any, as the latter might'.[124] Even as a child, More could not 'swallow down that hard Doctrine' of predestination,[125] and when he came to a man's estate it still seemed to him as 'black as the smoak of the bottomless Pit out of which the Locusts came'.[126] And quite naturally, for More, like all the group, erected his metaphysics and his morality on the axiom of knowledge. Underlying the warmth and tenderness of Whichcote's *Aphorisms*, or of More's own quaint dabbling in everything from Descartes' vorticism to Hebraic mysticism, or

---

[120] Whichcote, *Moral and Religious Aphorisms*, no. 24.
[121] Ibid., no. 99.   [122] Ibid., no. 76.
[123] Ibid., no. 925.
[124] *The True Intellectual System of the Universe*, IV, 161.
[125] See *Philosophical Writings*, p. xi.   [126] *Divine Dialogues*, p. 325.

of Smith's rapturous Neo-Platonism, or of Cudworth's dusty learning, is the conviction that man's well-being is rooted in piety and truth, whose principles, as Hooker said, are by reason investigable and may be known.

> Man's Observance of God in all Instances of Morality; these are Truths of first Inscription; and these have a deeper Foundation, greater Ground for them, than that God gave the Law on Mount Sinai; or that he did after ingrave it on Tables of Stone; or that we find the Ten Commandments in the Bible. For God made Man to them, and did write them upon the Heart of Man, before he did declare them upon Mount Sinai, before he ingraved them upon the Tables of Stone, or before they were writ in our Bibles; God made Man to them, and wrought his Law upon Mens Hearts; and, as it were, interwove it into the Principles of our Reason; and the things thereof are the very Sense of Man's Soul, and the Image of his Mind: So that a Man doth undo his own being, departs from himself, and unmakes himself, confounds his own Principles, when he is disobedient and unconformable to them; and must necessarily be self-condemn'd.[127]

Whatever the syntax of this passage, its fervor is unmistakable, and as an epitome of the Cambridge Platonists' cardinal conviction it illuminates and binds together all the disparate writings of the group. 'I desire only so to understand God', said More, 'that nothing be attributed to him repugnant to my Understanding, nor any thing found in the World repugnant to his Attributes.'[128]

To these men, God was a God of reason, and even fallen man retained those truths of first inscription sufficient to know that moral conduct is a function of reason. To reason, moreover, is added what Whichcote calls the truth of after-revelation, truths that though 'they be not of Reason's Invention, yet they are of the prepar'd Mind readily entertain'd and receiv'd'.[129] Under the aegis of this single truth that has a double mode the Cambridge Platonists tried to domesticate to the reciprocal uses of reason and goodness an astonishing variety of intellectual disciplines. Like Ficino and Pico della Mirandola nearly two centuries earlier, they regarded all imperfect systems and all partial truths as grist for their mill. To men of Tuckney's stripe – those who liked their religion straight – they seemed outrageously liberal, for in making theology rational they ran the risk of making it godless. What

[127] Whichcote, *Select Sermons*, p. 5. [128] *Divine Dialogues*, p. 29.
[129] *Select Sermons*, p. 7.

was to be done with a man like More, who calmly announced that moral principles 'are no less demonstrable than Mathematicks',[130] or like Cudworth, who compared the moral insights of the unaided human intellect to the Pythagorean theorem?[131]

But unlike the Tuckneys, the latitudinarians, even though their own values were humanistic and pre-scientific, realized that if Christianity could not come to terms with the new experimental philosophy it must be destroyed by it. With their powerful conviction of moral absolutes operative in the whole universe and susceptible to the instrument of human reason, they could only regard the irrational as the irreligious. There are, says Cudworth, 'things eternally just – which were not made such at certain times by law and arbitrary command, but being such in their own nature immutably, were from everlasting to everlasting'.[132] To the Cambridge Platonists these things, rather than theological hair-pulling, constituted the essence of religion, just as religion must be regarded as the finest distillation of truth. Since God Himself is 'the paradigm or platform, according to which this sensible world was made',[133] to know the world – even by the methods of experimental philosophy – is to know its creator.

It is no wonder, then, that they sought to adjust to their Christian values the instruments and data of the new philosophy. The dazzling successes of that philosophy had been achieved by the human mind ('so free, so rational, so intellectual' that it is like God's);[134] they seemed capable of geometrical demonstration; and they could, if properly construed, serve as paeans to a rational God. 'Thank God, that he doth uphold the Foundations of Nature; and continue us in the use of true and solid Reason.'[135] Although Cudworth's most systematic arguments for the existence of God are buttressed by the findings of experimental philosophy,[136] he insisted that the God who sustains nature in its orderly workings is transcendent to those workings, carrying things on 'in a still and silent path' which 'shows his art and skill in making things of themselves fairly unwind, and clear up at the last into a satisfactory close'.[137] Thus the recent gains in natural philosophy

---

[130] *Divine Dialogues*, pp. 3–4.
[131] *The True Intellectual System of the Universe*, III, 406–7.
[132] *Ibid.*, III, 409.   [133] *Ibid.*, III, 408.
[134] More, *Conjectura Cabbalistica*, p. 31.
[135] Whichcote, *Aphorisms*, no. 468.
[136] *The True Intellectual System of the Universe*, I, 27, 28, 38, 39.
[137] *Ibid.*, IV, 171.

could hold no terrors for him and no threat to the God whom he adored. 'The new celestial phenomena, and the late improvements of astronomy and philosophy made thereupon' can only confirm the sovereignty and wisdom of the Lord.[138]

In More's view, the facts of comparative anatomy – 'no Birds have Paps, as Beasts have' – are 'as certain a Pledge of the Existence of a God, as any Voice or Writing that contains such Specimens of Reason as are in Archimedes his Treatise are an Argument of the Existence of some Man or Angel that must be the Author of them'.[139] From man's innate idea of God we can only infer the existence of God, says More like a good Cartesian; likewise we must infer that the human soul is 'a compendious Statue of the Deity', so that we are able 'to contemplate the nature of the Almighty in this little Medal of God, the Soul of Man'.[140] In view of this theistic optimism More's early flirtation with Cartesian rationalism is very revealing. Though the Cambridge group rose as one man against the unblushing materialism of Hobbes – More's *Antidote against Atheism* and Cudworth's *Treatise Concerning Eternal and Immutable Morality* stand out importantly from the swarming rebuttals of that dreadful man – some of them, at least, hoped for much from Descartes. In the first tremor of excitement that passed over Europe at his works, it was thought he had at last reconciled – geometrically – the claims of matter and spirit, reason and faith. As his *Democritus Platonissans* (1646) shows, More's early enthusiasm was very high; and though he presently realized, as he should have earlier, that Cartesian metaphysics struck a fatal blow at the theistic tradition, he never lost his regard for Cartesian physics.

Although More made large concessions to contemporary philosophy – for example, he ascribed extension to Descartes' *res cogitans*, placing the seat of the soul in the fourth ventricle of the brain,[141] and he populated his spirit-world with substantial beings who satisfied their 'musical and amorous propension'[142] – he of

---

[138] *Ibid.*, IV, 179–80. In the same passage Cudworth goes on to advocate the doctrine – so terrifying to many – of a plurality of worlds: 'Now, it is not reasonable to think, that all this immense vastness should lie waste, desert, and uninhabited, and have nothing in it that could praise the Creator thereof, save only this one small spot of earth.'
[139] *Divine Dialogues*, p. 14.
[140] *Antidote against Atheism*, I.iii.4; cf. I.xi.12.
[141] *Divine Dialogues*, pp. 75 f.
[142] See Marjorie Nicholson, 'The Spirit World of Milton and More', *SP*, XXII (1923) 433–52.

course recognized that the segregation of mind from matter would ultimately jeopardize the fact of spirituality. And that, in turn, would destroy the synthesis of reason and faith, body and soul, from which he derived his metaphysical, epistemological, moral, and theological values. 'The phenomena of the world', he wrote to Boyle, 'cannot be solved merely mechanically.'[143] The thought of a universe merely of matter in motion dizzies and appals him. It would mean that

> it is impossible that there should be any God, or Soul, or Angel, Good or Bad; or any Immortality or Life to come. That there is no Religion, no Piety nor Impiety, no Vertue nor Vice, Justice nor Injustice, but what it pleases him that has the longest Sword to call so. That there is no Freedome of Will, nor consequently any Rational remorse of Conscience in any Being whatsoever, but that all that is, is nothing but Matter and corporeal Motion; and that therefore every trace of mans life is as necessary as the tracts of Lightning and the fallings of Thunder; the blind impetus of the Matter breaking through or being stopt every where, with as certain and determinate necessity as the course of a Torrent after mighty storms and showers of Rain.[144]

To save the universe from such mechanism More ran to embrace various theosophies and demonologies. He borrowed heavily from the Cabala, hoping thereby to reconcile the cosmology of Genesis with the facts of science; he advocated a curious Pythagorean dualism of masculine and feminine, reason and will; he postulated an *anima mundi* – 'a substance incorporeal, but without sense or animadversion, pervading the whole matter of the universe, and exercising a plastic power therein' – to account for those phenomena (like gravity, cohesion, magnetism) which he refused to regard as 'mere mechanical powers';[145] with Joseph Glanvill he vigorously argued for the existence of witches and their evil familiars, on the very sound assumption that if evil spirits are only imaginary, then so are good ones too.

This foolish eclecticism of More's has always operated against his reputation, and properly so; yet he and his like-minded contemporaries are important, not only for their influence on later British idealism, but for their intense if futile efforts to stem the

---

[143] Burtt, *Metaphysical Foundations*, p. 130; cf. *Enchiridion ethicum*, ch. ix-xv *passim*.
[144] *The Immortality of the Soul*, I.ix.1.
[145] *Ibid.*, III.xii.

tide of scientific materialism. Writing as a recent Catholic convert, Dryden has his milk-white Hind denounce such 'sons of latitude' to the Anglican Panther as 'far the worst of your pretended race', but the charge is grossly unfair. The good sense and moral clarity of Whichcote's *Aphorisms* or Cudworth's Parliamentary sermon reveal their authors as spokesmen for a tradition whose strength had always been a moral strength; and, although they failed to reconcile mechanism and morality, in the history of English thought they poignantly symbolize the dilemma confronting their age.

VI. MILTON

Although his rich and tireless genius resists easy classification, in this synoptic account Milton may fairly stand as the last great exemplar of Renaissance humanism in England. To call him this should explain both his significant departures from Calvinistic theology and his growing sense of isolation as the darkness closed in on him. Although he incarnates the characteristically intense individualism of the Puritan, and although there is a strong element of voluntarism in his theology,[146] none the less he takes his honored place alongside Hooker in that tradition of Christian humanism we have tried to outline. To justify the ways of God to man in a theocratic universe was his high resolve, and he used all the resources of his great art and learning to justify them on the truths of God's sovereignty and man's dignity. For Milton the cardinal concepts are the providence of God and the free will of man which makes rational choice the key to moral action; for him the highest wisdom is 'that whereby we earnestly search after the will of God, learn it with all diligence, and govern all our actions according to its rule';[147] for him nature is both the vitalistic *natura naturans* working toward moral ends and the *natura naturata* whose symmetry and order manifest to the mind of man God's supremely rational and therefore good designs.

Within this broad and flexible framework of values the role of reason is very great. Milton's rather Arminian theology tends to identify Christ with reason, and, thus minimizing the doctrine

---

[146] See, for example, his 'permissive' theory of evil, *PL*, I.212; VII.168-73. See Hooker, *Laws*, I.iii.3.
[147] *De doctrina*, II.ii (*PW*, V, 10).

of the Atonement, to make reason the agency of man's regeneration. As God tells Abdiel, those

> who reason for thir Law refuse,
> Right reason for thir Law, and for thir King
> Messiah, who by right of merit Reigns,

deserve their self-appointed destruction.[148] Just as Satan fell by choosing evil rather than good, so man, denying the dictates of nature, must be held accountable for his alienation from God. 'God and nature bid the same',[149] and what they bid we may know through reason – 'discursive' reason for drawing inferences from the data of sensory cognition, 'intuitive' reason for grasping, like the angels, the mysteries of God through faith.[150] For Milton, as for Hooker, reason is both a metaphysical and a moral principle, and as such it fuses truth with goodness. Right reason comprises both those moral absolutes which pattern the universe and man's capacity for apprehending these moral absolutes; they are made clear to his conscience[151] and operative by the law of nature.[152]

Of course, Milton repeats the traditional arguments for keeping reason properly subordinate to faith. Even when he asserts that if a man believes the truth on faith, 'the very truth he holds becomes his heresy',[153] he is defending, in terms of his general position, the prerogatives of both kinds of knowledge in their proper spheres; moreover, he is implying, as he makes explicit in the *De doctrina*, that identification of reason and faith which informs his epistemology: 'No one ... can have right thoughts of God, with nature or reason alone as his guide, independent of the word, or message of God.'[154] To the ignorance of the proper limits of human reason, he says, we may charge 'one huge half of all the misery that hath been since Adam'.[155] God, 'the

---

[148] *PL*, VI.41–3.   [149] *PL*, VI.176.
[150] *PL*, V.488–90.   [151] *De doctrina*, I.ii *passim*.
[152] *The Ready and Easy Way to Establish a Free Commonwealth*, *PW*, II, 111, where the law of nature is described as 'the only law of laws, truly and properly to all mankind fundamental'. See *Samson*, ll. 888–90; *PL*, XII.24–9; X.720–844 (a crucial passage where the fallen Adam questions God's designs, only to end in acquiescence to that justice which he assumes is implicit in the moral order but which he is unable to grasp intellectually). For an earlier humanist's views on natural law, see Thomas Wilson, *The Arte of Rhetorique*, p. 24.
[153] *Areopagitica*, *PW*, II, 85.   [154] I.ii (*PW*, IV, 16).
[155] *The Doctrine and Discipline of Divorce*, 'To the Parliament of England', (*PW*, III, 175).

great Architect', mocks man's efforts to comprehend all His plans,[156] and Adam sounds at once Puritan and Baconian in seeking to know only 'That which before us lies in daily life' lest he lose the name of action and of piety in maundering about 'things remote From use, obscure and subtle'.[157]

Perhaps the most notorious passage in all Milton is that, in *Paradise Regained*, where classical culture is denounced as impious[158] – and by a man who owed so much to that culture. Yet it is quite consonant with his general position on subordinating natural to supernatural truth. For all their great gifts the pagan philosophers and moralists worked in darkness without the gift of revelation, whereas

> he who receives
> Light from above, from the fountain of light,
> No other doctrine needs, though granted true;
> But these are false, or little else but dreams,
> Conjectures, fancies, built on nothing firm. . . .
> Alas! what can they teach, and not mislead;
> Ignorant of themselves, of God much more,
> And how the world began, and how man fell
> Degraded by himself, on grace depending?
> Much of the Soul they talk, but all awry,
> And in themselves seek virtue, and to themselves
> All glory arrogate, to God give none,
> Rather accuse him under usual names,
> Fortune and Fate, as one regardless quite
> Of mortal things.

For the Christian epic, fused into the thought and feeling of men like Milton, meant nothing if not that God is omnipotent, that man was created pure but is of his own responsibility fallen, that his task on earth is to rebuild his ruined faculties to know God aright, and that to his regeneration God by His watchful providence provides the inexplicable gift of grace. These are the essential truths for knowledge, as Michael outlines them to Adam at the close of *Paradise Lost*, and if one knows them he has reached the top of human knowledge. They bear the double sanctity of truth and goodness, and they suffice for contentment here, for salvation hereafter.

[156] *PL*, VIII.75–84.
[158] IV.285–364.
[157] *PL*, VIII.179–97.

This having learnt, thou hast attain'd the sum
Of wisdom; hope no higher, though all the Stars
Thou knew'st by name, and all th' ethereal Powers,
All secrets of the deep, all Nature's works,
Or works of God in Heav'n, Air, Earth, or Sea,
And all the riches of this World enjoy'dst,
And all the rule, one Empire; only add
Deeds to thy knowledge answerable, add Faith,
Add Virtue, Patience, Temperance, add Love,
By name to come call'd Charity, the soul
Of all the rest: then wilt thou not be loath
To leave this Paradise, but shalt possess
A paradise within thee, happier far.[159]

[159] *PL*, XII 574–87; cf. III.694–98, VII.70–5, 119–78.

IV

THE ATTACK ON AUTHORITY

I. OCKHAM

The axiom of knowledge which so majestically shaped the thought of St Thomas by no means lost its appeal in the centuries that stretched between him and Milton. But it is one of the ironies of intellectual history that the scholastic synthesis of faith and reason had hardly attained its fullest statement before it began to crumble. Not that St Thomas had failed to make a large accommodation for the supernatural in his natural theology: the long and bitter controversy over transubstantiation – a doctrine first strongly advanced by Radbertus Paschasius, futilely resisted by Bérengar of Tours, and finally declared an article of faith by the fourth Lateran Council in 1215 – symbolized the conflict between faith and reason for the medieval church. But it is significant that faith triumphed, and ironical that St Thomas had to resort to all his immense dialectical skill to establish the inadequacy of reason before the fact of miracle.[1] None the less, his main effort had been toward a reconciliation of faith and reason, and therefore the post-Thomistic eruption of voluntarism and nominalism posed a real threat to his delicately wrought synthesis.

In retrospect it appears ominous that Duns Scotus, within a generation of St Thomas' death, enlarged the catalogue of those mysteries beyond man's rational grasp to include the omnipotence of God, His infinity, His role as the object of man's ultimate knowledge, and the immortality of the soul – all established in the *Summa* as safely within the area of natural knowledge and thus derivable from the very nature of things themselves. But equally ominous was Scotus' insistence that to construe God, in Thomistic terms, as a being essentially rational was to delimit and debase His sovereignty. In Scotus' view the will – human or divine – is capable of self-determination quite independently of reason and sometimes even against it. St Thomas had enthroned

[1] *ST*, III.lxxv.2–5.

reason not only as the 'essence' of God,[2] but as the operative principle of the whole universe: reason is that *supremus motor*, which holds the stars in their courses, makes necessary the ordered hierarchies of being, and underlies the very strategy of God's vast designs. Its object is *verum* rather than *bonum* – 'since the true is related to knowledge, and the good to the appetite, the true must be prior in nature to the good'[3] – but from *verum* all other goods follow. This Dante realized when he described those thrones of the divine aspect ranged about the very presence of God Himself:

> And thou shouldst know that all have delight in proportion as their vision penetrates into the Truth [*quanto la sua veduta si profonda nel vero*] in which every understanding is at rest. Hence may be seen how beatitude is founded on the act which sees, not on that which loves, which follows after. And the merit, to which grace and goodwill give birth, is the measure of this seeing; thus is the progress from grade to grade.[4]

But if will be not superior to reason in both God and man, argued the Franciscan against the Dominican, then there can be no genuine freedom. 'Voluntas divina nihil aliud respicit necessario pro objecto ab assentia sua.'[5] Because God's will is *emperens intellectui* His acts are predetermined by nothing, certainly not by criteria of reason. What He wills is good of itself, not because it is rational. He did not create the universe as He did because He followed great preëxistent ideas (*universalia*): He acted indeterminately, and therefore the creation as it stands is good simply because He willed it so. As the ineffable mysteries of Christianity show us, the limits of reason are sharply drawn. As articles of faith they yield to no rational proof, and to believe them we must rely solely on *gratia infusa*.[6] In all this, of course, it is feasible to argue a difference of emphasis rather than a complete divergence between St Thomas and Scotus. On the basic questions of realism, and the limits of faith and reason, and the nature of God, Scotus' position, for all his great talents of skeptical analysis, is essentially scholastic, and it is possible that his iconoclasm has been exaggerated.[7] For he is reluctant to abandon the very archstone of scholastic thought – the notion that the essence of God

---

[2] *ST*, I.lxxxix.1.   [3] *ST*, I.xvi.5.
[4] *Paradiso*, xxviii.
[5] See C. R. S. Harris, *Duns Scotus*, I, 184, n. 1.
[6] See De Wulf, *History of Mediaeval Philosophy*, II, 81–6.
[7] See McGiffert, *A History of Christian Thought*, II, 297–9.

is intellect and that the archetypal scheme of things demands a *lex aeterna* without which the divine plan would be unknowable.

Not so William of Ockham. That great English Franciscan, surely one of the sharpest minds of the early Renaissance, was untimely struck by the Black Death in 1349; but before he died he crowded into a restless life of teaching, diplomacy, and political agitation a shattering attack on those very assumptions that had made scholasticism possible. When Anselm had, as he thought, established the existence of God ontologically – arguing that the reality of an infinitely perfect being is made necessary by our concept of Him – and had justified the dogma of the Incarnation on dialectical grounds of infinite sin calling for infinite atonement through a sinless being, he had inaugurated the high period of scholasticism. For his arguments had rested on logical proofs derived from the *a priori* assumption that when Adam sinned all men sinned and that when Christ suffered for that sin all men atoned. Such universal truth required actual implementation: if the doctrine of generic sin and generic atonement were valid, then the universal idea or Form of man had to have a reality apart from individual men, just as the Universal Church had to have a reality over and beyond the actual church as it existed in space and time. *Universalia sunt realia*; otherwise faith is impossible, and so is that natural reason of which ideas are the content. Without tracing the serpentine – and dialectically very interesting – controversy following the collision of Roscelinus and Anselm, we can see that when Ockham put the capstone on the nominalist tradition he struck a powerful blow at the orthodox scholasticism of the realists.

The nominalist would argue that whereas the objects of perception are individual, concrete presentations of sense (a view adopted by St Thomas himself, as we have seen), ideas or species are mere abstractions or concepts created by the mind and enjoying existence only in words. *Universalia*, then, are *vocalia* or *nomina*, but emphatically not *realia*. The mind has great power in juggling, assorting, and drawing inferences from the individual presentations of sense, and the resulting concepts and propositions and abstractions make rational thought possible; but such concepts – for example, of God, of the Church, of truth, of man – have no universal (or Platonic) reality; consequently there is no necessary relation between them and the data of sensation from which we abstract them. The implications for theology are boundless. As Kuno Fischer has said, if concepts 'neither have, nor apprehend, reality, there is no knowledge of the real, and, since the objects of faith are the truly real, no knowledge of faith'.[8] The edifice of rational theology, so painfully built up between Anselm and St Thomas, could totter and fall before the skeptical attack of Ockham and succeeding nominalists.

The attack was subtle, relentless, and successful. Since the problem of universals reduced itself to epistemology, Ockham, bred in the traditions of scholasticism, conducted his offense in terms of logic. The realists had succeeded in marrying logic to ontology; they sanctified the class concept or species (viewed by Plato and Aristotle as either the metaphysical content of reason or the inherent principle of actuality) as the anchor of both natural and revealed theology, and traditional logic as the process by which knowledge of such concepts could be attained. Ockham, strongly influenced by the *Summulae logicales* of Petrus Hispanus, tried to restore logic to its proper sphere of grammar and semantics by divorcing it from ontology.[9] To him logic was a *scientia sermonicalis*, a science whose objects are not the timeless aspects of truth and error which lie hopelessly beyond man's rational reach, but instead the meanings and significations which are arbitrarily and conventionally conferred upon words and propositions. That is, logic is rooted not in the ontologically real, but in the relations existing between a word and the supposition following it, the grammatico-logical properties such as *significatio, suppositio, ampliatio, appellatio, restrictio, distributio, exponibilia*. Consequently, the aim of logic must be regarded as not to teach *vere loqui*, but *recte loqui*; the *modi essendi et subsistendi* must give way to the *modi significandi et intelligendi*. Resisting even the modified realism of St Thomas and Scotus, Ockham insisted that between alleged universals and individual objects of cognition (or intuition, as he would say) there is neither a 'copy' nor an 'adequation' relationship; there is merely a sign or a signification, for since universals have no reality, our concepts are only mental signs – 'anything that, as apprehended, presents something else to cognition'[10] – which Ockham calls *termini*. Such *termini* seem to be nothing

---

[8] *History of Modern Philosophy*, p. 68.
[9] Throughout this discussion I am much indebted to the admirable analysis of Stephen Chak Tornay, *Ockham: Studies and Selections*.
[10] Tornay, p. 9; cf. Erdmann, *A History of Philosophy*, I, 512–3.

more or less than physiological responses to the data of sensation, and so, says Ockham, 'the passion of the soul is the act of intellect itself'.[11]

This is not to say that conceptual thought is impossible. Although man can apprehend sensibles only by 'intuition' – 'cognition by virtue of which it can be known that a thing is when it is, and that a thing is not when it is not'[12] – we can conceive the object as thought of by abstraction, and so abstractions come to take the place of (*supponere*) the welter of individual objects of intuitive cognition. As labels for cataloguing the concrete data of sensation into genera, species, and classes, they make inference possible. But the corollary is clear: if such ideas are the materials of knowledge, then knowledge itself can have no necessary relation to substantial reality. Such abstractions as being or law or cause or end become merely mental constructs, not the logical redactions of ontologically valid universals. Ockham pushes on to the relentless conclusion:

> The universal is not some real thing having a psychological being (*esse subjectivum*) in the soul or outside of the soul. It has only a logical being (*esse objectivum*) in the soul and is a kind of fiction having the same sort of entity in the logical realm as the external thing has in the psychological realm. Figments have no psychological being in the soul, for then they would be real things, and a chimera and centaur and other such things would all be real things. There are, then, certain entities which have only logical being. In the same way, propositions, syllogisms, and such other things as logic treats, have no psychological being but only a logical being: and so *their being is their being understood*.[13]

The mind is capable of deriving the most elaborate abstractions from the intuitions of sense, but their only validity is that of iteration. When we first 'intuit' a horse we of course experience a single horse, but by repetition and similarity of such intuitions we derive the concept *horse* which takes on a kind of universal significance in our minds. Repeated intuitions result in a *habitus* or trace in the mind, and such traces, grouped together through their common elements, can lead to *consimilia*. Universals, then, are only recurring acts of abstraction. In other words, without memory – a psychological, not an ontological, fact – universals would be impossible. 'Every science starts from individuals. From

---

[11] Tornay, p. 9.   [12] Tornay, pp. 119–20.
[13] Tornay, pp. 12–3.

sensation, which gives only singular things, arises memory, from memory experimentation, and through experimentation we get a universal which is the basis of art and science.'[14]

To confuse such mental constructs with reality is a desperate fallacy. 'Nullum universale est extra animam existens realiter in substantiis individuis, nec est de substantia vel esse earum.'[15]

> If 'humanity' were different from the particular individuals and a part of their essence [as we must infer from the realists' account of the Fall, for example] one and the same invariable thing would be in many individuals, and so the same numerically one and invariable thing would be at different places, which is false. In the same way, the same invariable thing would, say, be condemned in Judas and saved in Christ, and, hence, there would be something condemned and miserable in Christ, which is absurd. In much the same manner, God could not, then, annihilate an individual without destroying all the individuals of the same genus.[16]

Clearly, then, such abstractions can have no reality, whatever their convenience; and we are – or should be – always mindful that at their root lies the primal act of intuition. The act itself can give us no knowledge of the thing which is its object. There is no relation between the thing and our conception of it, and therefore no basis for absolute truth.

When Ockham applies his logic to questions which scholasticism had seemed to answer, the results are astonishing but inevitable. Perhaps it would be instructive to sketch as an example his vigorous analysis of the question, 'Does God know all things which are not Himself by means of their ideas?'[17] Such a question suggests one of the axioms of scholasticism: that behind the phenomena of sense lie the eternal and ontologically real ideas from which sensibles derive their existence and according to which they were created by God – in short, one of the essential corollaries of the axiom of knowledge. The first and perhaps most telling of Ockham's devious attacks is that God knows everything by means of His essence, rather than by ideas. Now, since the essence of God is unity, neither God nor His essence can be an idea, 'for, in that case just as there are many ideas there would be a number of essences, a thing which is impossible'. God does not need ideas as the ground of knowledge or as the (Platonic) forms or archetypal models for the creation of indivi-

[14] Tornay, p. 18.
[15] Quoted by De Wulf, II, 183.
[16] Tornay, pp. 127–8.
[17] Tornay, pp. 137–64.

dual things. The divine intellect knows all things 'which are not Himself without any aspect of reason'. Indeed,

> these aspects would be derogatory to His intellect. For if the divine intellect would understand things which are not Himself through these [aspects] so that the object itself would be the constitutive factor in the act of knowing, this fact would detract from His intellect. Therefore, if the divine essence alone were not a sufficient moving cause of His intellect for the understanding of all other things, it would require something else, and the result would be a disparagement of His intellect.

The notion that the divine intellect could be moved by an idea – for example, be moved to the act of creation on the model supplied by an idea – is impious: 'it would be contradictory to its very being to be moved by anything, just as it is contradictory to the divine cognition to be made or created by any one'. To regard the universe as created according to a framework of pre-existing ideas, themselves the object of God's cognition, impugns the nature of God. For He 'does not need ideas in order to enable Him to act. Only the knowledge of the ideas themselves is required, and that knowledge is identical with God in every way'. And the conclusion, after many pages of the most sinuous dialectic, is for Ockham's purposes triumphant: 'The principal proposition now is evident: The idea is not a ground of knowing, but is that which is known.'[18]

Just as he demolishes the realists' conception of a universe rationally ordered according to archetypal ideas, so he scrutinizes and rejects the other central propositions of scholasticism. Thus he denies the ontological reality of the intellectual soul (which to St Thomas confirmed the fact of immortality). To posit such an entity

> as an immaterial and incorruptible form which is totally in the whole and totally in every part, cannot be accepted as evident from either reason or experience. We cannot know whether such a form is in us, or that it is the nature of such substance in us to be intellectual, or that the soul is the form of the body. I do not care how Aristotle felt about this, because

---

[18] Note St Thomas' conclusion to the same question (*ST*, I.xiv.5): 'Hence whatever effects pre-exist in God, as in the first cause, must be in His act of understanding, and they must be there in an intelligible way.'

Two and a half centuries later Ockham's view had become so commonplace that Puttenham could glibly slip it into a treatise on literary theory. He compares the poet to God, 'who without any travell to his divine imagination made all the world of nought, nor also by any paterne or mould, as the Platonicks with their Idees do phantastically suppose' (*The Art of English Poesie*, I.i [*Elizabethan Critical Essays*, II, 3]).

everywhere he himself appears on this point to be uncertain. We hold the three foregoing propositions only by faith.[19]

Moreover, he, like Scotus, dislocates the scholastic relationship between will and reason, because he holds the act of loving (the function of will) superior to the act of understanding (the function of intellect). Since the intellect is passive rather than active,

> everything can be explained by the act of will or by the impression of things. Therefore, I say that the cause, as a result of which a true rather than a false proposition is formed, an affirmative rather than a negative, is the will, because the will wants to form the one and not the other.[20]

This is true of God as of man, for to regard reason as supreme places an intolerable limitation on freedom. What God wills becomes obligatory for man – who none the less retains his freedom to submit or not to such an obligation – and therefore sin can be

> nothing else than an act of commission or omission when there is an obligation for man. Only obligation constitutes one a sinner or not a sinner. But God cannot be obligated to any act. With Him a thing becomes right solely for the reason that He wants it to be so.[21]

Even what appear to man as the most unspeakable sins – hatred of God, theft, adultery – must not be regarded as contrary to the allegedly rational and preëxisting disposition of things; they can only be relative to God's volition, which is itself contingent on nothing. Consequently, 'they may be performed by God without any sinful circumstance attached to them. They may even be meritoriously performed by man if they fall under divine precept, just as now their opposites, as a matter of fact, fall under the divine precept.'[22] Predestination itself is wholly a matter of God's will, and not of rational predetermination. To try to explain it rationally is as impious as it is futile. 'The reason why Saint Paul was struck by God and converted without any previous merits of his own while others were not, is nothing else than the will of God.'[23]

And so on. Ockham's penetrating analysis of the axiom of knowledge deprived both God and man of that faculty of reason by which the world was thought knowable and the strategy of

---

[19] Tornay, p. 173.
[20] Tornay, pp. 174–5.
[21] Tornay, p. 180.
[22] Tornay, pp. 180–1.
[23] Tornay, p. 181.

salvation understandable. It tore apart the realms of grace and nature, denied the essential anthropomorphism of medieval theology, threw man back on his natural capacities for knowledge, and then maintained that his knowledge could have no necessary relation to reality. Ockham's pious intention, obviously, was to isolate the sovereignty of God safely beyond the picayune limits of natural reason, and thus to elevate faith as alone necessary for salvation. However convenient the fictions of abstraction may be when we try to manipulate and categorize the data of sensation, they can tell us nothing of reality, and they are ludicrously inadequate to explain those mysteries which God has made compulsory for salvation. Most of the hundred conclusions that comprise the *Centilogium* suggest either that 'rational' proofs for such dogmas as the existence, the unity, and the infinity of God are uncertain or that the essential mysteries of faith such as the Trinity, creation *ex nihilo*, the Incarnation, and transubstantiation flagrantly contradict the most cherished principles of human reason.

Before these inscrutable but necessary articles of faith the puny laws of thought – that nothing can exist before itself, that the whole is larger than its parts, that two bodies cannot occupy the same place at the same time – must all collapse.

> We cannot know in itself either the oneness of God, or His firstness, or His infinite power, or divine goodness and perfection. The things which we know about Him immediately, are certain concepts, which in reality are not God, which, however, we use in propositions for God. Through them we know by a general cognition many other things besides God; and, therefore that entity which is God, or that simple power or perfection which is God, cannot be known by us in itself.[24]

If, however, Ockham sterilized and isolated the realm of grace beyond all the inadequacies of sensory knowledge, he also established the realm of nature as the only legitimate object of man's comprehension. The consequences for the intellectual history of Europe were immense. When he wrote, fired by his Franciscan zeal against the worldly pretensions of John XXII and determined to strip away from the arcana of faith the contaminations of the Dominicans' natural theology, his intent was obviously to protect religion from the claims of secularism – epistemological, political, or other. He worked tirelessly to support the demands of Louis

[24] Tornay, pp. 186–7.

of Bavaria against the pope, and so he joins company with Marsiglio of Padua and John of Jandun as a churchman dedicated to demolishing the political aspirations of a church grown fat and secular with power. But as his long fight for the evangelical poverty of the Franciscans shows, his motives were impeccably religious. And it is the supreme irony that the man who of all his contemporaries sought most valiantly to preserve religion from the cancer of secularism should, by his labors, have done most to demolish that synthesis of faith and reason, church and state, grace and nature, which had marked the apogee of Christianity in Europe. Ockham resisted Thomism as he would have resisted Baconianism, and yet without his emancipation of the realm of nature from the claims of theology it is unlikely that Bacon would have written *The Advancement of Learning* or that the Church would have been put into that posture of defense signalized by the Council of Trent.

II. RENAISSANCE SKEPTICISM

In a sense, then, Ockham and succeeding nominalists emancipated nature, but the price of that emancipation was very great: nothing less than the discrediting of reason itself. Those who sought to exploit that emancipation had to make their way against the opposition of the Church no less than against the powerful pulls of inertia and habit. As we shall see, the axiom of knowledge was not destroyed at one blow; indeed, it forms the very core of Renaissance optimism. But the success of nominalism in the fourteenth and fifteenth centuries would have been less had the age not found in nominalism a sanction for those antirational assumptions that were burgeoning throughout all western Europe. For nominalism provided systematic statement for two of the most powerful convictions of the emerging modern world: that the individual thing alone enjoys true being and that voluntarism rather than rationalism most satisfactorily accounts for the workings of God as well as man.

Therefore nominalism may be construed as an attack on the anthropomorphism of scholastic thought, by which an inscrutable God was reduced to the level of human reason, and projected in terms which, if hardly warm and human, were comprehensible by human faculties. But in a more important sense it declared the independence of man and the emancipation of nature from all theocratic and theological claims. Realism had triumphed in an age when the corporate rather than the individual was the main object of concern. The Church, the state, man were in the Middle Ages conceived as universals which scholasticism had justified philosophically – or perhaps they were so justified because they were so conceived. But with the astonishing new emphasis on the individual that developed in the fourteenth century there was felt a need for philosophic nominalism. The emergence of the national state, the splintering of the universal church, the rise of vernacular literatures, all indicate the course of events. We need only to read Chaucer or Villon to realize that literature was finding new subjects and developing new forms: the sharp, factual, human detail – Criseyde's complicated state of character, the Yorkshire rustics of the *Secunda pastorum*, the acid realism of Jean de Meung – were supplanting the abstract and the depersonalized. In every department of life Europe was reaching out for the personal, the idiosyncratic, the concrete; and that wonderfully contrived symmetry of seen and unseen, secular and theological, that scholasticism had stated philosophically no longer served.

Ruskin, in a famous passage, has dated the modern world from the moment that Raphael put theology on one wall, poetry on the other, of the Stanza del Signatura. When Christ and Apollo could be conceived as governing separate provinces the medieval synthesis was rent, and 'from that spot, and from that hour, the intellect and the art of Italy date their degradation'.[25] Perhaps so. But long before Raphael the lines between Apollo and Christ, this world and the next, nature and grace, reason and faith, were laid down; and if Ruskin had sought an earlier moment of fission he would have found it in an English Franciscan's subtle demonstration that 'everything can be explained by the act of will or by the impression of things'.

Before a genuinely natural philosophy resulting from the emancipation of nature could develop, however, it was necessary for European thought to contrive a new methodology in the interests of merely natural knowledge. Once the old instruments of discursive reason and logic were discredited by the nominalists, and the cosmological status of reason was impugned by the voluntarism of the great Reformers, man was left with a whole new

[25] *Pre-Raphaelitism* in *The Works*, XII, 148–50.

area of legitimate natural knowledge without the means of exploiting his new freedom. The realm of nature, now loosened from the realm of grace, lay invitingly before him, but he had lost the traditional instruments of knowledge in the post-Thomistic onslaught against rationalism. For the artist the problem of knowledge was irrelevant. He needed no conceptual tools or methodology except sensation itself, and Renaissance art, pictorial and literary, is made glorious by the eagerness and audacity with which it revels in the surfaces and sounds and textures and colors of sensation. But systematic thinkers are duller and more doctrinaire: they seek sanctions and build systems, and throughout the Renaissance they were aware of the burden which they could not cast off.

From every quarter, then, there rose the mutters or the thunders of discontent with the Schoolmen and their 'notional' aridities. Occasionally, and especially among the naturalists trained or influenced by northern Italian Aristotelians like Pomponazzi or Zabarella, there began to appear cautious efforts (usually sterilized by the doctrine of the double truth) toward a new methodology of reducing experience to systematic knowledge. But though the Renaissance was enchanted by the kind of individualism and voluntarism that had motivated the nominalists, they were too close to the theocratic tradition of the Middle Ages to achieve a genuine naturalism. Therefore while it remained the great work of the seventeenth century to formulate a new mathematical and scientific methodology for ascertaining the 'truth' about nature and its processes, the skeptics and malcontents of the late Renaissance could only acknowledge the impotence of traditional rationalism and libel the Schoolmen – only dimly realizing that those very acute thinkers whom they refused to read and were emotionally incapable of comprehending had construed the ends of knowledge in terms no longer operative.

The skeptics of the Renaissance went as far as it was possible to go in this strategy of discontent. They were skeptics, but until a genuine alternative to scholastic rationalism was forthcoming their skepticism could have only one outcome: the symbolic suicide of reason in fideism. For skepticism has historically always proved to be a way-station, never an end in itself. As Strowski has said, it is, rather than a doctrine, 'un certain équilibre de tendances diverses d'opinions contradictoires, qui s'opposent et se neutralisent'.[26] It is hard, if not impossible, to maintain the delicate equilibrium of disbelief that a genuine philosophic skepticism demands, but it is very easy to slip into either the moral irresponsibility of the libertine or the arrogant humility of the *dévot*.

Both alternatives are discernible in the Renaissance. Donne's *Songs and Sonnets* is a familiar example of the naturalistic skepticism – or skeptical naturalism – which rationalizes sexual and other license on the ground that moral codes have only the sanction of obsolete convention. But the pious skepticism which elevated God's inscrutable sovereignty at the expense of human reason is more common. In point of fact, it became commonplace – a fashionable affectation of such savants as Petrarch and Burton and many others who had read everything but lacked a Bacon's or a Descartes' compulsion to beat a straight path through the jungle of their tangled 'authorities'.

Petrarch here as elsewhere strikes the note of *echt* Renaissance urbanity: ironically deferring to the pretensions of the irreligious intellectuals of his day – that is, the Averroists – who scorned his humanistic piety embracing both the Bible and the pagan moralists, he professes a disarming skepticism of all secular philosophy; but though he is impervious to their naturalistic and impious explanations of all events on earth and in the heavens, he can always fall back on the higher knowledge of faith.

> How copious and how ridiculous are the vanities of philosophers, how many contradicting opinions show up; how great is their obstinacy, how great their impudence! Innumerable are the sects, innumerable the differences.[27]

As he wrote to Francesco Bruni in 1362, he could not trust his faculties or believe in anything – 'with the single exception of what I believe is a sacrilege to doubt'.[28] At its best – in Hooker and Milton, for instance – this attitude is one of the main planks in the platform of Christian humanism: it is that reverent and uncritical acceptance of the limits of human reason which must be complemented by the mysteries signalizing the incapacity of the unaided human intellect to penetrate all the ways of God.

But this kind of piety can easily lead to obscurantism, a progress which appalled Petrarch much more than certain of his posterity.

---

[26] *Montaigne*, p. 119. [27] *On his own Ignorance* in *PR*, p. 125.
[28] *Ibid.*, p. 35.

It is generically related to the nihilism and misanthropy of Marston's seventh satire in *The Scourge of Villainy*, but it immediately suggests that common Renaissance antagonism to learning which Bacon so eloquently denounced. For example, in his influential *De incertitudine et vanitate scientiarum et artium* (1531) Henry Cornelius Agrippa von Nettesheim lovingly and systematically exploited all the obscurant implications of his pious skepticism. Like that of such seventeenth-century zealots as William Dell, Agrippa's anti-intellectualism is always at the service of his piety. A German soldier, doctor, and (according to rumor) magician who once visited John Colet in England, Agrippa wandered and taught all over Europe. He dabbled in medicine, espionage, and occult philosophy; and although his notorious treatise on magic, *De occulta philosophia*, got him in trouble with the Inquisition, he lived and died a good Catholic. In his *De incertitudine* Agrippa's defense of his faith is simple: he attacks secular learning and reason that he may elevate the mysteries of his revealed religion.

He ridicules those 'pufft up with Humane Knowledge and Learning' who 'contemn and despise' the truths of a suprarational faith.

> Therefore these audacious Giants, these Enemies of the Scripture, are to be set upon, their Bulwarks and Castles are to be stormed: And it behooves us to shew how intolerable the blindness of Men is, to wander from the truth, misguided by so many Sciences and arts, and by so many Authors and Doctors thereof.[29]

It is clear, says Agrippa, that 'there is nothing more pernicious, nothing more destructive to the well-being of Men, or to the Salvation of our Souls', than a distorted emphasis of and reliance on man's secular attainments.[30] His book, consequently, is an essay in abuse of those worldly skills that made the Renaissance glorious. Poetry is dismissed as an art invented to employ 'lascivious Rhythms' and the 'jingling noise of fine words' to 'allure and charm the Ears of men addicted to folly'.[31] Scholastic theology, a 'Hodge-podge, or Mixture, of Divine Precepts, and Philosophical Reasons', looks like a centaur to a man of genuine piety.[32] The *summum bonum* sought by pagan philosophers and

---

[29] *The Vanity of Arts and Sciences*, 'To the Reader', sig. A3r–A3v.
[30] pp. 1–2.
[31] p. 21. Agrippa's strictures on poetry became the object of attack and rebuttal by many Elizabethan theorists; for example, see Sir John Harington, 'Preface, or rather a Briefe Apologie of Poetrie' prefixed to his translation of *Orlando Furioso* in *Elizabethan Critical Essays*, II, 199–200.   [32] p. 352.

the rational theologians whom they have corrupted is 'not to be attain'd or acquir'd by Stoick vertue, Academical Severity, or Peripatetick Speculation; but by Faith and Grace'.³³

And so the cascade pours forth. Agrippa's diatribe is by no means unique, however. His kind of skepticism has always been the easiest kind, and its popularity in the Renaissance was wide. Behind it lay Cusanus' *De docta ignorantia* and Pico's *Examen vanitatis doctrinae gentium*; ahead lay Suarez's *Quod nihil scitur* and Fulke Greville's *Treatie of Humane Learning*. They are only a few of the many books that used skepticism as a club to bludgeon the rational optimism and natural theology of the Renaissance.

The crowning work of this genre, of course, is Montaigne's monumental *Apology for Raymond Sebond*, a glittering masterpiece that fused the anti-intellectualism of the late Renaissance with the revived Pyrrhonism of Sextus Empiricus. Only a few decades earlier Rabelais could ridicule mere bookish skepticism as pedantic affectation: Trouillogan's noncommittal advice to Panurge about marriage is a parody of Pyrrhonism.³⁴ But in 1576 Montaigne adopted for his motto 'Que sçais-je', and for two years thereafter he was engaged on his ironic refutation of a proud natural theology. When he had finished, Sebond's arrogant mythology seemed to lie in ruins, and all the skeptical traditions of the Renaissance had received their most emphatic statement.

Montaigne's attack in this, the greatest of his essays, is the venerable notion of man's supremacy as a rational creature crowning a universe rationally conceived and sustained. 'Let us then for the nonce consider man alone', he says after he has paid Sebond his meager and ironic lip-service,

> without outside assistance, armed only with his own weapons, and destitute of the divine grace and knowledge, which comprise all his honour, his strength and the foundation of his being. Let us see how he will hold out in this fine equipment. Let him explain to me, by the force of his reason, on what foundation he has built those great advantages he thinks he has over the other creatures. What has induced him to believe that that wonderful motion of the heavenly vault, the eternal light of those torches rolling so proudly over his head, the awe-inspiring agitations of that infinite sea, were established, and endure through so many centuries, for his service and convenience?³⁵

---

³³ p. 153.
³⁴ Panurge explains (II, 36): 'he evades and avoids, shifts and escapes me, and quite slips and winds himself out of my gripes and clutches'.
³⁵ *Essays*, I, 441.

For such a disorderly writer, Montaigne proceeds to his business of destruction very systematically. He first compares man to the other animals, only to find that the brutes have many faculties – such as communication and even art – which man has arrogated to himself alone.[36] Man may be properly understood only as a part of nature, not as a special creation, and his greatest folly is to elevate himself so vaingloriously. 'Whatever is not as we are, is not worth a rap.'[37] Since nothing is fixed and certain, who can be dogmatic about values? Who is sure, after all, that what we call knowledge is better than what we call ignorance, or that one man is better than another? 'I have in my time seen a hundred artisans, a hundred labourers, wiser and happier than the rectors of the University, and whom I had much rather resemble.'[38]

Having in effect abolished the distinction between man and animal, Montaigne, like Sextus Empiricus, pauses to evaluate the alleged marvels of the human intellect. Certainly the great philosophers show man 'in his highest state',[39] and yet it is hard to tell which is sillier and more dogmatic, a Peripatetic, a Stoic, or an Epicurean. With their pretensions and their rival claims to ultimate 'truth' they cancel each other out. 'How much more docile and tractable, both to the laws of religion and to the civil laws, are simple and incurious minds, than those wits who supervise and pedantically hold forth on divine and human causes!'[40]

After all, what kind of knowledge *is* available to man? He 'cannot be anything but what he is, nor imagine anything beyond the reach of his capacity',[41] and therefore he debases the majesty of God when he construes him in his own pitiable image.[42] We claim to know nature, and yet we hide behind unexamined authority, accepting the 'more probable and attractive' because we have no faculties for genuine knowledge.[43] We cannot even know ourselves. Man babbles about his soul in the jargon of Aristotle and Galen, and proceeds to fantastic dogmatisms, all because 'it is very easy, the postulates being admitted, to build whatever we please'.[44] And what nonsense has been sanctified under the aegis of 'reason' – a touchstone full of falsity, error, weakness, and impotence.[45]

Montaigne thus obliterates the distinction between man and

[36] I, 451.　　　　[37] I, 480.　　　　[38] I, 481.
[39] I, 497.　　　　[40] I, 502.　　　　[41] I, 518.
[42] I, 511.　　　　[43] I, 538.　　　　[44] I, 541.
[45] I, 543.

beast, discredits the pretensions of systematic thought, laughs at alleged authorities, and scorns the possibility of mere natural knowledge of either man or God. In the last part of the *Apology*, then, he embroiders his rich variations on the theme of pride: 'to what a pitch of presumption and insolence do we not carry our blindness and our folly!'[46] The fact is, as the long and penetrating discussion makes clear, that man can know nothing but what his senses tell him – and he can never be sure that they are telling him the 'truth' about their objects out in nature. Our reason is worthless because it functions only on the data of sensation, and our sensation is worthless because we have no way of checking it against 'reality'. 'Thus, both within and without, man is full of weakness and falsehood.'[47]

Thus Montaigne marshals his multitudinous evidence to his purpose –

> to crush and tread under foot human pride and arrogance, to make them sensible of the inanity, the vanity and insignificance of man; to wrest out of their fists the miserable weapons of their reason; to make them bow the head and bite the dust under the authority and reverence of the divine majesty.[48]

The *Apology* is the most compelling statement of Renaissance skepticism. Ending as it does on a note of piety – as if the whole relentless demonstration of human frailty had been *ad majorem Dei gloriam* – from it Montaigne could have passed on to that fideism which lay beyond Pascal's *Entretien avec M. de Saci*. But the conclusion is only a stale and toneless hope for man's elevation 'by purely celestial means'.[49] As it stands, the *Apology* may be most properly construed as a frontal attack on traditional Renaissance optimism; thus, as Villey has pointed out, its whole movement is toward Pyrrhonism.[50] Beyond it, Renaissance skepticism could hardly go.

There is nothing in English literature quite like the *Apology*, but there are enough lesser works to indicate that Montaigne's discontent was not unique. Sir Walter Ralegh's little essay called *The Sceptic* – derivative as it is – suggests that the epistemological questions of the last part of the *Apology* were troubling people across the Channel. Ralegh is concerned solely with the validity

---

[46] I, 556.   [47] II, 44.   [48] I, 439–40.
[49] II, 53.
[50] *Les Sources & l'évolution des essais de Montaigne*, II, 185.

of sensation, and he reaches the virtually solipsistic conclusion that since man's sensory knowledge of external nature is probably no more accurate than animals', and since he can never know whether the data of sensation correspond accurately to the objects of sensation, each man lives in a private world of his own imagining. The scraping of a goat's horn is white, but the horn is black. Single grains of sand are hard, but in heaps they are soft. 'I may then report how these things appear; but whether they are so indeed, I know not.'[51] Although 'I know not' is good orthodox Pyrrhonism – and helps us understand Ralegh's shadowy reputation as an 'atheist' among his contemporaries – *The History of the World* was orthodox enough for generations of Puritans. With a subtle blend of Augustinian historiography and incipient deism, the larger work refers all unanswerable questions to the 'power infinite and eternal' whose sovereignty is manifested in every act of history:

> To inquire further, as of the essence of God, of his power, of his art, and by what means he created the world; or of his secret judgment, and the causes, is not an effect of reason; *sed cum ratione insaniunt*; 'but they grow mad with reason that inquire after it'.[52]

Such a relapse into theism was the usual resort of the Renaissance skeptic. At the opening of *Nosce Teipsum* Sir John Davies is fashionably incredulous:

> What can we know? or what can we discerne?
> When Error chokes the windowes of the Minde;
> The divers formes of things, how can we learne,
> That have been ever from our birth-day blind?[53]

But he asks such questions only to answer them like a devout believer. We know what God gives us to know, what is enough for salvation. Fulke Greville's *Treatie of Humane Learning* is similarly skeptical and pious. The human animal, says Greville, is lamentable. His senses are deluding, his imagination vain, his memory corrupted, his understanding vitiated by his innate (Calvinistic) depravity. Moreover, none of these 'naturall Defects' can be 'supplyed by Sciences and Arts', since philosophy, music, poetry, geometry are all built upon 'the false foundation of his Guilt'.[54] Greville's bleak poem is interesting because it combines

[51] *Works*, VIII, 556. [52] 'Preface', *Works*, II, lix.
[53] *Complete Poems*, I, 18. [54] Stanza 55.

RENAISSANCE SKEPTICISM

both the skeptical obscurantism of Calvin and the skeptical distrust of 'authority' trumpeted by his friend Bacon. He insists that our traditional knowledge should be revised through experience ('briefe in bookes, in practise long');[55] he is interested in political reform; he, like Montaigne, advocates a kind of primitivism to counteract the evils of civilization. But Greville's view of man's natural prospects is invincibly morose. Only the elect, the saints of God, can acquire real wisdom, and that is given them from above,

> Their Arts, Laws, Wisedome, Acts, Ends, Honors being
> All stamp'd and moulded in th' Eternall breast.[56]

The rest of us, tainted with sin and blinded with error, can only throw ourselves on God's mercy and hope for His unmerited grace. Heaven and hell are real, and the earth is only a snare. Therefore

> we must not to the world erect
> Theatres, nor plant our Paradise in dust,
> Nor build up Babels for the Divels elect;
> Make temples of our hearts to God we must;
> And then, as Godlesse wisedomes follies be,
> So are his lights our true Philosophie.[57]

In short, as Cornwallis had tritely said, 'our discerning but beget Opinions; and when we have said we thinke thus, our Knowledge is at the farthest'.[58]

In the trackless jungle of *The Anatomy of Melancholy* we can trace the most formidable statement of this skepticism. Burton had obviously read too many books – ' 'Tis most true, *tenet insanabile multos scribendi cacoethes*'[59] – and consulted too many clashing authorities; the result, in an unoriginal mind like his, was a repudiation of them all. 'We are, *ad unum omnes*, all mad', like children, except that they play with 'clouts & such toys' while 'we sport with greater baubles'.[60] Man is a passion-ridden beast: 'folly, melancholy, madness, are but one disease, *delirium* is a common name to all';[61] and so our ludicrous claims to reason, our systems and our dogmatisms, are all insane. Glutted with the

---

[55] Stanza 68.   [56] Stanza 131.   [57] Stanza 147.
[58] 'Of Ambition', *Essayes*, no. 10 (Allen, pt. I, p. 3A). Like many others, Cornwallis oscillated between skepticism and the most fragrant Renaissance optimism; see 'Of the admirable Abilities of the mind', *Essayes*, no. 52 (Allen, pt. II, pp. 235–7).
[59] I, 20.   [60] I, 46.   [61] I, 39.

learning of the Renaissance, Burton despises it; and, confronted by the audacious novelties of the new science, he is too apathetic to denounce them. To snatch the veil from the mystery is no more possible for religious 'fanatics' than for the system-spinning Schoolmen, and to tease our feeble minds to distraction with our efforts at comprehension is a mark of our futility.

> If God be infinitely and only good, why should he alter or destroy the World? if he confound that which is good, how shall himself continue good? if he pull it down because evil, how shall he be free from the evil that made it evil? &c. with many such absurd and brainsick questions, intricacies, froth of human wit, and excrements of curiosity, &c. which, as our Saviour told his inquisitive Disciples, are not fit for them to know. But hoo! I am now gone quite out of sight, I am almost giddy with roving about: I could have ranged farther yet, but I am an infant, and not able to dive into these profundities, or sound these depths, not able to understand, much less to discuss. I leave the contemplation of these things to stronger wits, that have better ability, and happier leasure, to wade into such Philosophical mysteries: for put case I were as able as willing, yet what can one man do?[62]

To assume the mask of Democritus was not to answer these perennial and imponderable questions, but it symbolized a weary man's contempt for 'so much talk of Religion, so much science, so little conscience, so much knowledge, so many preachers, so little practice, such variety of sects'.[63]

III. CUSTOM AND ERROR

Nothing indicates better the tonality of seventeenth-century thought than its vigorous development of this traditional Renaissance skepticism. If Montaigne and Burton could find no alternative to the abrogation of human reason before the evidence of its inadequacies, there were those who could – and they are the men who best represent the thought of the age. Not all of those who, like Burton, were dizzied by conflicting dogmatisms resorted to the evasions of skepticism. Although men as radically dissimilar as Bacon and Chillingworth and Browne and Milton were agreed that the first step to wisdom is doubt – *de omnibus dubitandum*, decreed Descartes – their quest was a reconstruction of truth rather than intellectual annihilation. The object of doubt is error and untested authority rather than the capacity for know-

[62] II, 68–9.   [63] I, 56.

CUSTOM AND ERROR

ledge itself. The genuine skeptic whom Earle ridicules – he who 'hangs in the balance with all sorts of opinions, whereof not one but stirs him and none sways him'[64] – is indeed rare in an age so compulsively bent on attaining truth. Though they might differ *toto caelo* in their conceptions of truth, the most muscular minds of the century would insist on the necessity of man's attaining it.

That is why Bacon's attack on merely destructive skepticism[65] finds so many echoes. The disenchantment with obsolete authorities implied the necessity of reform. The antiauthoritarian protest is one of the most insistent motifs of the age, and the corollary is obvious: if the alleged authorities are so patently inadequate, then they must be scrapped; men in quest of certainty must cut through the swamp of custom and error. At the very beginning of the century Gilbert voices the defiance that was to become conventional. Launching into the *De magnete*, he warns the reader to look for no urbane citations from the classics, their language like their opinions being obsolete. 'Our doctrine of the loadstone is contradictory of most of the principles and axioms of the Greeks' is a pronouncement that, projected against the background of most Renaissance 'science', rings like a brazen bell.[66]

Men like Gilbert and Galileo were movers and shakers, determined to reconstruct not only the objects but also the ways of knowledge; and their attack on authority was made imperative by their programs. But even though lesser thinkers, securely within the tradition of Renaissance culture, increasingly demanded the scrutiny of inherited values, we must not claim for them an intellectual independence which they would reject. The axiom of knowledge was too strong; Hooker's defense of epistemological optimism was too influential. Elizabethans as antipodal as Spenser and Nashe had agreed that a morality not founded on reason was an affront to both God and man – it would take but 'small learning' to 'confute so manifest a scandale' as Agrippa's *De incertitudine*, boasted Nashe[67] – and one of the main intellectual legacies of the new century was that Christian humanism informing the work of Chapman and Drayton and many others. For such men, nature still had a sacramental function of attesting the glory of God and a cognitive function of providing the

[64] *Microcosmography*, no. xxv.
[65] *NO*, I.xxxvii; cf. I.lxvii.
[66] *Of the Loadstone*, 'Author's Preface', p. l.
[67] *Pierce Pennilesse*, *Works*, I, 191.

grounds of moral truth. As Fuller tritely said, man's understanding and will 'are kept as it were in *Libera Custodia* to their objects of *Verum & Bonum*'[68] – an allocation that had served St Thomas and that could still serve many of his posterity.

Within this broad tradition, however, there was possible a good deal of discontent with various disciplines and authorities. For example, the anticlericalism which Erasmus had long before exploited so urbanely came to acquire new emphasis in the seventeenth century. When Milton inveighs against ecclesiastical authority – 'the dark, the bushy, the tangled forest' where the prelates would 'imbosk' to protect their sinecures[69] – or when Taylor gravely itemizes the dangers of compulsory doctrinal conformity,[70] both could find ample precedents in the Renaissance. Like their predecessors they can question an obsolete authority without denying man's proper thirst for truth. As we can learn from Chillingworth and Whichcote and More the course of events had forced a new flexibility in men's thinking, but it had not shaken their conviction that the coalescence of truth and goodness constituted the *summum bonum*. Their universe was still constructed along essentially moral lines, and for them *recta ratio* still retained its divine function of yielding to man that knowledge of nature from which he might infer the knowledge of God, and so, buttressed by faith and revelation, approach the throne of grace. Thus their antiauthoritarianism was directed not at the central and immemorial axiom of knowledge, but at the distortions and accretions which obscured the nature of truth and blocked man's progress toward it. Their aim was to restate the tenets of the old epistemology, not to forge a new one.

Consequently a good deal of more or less traditional antiauthoritarianism was without real significance in the seventeenth-century effort to establish new methods and objects of knowledge. As in the Renaissance, it was often antischolastic, but it was also extremely optimistic; for it was predicated on the assumption that error is not invincible, that truth, as Milton says, is the daughter of heaven which will be delivered by the midwife time. In England the Reformation had been a powerful stimulus to this sort of historical optimism, and the seventeenth century produced

---

[68] *The Holy State and the Profane State*, III, 11.
[69] *Of Reformation in England*, bk. I (*PW*, II, 389).
[70] *The Liberty of Prophesying*, VIII, 1–6 (*Works*, V, 483–93).

many men content, on the whole, to stay within the comfortable assumptions of a traditional optimism but none the less eager to expose and eliminate the errors inherited from a darker age.

Unquestionably the grossest of these errors, in the opinion of the average Englishman, were those represented by the dogma and discipline of the Catholic church. From the accession of Elizabeth until the inglorious exit of the last Stuart in 1688, fear and hatred of Rome, on both political and theological grounds, informed virtually every aspect of English thought. Certainly there can be little doubt that these passions generated much of the antischolastic and antiauthoritarian fervor of the seventeenth century. Apart from obscure recusants and Jesuit missionaries like Campion and Parsons and Fisher and Knott (the last two participants in notable controversies with Laud and Chillingworth), most of his contemporaries would agree with Hobbes that the Catholic hierarchy was a kingdom of darkness, and that the papacy was 'no other, than the Ghost of the deceased Romane Empire, sitting crowned upon the grave thereof'.[71] Anglicans like Hooker[72] and Browne might hold that not all things in the Council of Trent were to be condemned, nor all things in the Synod of Dort approved,[73] but the currents of nationalism and religious individualism were sufficiently strong to make such sophisticated views impossible for the vast majority.

Although we may turn to the increasingly oppressive Elizabethan statutes to trace the growing fear of Rome – statutes which in effect identified Catholicism with treason, and which brought nearly two hundred papists to a horrible death in the late sixteenth century[74] – such data are dull when compared, say, to the virulence of Spenser's portrait of Duessa. And Spenser, touched as he was with Puritanism, was only one among many. The obscene and artless abuse of Joan of Arc in *Henry VI*, or Deloney's heavy-handed intolerance,[75] or Nashe's view of Philip

[71] *Leviathan*, ch. xlvii (p. 381). For Hobbes's systematic indictment of Catholic error – religious and political – see *ibid.*, ch. xliv (p. 332), ch. xlvii (pp. 377–9).
[72] See the *Laws*, IV.viii.2, for example.
[73] *Religio Medici*, p. 6.
[74] See Smith, *A History of Modern Culture*, I, 473; Davies, *The Early Stuarts*, p. 202; Clark, *The Seventeenth Century*, p. 227. Conservative Puritan though he was, Richard Rogers was by no means an alarmist in noting (Knappen, *Two Elizabethan Puritan Diaries*, p. 80) that there were 'papistes in multitudes ready to come uppon us unawares'. The date of this entry, significantly, was August 1588.
[75] See *The Gentle Craft*, II.vii (*Works*, pp. 181 f.); 'A pleasant Dialogue betweene plaine Truth, and blind Ignorance', *The Garland of Good Will*, pt. II (*Works*, pp. 351–5).

II as a 'wolvish unnatural usurper'[76] suggest the popular taste to which popular writers catered. And not only popular writers: Burton describes recusants as 'collapsed Ladies, some few tradesmen, superstitious old folks',[77] and gleefully rehearses the common calumnies (if they were calumnies) about monastic practices: 'mastupration, satyriasis, priapismus, melancholy, madness, fornication, adultery, buggery, sodomy, theft, murder, and all manner of mischiefs'.[78] Donne – born a Catholic – wittily makes fun of Purgatory as a place decreed fashionable by the Council of Trent (a body whose business it was to change 'fables into Articles of faith');[79] Bacon denounces saints' lives and similar pious frauds as a major 'scandal and detriment of religion';[80] Jeremy Taylor first came to the notice of Laud with his famous sermon on the Gunpowder Plot, in which he learnedly and tediously underscored the Catholic threat. Milton, who detested Catholics as he detested atheists, brought against them the grievous charge of destroying the true inwardness of religion with their superstitious and compulsory rituals: they pervert baptism, he sneers, into 'a kind of exorcism', in which the water sanctified by Christ's own institute is thought ineffectual without 'the scratch or cross impression of a priest's forefinger'.[81] And if we tend to smile sometimes at Milton's crude and angry invective we must remember that both he and Locke (whose political liberalism makes Milton's look spotty and spasmodic) concurred in denying civil and religious toleration to atheists and Catholics alike. During the grave constitutional crisis of the late 'seventies, when fear of Rome degenerated into an obscene hysteria, even Tillotson, the apostle of the Latitudinarians, solemnly warned Commons that pagans, illumined only by the light of nature, were more trustworthy than papists.

Anti-Catholicism was, however, only one factor, if a very powerful one, in the seventeenth-century reconstruction of knowledge. The 'noble Eluctation of Truth; wherein, against the

---

[76] *Pierce Pennilesse, Works*, I, 184–5.   [77] *Anatomy*, III, 389.
[78] *Ibid.*, III, 280.
[79] *Ignatius His Conclave* in *Complete Poetry and Selected Prose*, pp. 360–1.
[80] *AL*, bk. I (*Works*, VI, 126).
[81] *Of Reformation in England*, bk. I (*PW*, II, 366). Perhaps because he was insufficiently aware of his monarch's machinations with Louis XIV, Bunyan could take a much more complacent view of the Catholic threat. Christian passes safely by the cave where the giants Pope and Pagan had holed up together, for Pagan was dead and Pope was grown so old and impotant that he could only bite his nails in frustration (*The Pilgrim's Progress*, p. 76).

CUSTOM AND ERROR

tenacity of Prejudice and Prescription, this Century now prevaileth', was in Browne's view a gradual process: the obscured Virgin was only half out of the pit, and each succeeding age must make its own contribution to the 'exaltation of Truth'.[82] The same melioristic motive informs Henry More's *Antidote against Atheism*, written so seasonably when the minds of men have at last been loosened 'from the awe and tyranny of mere accustomary Superstition'.[83] The twin villainies that young Milton repeatedly attacks are custom and error, that 'double tyranny' in church and state which it is the function of his age to demolish. For these evils would 'persecute and chase away all truth and solid wisdom out of human life' did not God, 'once in many ages', call upon His saints to 'repress the incroachments, and to work off the inveterate blots and obscurities wrought upon our minds'.[84] This passage strikes the genuine note of Milton's antiauthoritarianism: that strong, sometimes arrogant, conviction that nothing blocks man's well-being but a certain external and internal disequilibrium – custom over truth, passion over reason – which piety and education can speedily set right. As Donne had said long before in his third satire, truth is available to man, but through effort and seeking rather than prescription.

> On a huge hill,
> Cragged and steep, Truth stands, and hee that will
> Reach her, about must, and about must goe.

The characteristic tone of seventeenth-century thought – vigorously if sometimes philosophically naive – derives mainly from this discontent with compulsory instruments and objects of knowledge. Revealed truth excepted (and even Hobbes, in that devastating fourth book of the *Leviathan*, can cite Scripture to his purpose), there was an increasing reluctance to yield unanimous and uncritical allegiance to any inherited set of values. In the rolling rhetoric of *The Advancement of Learning* Bacon surveys, only to dismiss as 'impediments' to the great instauration which he was demanding, most of the intellectual disciplines of the European tradition. In the metaphor of the four idols in the *Novum Organum* he embellishes the same text:

---

[82] *Christian Morals*, II.v.   [83] I.i.1.
[84] *The Doctrine and Discipline of Divorce*, 'To the Parliament of England' (*PW*, III, 172).

> In order to penetrate into the inner and further recesses of nature, it is necessary that both notions and axioms be derived from things by a more sure and guarded way; and that a method of intellectual operation be introduced altogether better and more certain.[85]

Pascal ironically comments that 'en verité, le monde devient méfiant et ne crois les choses que quand il les voit',[86] but the quip, coming from a Jansenist, was truer than he wished. Dr Donne of St Paul's, though certainly no Baconian, made it a cardinal principle of his theology that, if man despaired of his capacity for rational knowledge, he could only sink into an 'incapable and barren stupidity'.[87] *Mutatis mutandis*, it was an attitude that is discernible almost everywhere.

The man who in the *Religio Medici* had skirted the fringes of fideism in his desire to follow the great wheel of his church also wrote the *Pseudodoxia Epidemica* on the most approved Baconian principles: Browne grimly catalogues many causes for man's proneness to err – the Fall of Adam, credulity, supinity, the unceasing work of Satan[88] – but he trains his heaviest guns on the monster of authority. Most books and doctrines that command respect from the vulgar we must regard 'as things unsaid, and account them but in the list of nothing'.[89] In mathematics and natural philosophy – the proper areas for man's intellectual efforts – authority can carry no weight whatever, and though 'allowable' in moral philosophy, rhetoric, law, and history, even there it 'admitteth many restrictions'.[90] The reason is clear: 'an argument from Authority to wiser examinations is but a weaker kind of proof; it being but a topical probation, and as we term it, an inartificial argument, depending upon a naked asseveration . . . it carrieth not with it the reasonable inducements to knowledge'.[91]

Truth was the celestial city of the seventeenth century, and the urge to attain it was no less ardent than the conviction that it was attainable. The moving words of the ever-memorable Mr John Hales could stand as an epitaph for his generation:

> For the pursuit of truth hath been my only care, ever since I first understood the meaning of the word. For this I have forsaken all hopes, all

---

[85] *NO*, I.xviii (*Works*, VIII, 71).
[86] *Lettres Provinciales*, no. i (*Œuvres*, pp. 436–7).
[87] *Works*, II, 277.   [88] I.i-x.
[89] I.vii (*Works*, II, 55).   [90] I.vii (*Works*, II, 52).
[91] I.vii (*Works*, II, 50).

friends, all desires, which might bias me, and hinder me from driving right at what I aimed. For this I have spent my money, my means, my youth, my age, and all I have, that I might remove from myself that censure of Tertullian – *Suo vitio quis quid ignorat?*[92]

Henry More refused the luxury of a religion that turned its back on reason – 'to give no other account of the Nature of God and his ways than that they are unintelligible, is to encourage the Atheist, and yield him the day'[93] – for however wide their differences, he and most of his contemporaries clung fast to the central legacy of Renaissance thought: that as a rational creature man finds his highest good in knowledge. The significant seventeenth-century contribution to the tradition, however, was that a healthy skepticism of untested authority must precede the fruition of knowledge. All men sought truth, and most of them were sure they could find it, but they were agreed that a truth resting supinely on authority or one incompatible with reason was no better than error.

On this point, as on so many others, Descartes speaks for his age. His education by the Jesuits at La Flèche had left him glutted with knowledge but skeptical of all he had been taught. 'For I found myself embarrassed with so many doubts and errors that it seemed to me that the effort to instruct myself had no effect other than the increasing discovery of my own ignorance.'[94] Consequently, as he thought, his course was clear: to sweep 'completely away' his former opinions accepted by the habit of authority, 'so that they might later on be replaced, either by others which were better, or by the same, when I had made them conform to the uniformity of a rational scheme'.[95] And again he echoes Bacon:

> Not that indeed I imitated the sceptics, who only doubt for the sake of doubting, and pretend to be always uncertain; for, on the contrary, my design was only to provide myself with good ground for assurance, and to reject the quicksand and mud in order to find the rock or clay.[96]

It was with the same self-sufficiency that Spinoza, in a letter to Hugo Boyel, remarks that the 'authority of Plato, Aristotle, and Socrates has not much weight with me',[97] that Milton launches

---

[92] Quoted by Tulloch, *Rational Theology and Christian Philosophy*, I, 213.
[93] *Divine Dialogues*, p. 29.   [94] *Discourse*, pt. I (*Works*, I, 83).
[95] *Discourse*, pt. II (*Works*, I, 89).   [96] *Discourse*, pt. III (*Works*, I, 99).
[97] *Letters*, no. LVI (Wild, p. 457). But observe Spinoza's acute analysis of the errors of a sterile skepticism in *On the Improvement of the Understanding*, Wild, p. 17.

his attack on the twin evils of custom and error, that Glanvill does battle with Stubbe. By the timorous acquiescence of authority we must conclude that its stamp 'can make Leather as current as God; and that there's nothing so contemptible, but Antiquity can render it august, and excellent'.[98]

IV. NATURE AND GRACE

This endemic antiauthoritarianism of the seventeenth century found its main target in the tradition of scholasticism. Here, as so often when we try to follow the sinuous paths of intellectual history, we must allow for a certain looseness of language. Just as 'reason' meant very unlike things to Bacon, to Milton, to Hobbes, to Taylor, to Descartes, so such roughly synonymous words as 'scholastic', 'Aristotelian', 'notional', and 'peripatetic' resist rigid definition. They served as triggers for the release of emotion rather than as signs for that body of Christian philosophy between Erigena and Ockham; but because they were made to bear the brunt of the immense discontent with certain inherited attitudes and assumptions they can tell us much about the intellectual temper of the age.

Under all the smoke and noise of the attack on scholasticism we can discern some basic points of friction between the values that had sustained the Middle Ages and those that the seventeenth century was slowly evolving. If, as T. E. Hulme has said, the Middle Ages could accept certain propositions as facts,[99] we may now see that the late Renaissance could at best view them as doctrines, at worst as fictions of the ill-disciplined human mind. For an age with so strong a compulsion to demolish error and achieve truth the whole fabric of medieval thought could only be gravely suspect. In the great nominalistic reaction to scholastic rationalism, Europe had shifted its center of intellectual gravity from God to man, from grace to nature, from theology to philosophy, from supernaturalism to naturalism; consequently a readjustment of the objects and methods of knowledge was made inevitable.

Mr Willey has commented on the 'transference of interest from metaphysics to physics, from the contemplation of Being to the

---

[98] *The Vanity of Dogmatizing*, p. 186
[99] *Speculations*, p. 51.

NATURE AND GRACE

observation of Becoming'.[100] The same thesis informs Whitehead's interpretation of modern intellectual history. Although it is a transference easier to summarize than to trace, an obvious factor – which may be regarded both as a symptom and a cause – was the cordial vilification poured on the obsolescent tradition of scholasticism after the fifteenth century. For all its conceptual sophistication, medieval thought was essentially anthropomorphic. In a way that Protagoras and Gorgias would not have liked, the Schoolmen made man the measure of all things, disciplining their imaginative and intellectual constructs to the wants and needs of the human soul as contained within the limits of Christian dogma. Like Aristotle, they viewed nature as an organism in which purpose and end were the supreme considerations; and, in a way that their posterity found increasingly repugnant, they tended to locate these purposes and ends within those values projected from human fears, fancies, and aspirations. Under the habit of theological, political, and intellectual authority, and because they preferred to place man above rather than in nature, they were content to construe all experience in the hallowed Aristotelian categories of substance, essence, quality, and the like – categories formulated by and dependent for their validity upon the fertile mind of man.

By the middle of the seventeenth century, however, the sacramental view of nature was waning, so that, as Descartes' dualism makes clear, mind and matter were thought to represent two distinct kinds of reality. Moreover, the knowledge of matter – or of matter in motion – came to be regarded as virtually if not entirely without moral implications. In short, men were coming to look upon nature as finally loosened from moral or theological anchors, and therefore in mechanistic rather than organic terms. Viewing nature as a machine constructed (perhaps by God) in accordance with certain abstract and mathematically describable principles, the most influential minds of the seventeenth century were increasingly interested in space, mass, and energy. For them the great foci of medieval thought – which an eminent and sympathetic historian has called 'the finite and the infinite, act and potency, matter and form, essence and existence, individuality and individuation, efficiency and finality, sensation and thought, the spiritual soul and the material body'[101] – had lost their fascina-

[100] *The Seventeenth Century Background*, p. 6.
[101] De Wulf, *History of Mediaeval Philosophy*, II, 315.

tion. It is true, as we learn from Bacon and Descartes, that the 'new men' were not able to dispense entirely with the intellectual habits they came to despise, nor is it likely that they were aware of all the implications of their protests against scholasticism. But to an extraordinary degree they knew what they wanted to do, and why. Their success justifies Whitehead's famous tag, the century of genius.

In the nature of things, intellectual revolutions of such dimensions cannot be precipitate. We may carefully separate out the strands of novelty in the thinking of a Galileo or a Descartes, but we must remember that even such giants as they still operated within an ancient and very powerful framework of ideas, while many, perhaps most, of their lesser contemporaries went about their business without realizing at all that they were living through a crisis in the history of thought. When Thomas Kyd has the mother of the murdered Horatio invoke heaven, she does so without reference to either St Thomas or Thomas Digges, yet we can only believe that she represents the immense and silent majority of the age.

> Ay, there sits my Horatio,
> Backed with a troop of fiery cherubins,
> Dancing about his newly healed wounds,
> Singing sweet hymns and chanting heavenly notes,
> Rare harmony to greet his innocence,
> That died, ay died, a mirror in our days.[102]

For her and people like her, questions of essence and substance were as remote as those of mass and energy: she was finding what comfort she could in an ancient religion whose values were human, pictorial, almost tactile. But allowing for the obvious fact that most people of the sixteenth and seventeenth centuries were incapable of understanding and uninterested in the refinements of conceptual thought, we must also take account of those who knowingly defended the old against the new.

For one thing, even scholastic logic – which came to be the most despised element of scholasticism – could claim the allegiance of many intelligent men. It was a system that worked after a fashion, and it was a prized component of those values that had largely sustained the Renaissance. Based on the essentials of the

[102] *The Spanish Tragedy*, IV.i.

NATURE AND GRACE

ten Aristotelian categories and the syllogism, it seemed to give men a kind of truth sufficient for their needs. Beginning with the 'predicables' constituting the content of logical discourse – which, according to Thomas Wilson, 'shewe the largenesse & the narrownesse of woordes, how ferre thei dooe extende, and how moche thei comprehende in them'[103] – one could proceed systematically and majestically toward the syllogism, and so to truth. There were the antepredicaments (genus, species, difference, property, accident) which define anything whatever; the ten categories which were the predicaments proper; and the postpredicaments, that is, the 'affections' of things depending on their disposition in the categories (for example, cause and effect, contradiction). Having learned the first two by rote, one could apply the syllogism to work his way through the third to certainty. For with a confidence at once sublime and naive, the advocates of this logic could insist that its end was certainty. 'There is none other difference' between logic and reason itself, says Wilson, except that 'Logique is a Greke woorde, and Reason is an English woorde'.[104] Logic is nothing more nor less than God's gift to fallen man, who through the sweet discourse of reason might repair the ravages of Adam's sin and restore his corrupted faculties. Moreover, in those areas where logic was inoperative, there was ready at hand the higher truth of revelation.

Wilson, whom I have been quoting, wrote in the middle of the sixteenth century. A hundred years later we find the irascible Alexander Ross damning Sir Kenelm Digby for his strictures on Aristotelian logic[105] and the more temperate Seth Ward answering John Webster's influential *Academiarum Examen* in terms which Wilson would have approved.[106] But we must remember that it was university dons, the panjandrums of conservatism, who clung most tenaciously to that logic which Bacon and Descartes and Hobbes – to say nothing of Ramus – held in contempt. Toward the end of the sixteenth century Gabriel Harvey observed that Wilson's *Rule of Reason* was 'the dailie bread of owr common pleaders, & discoursers';[107] in his effort to save the Elizabethan settlement Archbishop Parker, in his Advertisements of 1566 and

---

[103] *The Rule of Reason*, fol. 3ᵛ.
[104] *Ibid.*, fol. 1ʳ.
[105] *The Philosophical Touch-stone*, pp. 63–4.
[106] For example, see *Vindiciae Academiarum*, pp. 23–6.
[107] *Marginalia*, p. 122.

in his other attacks on Puritan dissidents, tried to salvage a large part of the scholastic tradition;[108] an Oxford statute provided a fine for those students daring to depart from the method of Aristotle's *Organon*;[109] such popular and unlearned writers as Dekker drew uncritically on the scholastic lore of Thomas Hibernicus' *Flores doctorum*; John Earle ridiculed the 'self-conceited man' who would prefer Ramus to Aristotle or Paracelsus to Galen;[110] the mighty Selden thought that without 'schoole Divinity a Divine knowes nothing Logically, nor will be able to satisfye a rationall man out of the pulpitt'.[111] In short, the tradition of reason and authority which Hooker so nobly argued and which Laud died in trying to preserve had by no means spent its force at the end of the Renaissance. 'We should be slow and unwilling to change, without very urgent necessity, the ancient ordinances, rites, and long approved customs, of our venerable predecessors.'[112]

And yet within a couple of generations after Hooker's death an Anglican bishop could make merry sport of the Schoolmen's absurdities.

> They began with some general Definitions of the things themselves [i.e. 'those Arts, which Aristotle had drawn into Method, or the more speculative parts of our Divinity'], according to their universal Nature: Then divided them into their parts, and drew them out into several propositions, which they laid down as Problems: those they converted on both sides: and by many niceties of Arguments, and citations of Authorities, confuted their Adversaries, and strengthened their own dictates.[113]

Sprat's conventional contempt shows that in the earlier seventeenth century opposition to the whole tradition of scholasticism had mounted steadily. Moreover, it had mounted on two great fronts at once: the secular and the religious. As the century advanced it was urged, with increasing emphasis, that a servile reliance on the medieval tradition was inimical to both natural philosophy and piety.

The attack on scholastic logic as an inadequate instrument of natural truth was directed *au fond* at scholastic rationalism. As we

---

[108] See Bettenson, *Documents of the Christian Church*, pp. 338–40; cf. Tulloch, *Rational Theology and Christian Philosophy*, I, 56.
[109] Jones, *Ancients and Moderns*, p. 287, n. 2.
[110] *Microcosmography*, no. xi.
[111] *Table Talk*, p. 80. See his remarks on Aristotle (p. 131): 'There never breath'd that p[er]son to whom mankind was more beholding.'
[112] *Laws*, V.vii.3.
[113] Sprat, *The History of the Royal Society*, p. 16.

NATURE AND GRACE

have seen, this rationalism construed God, His works, and the operations of the human mind as all exemplifying the essentially rational order of the universe. For English-speaking peoples, it is the view that has been given its consummate statement by Hooker; in the larger European tradition its greatest spokesman is St Thomas. But whatever its lineage and its prestige, it collided squarely with the emerging naturalism of the seventeenth century. The crucial point of opposition was the scholastic assumption that the realm of nature is to be understood by those allegedly *a priori* ideas of order and reason and purpose that are actually spun out of the mind of man. If, as Ockham and Calvin had argued, the inscrutable ways of God lie beyond the scope of man's reason, then he must seek to understand those things which he can. The Averroists, the northern Italian naturalists like Pomponazzi and Zabarella and Galileo, and the English empiricists headed by Bacon agreed that such things lay within the realm of nature. This was a realm scrupulously discriminated from that of theology and the supernatural; for it was a realm whose workings, while supremely orderly (and probably mechanistic) were in no way dependent on the 'notional' or rational presuppositions of the human mind. Conversely, truths proper to faith were supernatural and therefore not amenable to the methods and demonstrations of natural knowledge. Since it is an article of faith that the soul is immortal, said Pomponazzi at the close of his remarkable treatise in which he had jeopardized that 'truth' by purely natural reason, it ought to be proved only by the instruments proper to faith – 'revelation and canonical Scripture'. Any other reasons are 'foreign' and inadmissible, and philosophers would do well to remember that the two orders of truth – revealed and natural – have their sharp limits and yield no reciprocal proof.[114]

Such a bifurcation of truth made inevitable the incessant attacks on the notional and syllogistic method of the Schoolmen, the incessant demands that men evolve a new method of observing and describing the truths of nature. To say, as St Thomas had said,[115] that heavenly bodies are incorruptible because their movement is circular and therefore perfect does violence to the observable facts; it is to superimpose upon the processes of nature a set of spurious and rational presuppositions for ulterior theological

[114] *On the Immortality of the Soul*, ch. xv (*RP*, p. 379).
[115] *ST*, II.lxxxv.6.

ends. Let theology and nature be properly segregated, and both will benefit. As the Reformers had insisted, the ways of God must be believed through revelation, not inferred from quasi-moral philosophy; and, as others went on to say, such moral philosophy can be neither very moral nor very philosophical. When man can learn to believe what he must believe for salvation and to know what he may know by the instruments of natural knowledge, then the great instauration will be at hand:

> For if any man shall think by view and inquiry into these sensible and material things to attain that light whereby he may reveal unto himself the nature or will of God, then indeed is he spoiled by vain philosophy: for the contemplation of God's creatures and works produceth (having regard to the works and creatures themselves) knowledge; but having regard to God no perfect knowledge, but wonder, which is broken knowledge.[116]

To understand the temper of seventeenth-century thought it is, I think, impossible to stress too strongly this segregation of the natural from the supernatural. Both Calvin and Bacon were potent in causing that segregation, and they both – otherwise so dissimilar – hammered ceaselessly on its necessity. Calvin labored to save supernaturalism from aggressive Renaissance secularism and skepticism, Bacon to free nature from the decadent though still powerful scholastic supernaturalism. Calvin revived an Augustinian God of unqualified will whose secret counsels, such as election and reprobation, imposed awful limits on man's rational comprehension; Bacon trumpeted the emancipation of a nature which man could hope to observe, describe, and understand for his own 'commodity'. But both insisted that to segregate the realms of grace and nature was the beginning of wisdom.

Thus the second book of the *Institutes* is a sustained attack on naturalism. Like Montaigne later, Calvin presents man as he is, not as he thinks he is; and against the view that his natural knowledge (even though supplemented here and there by revelation) suffices for well-being in this world and salvation in the next Calvin hurls the doctrine of innate depravity. For the outrageous pretensions of the 'sophists of the Sorbonne, those Pelagians of the present age',[117] he has only contempt. Even in his fallen state man still retains such glimmerings of his pristine virtue as are

---

[116] *AL*, bk. I (*Works*, VI, 95–6).   [117] *Institutes*, II.iii.13.

sufficient for the conduct of civil polity, domestic economy, and the mechanical arts and sciences. But when the faculty of reason is illegitimately used to seek out the ultimate designs of God in creating and sustaining His universe, its impotency is at once revealed. 'Human reason, then, neither approaches, nor tends, nor directs its views toward this truth, to understand who is the true God, or in what character he will manifest himself to us.'[118] All the central doctrines of Calvinism signalize this dichotomy between God's will and man's reason. Predestination, for example, poses insurmountable obstacles to man's comprehension: 'If, therefore, we can assign no reason why he grants mercy to his people but because such is his pleasure, neither shall we find any other cause but his will for the reprobation of others. For when God is said to harden or show mercy to whom he pleases, men are taught by this declaration to seek no cause beside his will.'[119]

Calvin tried to save dogma from reason, Bacon to free natural knowledge from theology, and the efforts of both led to what Mr Woodhouse has called the Protestant principle of segregation. This means the rigid discrimination of the spiritual and the secular, the supernatural and the natural, theology and morality, faith and works, goodness and knowledge; and although its initial impulse, in the great Reformers, was to combat the drift toward a natural religion of overreaching rationalism, its result in the next century was to isolate religion beyond such secular concerns as money-making, politics, and science.

V. BACON

It is at this point that Bacon's true significance emerges. Although his vaunted methodology could lead nowhere and his 'science' was at best questionable, he was a born propagandist. He made a powerful case for that bifurcation of nature and grace, arguing on secular grounds the principle which Ockham and Calvin had argued on religious grounds. As the second book of the *Novum Organum* shows, his cumbersome methodology for exploiting man's franchise for natural knowledge is often ludicrous, but his powerful defense of that franchise provided a rationale for some of the most characteristic thought of the seventeenth century. As

[118] *Ibid.*, II.ii.18.   [119] *Ibid.*, III.xxii.11.

Cowley told the Restoration, English thinkers had wandered helplessly in scholastic error until

> Bacon, like Moses, led us forth at last,
> The barren wilderness past,
> Did on the very Border stand
> Of the blest promis'd Land,
> And from the Mountain's Top of his Exalted Wit,
> Saw it himself, and shew'd us it.[120]

Not without reason did Thomas Sprat, in recording the history of the Royal Society, urge that there was no more appropriate preface than the works of the learned Verulam.

The antirationalistic – that is, the antischolastic – bias of Bacon's thought, though not as deep as he believed, was what most impressed his contemporaries and immediate posterity. His contempt for the system-spinning abstractions of the Schoolmen is matched only by his confidence in the possibilities of man's emancipated intellect. Once he abandons the futile and impious search for first causes, relinquishes the effort to make theology rational and knowledge moral, and shakes off the dead weight of scholastic authority, he can then proceed to the observation, description, and control of natural processes. Divinity is 'grounded only upon the word and oracle of God, and not upon the light of nature: for it is written, *Coeli enarrant gloriam Dei*, but it is not written, *Coeli enarrant voluntatem Dei*'.[121] Indeed, one of the main tokens of God's wisdom is that in closing to man's questing mind certain areas of truth which He has chosen to give us through revelation, He has left us free to explore others by our natural faculties. Thus are both piety and knowledge served. It is to the glory of Christianity that 'it excludeth and interdicteth human reason, whether by interpretation or anticipation, from examining or discussing of the mysteries and principles of faith'.[122] The reaches of human reason are not boundless, as the Schoolmen had seemed to suggest; and it is imperative that we remember its limitations.

> The first, that we not so place our felicity in knowledge, as we forget our mortality. The second, that we make application of our knowledge to give ourselves repose and contentment, and not distaste or repining. The third, that we do not presume by the contemplation of nature to attain to the mysteries of God.[123]

[120] 'To the Royal Society' in Sprat, *The History of the Royal-Society*, sig. B2ᵛ.
[121] *AL*, bk. II (*Works*, VI, 394). [122] *Valerius Terminus*, *Works*, VI, 65.
[123] *AL*, bk. I (*Works*, VI, 94–5).

It was in ignoring such checks that the Schoolmen had vitiated European thought for long centuries. They were guilty of the intellectual pride which jeopardized both piety and sound natural knowledge:

> But as in the inquiry of the divine truth their pride inclined to leave the oracle of God's word and to vanish in the mixture of their own inventions, so in the inquisition of nature they ever left the oracle of God's works and adored the deceiving and deformed images which the unequal mirror of their own minds or a few received authors and principles did represent unto them.[124]

Thus, foisting off their radical errors as truth, they have shown the modern age

> the extreme prejudice which both religion and philosophy have received and may receive by being commixed together; as that which undoubtedly will make an heretical religion, and an imaginary and fabulous philosophy.[125]

All this, it is hardly necessary to say, is ancillary to Bacon's main purpose of enfranchising man's pursuit of natural knowledge. In preaching the great instauration he draws together those strands of empiricism and utilitarianism which were to dominate English thought of the seventeenth century. Not only does he demand the emancipation of natural knowledge; he insists that it is man's great mandate to employ it for his 'commodity'. Bacon's thought is secular through and through. He denies the Socratic identification of knowledge with virtue in order to make his new equation of knowledge and power. 'But man must know, that in this theatre of man's life it is reserved only for God and angels to be lookers on.'[126] The Thomistic ideal of a life dedicated to the contemplation of truth gives way to a pulsating concern with man's immediate well-being, a concern which, by some strange alchemy, is itself invested with divine sanction. Philosophy comes to mean natural philosophy: 'the Inquisition of Causes, and the Production of Effects; Speculative, and Operative; Natural Science, and Natural Prudence'.[127] Man's first

---

[124] *AL*, bk. I (*Works*, VI, 124); cf. *NO*, I.lxxxix.
[125] *AL*, bk. II (*Works*, VI, 213).
[126] *AL*, bk. II (*Works*, VI, 314). Note Bacon's criticism of Telesio (whom he generally admired as one of the 'new men'): Telesio's philosophy is ultimately unsatisfactory simply because he 'contemplates the world placidly and at its ease' (*On Principles and Origins*, *Works*, X, 385).
[127] *AL*, bk. II (*Works*, VI, 214).

offense was not the pursuit of knowledge, but the pursuit of the wrong kind of knowledge – divine rather than natural.[128] It is God's will that man should discover and control those processes by which He sustains His temporal creation, that he seek to know not wherefrom but the 'moving principle' whereby natural effects are produced. 'For the former tend to discourse, the latter to works.'[129] The one impiously seeks first causes, the other glorifies God by disciplining nature to the advantage of His creatures. 'And although the highest generality of motion or summary law of nature God should still reserve within his own curtain, yet many and noble are the inferior and secondary operations which are within man's sounding.'[130]

The knowledge within man's sounding is the knowledge proper for man, and to acquire it means the purposeful observation of those natural effects from which may be inferred natural causes. All else is bigotry and superstition. To relapse comfortably into explanations which explain nothing – to ascribe the events of nature to the providence of God,[131] to search vainly for the final cause or the secret will of God,[132] to derive knowledge from *a priori* assumptions rather than closely observed 'facts' – is to ignore our divine mandate for understanding and thus controlling nature. 'But for my part I do not trouble myself with any such speculative and withal unprofitable matters. My purpose, on the contrary, is to try whether I cannot in very fact lay more firmly the foundations, and extend more widely the limits, of the power and greatness of man.'[133] The Schoolmen, attempting an unholy marriage of divine and natural knowledge, had done disservice to both God and man with their baseless abstractions; Bacon is content, and generally he taught his seventeenth-century disciples to be content, with a knowledge more circumscribed but more immediately profitable. 'I am not raising a capitol or pyramid to the pride of man, but laying a foundation in the human understanding for a holy temple after the model of the world.'[134] The

---

[128] *AL*, bk. I (*Works*, VI, 138).
[129] *NO*, I.lxvi (*Works*, VIII, 95–6).
[130] *Valerius Terminus*, *Works*, VI, 32.
[131] *AL*, bk. II (*Works*, VI, 228). In his study of Henry VII Bacon is characteristically ironical in treating providence as a principle of historical causality (*Works*, XI, 190, 246–67, for example).
[132] *Valerius Terminus*, *Works*, VI, 29; cf. *NO*, I.xlviii.
[133] *NO*, I.cxvi (*Works*, VIII, 147).
[134] *NO*, I.cxx (*Works*, VIII, 151).

model of the world: the phrase suggests how hopelessly fractured was St. Thomas's large, round vision; but it also announces that man, in his long effort to understand himself, was taking a significantly new direction.

VI. ANTI-SCHOLASTICISM

Bacon's double-pronged attack on both the theology and the philosophy of the Schoolmen gathered many followers. In a century trying to feel its way toward a new conception of truth there was a broad movement to reduce religion to those few clear and distinct essentials which were proving so fruitful in science. It is too much to say that all who cried out against the tortuous subtleties of scholastic theology were verging toward deism, but there was an increasing demand for a religion without the miniscule refinements of doctrine which had been the glory and the bane of medieval theology and which were splintering Puritanism into dozens of competing sects. The generating impulse of the Reformation had been to restore the primal authority of the Scriptures from the clashing dogmatisms of scholastic rationalism. In the reaction to the interminable controversies over realism and nominalism, essence and potentiality, individuality and individuation, men like Luther and Tyndale and Calvin could only restate the unique, divine importance of the Bible over the self-indulgent theorizing of the Schoolmen.

At the Leipzig Disputation, so one of his scandalized opponents reported, Luther had denied

> that the Church was built upon Peter: 'Upon this rock, etc.' And though I quoted to him Augustine, Jerome, Ambrose, Gregory, Cyprian, Chrysostom, Leo and Bernard, with Theophilus, he contradicted them all without a blush; and said he would stand alone against a thousand, though supported by no other, because Christ is the only foundation of the Church, for other foundation can no man lay.[135]

Erasmus, though certainly no Reformer, never tired of ridiculing the absurdities of the Schoolmen. He unceasingly preached the simple essentials of a good life, and he marshaled all his erudition to restore the Bible itself to its textual purity; but he had no head for scholastic disputation. 'The Freedom of the Will is a thorny question which it profits us little to debate; let us leave it to the

---

[135] Bettenson, *Documents of the Christian Church*, p. 272.

professed theologians.'¹³⁶ Tyndale was characteristically more blunt:

> Twenty doctors will expound one text twenty ways, as children make descant upon plain song. Then our sophisters . . . with an ante-theme of half an inch, will draw out a thread of nine days long. Yea, thou shalt find enough that will preach Christ and prove whatsoever point of the faith thou wilt, as well out of a fable of Ovid or any other poet as out of St John's Gospel or Paul's Epistles.¹³⁷

In the seventeenth-century recoil from the intricacy and violence of contemporary theological controversy this kind of anti-scholasticism received a new impetus. When Chillingworth complained that the scholastics exterminate reason and common sense in 'weaving and unweaving subtle cobwebs, fitter to catch flies than souls', he was calling for a return to that simple but active piety jeopardized in an age of incessant doctrinal warfare.¹³⁸ Although the Schoolmen had been a formative influence on Donne's theology, he was sufficiently of his age to insist that man's first duty was not 'a contemplation of God sitting in heaven, but of God working on earth'.¹³⁹ For him, religion should give tone and color to every act; a true piety is manifested by purposeful moral conduct. 'Thinkest thou that thou wast made to be *Cos Amoris*, a Mole in the Face for Ornament, a Man of delight in the World?'¹⁴⁰ In a way suggestive of Whichcote's incessant concern with practical morality Jeremy Taylor, one of the greatest preachers in his or any other century, refused to discuss 'the evils of sin by any metaphysical and abstracted effects', but only by its corrosive effects in daily life.¹⁴¹ The arid intellectualism of the Schoolmen can mean nothing in time of trouble; and

> when in sickness we forget all our knotty discourses of philosophy, and a syllogism makes our head ache, and we feel our many and loud talkings served no lasting end of the soul, no purpose that now we must abide by, and that thy body is like to descend to the land where all things are forgotten; then she lays aside all her remembrances of applauses, all her ignorant confidences, and cares only to know Christ Jesus and him crucified, to know him plainly, and with much heartiness and simplicity.¹⁴²

---

[136] Allen, *Erasmus: Lectures and Wayfaring Sketches*, p. 90.
[137] Quoted by Tulloch, *Rational Theology and Christian Philosophy*, I, 39.
[138] *Works*, I, 47.   [139] *LXXX Sermons*, p. 376.
[140] *XXVI Sermons*, p. 343.   [141] *Sermons*, p. 61.
[142] *Holy Dying*, III.vi.

ANTI-SCHOLASTICISM

Since the Bible, which tells us all we need to know for salvation, is available to 'the most unlearned person', why do we perplex our minds and affront our God with sophistries? 'The wit of man cannot more plainly tell us our duty, or more fully, than the Holy Ghost hath done already.'[143] 'Bring me a Soul,' cries John Hales,

> not one deeply learn'd, sharp and subtil, *Sed simplicem, rudem, & impolitam, & qualem habet, qui eum solum habet,* as Tertullian speaks, a dull, a silly, an unletter'd one, and such an one as that Man hath, that hath nothing else but his Soul to witness him to be a Man, and even this shall with ease apprehend what is necessary to save him.[144]

We are not surprised to hear a good Baconian like Henry Power remark that the 'old Dogmatists and Notional Speculators' with their subtle inferences could learn no more of the workings of God than a country bumpkin could of the structure of a watch by watching its hands go round,[145] or to hear a left-wing Puritan like William Walwyn cry out against the doctrinal absurdities that obscure the simplicity of regenerative love: 'good God! that free love should be suspected: that because it is easie to be had, we should put it farre from us'.[146] But Milton himself punishes the fallen angels by making them argue questions of fate, free will, and providence, 'in wand'ring mazes lost';[147] and it is surely a sign of the times when Richard Baxter, mellowing into old age, lost his interest in the Schoolmen who had been his youthful passion and instead came to seek the essentials of salvation: 'The Creed, the Lord's Prayer and the Ten Commandments do find me now the most acceptable and plentiful matter for all my meditations.'[148] At the other edge of the spectrum Hobbes agrees in making salvation simply a matter of faith in Christ and obedience to laws.[149]

For various reasons, then, and from many different directions, men of the most dissimilar interests were converging to that position which Locke, at the end of the century, could state as a commonplace:

> The greatest part of mankind have not leisure for learning and logic and superfine distinctions of the schools. Where the hand is used to the plough and the spade, the head is seldom elevated to sublime notions, or exercised in mysterious reasoning.... Had God intended that none but the learned

---

[143] *Holy Living,* IV.iv.
[145] *Experimental Philosophy,* p. 193.
[147] *PL,* II, 557–65.
[149] *Leviathan,* ch. xliii (p. 319).

[144] *Golden Remains,* p. 235.
[146] *The Power of Love,* Haller, II, 294–5.
[148] *Autobiography,* p. 107.

scribe, disputer, or wise of this world should be christians or be saved, thus religion should have been prepared for them, filled with speculations and niceties, obscure terms, and abstract notions. But men of that expectation, men furnished with such acquisitions, the apostle tells us, 1 Cor. i, are rather shut out from the simplicity of the gospel; to make way for those poor, ignorant, illiterate, who heard and believed promises of a Deliverer and believed Jesus to be him; who could conceive a man dead and made alive again; and believe that he should, at the end of the world, come again and pass sentence on all men, according to their deeds.[150]

Apart from the mounting discontent with the theology of scholasticism there was even stronger protest against its logic. When a popular dramatist like Middleton could get laughs by making an Oxford undergraduate and his tutor chop logic together[151] it would seem that the scholastic tradition had reached its nadir. But the strength and frequency of more systematic attacks show that the tradition was still powerful enough to stimulate intemperate reaction. There were still those jaded Renaissance skeptics like Burton who wanly despaired of any certainty, scholastic or other, as being more than 'a Labyrinth of opinions, idle questions, propositions, metaphysical terms';[152] but men with programs of their own to advance took a firmer line. Bacon tersely concluded that the syllogism – which, starting from the known, can never teach anything new – 'does more harm than good'.[153] In his third prolusion (*Contra philosophiam scholasticam*) young Milton urged his college fellows to abandon their sterile pursuit of scholastic logic so they might turn their attention to history, geography, astronomy – studies concerned with man and his immediate environment. When he grew older he returned to the attack with more vehemence than good taste, ridiculing those 'prelatical' universities where boys,

> fed with nothing else, but the scragged and thorny lectures of monkish and miserable sophistry, were sent home again with such a scholastic bur in their throats, as hath stopped and hindered all true and generous philosophy from entering, cracked their voices for ever with metaphysical gargarisms, and hath made them admire a sort of formal outside men prelatically addicted, whose unchastened and unwrought minds were never yet initiated or subdued under the true lore of religion or moral virtue, which two are the best and greatest points of learning.[154]

[150] *The Reasonableness of Christianity, as delivered in the Scriptures, Works*, VII, 157-8.
[151] *A Chaste Maid in Cheapside*, IV.i.
[152] *Anatomy*, I, 421.
[153] *NO*, I.xii (*Works*, VIII, 69).
[154] *The Reason of Church Government*, bk. II (*PW*, II, 504).

ANTI-SCHOLASTICISM

This invective matches that of the famous encomium of 'our Learned Selden' at the expense of Gratian and Peter Lombard – 'him the compiler of canon iniquity, the other the Tubalcain of scholastic sophistry' – whose 'bastardy' has corrupted human learning, 'dejected' the clear light of nature, and polluted the very fountains of Scripture'.[155]

More urbanely, Browne could only deplore those many scholastic centuries which 'were lost in repetitions and transcriptions sealing up the Book of Knowledge',[156] but Hobbes polished off the political theory of the great Cardinal Bellarmine with a vigor and a glittering hatred unmatched elsewhere in our language.[157] As a nominalist, Hobbes was fundamentally antagonistic to scholasticism. In his memorable attack on the Kingdom of Darkness – that is, the Catholic church – he sees the effort to make theology 'rational' as the basis of most political and ecclesiastical disorders;[158] the endless and empty words of the Schoolmen are good for nothing but to frighten men from their civil duties of obedience 'as men fright Birds from the Corn with an empty doublet, a hat, and a crooked stick'. Scholastic natural philosophy is vitiated by its ignorance of geometry, its theology is blasphemous, its metaphysic is beneath contempt, its jargon nothing but 'insignificant Traines of strange and barbarous words' – and so on for many angry pages.

Lesser men enthusiastically joined the attack. Nathaniel Carpenter sneered that Aristotle himself would repudiate the stupidity of his modern advocates – 'quos (opinor) Philosophus ipse, si revivisceret, tanq[u]am spurios abdicaret; aut saltem, ut Degeneres, indignaretur'.[159] In an appendix to Thomas James's *Strange and Dangerous Voyage* William Watts used James's exploits as a stick to beat the servile Aristotelians: they sought knowledge not by going out to seek experience and to master nature, but by hiding in discredited texts; and even though James had failed to find the Northwest Passage he had broadened man's knowledge of his planet, so that we may hope 'the same improvement may by this meanes accrew unto our Physicks, that hath advaunced our Geography, our Mathematicks, and our Mechan-

---

[155] *The Doctrine and Discipline of Divorce*, II.xxii (*PW*, III, 269).
[156] *Christian Morals*, II.v.
[157] *Leviathan*, ch. xlii.
[158] *Ibid.*, ch. xlvi.
[159] *Philosophia Libera*, 'Praefatio ad Lectorem'.

icks'.¹⁶⁰ In his *Free and Impartial Censure of the Platonick Philosophie* Samuel Parker attacked all 'notional' philosophy which spurned sensory cognition for *a priori* abstractions, quantity for quality, observation for system-spinning. Since it is 'infinitely notorious' that Platonic ideas and Aristotelian forms are one in 'their obscurity and remoteness from sence', Parker chooses to pin his hopes for the advancement of learning on experimental philosophy 'not so much because of its greater certainty, but because it puts inquisitive men into a method to attain it, whereas the other serves only to obstruct their industry by amusing them with empty and insignificant Notions'.¹⁶¹

To quote Parker brings us to that glorious dawn which Dryden celebrates in his *Annus Mirabilis* – the age that was to produce Locke and Newton, but that would not have to answer Hume and Kant.

> This is the Age wherein (me-thinks) Philosophy comes in with a Springtide; and the Peripateticks may as well hope to stop the Current of the Tide, or (with Xerxes) to fetter the Ocean, as to hinder the overflowing of free Philosophy: Me-thinks I see how all the old Rubbish must be thrown away, and the rotten Buildings be overthrown, and carried away with so powerful an Inundation.¹⁶²

So strong was the current of the tide that even Ralph Cudworth, though intent on salvaging Christianity from the atheistical monsters of his age, refused to do so at the price of embracing scholastic rationalism; for to do so requires us to say, of natural phenomena, 'that is done we know not how; or, which is yet more absurd, to make our very ignorance of the cause, disguised under those terms of forms or qualities, to be itself the cause of the effect'.¹⁶³ If such an unblushing rationalist as Cudworth thus denounced his intellectual forebears, what might we not expect from the utilitarians, the experimental philosophers, and the empiricists? To bring this catena of disparagement to a close we may glance at a representative of each class.

John Webster's *Academiarum Examen*, an important statement of Baconian utilitarianism, is a vigorous and systematic assault on scholasticism from the Puritan position. The men who dared to raise their arms against the Lord's anointed were not un-

---
¹⁶⁰ Sig. S4ʳ.   ¹⁶¹ pp. 41–2, 45.
¹⁶² Power, *Experimental Philosophy*, p. 192.
¹⁶³ Quoted by Burtt, *Metaphysical Foundations*, pp. 143–4.

ANTI-SCHOLASTICISM

naturally attracted by the empirical and utilitarian sanctions they found in Bacon and Comenius; and a whole school of Baconian Puritans – headed by the indefatigable Samuel Hartlib and including Durie and John Hall and Petty and many others – labored ceaselessly for man's temporal and secular well-being by cultivating the useful arts and sciences. Webster's book belongs in their history as an assessment and rejection of the 'notional' tradition perpetuated by the universities – doubly damned by their traditional curriculum and Anglican sympathies. The assessment is not temperate, and the rejection is vehement, but that is why the book is typical of its age.

The fourth chapter, 'Of Scholastick Philosophy', is a sustained attack on Aristotle's character, intelligence, canon, methodology, and followers. 'This Philosophy is meerly verbal, speculative, abstractive, formal and notional, fit to fill the brains with monstrous and airy Chymæras, speculative, and fruitless conceits.'[164] The dreadful epithets 'notional' and 'speculative' carry the weight of the opprobrium. Webster was not a subtle or perhaps even intelligent man – he celebrated the astrologist Robert Fludd while denouncing Aristotle as a barefaced fool – but as God gave him strength he tried to lay the ghost of scholasticism forever. Whereas rational theology impiously reduces the mysteries of religion to logical demonstration, true religion teaches us to 'go out of our selves, and out of the weak and rotten vessel of humane reason, into that ark of Noah, which guided by the divine magnetick needle of Gods Spirit, can onely direct us to rest upon the mountains of Ararat'.[165] Clearly, Webster is in the main tradition of Calvin's antirationalism in allocating to grace the things belonging to grace, to man's faculties for industry and self-improvement the search for practical knowledge. As both a Sectarian 'fanatick' and a Baconian he represents two of the most powerful forces of the century, and on two fronts – that of piety and of utility – he waged war on the scholastic tradition.

The wayfaring Christian must attain his salvation by inwardness and grace, for from the 'putrid and muddy fountain' of human reason

> arise all those hellish and dark foggs and vapours that like locusts crawling from this bottomlesse pit have overspread the face of the whole earth, filling men with pride, insolency, and self-confidence, to aver and main-

[164] p. 67.   [165] p. 14.

tain that none are fit to speak, and preach the spiritual, & deep things of God, but such as are indued with this Scholastick, & mans idol-made learning.[166]

Against the efficacy of God's grace scholastic logic is both blasphemous and useless,

> *bellum intestinum Logicum*, a civil war of words, a verbal contest, a combat of cunning, craftiness, violence and altercation, wherein all verbal force, by impudence, insolence, opposition, contradiction, derision, diversion, trifling, jeering, humming, hissing, brawling, quarreling, scolding, scandalizing, and the like, are equally allowed of, and accounted just, and no regard had to the truth.[167]

And in brief – though Webster is never brief – a man of true wisdom and piety will forego the frippery of the Schoolmen: for his soul's health he will hope for that regeneration which comes through grace alone; for his secular commodity he will develop those useful (even 'mechanick') arts and sciences which comprise his proper natural knowledge.

A more judicious attack than Webster's came from the latitudinarian Anglican clergyman Joseph Glanvill. Broadly speaking, Webster is in the Calvinistic, Glanvill in the Baconian, tradition of protecting both secular and religious knowledge from scholastic rationalism. One a Puritan, the other an Anglican, they were agreed, against all varieties of notional philosophy, that the advancement of learning must derive from the observation and control of nature, whereas the progress of piety must be left to the workings of God's grace or to the safe discipline of the established church.

Glanvill is a slicker and more sophisticated writer than Webster. His style, as Mr Willey has pointed out, is wonderfully full of surprises, and he has the advantage of being thoroughly (if uncritically) *au courant* with the most fashionable thought of his age. Ostensibly a skeptic, by playing off Sir Kenelm Digby against Descartes, and both against Henry More,[168] he seeks to demonstrate that philosophical objectivity and detachment which he urged against all dogmatists. To answer even the most rudimentary questions of man's physiology must, in our present state of uncertainty, 'be left to the coming of Elias'. We can as easily explain how a thought could be united to a marble, or a sunbeam

---

[166] p. 12.   [167] p. 33.
[168] *The Vanity of Dogmatizing*, p. 42.

ANTI-SCHOLASTICISM

to a lump of clay, as explain the interaction of soul and body. 'To hang weights on the wings of the winde seems far more intelligible.'[169] But Glanvill's skepticism is only thinly disguised anti-scholasticism, and it soon becomes clear that his main purpose is to advance the claims of experimental philosophy against traditional rationalism. Although he wittily and learnedly points out epistemological difficulties which would never occur to Webster,[170] he shares the conviction of his century that the mind of man is 'naturally amorous of, and impatient for Truth';[171] and he proceeds on the common assumption that truth will come when the proper methodology is established.

Such an assumption makes possible the conventional attack on custom and error. 'There is nothing so monstrous, to which education cannot form our ductile minority; it can lick us into shapes beyond the monstrosities of those of Affrica.'[172] The dead hand of authority is the enemy of progress, reverence for antiquity the chief source of error.

> We look with a superstitious reverence upon the accounts of praeterlapsed ages: and with a supercilious severity, on the more deserving products of our own. A vanity, which hath possess'd all times as well as ours; and the Golden Age was never present.[173]

Actually, there are only two areas in which truth is inviolate. These are religion and mathematics, for both are 'superstructed on principles that cannot fail us, except our faculties do constantly abuse us. Our religious foundations are fastned at the pillars of the intellectual world, and the grand Articles of our Belief as demonstrable as Geometry'.[174] In Glanvill the segregation of religious from secular truth is made the necessary condition for progress. Each has its province, and to apply the authoritarian test of revelation or of *a priori* rationalism to the observable (and mathematically describable) truths of nature is the most desperate folly. Indeed, the fact that mathematics and the 'Mechanick Arts' have finally been freed from the silly presuppositions of the Schoolmen is the reason for their progress in the present age.

---

[169] p. 20. [170] pp. 93–8.
[171] p. 112. Note the specific disclaimers of philosophical skepticism, p. 223; cf. 'Skepticism and Certainty', *Essays*, pp. 37 f.
[172] p. 128. [173] p. 137.
[174] p. 209.

'Galileus without a crime out-saw all Antiquity; and was not afraid to believe his eyes, in spight of the Opticks of Ptolomy [sic] and Aristotle.'[175]

And thus in his long peroration Glanvill concludes his indictment of those Aristotelians who obstruct the progress of natural knowledge. 'That the Aristotelian Philosophy is an huddle of words and terms insignificant, hath been the censure of the wisest.'[176] To plow through the endless folios of the Schoolmen is 'laborious idleness', for in them all things are 'crumbled into notional Atomes; and the substance evaporated into an imaginary Æther. The Intellect, that can feed on this air, is a Chamælion; and a meer inflated skin. From this stock grew School-divinity, which is but Peripateticism in a Theological Livery. A Schoolman is the Ghost of the Stagirite, in a Body of condensed Air: and Thomas but Aristotle sainted'.[177] The greatest barrier to truth has ever been the 'nugacious Disputations' of the Aristotelians, and Luther spoke well when he said 'Quam primum apparuit Theologia Scholastica, evanuit Theologia Crucis'.[178] In place of the careful scrutiny of natural processes, the Aristotelians advocate the most flatulent verbiage: 'That heavy Bodies descend by gravity, is no better an account then we might expect from a Rustick: and again; that Gravity is a quality whereby an heavy body descends, in an impertinent Circle, and teacheth nothing.'[179] In short, because the notional philosophy of the Schoolmen is 'inept for New Discoveries' it therefore is 'of no accomodation to the use of life'.[180]

Webster and Glanvill, though interesting, are pygmies, and their antischolasticism is partial and weak when compared to Locke's. Whatever the inadequacies of that empiricism which he bequeathed the eighteenth century, he summarized his century's discontent with scholastic rationalism. His refutation is the most studied and magisterial of the age. Whereas other men had sniped at this and that extravagance of the Schoolmen, Locke trained his artillery on their deepest bulwark, their epistemology. Contemptuously dismissing the claims of *a priori* truth, innate ideas, and all the obsolete baggage of rationalism, he firmly anchors knowledge in sensation.

[175] p. 140. [176] p. 150.
[177] p. 152. [178] p. 166.
[179] p. 171. [180] p. 178.

ANTI-SCHOLASTICISM

Let us then suppose the mind to be, as we say, white paper, void of all characters, without any ideas; – How comes it to be furnished? Whence comes it by that vast store which the busy and boundless fancy of man has painted upon it, with an almost endless variety? Whence has it all the materials of reason and knowledge? To this I answer, in one word, from EXPERIENCE. In all that our knowledge is founded; and from that it ultimately derives itself.[181]

Man entertains simple ideas which, on reflection, yield patterns of inference and relatedness, but that is all: he cannot 'invent or frame' a single simple idea apart from sensation, nor can 'any force of the understanding destroy those that are there'.[182] Universals, then, are merely verbal; they have no reference to anything real, and a logic constructed on such alleged references is foolish. 'Right reasoning is founded on something else than the predicaments and predicables, and does not consist in talking in mode and figure itself.'[183] Such terms are not metaphysical entities, but 'artificial ignorance, and learned gibberish'.[184] Reality belongs only to things, and things are 'all of them particular in their existence'.[185] Consequently, we must base our knowledge on the things our faculties permit us to experience.

The senses at first let in particular ideas, and furnish the yet empty cabinet [of the mind], and the mind by degrees growing familiar with some of them, they are lodged in the memory, and names got to them. Afterwards the mind proceeding farther, abstracts them, and by degrees learns the use of general names. In this manner the mind comes to be furnished with ideas and language, the materials about which to exercise its discursive faculty. And the use of reason becomes daily more visible, as these materials that give it employment increase.[186]

In his effort to extirpate, root and branch, an epistemology based on innate ideas, Locke repeatedly invokes 'every man's experience' and what 'one may call large, sound, roundabout sense'.[187] Thus if one wishes to know what solidity is, why should he contrive and juggle meaningless abstractions? 'Let him put a flint or a football between his hands, and then endeavour to join them, and he will know.'[188] Man's sensory knowledge is prone

---
[181] *Essay*, II.i.2 (Fraser, I, 121–2).
[182] *Ibid.*, II.ii.2 (Fraser, I, 145).
[183] *Some Thoughts Concerning Education*, sect. 188 (*Works*, IX, 177).
[184] *Essay*, III.x.9 (Fraser, II, 128).
[185] *Ibid.*, III.ii.11 (Fraser, II, 21).
[186] *Ibid.*, I.i.15 (Fraser, I, 48–9).
[187] *Conduct of the Understanding*, sect. 3 (*Works*, III, 190).
[188] *Essay*, II.iv.4 (Fraser, I, 156–7).

to error, but such as it is it suffices, if properly disciplined, to attain at least limited truth; that is all one may hope for. As for the notion that truth is to be derived deductively from innate moral or metaphysical principles in the human mind which command universal assent, 'I appeal to any who have looked abroad beyond the smoke of their own chimneys'.[189] All intellectual systems are fallible; they should be entertained as 'hypotheses' rather than paths to a 'comprehensive, scientifical, and satisfactory knowledge of the works of nature'. Even the best of them, that of 'the incomparable Mr Newton', has only a limited utility in showing how far mathematics can 'carry us in the knowledge of some, as I may so call them, particular provinces of the incomprehensible universe'.[190]

Since the universe is incomprehensible, and since we can never even have direct experience of primary qualities of mass and substance, the pretensions of rational theology are as ridiculous as they are impious. However, since man does possess faculties of sense and the power to assimilate and arrange the data of sensation for the drawing of inferences, he can achieve a morality of prudence if not one of ethical absolutes.

> The Candle that is set up in us shines bright enough for all our purposes. The discoveries we can make with this ought to satisfy us; and we shall then use our understandings right, when we entertain all objects in that way and proportion that they are suited to our faculties, and upon those grounds they are capable of being proposed to us; and not peremptorily, or intemperately require demonstration, and demand certainty, where probability only is to be had, and which is sufficient to govern all our concernments.[191]

For our purposes we can isolate two principal effects of this positivism: it tended to restrict man's intellection to those objects about which he could hope to gain empirical knowledge, and it tended to discredit further the notional philosophy of the rationalists – scholastic or Cartesian or other. If everything that man knows derives from his sensations, then most of the theological notions of the past are demonstrably foolish. In the eighteenth century Locke was widely acclaimed for having thus demolished the specter of total depravity: he was thought to have restored

---

[189] *Ibid.*, I.ii.2 (Fraser, I, 66).
[190] *Some Thoughts Concerning Education*, sect. 194 (*Works*, IX, 186).
[191] *Essay*, 'Introduction', sect. 5 (Fraser, I, 30).

at long last men's primal innocence – of good as well as of evil – from which they could, 'barely by the use of their natural faculties', achieve sufficient knowledge to live well and sociably together. The direction of Locke's thought is, then, secular, sensible, and utilitarian. Whatever violence his epistemology does to the Christian epic, it enables man, securely established in a benevolent nature, to exploit his natural resources with cheerful zeal.

> Every man carries about him a touchstone, if he will make use of it, to distinguish substantial gold from superficial glitterings, truth from appearances. And indeed the use and benefit of this touchstone, which is natural reason, is spoiled and lost only by assuming prejudices, overweening presumption, and narrowing our minds. The want of exercising it, in the full extent of things intelligible, is that which weakens and extinguishes this noble faculty in us.[192]

If reason, then, has lost its metaphysical validity, it none the less retains a most useful functional status as part of man's natural equipment. His well-being – social, political, economic – depends on his using it wisely. We have discerned in earlier seventeenth-century thought a movement toward secular morality; Locke accelerates that movement prodigiously. He makes the customary concessions to revelation, of course: the mysteries of Christianity 'are the fundamentals, which it is not enough to disbelieve: every one is required actually to assent to them'.[193] But he reduces the essentials of salvation to faith in Christ and the living of a good life. It is significant that a 'good life' assumes this role in attaining eternal bliss; it casts great weight on the side of practical morality, and practical morality itself becomes a matter of reason and prudence, almost of enlightened self-interest. Faith without works, in Locke's inversion of Calvin, is worthless.[194] Man is a creature who lives in society, and society is ordered by a law of nature discernible through the process of reason; it teaches 'all mankind who will but consult it that, being all equal and independent, no one ought to harm another in his life, health, liberty or possessions'.[195] These public virtues make for peace and justice, and they lie within each man's capacities in quite the same degree, and are attainable by the same means, as the private virtues that order his passions and affections.

[192] *Conduct of the Understanding*, sect. 3 (*Works*, III, 193).
[193] *The Reasonableness of Christianity*, *Works*, VII, 156.
[194] Ibid., *Works*, VII, 111–2.
[195] *Of Civil Government*, II.i.6 (*Works*, V, 341).

THE ATTACK ON AUTHORITY

This is no place even to sketch Locke's wide and complex significance in English thought. In this survey it is enough to remind ourselves that he climaxed his century's repudiation of scholastic authority. Though it is true that he could, as explicitly and angrily as his contemporaries, condemn the grosser absurdities of theological rationalism,[196] he went further than they in rejecting the very assumptions which made it possible. Thus he not only crowns the antiauthoritarian protest with which Bacon had opened the century, but also brings to a full cadence that incisive attack with which William of Ockham had initiated the revolt against scholasticism.

[196] For example, see his withering attack on scholastic jargon, *Essay*, III.x, *passim*.

V

ANGLICAN AND PURITAN

1. 'THE BIBLE ONLY'

The movements of intellectual history, never sharp or unilateral, were in the seventeenth century notably complex. The intricate meshing of inherited and slowly emerging attitudes give the thought of the period an extraordinary richness, not to say difficulty; yet it is the business of studies like this to try to untangle the snarled strands, and to find, beneath the antinomies and inconsistencies, continuity and pattern. In the last chapter we sketched one of the most powerful forces of the century – its discontent with what may be called the scholastic conception of truth. It was a discontent shared by the most unlike persons and utilized for the most antagonistic purposes, and it left no major thinker of the period untouched. Yet elements of tradition, even of reaction, persisted long.

Notably, the long habit of belief in the Christian epic was too strong to be shaken off overnight. Although the inherited views of God and nature and man were subjected to attacks of increasing intensity, the values persisted, after a fashion, modified now here, now there, to meet the demands of secularism, science, civil disobedience. In this chapter we shall examine those configurations of religious emotion called Anglican and Puritan as the two main foci of such inherited values in seventeenth-century England. Both were committed to perpetuating the Christian tradition, and yet both were forced to make important concessions in reconciling to that tradition the new interests generated in the new century.

Since we are mainly concerned in this book with seventeenth-century notions about truth, and only incidentally with political or ecclesiastical history, we should keep in mind that for both Anglicans and Puritans the Bible constituted the revealed word of God. That is a truism which we sometimes tend to forget. Whatever their differences – and the two disciplines split rancorously on the nature and scope of extra-Biblical truth – they were agreed that, in Hooker's words, there is 'no part of true philosophy, no art of account, no kind of science rightly so called, but the Scripture must contain it'.[1] As a Protestant, Hooker could hardly have said less. The initial theological impulse behind the Reformation had been the desire to restore the faith to its apostolic – that is, ante-Catholic – purity; the strategy for doing so was to use the Bible as a detergent to all the accretions of councils and creeds and philosophical systems that had come to obscure the naked truth of God's own words. The absolutely literal acceptance of the Bible was the only recourse against the intolerable pretensions of natural philosophy and a corrupt ecclesiastical monopoly, the only path to certainty for man who by his Fall lay grovelling in sin and impotence. In the Bible, as Calvin said, God 'opens his own sacred mouth',[2] thus providing man's only irrefragable source of truth. Reason is frail, private inspiration is dubious, natural science is as fallible as the senses on which it is based, scholastic concepts are impious absurdities, classical morality is heathen. The 'doctrine of heaven' is, therefore, man's only refuge, and the Bible is the only repository of that doctrine. Consequently, the Scripture 'obtains the same complete credit and authority with believers, when they are satisfied of its divine origin, as if they heard the very words pronounced by God himself'.[3] When Milton said that 'the rule and canon of faith is Scripture alone' he was repeating the cardinal tenet of Protestantism.[4]

At least in principle, all Protestants in the seventeenth century could only concur. Although the Puritans, as one of their early historians put it, could be defined by their belief in the 'absolute perfection' of the Scripture,[5] no Anglican would dare to question such a belief. Even Chillingworth, whom the Presbyterian Cheynell buried with curses and execrations as a Socinian, built the whole of his noble defense of Protestantism on the proposition, 'The Bible, I say, the Bible only, is the religion of protestants!'[6] Similarly, Milton based both his religion and his art on the conviction that truth is 'the daughter not of time, but of Heaven, only bred up here below in Christian hearts between two grave

---

[1] *Laws*, I.xiv.1.   [2] *Institutes*, I.vi.1.
[3] *Ibid.*, I.vii.1.
[4] *De doctrina*, I.xxx (*PW*, IV, 455).
[5] Ames, *English Puritanisme*, sig. A2r.
[6] *Works*, II, 450.

and holy nurses, the doctrine and discipline of the gospel'.[7] One of the most conspicuous features of the sermons of the period, Puritan or Anglican, is the incredible and microscopic knowledge of the Bible that they reveal; and, lest we think that only preachers and scholars – Hooker, Andrewes, Perkins, Sibbes, Donne, Milton, Taylor – had such extraordinary command of a text, we should remember the vast majority of unread and unlearned people, like Bunyan, who knew only one book, but that one almost by heart. However, that one book, as Taylor said, was enough:

> The word of God is all those commandments and revelations, those promises and threatenings, the stories and sermons recorded in the Bible: nothing else is the word of God, that we know of by any certain instrument.[8]

It was inevitable that this conviction should be so common. When the intricate and massive machinery of Catholicism was summarily scrapped by the Reformers, religion was reduced to its components of God and His word, sinful man and his hope of heaven. The divinely sanctioned authority of the hierarchy once denied, Protestants were forced to take their stand upon the Bible and upon their individual conscience. With the Bible as their guide they were forced to contrive a substitute for those rites and rituals (such as auricular confession and penance) which the Catholic church had declared essential for salvation. Thus the strong Protestant emphasis on the conscience as an invincible instrument of self-knowledge: in point of authority, said Perkins, 'it is placed in the middle between man and God, so as it is under God, and yet above man'.[9] All the great English casuists – Perkins, Ames, Baxter among the Puritans, Hall, Sanderson, Taylor among the Anglicans – sought the same end: to resolve the moral and religious questions of the perplexed by a discussion of divinely sanctioned principles and their application to particular cases of conscience. Their great appeal was to the Scripture, as searched by the conscience and seeking spirit of the individual suppliant; and their intent was to bring Biblical truth to bear on daily conduct. Perkins' remark in his *Treatise of Conscience* indicates the central strategy of all the casuists:

---

[7] *Of Prelatical Episcopacy, PW*, II, 428.
[8] *Holy Living*, IV.iv.
[9] *Cases of Conscience*, I.iii.

Inferior authority cannot bind the superior; now the courts of men and their authority are under conscience. For God in the heart of every man hath erected a tribunal seat, and in his stead he hath placed neither saint nor angel, nor any Creature whatsoever, but conscience itself, who therefore is the highest judge that is, or can be, under God; by whose directions also courts are kept and laws are made.[10]

In spite of the formidable problems posed by this kind of religious individualism it remained the base of all reformed theology.

'Not the Church of England only', Laud told the Jesuit Fisher, 'but all Protestants, agree most truly and most strongly in this, "That the Scripture is sufficient to salvation, and contains in it all things necessary to it".'[11] It is with the same invulnerable conviction of truth that Richard Sibbes, a man otherwise very unlike the archbishop, could say that 'truth is truth, and error, error, and that which is unlawful is unlawful, whether men think so or no'.[12] Just as Sir Henry Wotton told a mocking priest that he found his religion 'in the written Word of God',[13] Bishop Jewel had long before rejoiced that the old bad days were gone

> when all the bishops of Rome's sayings were allowed for gospel, and when all religion did depend only upon their authority. Now-a-days the holy scripture is abroad, the writings of the apostles and prophets are in print, whereby all truth and catholic doctrine may be proved, and all heresy may be disproved and confuted.[14]

Since the 'very essence of truth is plainness and brightness', and since God has given to every man an understanding 'fit and proportionable to truth', argued Milton, then our course is clear:

---

[10] Quoted by Henson, *Studies in English Religion in the Seventeenth Century*, p. 184. John Aubrey (*Brief Lives*, pp. 6–7) amusingly illustrates the vogue for casuistry in an anecdote about Lancelot Andrewes: 'There was then at Cambridge a good fatt Alderman that was wont to sleep at Church, which the Alderman endeavoured to prevent but could not. Well! this was preached against as a signe of Reprobation. The good man was exceedingly troubled at it, and went to Andrewes his Chamber to be satisfied in point of Conscience. Mr Andrewes told him, that was an ill habit of Body, not of Mind, and that it was against his Will; advised him on Sundays to make a more sparing meale, and to mend it at Supper. The Alderman did so, but Sleepe comes on again for all that, and was preached at; comes againe to be resolved with Teares in his eies. Andrewes then told him he would have him make a good heartie meal as he was wont to doe, but presently take out his full sleep. He did so, came to St Maries, where the Preacher was prepared with a Sermon to damne all who slept at Sermon, a certaine Signe of Reprobation. The good Alderman, having taken his full nap before, lookes on the Preacher all Sermon time, and spoyled the design.'
[11] *A Relation of the Conference*, Works, II, 61.
[12] *The Bruised Reed and Smoking Flax*, ch. xx (*Works*, I, 80).
[13] Walton, *Lives*, I, 170.
[14] *Apology*, Works, III, 57.

If we will but purge with sovereign eye salve that intellectual ray which God hath planted in us, then we would believe the scriptures protesting their own plainness and perspicuity, calling to them to be instructed, not only the wise and learned, but the simple, the poor, the babes, foretelling an extraordinary effusion of God's Spirit upon every age and sex, attributing to all men, and requiring from them the ability of searching, trying, examining all things, and by the Spirit discerning that which is good; and as the scriptures themselves pronounce their own plainness, so do the fathers testify of them.[15]

If the Protestants had, as they thought, so invulnerable a repository of sacred truth, it may be wondered why the history of Protestantism has been one of conflict, schism, and splinter-movements; and why for nearly a century English history was made hideous by the incessant warfare between Anglican and Puritan. Both persuasions were united in their fear and hatred of Rome ('religion mixt as well of Treason, as of Idolatry', sneered Donne),[16] both were committed to Genevan theology and built their creeds around that dark dogma, both (as Fuller pointed out) appealed to the practice of the primitive church for their discipline,[17] both took their stand on all matters – ecclesiastical and secular – on the presumed authority of the Scripture. Why, then, their most unchristian wrangling? Beneath all the words and fury, the learning and the sometimes fanatical zeal, of their interminable controversies we may see that on one all-important but inevitable weakness the great moral fervor and inner strength of Protestantism has always fractured and spent itself: it has lacked a generally accepted method for interpreting, for purposes of church discipline and morality, the truth which God reveals in His Scripture.

The Continental Reformers had succeeded in tearing most of northern Europe away from a church that seemed too worldly, too secular, too rational, and too corrupt; and they offered as an alternative the indisputable truth of God's naked word. But they had failed to prescribe the way to interpret that word. In order to assure the priesthood of each believer they had scrapped what seemed to them a spurious and decadent mechanism for bringing men to God. Angrily demolishing an ancient, stylized, and ritualized strategy of grace, they had insisted that each man come to

[15] *Of Reformation in England*, bk. I (*PW*, II, 387–8).
[16] *LXXX Sermons*, p. 375.
[17] The virtually canonical source of Puritan discipline was Calvin's *Institute* (IV.xii).

God alone and wrestle for salvation with the fiercest subjective intensity. In doing this they had, as they wished, renewed the tone and temper of apostolic Christianity, and with a tremor of both horror and elation they had injected into European thought an almost forgotten poignancy of religious emotion. All this they had done with 'the Bible only'. In it they found the sanction for their iconoclasms, and with it alone they met and conquered the massive power of Rome.

The price, however, was very great. They had gained, as they thought, a new purity; certainly they had gained a new kind of religious individualism; but they had lost unity, and as the subsequent history of Protestantism shows, for that loss their posterity have paid very dear. For Reformed theology could, and eventually did, lead to a religious subjectivism incompatible with any formal ecclesiastical organization. Milton recognized two Scriptures – the external one written in God's word and the internal one imprinted on our conscience; and significantly he declared the latter to be the final court of appeal for questions of moral and religious truth. 'Every believer has a right to interpret the Scriptures for himself, inasmuch as he has the Spirit for his guide, and the mind of Christ is in him; nay, the expositions of the public interpreter can be of no use to him, except so far as they are confirmed by his own conscience.'[18] For all its faults – and in time they came to be intolerably gross – the Roman church had given to the Middle Ages a corporate sense that the modern world has never regained (not even in the new secular dogmas of political theory).

Perhaps it is just as well: medieval unity derived from a ruthless authoritarianism, and modern multiplicity is made possible by concepts of human freedom that would have been denounced as heretical by Boniface III. Those who yearn nostalgically for the medieval synthesis perhaps forget its cost – or perhaps they do not, which is sufficiently damning. At any rate, that cost seemed too great for the Reformers. Not that they were impelled by any ardor for civil or religious freedom: the Genevan theocracy remains a chamber of horrors, and Luther's political thinking was so reactionary as to be archaic; yet they shifted the whole base of religious authority from ecclesiastical tradition to the Bible, and their seventeenth-century heirs gradually forced that separa-

[18] *De doctrina*, I.xxx (*PW*, IV, 444).

tion of church and state which is the necessary condition of religious freedom. Thus they made possible the development of a political and ecclesiastical liberalism that would have appalled them could they have foreseen its consequences. Reducing religion to its basal factors of sin and regeneration, they insisted on individual rather than corporate religious experience. The resulting loss of authority in ecclesiastical and disciplinary matters is the central fact of European history for the next two centuries. The mere bulk of religious controversy in the late Renaissance – to say nothing of the resulting violence, bloodshed, and cruelty – was enough to make a strong man blanch. What certainty is possible, asks Gabriel Harvey.

> You that have read Luther against the Pope; Sadolet, Longolius, Omphalius, Osorius against Luther; Calvin against Sadolet; Melanchthon against Longolius; Sturmius against Omphalius; Haddon against Osorius; Baldwin againste Calvin; Beza againste Baldwin; Erastus against Beza; Travers against Erastus; Sutcliff against Travers; and so foorth (for there is no ende of endlesse controversies: nor Bellarmine shall ever satisfye the Protestantes; nor Whittaker contente the Papistes; nor Bancroft appease the Precisians; nor any reason pacify affection; nor any authority resolve obstinacy).[19]

The tumultuous religious history of seventeenth-century England copiously illustrates the Protestant genius for schism. Given the Protestant Bible as the unchallenged repository of truth, and given the doctrine of original sin as the central Protestant creed, what allowance was to be made for varying interpretations of that Bible, or for the claims of extra-Biblical truth available to even the corrupted cognitive faculties of sinful man? To summarize too broadly a tortuously complicated question we may say that the Anglicans generally were more flexible, the Puritans more rigid, in adapting to matters of morality and church discipline varieties of truth not specifically contained in the Scripture. Whereas the early Reformation was in large part a studied reaction to Renaissance humanism, and the English Presbyterians were the most ardent agents of that reaction, the Anglicans built their defense of the *via media* on the broad epistemological base that had made such humanism possible. After their fashion – and making the necessary allowances for the political exigencies of their Erastian church – they carried on the central European tradi-

[19] *Pierce's Supererogation, Elizabethan Critical Essays*, II, 248.

tion of the dignity of man as deriving from his capacities for rational truth. On this point the monuments of Anglican theology are consistent. Hooker's *Laws*, Donne's sermons, Chillingworth's *Religion of Protestants*, Taylor's *Ductor Dubitantium* – to name only four out of hundreds – all proceed on the assumption that man may know God in various ways: by natural law, by the discourse of reason, by civil and ecclesiastical law, by the dictates of right reason, by the tradition and antiquity of human institutions, by the Scripture. As a creature in whom there still remain, in spite of the Fall, certain usable cognitive faculties, it is man's duty to use them all in attaining wisdom, social well-being, and salvation.

The Puritans, on the other hand, denied any extra-Biblical approach to God. On the single but sufficient argument that by his Fall man has been rendered odious and impotent, they rejected the claims of natural reason or apostolic succession, inexorably forcing him to use the revealed truth of the Bible alone as the explicit and literal commandment of God on all matters of theology and church discipline. It was not that man did not enjoy at least limited rational faculties, but that these, not guided and informed by the Bible, are worthless, just as his natural piety is worthless without regeneration, or his works without faith.

From this fundamental divergence, then, developed that complicated and tediously acrimonious controversy between Anglican and Puritan that seethed throughout most of Elizabeth's reign, disturbed the domestic policies of the heavy-handed Stuarts, and at last erupted bloodily in the Great Rebellion. Although it would be a formidable task to trace its development closely, to understand its principal points and to observe its shaping power on the thought and emotion of the period is to get close to the intellectual problems of the seventeenth century.

II. THE *VIA MEDIA*

When we compare the timeservers and toadies of the Jacobean church with men like Parker and Jewel and Hooker we realize that there were all kinds of Anglicans; when we try to include Perkins and Ames and Prynne and Milton and Lilburne and Walwyn under a single rubric we despair of ever contriving a sufficiently broad definition for Puritan; and yet it is possible to discriminate the two persuasions on the basis of their attitudes toward Biblical truth. The Anglican establishment, an Erastian church legislated into being by the Elizabethan Settlement, built its doctrine on Geneva and its prelatical discipline on Rome; its defense of such a discipline necessarily rested on tradition and extra-Biblical authority. The Puritan dissent, reformist but not separatist, demanded a total reconstruction of the organization and discipline of the church along lines thought to be strictly Biblical.

More specifically, the Anglicans, appealing to the apostolic tradition and to the demands of reason and civil polity, sought to preserve the prelatical structure, the ritual, and the rites – all under the monarch as 'governor' of the church – that to their opponents looked like Roman idolatry. The Puritans, appealing to Genevan practice ostensibly derived directly from the Scripture and codified in Calvin's *Institutes*, would substitute the Presbyterian discipline of classis and synod, abolish the office and functions of bishops, eliminate the ritual, and vest supreme ecclesiastical authority with the church rather than with the chief of state.

As the Vestiarian controversy of the 'seventies shows, the conflict between the two groups was originally one of church discipline, but it quickly became apparent that questions of discipline involved much larger questions of civil and religious authority which the Reformers, in spite of their strenuous efforts, had left wide open. All men agreed that the church existed to explore and articulate the truth divinely revealed in the Bible; but there their agreement ended. The specific means of organizing and governing such a church, the specific application of Biblical truth to the mechanics of ecclesiastical and political administration posed problems of the gravest importance and difficulty. As Anglicans and Puritans sought to resolve such problems they were compelled to seek the ultimate basis of authority in truth, and to make clear the kinds of truth available to men. Hence the opposition of Cartwright and Travers to Jewel and Hooker, or of Milton and Lilburne to Laud and Sanderson. Was truth to be derived solely from the Bible as the 'sacred mouth' of God, or from tradition, natural reason, nature, and custom in addition to the Bible? Such a question very quickly led the Elizabethan controversialists beyond matters of surplices and altar-cloths and feast days to the basic epistemological problem of what man can know and how he can know it.

Bleakly stated, the doctrine of predestination would seem to make the problem unnecessary, and if we may believe the testimony of such unyielding Presbyterians as Prynne and Thomas Edwards it was, in fact, unnecessary. However, Hooker had staked out a wide area of natural truth which the latitudinarian theologians of the next century extended greatly; and the liberal wing of the Puritan party, seeking in the law of nature and the covenant of works sufficient sanctions for the political and ecclesiastical reforms, achieved a secular morality that would have repelled Calvin. It will be the business of this chapter and the next to explore these developments, and to show what a radically subversive effect they had on the traditional attitudes toward nature and truth.

When in his *Eius qui immobilis* (1535) Paul III smote Henry VIII with 'the sword of anathema, malediction and eternal damnation',[20] it was already too late to check the course of Henry's ecclesiastical policy. The English Reformation was unique in being the work of a single wilful and ruthless monarch rather than an upswelling popular movement, and Paul III was right in heaping his anathemas on that monarch. The church which Henry then established bore the stamp of its maker: the enabling legislation which a complaisant or a terrified Parliament provided firmly fixed its Erastian principles, and it has never lost its secular coloring as the ecclesiastical arm of the civil government. Not until a generation later, with the Elizabethan Settlement, were the main doctrinal and disciplinary lines of that church definitely laid down. As the Thirty-Nine Articles and the Book of Common Prayer show, the doctrine was Genevan and the discipline prelatical, but it was thus that Elizabeth hoped to steer a middle path between the demands of the Hot Gospelers of the left and the unreconstructed papists of the right. Paul V's *Regnans in excelsis* (1570) made it clear that the die was cast between Rome and Canterbury; the whole of Catholic Europe was lined up against Protestant England, and heresy and recusancy were broadened from merely ecclesiastical to political offenses.

None the less, a string of remarkably able prelates – Parker, Jewel, Bancroft, Whitgift – managed to maintain Elizabeth's policy against the increasing pressure of the Puritan minority and the open hostility of Continental Catholicism. Jesuit missionaries

---
[20] Bettenson, *Documents of the Christian Church*, p. 324.

THE VIA MEDIA 197

like Campion and Parsons, and even such Brownists[21] as were caught, were ostentatiously butchered. Meanwhile, the laws against recusancy and nonconformity mounted in ferocity until, as Bacon said with notable understatement, the queen's subjects had learned the habit of obedience and the moderation of discontents. However, the fact that the extremely Calvinistic Lambeth Articles (1595) failed to receive the official sanction of the Anglican church (even with Whitgift's powerful support) was simply one more proof that Elizabeth until the end of her days never abandoned her *via media*.

Elizabeth used terror because, as Milton said, she thought an attack on her bishops was an attack on her prerogatives; as for the bishops themselves, they consulted only their 'bellies'. ('They had found a good tabernacle, they sat under a spreading vine, their lot was fallen in a fair inheritance.')[22] At any rate, by the time James came to the throne it was obvious even to that muddle-headed Scotsman that the Erastian and prelatical discipline could not be changed without serious injury to the crown. No bishop, no king. Of course, there had been mounting discontent with that discipline ever since the opening of Elizabeth's reign. Very early (December 27th, 1558) she had banned preaching which caused 'unfruitful dispute' and even worse among the 'common sort' of people; a year later she emphatically denounced the soul-searching and gospel-searching Puritans who might upset the delicate status quo:

> Because in all alterations, and specially in rites and ceremonies, there happen discords amongst the people, and thereupon slanderous words and railings, whereby charity, the knot of all Christian society, is loosed; the queen's majesty . . . wills and straitly commands all manner her subjects to forbear all vain and contentious disputations in matters of religion, and not to use in despite or rebuke of any person these convicious words, papist or papistical heretic, schismatic or sacramentary, or any suchlike words of reproach.[23]

---

[21] The followers of Robert Browne represented the extremest form of Tudor Puritanism. A pupil of Cartwright who found his master too tame, Browne advocated the complete separation of church and state, denying to any magistrate any ecclesiastical power. He outraged both Anglicans and Presbyterians, of course, and it was made a capital offense to possess those inflammable works – *Reformation without Tarrying for Any, Order for Studying the Scripture, Life and Manners of all true Christians* – which he published in Holland, where he had sought refuge. On the Jesuit missionaries, see Fuller, IX.iv.6–12.
[22] *Of Reformation in England*, bk. I (PW, II, 374).
[23] Gee-Hardy, *Documents Illustrative of English Church History*, pp. 416–7, 435–6. On the Lambeth Articles, see Fuller, IX.viii.23–8.

The workings of the spirit and the fury of Rome were not to be stilled by proclamations, of course. The vehement Vestiarian controversy at Cambridge in the 'seventies, the terror aroused by the Jesuit missionaries in the 'eighties, the constant threat of Spain and France and Mary Stuart, the increasingly severe reprisals against both papists and Puritans, all suggest that the Anglican *via media* was maintained with the utmost vigilance and difficulty. Yet maintained it was, after a fashion – if not by moral suasion then by terror – and when James succeeded in 1603 he found an established church which boasted both a working organization and also an eruditely argued rationale in Hooker's *Laws*.

It is clear that Hooker fully realized the implications of the Puritan attack, and it is significant that he based his defense on the ancient tradition of Christian rationalism. As he wrote to Whitgift in the dedication, in the Puritan opposition he was confronted by 'confident and bold-spirited men' who, it was to be hoped, could best be persuaded by that method 'which searches the truth by the causes of truth'. Both before and after Hooker the argument was often intolerably rude and arid – Whitgift *versus* Cartwright shares the laurel with Cartwright *versus* Whitgift – but his high design cast the whole question on the highest possible plane.

> Our desire is ... not to be carried up and down with the waves of uncertain arguments, but rather positively to lead on the minds of the simpler sort by plain and easy degrees, till the very nature of the thing itself do make manifest what is truth.[24]

---

[24] *Laws*, V.xxi.2. Perhaps we should at least itemize the main documents in the controversy to which Hooker brought his great talents. The first important statement for the defense of the Elizabeth Settlemant was John Jewel's *Apologia ecclesiae Anglicanae* (1562, in English 1562 and 1564). The Puritans first made their demands explicit in *An Admonition to the Parliament* (1571); the next year Thomas Cartwright issued his *Second Admonition to the Parliament*, followed two years later by his translation of Walter Travers' *A Full and Plain Declaration of Ecclesiastical Discipline out of the Word of God* (i.e. *Ecclesiasticae disciplinae . . . explicatio*). John Whitgift had entered the fray in 1572 with *An Answer to a Certain Libel Intitled An Admonition to the Parliament*; this elicited Cartwright's *A Reply to an Answer* (1574), which led to Whitgift's *The Defense of the Answer*, which led to Cartwright's *Second Reply of Thomas Cartwright* (1575) and finally (1577) *The Rest of the Second Reply*.

In briefest form the Presbyterians demanded that the national church – completely independent of the monarch's authority – be reorganized along Genevan lines (that is, with elders and deacons rather than bishops and deans as the governing body); that all its members have an equal voice in naming their elders and deacons as well as in calling their ministers; that nationally the church be organized by classes and synods; and that such rites as kneeling to receive Holy Communion, using a ring in marriage, the churching of women, private communions and baptisms, observation of saints' days, etc., be immediately abolished as Catholic idolatries with no Biblical sanction.

We have already examined the broad outlines of Hooker's position. Here we need only say that within his rationalist position he tried to accommodate such rites and practices of the Anglican church as, though not specifically demanded by the Scripture, nevertheless could be justified by learning, reason, and tradition. To do so was to extend significantly the prerogatives of natural reason beyond the limits set by Calvin; it was to admit a whole set of epistemological criteria for determining the validity of extra-Biblical truth. For Hooker, God is supremely rational, and He orders and sustains His creation by a majestic hierarchy of laws. Some, like the divine law, are plainly written down for every man to see and observe; others, like the natural law, are implicit in the processes of nature and therefore must be inferred by the discourse of reason; others, like 'positive' civil laws, are left to the discretion of those eminent persons to whom is entrusted (by general consent) the management of the body politic. To formulate such civil or ecclesiastical laws is the work of human reason, operating on the knowledge of history and the needs of the time. Such laws have, as it were, a sort of pragmatic sanction: their utility is in being obeyed for the health and tranquility of the body politic, and though they obviously may not run counter to the great natural and eternal and divine laws which subsume them, they demand assent rather than belief to be operative. For even if they have no explicit Scriptural sanction, they are so supremely useful in ordering the affairs of men that, even though inhibitory, they bring order out of chaos.

> Those things which the law of God leaveth arbitrary and at liberty are all subject unto positive laws of men, which laws for the common benefit abridge particular men's liberty in such things as far as the rules of equity will suffer. This we must either maintain, or else overturn the world and make every man his own commander.[25]

In this area, then, lie those rites and rituals and disciplinary ordinances which have for so long sustained and adorned the church of God. Man has created them and man may change them, but if their beauty and utility have once been proved they should be disturbed only for the most compelling reasons. Such points of doctrine as the unity of God, the Trinity, and the Atonement 'have been since the first hour that there was a Church in the

[25] *Laws*, V.lxxi.4.

world, and till the last they must be believed'; but points of discipline and 'regiment' enjoy no such eternal sanction.

> To make new articles of faith and doctrine no man thinketh it lawful; new laws of government what commonwealth or church is there which maketh not either at one time or another?[26]

The great articles of faith are indispensable: they have been put down in black and white in the Bible, but all else are things indifferent. In matters 'which belong to discipline and outward polity, the Church hath authority to make canons, laws, and decrees, even as we read that in the Apostles' times it did'.[27]

On this distinction between the things necessary and the things indifferent Hooker – and Anglicans generally – built the defense of the establishment. Although the Bible contains all things necessary to salvation, the converse is not true; and not everything in the Bible is necessary to salvation, however profitable for morality and edification. Hooker sees the establishment as, of course, 'reformed' from the doctrinal and idolatrous errors of Rome, but none the less as continuing and even perfecting that long and flexible tradition of ecclesiastical discipline which stretched back to the apostolic church. The strength and beauty of that tradition is potent in his thought. Even though tradition is in a way inhibitory, its beauty is as compelling as its utility. Those who would summarily reject it threaten the very base of civil and ecclesiastical stability. For the program of the Puritan dissidents, derived from a rigorous literalism and from private judgment of interpretation,

> shaketh universally the fabric of the government, tendeth to anarchy and mere confusion, dissolveth families, dissipateth colleges, corporations, armies, overthroweth kingdoms, churches, and whatsoever is not through the providence of God by authority and power upheld.[28]

Apart from this advantage of positive law, Hooker is profoundly moved by the sheer beauty of the traditional rites and rituals to which the Puritans objected. They are the outward signs of inner grace, and even without that sanction demanded by the zealots they have with the passage of time acquired a sanctity all their own. With no intrinsic 'vital force or efficacy', they are none the less 'moral instruments of salvation' by common assent.[29]

---

[26] *Laws*, III.x.7. [27] *Laws*, III.x.7.
[28] *Laws*, V.lxxi.4. [29] *Laws*, V.lxxi.4.

THE *VIA MEDIA*

The very law of nature demands that we sanctify to God's worship certain times, places, persons, and things;[30] the traditional rites of the Christian church meet this demand; and we should therefore retain them.

> They are the splendour and outward dignity of our religion, forcible witnesses of ancient truth, provocations to the exercise of all piety, shadows of our endless felicity in heaven, on earth everlasting records and memorials, wherein they which cannot be drawn to hearken unto that we teach, may only by looking upon that we do, in a manner read whatsoever we believe.[31]

In Hooker's great and influential work we find the noblest statement of the Anglican case. It was, as no less a personage than that amateur theologian King James said, 'a grave, comprehensive, clear manifestation of reason, and that backed with the authority of the Scripture, the Fathers, and Schoolmen, and with all Law both sacred and civil'.[32] Hooker's measured defense of the discipline and of the epistemological assumptions which the Puritans so fiercely resented leaves its mark everywhere in the seventeenth century, not only in doctrinal and disciplinary details (which we cannot go into) but more fundamentally in that habit of spacious moderation and reasonableness which came to be the real strength of Anglican thought. Not even the sycophancy of a Mainwaring or the bloody terrors of a Laud could quite obscure the merits of Hooker's position. Habit and tradition are always powerful forces in men's thinking, and never more so than when justified so beautifully. 'The things which so long experience of all ages hath confirmed and made profitable, let us not presume to condemn as follies and toys, because we sometimes know not the cause and reason of them.'[33] When Herbert rejoices in the 'perfect lineaments, and hue Both sweet and bright' of the Anglican tradition,[34] when Browne so eloquently follows the 'great wheel of the Church',[35] when Sanderson recoils from the *ex tempore* prayers and bleak doctrinal haggling of the Sectarians to the pursuit of 'meekness and charity, and a frequent practice of devotion',[36] when Taylor remembers in the time of troubles the age-old beauties of the Anglican ritual, then we understand Hooker's continuing strength.

[30] *Laws*, V.lxx.9.
[31] *Laws*, V.lxxi.11.
[32] Walton, *Lives*, II, 75.
[33] *Laws*, IV.i.3.
[34] 'The British Church', *Works*, p. 111.
[35] *Religio Medici*, pp. 7–8.
[36] Walton, *Lives*, II, 283–4.

> I shall onely crave leave that I may remember Jerusalem and call to minde the pleasures of the Temple, the order of her services, the beauty of her buildings, the sweetness of her songs, the decency of her Ministrations, the assiduity and Oeconomy of her Priests and Levites, the daily sacrifice, and that eternal fire of devotion that went not out by day nor by night; these were the pleasures of our peace, that there is a remanent felicity in the very memory of those spiritual delights which we then enjoyed as antepasts of heaven, and consignations to an immortality of joyes.[37]

The instinctive reliance on order, propriety, custom, and tradition was to remain the bulwark of the Anglican tradition, and though it could lead to the compulsions of Laud and the arid formalism of the Hanoverian establishment, it could also, in times of strife and urgency, quicken into a kind of religious sentiment quite as powerful as the Puritans' tortured, subjective intensity. There were many good men like Earle's divine: he 'thinks he owes that reverence to the church to bow his judgment to it, and make more conscience of schism than a surplice'.[38] Hooker's sweet reasonableness could serve as the base for Chillingworth's plea for toleration,[39] and even for that defense of the establishment which the martyred Charles was thought to have written in *Eikon Basilikon*:

> For I conceive, that where the Scripture is not so clear and punctuall in precepts, there the constant and Universall practice of the Church, in things not contrary to Reason, Faith, good Manners, or any positive Command, is the best rule that Christians can follow.[40]

The Anglican church and the English crown had both suffered terribly – perhaps justly – since Hooker laid down his defense of the *via media*; yet his words remained a monument to the hope that in reason and decorum men might yet find peace. 'Spend the time in reëxamining more duly your cause', he told his antagonists,

> and in more thoroughly considering of that which ye labour to overthrow. As for the orders which are established, sith equity and reason, the law of nature, God and man, do all favour that which is in being, till orderly judgment of decision be given against it; it is but justice to exact of you, and perverseness in you to deny, thereunto your willing obedience.[41]

---

[37] *A Collection of Offices, The Golden Grove* (ed. L. P. Smith), p. 6.
[38] *Microcosmography*, no. iii.
[39] For example, see 'The Apostolical Institution of Episcopacy Demonstrated', *Works*, II, 531.
[40] p. 121.   [41] *Laws*, 'A Preface', VI.5.

III. THE PURITAN DISSENT

To the rationalist, corporate, ritualized, and Erastian church discipline of the Anglican establishment the Puritan dissidents were a real menace. 'But let them chant while they will of prerogatives', thunders Milton against the prelates,

> we shall tell them of scripture; of custom, we of scripture, of acts and statutes, still of scripture; till the quick and piercing word enter to the dividing of their souls, and the mighty weakness of the gospel throw down the weak mightiness of man's reasoning.[42]

To Milton – and in this regard, at least, his Puritanism was typical – the Anglican argument from reason and tradition was an affront to the inwardness and subjectivism of true devotion. For 'near twelve hundred years' the odious bishops have been the curse of England, 'a wasteful band of robbers' to our purses, a 'continual hydra of mischief and molestation' to the state; 'this is the trophy of their antiquity, and boasted succession through so many ages'.[43]

It cannot be claimed for the Puritans that they were men of original minds or that they attempted and achieved a genuine reconstruction of religious or secular thought; but their revival of a pulsating Augustinian theology came in time to jeopardize the whole structure of a society built on the Renaissance values of order, reason, and theistic optimism. Early Presbyterians like Cartwright and Travers could not have foreseen the secular extension to which Independents like Lilburne and Overton would push their views, and, if they could, they would have been dismayed. But the seeds of Independency and democracy lay in the very nature of Protestantism, and it needed only the germination of time and history to fructify them. In a work like this we cannot hope to follow the tangled history of Puritan doctrine, or to trace properly from the original Calvinistic impetus of the Elizabethan Puritans the emergence of Brownists, Separatists, Independents, Baptists, Levelers, Diggers, Fifth Monarchy Men, assorted Sectarians, and all the rest. But we should attempt to isolate their common attitudes, and to show the relevance of these attitudes to the main patterns of seventeenth-century thought. The most important of these, perhaps, is what we shall call Puritan intensity.

---

[42] *The Reason of Church Government*, II.ii (*PW*, II, 485).
[43] *Of Reformation in England*, bk. II (*PW*, II, 411).

A distinguished modern historian has said that Puritan piety comprised the components of God, sin, and regeneration. In the generic Puritan consciousness – if there was such a thing – each of these factors of religious emotion was experienced with an intensity and a passion that seemed to obliterate all else. The Puritan's God was Calvin's – omnipotent, unknowable, terrifying. Although he was a God of infinite mercy, as witnessed by His election of sinners to undeserved salvation, He was also a God of wrath and awful justice: the joys of heaven no less than the fiery anguish of hell were at His disposal.

> The principal author of hell-torments is God himself. As it was no less than God whom the sinners had offended, so it is no less than God who will punish them for their offences. He hath prepared those torments for his enemies. His continual anger will still be devouring them. His breath of indignation will kindle the flames. His wrath will be an intolerable burden to their souls.[44]

For God's was an absolute sovereignty, and it was the crushing duty of fallen man to come to terms with him. Man is the absolute antithesis of God – sinful, depraved, impotent – and of himself or through his own puny efforts he can hope for no amelioration of his polluted soul. Such amelioration is possible, if at all, through regeneration, that is, through the actual rebirth of the Old Adam into the New Adam by the agency of Christ's atonement.

This regeneration cannot be earned, nor can it even be calculated on any curve of probability; it comes as the free gift of God, arbitrarily bestowed, made operative through His divine grace, and resulting in the justification and eventually the sanctification of the reclaimed sinner. 'Regeneration', says Milton, 'is that change operated by the Word and the Spirit, whereby the old man being destroyed, the inward man is regenerated by God after His own image, in all the faculties of his mind, insomuch that he becomes as it were a new creature, and the whole man is sanctified both in body and soul, for the service of God, in the performance of good works.'[45] In this transaction, the significance of which dwarfs every other fact of life, the initiative is always God's and man's role is that of seeker and supplicant. Yet when the transaction is successfully completed by God's irresistible grace, and man is elected a candidate for salvation, he has achieved

---
[44] Baxter, *The Saints' Everlasting Rest*, VI.9.
[45] *De doctrina*, I.xviii (*PW*, IV, 328).

THE PURITAN DISSENT

the imputed righteousness of Christ, and he is therefore a dedicated creature set apart.

If, on the other hand, he is chosen for reprobation, and left among the vast majority cut off from grace, he is doomed to a life of futility and an eternity of nameless horrors. Thus viewed, the Christian epic, though retaining its broad outlines, was brought to focus on the overwhelming anguish of man alienated from God, the ineffable joy of man reunited with God. Thus the main impulse of Puritan theology was to achieve that influx of unmerited grace which alone could relieve man's natural depravity. Preaching before the army headquarters at Putney in 1647, Thomas Collier made this apotheosis of God's elect the compelling Puritan dream. By this sanctification the saints of God achieve

> that union which the divine nature, the Spirit, hath with us and in our spirits, by which union it transforms our spirits into its own glory, and shall in conclusion wholly swallow up the Saints in that spiritual glory, which will be their eternal perfection, their heaven, their kingdom, their glory.[46]

Of course, the main articles of Puritan theology had been the common property of Christendom ever since the days of the apostles; certainly they occupied a central place in Anglican doctrine. But the Puritan was set apart from other men by the unremitting, sometimes maniacal, fervor with which he held these articles. The Puritan's distinction was perhaps one of tonality and degree, but it was enough to make him a marked man. Set against the traditional and formalized religious emotion of the Anglican, for instance, it flamed like a torch, and it illumined every aspect of his religious experience. His 'peculiar ferocity', as Mr Miller has said, came from the absolutism of his religious temper – from 'its refusal to make allowances for circumstance and weakness, from its judging by the highest possible standard, its unremitting measurement of the human by the divine'.[47] For the intensity of this religious subjectivism, as for the other basic elements in the Puritan ethos, Calvin was, of course, mainly responsible.

> It is necessary, therefore, that the same Spirit, who spake by the mouths of the prophets, should penetrate into our hearts, to convince us that they faithfully delivered the oracles which were divinely intrusted to them.

[46] Woodhouse, p. 390.
[47] *The New England Mind*, p. 57.

> ... We seek not arguments or probabilities to support our judgment, but submit our judgments and understandings as to a thing concerning which it is impossible for us to judge; and that not like some persons, who are in the habit of hastily embracing what they do not understand, which displeases them as soon as they examine it, but because we feel the firmest conviction that we hold an invincible truth; nor like those unhappy men who surrender their minds captives to superstition, but because we perceive in it the undoubted energies of the Divine power, by which we are attracted and inflamed to an understanding and voluntary obedience, but with a vigour and efficacy superior to the power of any human will and knowledge.[48]

Given this 'deepest conviction', this 'vigour and efficacy superior to the power of any human will and knowledge', the Puritan could – and often did – become an extremely unpleasant character. In his purest form he was a zealot, and his zeal derived from his absolute certainty that he, as one of the elect, had access to a body of divine truth compared to which the relative truths of the world – political, ecclesiastical, moral, natural – were thin and paltry. 'The Spirit of Christ is no fancy, dream, or delusion, nor worketh an imaginary change on the soul, but a real change, making the soul alive that was dead in sin, and becomes a principle of life within us.'[49] Like St Paul, Calvin had in a fashion democratized salvation, bringing each man face to face with God. But also he had created a spiritual élite: the saints of God were initiates, and their unyielding arrogance – communal among Presbyterians, personal among Sectarians – came to be one of the most disruptive forces of the late Renaissance.

Thus the inevitable collision between Puritan and Anglican notions of church government. With the passionate conviction that his enjoyed the sanction of God Himself the Puritan was temperamentally unable to make concessions to political expediency, or history, or tradition.

> The Discipline of Christs Church that is necessary for all times is delivered by Christ, and set downe in the holy Scriptures. Therefore the true and lawfull Discipline is to be fetched from thence, and from thence alone. And that which resteth upon any other foundation ought to be esteemed unlawfull and counterfeit.[50]

Thus Cartwright himself had spoken; and Milton, with sweet

---

[48] *Institutes*, I.vii.4–5.
[49] Baxter, *The Unreasonableness of Infidelity*, II.xiii (*Works*, XX, 153).
[50] Cartwright, *A Directory of Church-government*, sig. A2r.

THE PURITAN DISSENT

reasonableness, added that the 'queazy temper of lukewarmness' resulting from a prelatical discipline 'gives a vomit to God himself'.[51] His need for, or his sense of, initiation also accounts for the peculiar urgency of the Puritan's religious emotion. Judging by the highest possible standard – that is, the revealed word of God and the 'deepest conviction' of the Holy Spirit – his own conduct became to him a matter of agonizing inadequacy; his sense of sin and his need for grace were too searing to be assuaged by the hollow and perfunctory rituals of any ecclesiastical tradition. He was endlessly and tediously absorbed in the state of his soul, and the state of his soul was a matter strictly between him and God. Since he yearned to burn always with the white heat of religious fervor, when he lapsed into the ways of the world he was made wretched. Richard Rogers grieves that, although the month of July 1587 began well for him, his absorbing sense of God's presence steadily declined. 'I litle and litle fell from the strenghth which I had gotten and became unprofitable in study, and praier and med[itation] were not continued privatly of me with such joy as the first week, yet not broken of.'[52] This agonizing sense of spiritual weakness strikes the real note of Puritan introspection, and the habit of introspection was made compulsory by the very nature of Puritan theology.

For as every Puritan realized, and as Richard Sibbes said, it is 'no easy matter to bring a man from nature to grace, and from grace to glory, so unyielding and untractable are our hearts'.[53] The actual mechanics of that miraculous development depended ultimately, obviously, on the secret will of God; none the less, to describe the change from its inception through all its most minute stages to its consummation in glory became one of the favorite tasks of Puritan divines. The drama of man's election, vocation, justification, sanctification, and glorification was one of endless fascination and unutterable significance. As a drama in which every single man could be the protagonist, it represented the agony and the triumph of Puritan theology. 'What an eternal Sabbatism', breathes Baxter fervently, 'when the work of redemption, sanctification, preservation, glorification, is all finished, and

[51] *Of Reformation in England*, bk. I (*PW*, II, 373). For further expressions of Milton's typically Puritan contempt for the outward and garish rituals of stylized devotion, see *PL*, IV.736–7, V.144–52.
[52] Knappen, *Two Elizabethan Puritan Diaries*, p. 55; cf. p. 58.
[53] *The Bruised Reed and Smoking Flax*, ch. ii (*Works*, I, 44–5).

perfected forever!'⁵⁴ As a giant of systematic theology William Perkins gave a typically complex analysis of the process. Man's first access of grace has 'ten severall actions': God breaks man's spirit, then brings him to a consideration of sin in general, then of his own particular sins, then 'smites his heart with a Legall feare' so that the sinner fears punishment. These four 'actions' are preparatory; by the positive action of grace God stirs the mind to a serious consideration of the gospel promise of salvation, then kindles in the heart 'some seedes or sparkes of faith' (thus beginning the process of sanctification), this faith then combats doubt and mistrust, God then settles the conscience concerning the salvation of the soul, next He stirs the heart to 'Evangelicall sorrow' or grief for sin, and lastly He gives to the justified man the grace to obey His commands 'by a new obedience'.⁵⁵

Perkins' mechanistic, almost tabular, analysis of regeneration may seem stale and wearisome, but the process itself was of the most passionate concern to generations of Puritans. We need only read Bunyan's *Grace Abounding* to see how a man of genius could make it the center of his life, or *The Pilgrim's Progress* to find it transformed into art when Hopeful describes his salvation to Christian. Although he was aware of his evil ways – 'rioting, revelling, drinking, swearing, lying, uncleanness, Sabbath-breaking, and what not' – he hardened his heart and resisted the absolutely essential requisite of regeneration: that burning inward conviction of sin. Mere leaving off sin, weeping, and ostentatious prayer brought him no real relief. But when he learned that the righteousness of Christ would cancel his own unrighteousness he was at last pointed toward heaven.

> One day I was very sad, I think sadder than at any one time in my life, and this sadness was through a fresh sight of the greatness and vileness of my sins. And as I was then looking for nothing but hell, and the everlasting damnation of my soul, suddenly, as I thought, I saw the Lord Jesus Christ look down from heaven upon me, and saying, 'Believe on the Lord Jesus Christ, and thou shalt be saved'.

From this corrosive conviction of his infamy and of Christ's perfection two results followed: a great sense of spiritual well-being and a compulsion to cleanse the world's iniquity by bringing others to salvation. 'It made me love a holy life, and long to do

---

⁵⁴ *The Saints' Everlasting Rest*, I, 14.
⁵⁵ *Cases of Conscience*, I.v.7.

something for the honour and glory of the name of the Lord Jesus; yea, I thought that had I now a thousand gallons of blood in my body, I could spill it all for the sake of the Lord Jesus.'[56]

The Puritan saw life as struggle. Satan without and the Old Adam within lurked ever ready to drag him down to hell. His pilgrimage toward grace, even though futile without God's election, was a conscious, muscular effort to overcome the world and the flesh. As William Perkins said about 'the right way of fighting the Spirituall battell', there was needed the armor of truth, justice, evangelical obedience, faith, the word of God, and 'continuall and fervent prayer with watching'.[57] But even with such aids the good man's life was a torture of remorse, and not for nothing did Baxter enjoin the faithful to 'spend all your days in a skilful, vigilant, resolute, and valiant war' under the banners of 'Christ the Captain of your Salvation'.[58] In the regenerate man himself, as Calvin had warned, there still remains 'a fountain of evil, continually producing irregular desires, which allure and stimulate him to the commission of sin'.[59] Like Samuel Sewall of Boston, Milton, and many others, the diarist Rogers was an incorrigibly connubial man, and he periodically prescribed for this carnal weakness: 'Want of stricter diet, and the takeing of too much liberty in godes lawful bless[ings], and a contenting my selfe to kepe a comon course and takeing to much ease.'[60]

The felt discrepancy between the natural man and man in a state of grace was the most immediate object of the Puritan's thought, and his unspeakable longing for release from the body of this death the compelling motive behind his every action. 'Alas! What a disproportion is there between our light and heat!' exclaims Baxter, 'our profession and prosecution! Who makes that haste as if it were for heaven? How still we stand! How idly we work! How we talk, and jest, and trifle away our time!'[61] As Bunyan's great allegory tells us, life was a pilgrimage in which not a moment was to be wasted. If one attained the Celestial City one did so with agony of soul, with seeking, and with torment – but also with ineffable exultation. However, the saint's ever-

---

[56] *The Pilgrim's Progress*, pp. 162–71.
[57] *A Golden Chaine*, pp. 406 f.
[58] *Christian Directory*, I.iii.9 (*Works*, II, 258).
[59] *Institutes*, III.iii.10.
[60] Knappen, *Two Elizabethan Puritan Diaries*, p. 85.
[61] *The Saints' Everlasting Rest*, VII.5.

lasting rest was not for all who sought it, nor did the vision of it ease the intolerable sense of sin that was the first step toward heaven. 'When conscience is under the guilt of sin', said Richard Sibbes in a vastly popular treatise, 'then every judgment brings a report of God's anger to the soul, and all less troubles run into this great trouble of conscience for sin.'[62] The godly man stared upon his sins and writhed in his guilt, for as Bunyan said, if 'the power of guilt weareth away' then he has lost his vision of God.[63] Thus Samuel Ward's diary becomes a grim litany of his offenses: wearisome in God's service, dullness in morning prayers, 'My adulterous dream', anger against Mr Newhouse for his long prayers, desire of preferment 'over much', 'wandring mynd in the Chapell at prayer time', his gluttony the night before, his day-dreaming 'on herbals' at prayers, and so on. After several pages of this it comes as a surprise to read, among his other faults, 'My forgetfulness in noting my sinnes'.[64]

Such self-scrutiny helps us to understand the Puritan's insistence on good works and a moral life as the outward signs – but emphatically not the cause – of his justification. Socially and economically he was a man of action; his religion was a militant, aggressive force fundamentally incompatible with contemplation and ritualized devotion. No genuine piety, said Milton to his Anglican opponents, can 'run out lavishly to the upper skin, and there harden into a crust of formality'.[65] Although morality meant nothing without regeneration – justification had to precede sanctification, in the Puritan's jargon – regeneration made moral conduct possible. Although Milton had come far from Calvin, on this point his is the typical Puritan view: what he calls 'works' can come only as a result of the holy spirit working in the regenerated man, never as a result of man's own unaided attempts at virtue.

> Hence may be easily discerned the vanity of human merits; seeing that, in the first place, our good actions are not our own, but of God working in us; secondly, that, were they our own, they would still be equally due;

[62] *The Bruised Reed and Smoking Flax*, ch. iv (*Works*, I, 46). This was the book that Richard Baxter's father bought from a pedlar who came to the door with 'ballads and some good books'. Baxter names it as one of the principal agencies in bringing him to grace (*Autobiography*, p. 7).
[63] *The Pilgrim's Progress*, p. 181. For Burton's opinion of this Puritan melancholia, see *Anatomy*, III, 456.
[64] Knappen, *Two Elizabethan Puritan Diaries*, pp. 103–4, 106.
[65] *Of Reformation in England*, bk. I (*PW*, II, 365–6).

and, thirdly, that, in any point of view, there can be no proportion between our duty and the proposed reward [of eternal bliss].[66]

The virtues that man might acquire through exercise of his reason or education or self-control might (or might not) contribute to a good life, but they had no bearing whatever on the question of his salvation. For that, nothing less than regeneration through an access of divine grace was compulsory. Although the saints of God could not prove their election, by their intense introspection they knew it, and the fruit of this knowledge was a life of goodness. If the Puritan's creed made no allowance for works as a *means* of salvation, it insisted on their significance as *signs* of salvation; and every Puritan thus labored under a compulsion – frequently offensive to the ungodly – to assume personal responsibility for advancing the kingdom of God.

This reformist zeal, together with the historical fact of the ridicule and opposition that they encountered, led to a strong communal feeling among the saints. Their very exclusiveness was a source of strength. Since, in the nature of things, the elect constituted a tiny minority of the human race – 'that they are but a small part of mankind is too apparent in Scripture and experience', said Baxter smugly[67] – the happy few were forced into intimate spiritual association, so that from the very beginning the Puritans tended to band together in 'holy communities' under godly ministers.

As much through their piety and presence as through their writings, these great Puritan preachers influenced thousands of mute, inglorious Miltons. Academically radiating from Cambridge – Emmanuel College was the seedbed of Elizabethan and Jacobean Puritanism – they formed something of a ministerial succession from Cartwright. As the author of *A Golden Chain* and *Cases of Conscience*, William Perkins was the most important Puritan writer of the late sixteenth century. Though he published little, Laurence Chaderton preached for fifty years at St Clement's Church in Cambridge until he was succeeded by John Preston, whose short but dazzling career at Cambridge and Lincoln's Inn made him the Pico della Mirandola of Puritanism. From his

---

[66] *De doctrina*, II.i (*PW*, V, 8).
[67] *The Saints' Everlasting Rest*, IV. 2. Pierre du Moulin, the prominent Huguenot, calculated that only one person in 100,000 had any chance of salvation (Smith, *A History of Modern Culture*, I, 379).

Leicestershire parish Arthur Hildersham shaped the thinking of men like William Gouge (a famous preacher at Blackfriars), John Cotton (who after twenty-one years in Lincolnshire fled to America in the same ship with Thomas Hooker), and Preston. John Dod, whose sermons helped to set the Puritan 'plain style', preached in Cambridge, Oxfordshire, and Northamptonshire; he was a close associate of Richard Sibbes, whose *Bruised Reed and Smoking Flax* was prodigiously admired throughout the century. Thomas Goodwin, Preston's most notable disciple and his successor as Trinity lecturer, was driven by the Laudian oppression to Holland in the 'thirties, but he returned to become the hero of the Westminster Assembly when Charles was at the very gates of London; subsequently one of the most effective spokesmen for the Independents, he finally became president of Magdalen College in 1650. Of course, there were many others – some great celebrities, and many more whose very names have been forgotten – and collectively they were the motor energy of Puritanism.

With the 'holy communities' the basis of church organization was broadly equalitarian: since all men were as one in their iniquity, they could strive together; moreover, as earnest seekers their sense of vocation and spiritual dedication put them all on equal footing.[68] Their emphasis on preaching, exhortation, and Scriptural searching colliding as it did with the formality of Anglican ritual, the communal and theologically democratic aspects of Puritan discipline aroused the most vehement opposition. After the turn of the new century, when the Puritans began agitating political as well as ecclesiastical reforms as a countermeasure to Stuart oppression, their pulpits came to be regarded as a prime source of sedition as well as of 'fanatick' zeal. It was one of their most grievous charges against Laud and his spies that they suppressed public preaching and *ex tempore* prayers, the two essential adjuncts of Puritan piety.

What Bunyan calls the 'company of lively and warm Christians'[69] came to be viewed by the bishops with the gravest alarm, but the freedom of preaching and seeking was inevitably one of

---

[68] For a standard account of this discipline, see Cartwright, *A Directory of Church-government*, sig. A2ᵛ-A3ᵛ.

[69] *The Pilgrim's Progress*, p. 183. See Baxter's full discussion of the necessity of a 'judicious, faithful, serious, searching, powerful minister', *Christian Directory*, I.ii.7 (*Works*, II, 113-8).

THE PURITAN DISSENT

the Puritans' main demands. As Lord Brooke said,

> through the whole Kingdome, Preaching, Praying, Expounding, and the like exercises, both in publick & private, are severely suppressed, and in many places altogether forbidden (except such and such, more pernicious than profitable;) and al this by the Fathers of our Church, the Lords our Bishops.[70]

Such fathers, all Puritans would agree, were parasites sapping the strength of the kingdom, 'like the weake Fruitlesse Ivy, that must be propt up by some Elme, or mighty Oake, and yet most unnaturally destroyeth That prop which holdeth it up. And of This kind is that Humane (or rather Demonical) Episcopacie'.[71]

Against such charges, Jeremy Taylor advanced the customary Anglican defense. In place of the legal and decorous order of public worship, the Puritan zealots would force men

> under the harrows and saws of impertinent and ignorant Preachers, who think all Religion is a Sermon, and all Sermons ought to be Libels against Truth and old Governours, and expound Chapters that the meanings may never be understood, and pray, that they may be thought able to talk, but not to hold their peace, they casting not to obtain any thing but Wealth and Victory, Power and Plunder.[72]

As an Anglican, Taylor could never hope to understand the strength and solace that wrestling with the spirit brought to the Puritan, and as a Puritan Lord Brooke could never subjugate his need for spiritual health to the prescriptions of worldly prelates.

If Lord Brooke could have done so, or relaxed in the assurance of ritualized devotion, he would have been no Puritan. If he had not burned with a conviction of his sins he would not have been capable of the peculiar despair and elation which comprise the Puritan sensibility. Perhaps Sir John Harington recognized this sensibility when he defined Puritans as 'Protestants scar'd out of their wits'.[73] At any rate, they knew that man is a sinful worm and incapable of good; but they also knew he may hope for heaven. 'We have more for us than against us', exhorted Sibbes. 'What coward would not fight when he is sure of victory? None

---

[70] *A Discourse opening the Nature of Episcopacy*, II.vi (Haller, II, 136).
[71] *Ibid.*, I.ix (Haller, II, 89).
[72] *The Golden Grove*, 'To the Reader' (*The Golden Grove* [ed. L. P. Smith], pp. 31-2. Note Selden's wry comment (*Table Talk*, p. 104): ' 'Tis hoped wee may bee cur'd of our extempore prayers, the same way the Grocers boy is cur'd of his eating plums, when wee have had our belly full of them').
[73] *Nugae Antiquae*, I, 8.

are here overcome, but he that will not fight.'[74] He who did fight, and conquer, could hope for a blissful eternity in the very presence of God. For the Puritan's heaven, like his hell, was very real to him – 'What is heaven to us, if there be no love and joy?'[75] – and there he could hope at last to lay down the burden of his sin. Heavenly rest, said Baxter, is 'the ceasing from means of grace: When we have obtained the haven, we have done sailing. When the workman receives his wages, it is implied he has done his work. When we are at our journey's end, we have done with the way.'[76] In the great epic of Puritanism it is God Himself, speaking to His Son, who summarizes the aim and method of Puritan piety:

> And I will place within them as a guide
> My umpire Conscience, whom if they will hear,
> Light after light well us'd they shall attain,
> And to the end persisting, safe arrive.

Long after the first agony and ecstasy of English Puritanism had spent itself, Joseph Addison ridiculed its excesses. He shows a young man, just come up to Oxford, being interviewed by a Puritan minister. Latin and Greek are all very well, the youth is told, but what about the state of his soul? He is earnestly asked

> whether he was of the Number of the Elect; what was the Occasion of his Conversion; upon what Day of the Month, and Hour of the Day it happened; how it was carried on and when compleated. The whole Examination was summed up with one short Question, Namely, Whether he was prepared for Death?[77]

This is all very witty and urbane, and no doubt most of us find it easier to side with Addison than with Prynne. But unless we can understand the peculiar poignancy and even terror with which the Puritan asked himself these questions, and the significance of his answers, we miss one of the seminal forces in seventeenth-century thought.

[74] *The Bruised Reed and Smoking Flax*, ch. xxviii (*Works*, I, 98).
[75] Baxter, *Autobiography*, p. xxii.
[76] *The Saints' Everlasting Rest*, I. 5.
[77] *The Spectator*, no. 494 (IV, 76–7).

IV. DISPUTANDI PRURITUS ECCLESIARUM SCABIES

The respect for tradition, a dominant characteristic of Anglican thought, has obvious epistemological implications. It rests on the assumption that tradition represents the accumulated wisdom of the universal church, and that this wisdom may be defended on rational grounds as a repository of legitimate religious truth. Quite apart from its immense aesthetic appeal – so endearing to Hooker and Herbert and Taylor, so repugnant to the Puritans – it served other purposes. As a sort of religious *sensus communis* it preserved the slow precipitation of centuries of religious experience, at last cleansed from the errors of Rome and now deposited in the reformed discipline of the Anglican establishment. The bishops of that establishment, sanctioned by the apostolic succession and by their intimate Erastian alignment with the crown, were thus preëminently fitted to determine the nature, limits, and efficacy of practices not specifically called for in the Bible. It was their high function to adjudicate the claims of reason and revelation, to determine the articles of faith and the sacraments, to bring order and decorum to the ritual, and to enforce such conformity in things indifferent as would assure ecclesiastical and political stability.

As bishops in the apostolic succession and thus men illumined by grace, they were obliged to prove, said Laud, that Christianity, 'which rests upon the authority of this book [the Bible], stands upon surer grounds of nature, reason, common equity, and justice, than any thing in the world which any infidel or mere naturalist hath done, doth or can adhere unto, against it, in that which he makes, accounts, or assumes as religion to himself'.[78] Since reason and grace inevitably work together,[79] man can exercise his reason to no higher purpose than 'to discover, or to judge and allow, within the sphere of its own activity, and not presuming further', the way to salvation.[80] It is the divine mandate of the reformed church, properly guided by its bishops as men of grace and learning and experience, to determine the rites, rituals, and ordinances for maintaining this delicate equilibrium between faith and reason, and thus assure the salvation of souls, the piety of the realm.

[78] *Relation of the Conference, Works*, II, 88–9.
[79] *Ibid., Works*, II, 87.
[80] *Ibid., Works*, II, 91.

Although the logic of this tacit identification of apostolic tradition, reason, and the Anglican establishment is not always clear, its consequences are everywhere apparent in the seventeenth century. Against the presumptuous claims of private inspiration, the Puritan repugnance for ritual, the latent antirationalism of reformed theology, and the exfoliation of sects and parties, the national church stood as a bulwark for conformity, decorum, and tradition. It consistently maintained against the vagaries of this or that inspirational sect the massive and accumulated wisdom of the universal church; and it consistently combated the inherent Protestant tendency to refer all questions of religious truth and discipline to the inner light, or conscience, or private judgment. As Hooker warned, such alleged illumination, especially among the 'vulgar sort',

> hath already made thousands so headstrong even in gross and palpable errors, that a man whose capacity will scarce serve him to utter five words in sensible manner blusheth not in any doubt concerning matter of Scripture to think his own bare *Yea* as good as the *Nay* of all the wise, grave, and learned judgments that are in the whole world: which insolency must be repressed, or it will be the very bane of Christian religion.[81]

Similarly, Donne regarded those self-elected 'saints' who thought they alone had the key to salvation as the white spots of leprosy in the church;[82] Browne, deploring the vehemence and rancor of sectarian controversy, concluded that 'Every man is not a proper Champion for Truth, nor fit to take up the Gauntlet in the cause of Verity';[83] Burton prayed that God might destroy all the 'fopperies' of private religious judgment, but he feared the worst: 'As a dam of water stopt in one place breaks out in another, so doth superstition';[84] Sir Henry Wotton laid it down in his epitaph that 'Disputandi pruritus ecclesiarum scabies'.[85]

In this regard the rationalism, or at least the *bon sens*, of the Anglican establishment led certain men to take an increasingly dim view of all varieties of zeal and enthusiasm. Long before Locke ridiculed 'the conceits of a warmed or over-weening brain' and sneered at the 'ease and glory it is to be inspired',[86] or before Swift wrote *A Tale of a Tub*, there had been a steady Anglican movement against religious individualism. As a legalist Selden

[81] *Laws*, II.vii.6.
[82] *Works*, IV, 511.
[83] *Religio Medici*, p. 7; cf. p. 62.
[84] *Anatomy*, III, 372.
[85] Walton, *Lives*, I, 184.
[86] *Essay*, IV.xix.8 (Fraser, II, 433).

shuddered at the consequences of subordinating law to private conscience;[87] as an Erastian Hobbes could only regard highly subjective religion as a form of treason.[88] Samuel Butler spoke well and wittily for his age in caricaturing in his Ralph that sort of religious enthusiast whose inspiration defied reason, or common sense, or political loyalty.

> Some call it Gifts, and some New-light;
> A liberal art, that costs no pains
> Of study, industry, or brains.[89]

The Anglican *via media* represented, after its fashion, what was left of the corporate religious emotion of the Middle Ages (significantly conceived in national, not universal, terms), and to the modern heresies, political and religious, spawned by Puritan individualism it could give no quarter. If one is free to refer all questions of faith, or church discipline, or even political allegiance merely to conscience, then clearly church and state must fall together with the wisdom and the unifying tradition of the centuries. This was a common theme of Taylor's.

> Nothing is more usual, then to pretend Conscience to all the actions of men which are publick, and whose nature cannot be concealed. If arms be taken up in a violent warre; inquire of both sides, why they ingage on that part respectively? they answer, because of their Conscience. Ask a Schismatick why he refuses to joyn in the Communion of the Church? he tells you, it is against his Conscience: And the disobedient refuse to submit to Laws; and they also in many cases pretend Conscience. . . . And so Suspicion; and Jealousie, and Disobedience, and Rebellion are become Conscience; in which there is neither knowledge, nor revelation, nor truth, nor charity, nor reason, nor religion.[90]

To those who found in the Anglican communion a focus of conservative and traditional values, the various dissenting movements were objectionable on the most serious grounds. The Puritan's tendency to weigh his own reading of the Bible against the divinely and politically established authority of the episcopacy constituted the gravest threat to ecclesiastical and political conformity. The comic aspects of Puritan sanctity and hypocrisy

---

[87] *Table Talk*, p. 35.
[88] *Leviathan*, ch. viii (p. 37); cf. *Behemoth*, pt. I (*English Works*, VI, 167).
[89] *Hudibras*, I.i.482-4.
[90] *Ductor Dubitantium*, *The Golden Grove* (ed. L. P. Smith), p. 145. Taylor repeatedly attacks, in his sermons as in his more formal doctrinal works, the 'zeal' of misguided enthusiasts. See *Sermons*, pp. 37, 109; *Holy Living*, IV.iii; cf. Hooker, *Laws*, V.iii.1.

were exploited richly: Earle smiles at the 'shee precise hypocrite' who will not 'cudgel her maids without scripture',[91] and a whole generation of playwrights made characters like Zeal-of-the-Land-Busy into the grossest buffoons. But much more was at stake than such caricatures indicate. For one thing, it quickly became apparent that the Puritans, seeking Scriptural authority for every action, would resort to the most far-fetched interpretations of the Bible. Hooker held it a 'most infallible rule' that 'where a literal construction will stand, the farthest from the letter is commonly the worst',[92] and every good Anglican would echo his strictures on the 'licentious and deluding art' of wresting the Scripture. 'Make noe more Allegoryes in Scripture; then needs must', says Selden bluntly: given a fertile brain and a seditious temper, the Puritan could allegorize error from truth and justify treason from the naked word of God.[93] Similarly, John Hales speaks with unwonted severity against the sin of twisting the Scripture to one's own passions and prejudices.

> When we strive to give unto it, and not receive from it the sense: when we factiously contend to fasten our Conceits upon God; and, like the Harlot in the Book of Kings, take our dead and putrified Fancies, and lay them in the bosom of Scripture, as of a Mother; than are we guilty of this great sin of wresting of Scripture.[94]

The judicious Hooker had realized that the itch to 'draw all things under the determination of bare and naked Scripture' could jeopardize the realm, but he, after all, was dealing mainly with sober Presbyterians and so was spared the excesses of later Sectarians. But he recognized the danger: a fanatic fundamentalism, he argued, involves the rejection of all authority, and thus overthrows the 'orders, laws, and constitutions' without which the establishment would perish.[95] The Precisians who hold 'that one only law, the Scripture, must be the rule to direct in all things, even so far as to the "taking up of a rush or straw"', outrage decorum; they debase the Bible by applying it to things unworthy or indifferent, and they exact of their opponents minute Scriptural authority even for those practices on which the Scripture is properly silent. If God has made men reasonable, why cannot the Puritans use their reason in modifying their unwar-

[91] *Microcosmography*, no. xxxiv. [92] *Laws*, V.lix.2.
[93] *Table Talk*, p. 12. [94] *Golden Remains*, pp. 3-4; cf. p. 23.
[95] *Laws*, II.vii.1; cf. III.viii.5.

ranted and dangerous application of the Bible to every detail of life?[96]

This was the question that the Anglicans asked with more vehemence as the Puritans' demands became more dangerous. 'Scrutamini Scripturas, These two words have undone the world', groaned Selden.[97] Hobbes, of course, agreed. Like all his contemporaries he had a prodigious knowledge of Scripture, and like the devil he could cite it to his purpose; but he detested the Puritans' habit of casting 'atomes' of the Bible like 'dust before mens eyes' to obscure the truth and gain their own treasonous advantage.[98] In *Behemoth* he derives all the woes of the Great Rebellion from the Puritans' fundamentalism and individualism. Taught sedition by their preachers and presuming to weigh their reading of the Bible against their betters', they have run the gamut from folly to treason. Every boy and wench who could read English thought they spoke with God Almighty – a calamitous and inevitable result of exposing the Scripture 'to every man's scanning in his mother-tongue'.[99] Hobbes' scorn for Puritan subjectivism suggests Walton's story of an 'ingenious Italian' who, visiting England, marveled at the intensely personal religion of even the commonest people. Even the 'women and shop-keepers' dared to argue about predestination and 'to determine what laws were fit to be made concerning Church-government'.[100]

As usual, Taylor beautifully states the position of his church. Do not inquire, he intones majestically,

> into the things which are too hard for thee, but learn modestly to know thy infirmities and abilities; and raise not thy mind up to inquire into mysteries of state or the secrets of government, or difficulties theological, if thy employment really be, or thy understanding be judged to be, of a lower rank.[101]

But this was an injunction that, in the time of Lilburne and Overton, was hopelessly anachronistic. Even as Taylor wrote it events were moving with terrible speed toward that bloody consummation which neither Hooker's reason nor Laud's thorough

---

[96] *Laws*, II.i.2.
[97] *Table Talk*, p. 11; cf. p. 119: 'The puritan would bee judg'd by the word of God (if hee would speake cleerly hee meanes himselfe, but that hee is asham'd to say soe).' For Dryden's brilliant attack on the Protestant doctrine of searching the Scripture, see *The Hind and the Panther*, ll. 680 ff.
[98] *Leviathan*, ch. xliii (p. 329).
[99] *Behemoth*, pt. I (*English Works*, VI, 167).
[100] *Lives*, II, 41.   [101] *Holy Living*, II.v.

policy could avert. With all the arrogance and passion of his party young Milton invoked his God to smite the 'wild boars' of the episcopacy:

> O let them not bring about their damned designs, that stand now at the entrance of the bottomless pit, expecting the watchword to open and let out those dreadful locusts and scorpions, to reinvolve us in that pitchy cloud of infernal darkness, where we shall never more see the sun of thy truth again, never hope for the cheerful dawn, never more hear the bird of morning sing. Be moved with pity at the afflicted state of this our shaken monarchy, that now lies labouring under her throes, and struggling against the grudges of more dreaded calamities.[102]

The prayer went unanswered.

V. ANGLICAN RATIONALISM

Without much reference to specific points of doctrine or of ecclesiastical discipline we have thus far attempted to sketch the basic emotional drives behind Anglicanism and Puritanism. Although both parties took their stand, as they thought, on the Bible, each brought to bear on their interpretation of the Bible a characteristic temper and quality of emotion. The history of their differences is virtually the history of English thought for a half century or more. If we may take the Thirty-Nine Articles and the Westminster Confession as the fullest statements of their respective doctrinal positions, it is obvious that between them there was a very large area of agreement on the broad principles of reformed theology. Credally, both were committed to the Augustinian view of man as a fallen creature, incapable of salvation without the unmerited aid of divine grace; both regarded merely natural knowledge as in every respect inferior to the revelation of God's truth in the Scripture; both distinguished carefully between the claims of reason and faith, and agreed that the knowledge which comes by faith was the *sine qua non* of salvation. But within this area of agreement, there was room for very significant differences in emphasis, in tonality, and in temper.

Hooker had argued that goodness (and therefore truth) may be known in two ways: by the causes that effect it (which are ordinarily beyond the scope of man's enfeebled cognitive faculties), and by its signs, discernible to sense and amenable to the

[102] *Of Reformation in England*, bk. II (*PW*, II, 417).

discourse of reason. Reason, then, is the general and perpetual voice of men, available to all men at all times and therefore natural to man *qua* man. To know these dictates of reason, inferred from the ordinary data of sensation, he needs no special revelation; however, they are perfectly consonant with the higher truth of revelation, and together with it they constitute his total cognitive experience.

Now this epistemology lends itself very easily to the development of a natural theology. It reclaims for fallen man a significant function of ascertaining natural truth by his native faculties, and it goes further in aligning that truth with the supreme truth of revelation. Since it is based ultimately on inferential reason, it requires that man exercise choice and free will, and thus it places upon him a very large responsibility in choosing the proper inferences to arrive at truth. Thus it takes an optimistic view of natural man, establishes the most intimate correlation between natural and supernatural knowledge. '*Nihil in gratia, quod non prius in natura*', declares Donne:

> There is nothing in grace, that was not first in nature, so farre, as that grace always finds nature, and naturall faculties to work on; though that nature be not disposed to the receiving of grace, when it comes, yet that nature, and those faculties, which may be so disposed by grace, are there, before that grace comes. And the grace of God doth not work this cleansing, but where there is a sweet, and souple, and tractable, and ductile disposition wrought in that soule.[103]

The fundamental rationalism and optimism of Hooker's theology come to some sort of fruition in the latitudinarians of the seventeenth century.[104] If man may arrogate to himself a large

[103] *Fifty Sermons*, p. 63. See *ST*, I.ii.2.
[104] The complex Continental movement toward a more liberal Protestantism should not be forgotten. After about 1550 Protestant doctrine became stationary and dogmatic, with all the great Protestant creeds in existence. The rise of Arminianism around the turn of the century was an effort to escape from, or at least make more flexible, the rigidities of these creeds. In Holland, where the conflict between the conservatives and the latitudinarian Calvinists was sharpest, Jacobus Arminius (1560–1609) heretically proclaimed that though God has foreknowledge, He does not predestine men to salvation or reprobation, that all men are candidates for salvation through Christ the Mediator, that works are operative in earning salvation, that unbaptized infants who die without sin will be saved, that certain virtuous heathens may not only escape hell but even be granted grace for salvation. The subsequent controversy over these articles agitated all the United Provinces and was eagerly followed by the rest of Protestant Europe (as John Hales's famous letters from the Synod of Dort make clear). Inevitably, the theological camps assumed political importance: the Precisians or conservative Calvinists were aligned with the nationalists, who wanted a strong central government under the House of Nassau; the Latitudinarians favored a decentralized government under the republican leadership

capacity for ascertaining natural truth, it follows that no such truth compatible with piety should incur any derogation. Accepting the unquestioned essentials of faith as revealed by the Scripture, he is then free to employ his natural reason in determining things indifferent. Since details of church discipline, for example, are prescribed by no specific Scriptural authority, the inference is clear that man may determine them by the processes of reason. This view has two very significant consequences: the sacrosanct area of revealed truth is reduced to those few obvious and simple essentials laid down in the Bible, and the area of natural truth is extended to include everything else. In Chillingworth's tedious but very important *Religion of Protestants*[105] we find the fullest statement of this epistemology. There he takes the position that all necessary religious truth – as Protestants understand it – is clearly revealed by Scripture, and that since no doctrinal or disciplinary view not prescribed by the Bible is protected by divine sanction, it must be determined and defended by the instruments of natural truth.

> The Bible, I say, the Bible only, is the religion of protestants! Whatsoever else they believe besides it, and the plain irrefragable, indubitable consequences of it, well may they hold it as a matter of opinion: but as matter of faith and religion, neither can they with coherence to their own grounds believe it themselves, nor require the belief of it of others, without most high and schismatical presumption.[106]

of Barneveldt, peace with Spain, and a liberal domestic policy. Arminius died before the storm he raised had subsided. When the Precisians tried to impose their orthodoxy they were countered by the Remonstrance of 1610 which defined the latitudinarian dissent in five articles. This was answered by a Counter-Remonstrance, and at last the States-General were compelled to call a synod at Dordrecht, or Dort, in November 1618. The synod sat for six months, and, packed as it was with the rigid Calvinists, it overwhelmed its liberal opposition in promulgating the famous five articles: predestination, limited atonement, total depravity, irresistibility of grace, and perseverance of the saints. Maurice of Nassau, seizing his chance, put Barneveldt to death, imprisoned Grotius, removed two hundred Remonstrant ministers. In England, if we may believe the groans of the Presbyterians, Arminianism gained a sinister following among the Anglican clergy of the early Stuarts. On the English repercussions, see Godfrey Davies, 'Arminian versus Puritan in England, ca. 1620–1640', *The Huntington Library Bulletin*, no. 5 (1934), 157–79.

[105] This famous *apologia* has a complicated history. In 1630 Edward Knott, a Jesuit, published *Charity Mistaken*, in which he advanced the proposition that all Protestants are damned. He was answered by Dr Potter, provost of Queen's, Oxford, in *Want of Charity Justly Charged on all such Romanists as dare (without truth or modesty) affirm that Protestancy destroyeth Salvation* (1633). Knott replied in *Mercy and Truth, or Charity maintained by Catholics* (1634); and this, in turn, was answered by *The Religion of Protestants* (1637). While Chillingworth was writing his book, Knott attacked him (and accused him of Socinianism) in *A Direction to be observed by N.N.* (1636)

[106] *Works*, II, 450.

ANGLICAN RATIONALISM

Since Chillingworth is defending Protestant individualism against Catholic absolutism, he relentlessly pushes home the implications of this epistemology. No church, no council, no tradition can command absolute authority. The really essential points of divine truth – what we are to believe about God and what He requires of us – are made unmistakably clear in the Bible, and they alone are necessary for salvation. On points about which the Bible is obscure or silent, as it often is, man may exercise his natural reason: they lie in the realm of speculation, and are therefore inevitably subject to various interpretations. Indeed, to demand conformity of belief about them is contrary to God's clear purpose that man as a rational creature should assume large, personal responsibility for his opinions and his conduct. It follows, then, that every man should interpret the Bible for himself, and bring to the uses of discipline and morality the full play of his own intelligence.

Chillingworth's assumption that basic truth is thus available to man suggests Descartes' 'clear and distinct ideas' – or even Milton's inexorable moral sense – and his demand for a simple creed suggests the reduction of such truth to its simplest axioms. Although he shares the scholastic notion that natural knowledge is compatible with religious truth, he tends to reduce religious truth (that is, the articles of faith) to their most rudimentary terms: the simplest creed is the best, and therefore the Apostles' Creed is best of all. Whoever believes it sincerely cannot possibly offend God whatever else he may believe.[107] For apart from these irreducible necessities of faith, each man is free to seek and find truth for himself. Chillingworth will take away no man's liberty of judgment, nor will he surrender his own. Except for God's holy word he is unable 'to take any thing upon trust, and to believe it without asking myself why'. On the other hand, he is 'most apt and most willing to be led by reason to any way, or from it, and always submitting all other reasons to this one – God hath said so, therefore it is true'.[108]

The case for Protestant individualism has rarely been stated more clearly. Indeed, Chillingworth's attack on religious absolutism led him far beyond the limits of his own church's toleration – after all, he lived and wrote in the age of Laud, who was his patron – to that more or less natural morality which is one of the

[107] Ibid., II, 98–9.   [108] Ibid., I, 27.

last flickers of Renaissance optimism. His theology, which made such a large allowance for the claims of human freedom and natural piety based on reason, had little room for dogma and none for the ferocity of sectarian controversy. He strenuously objected to the Athanasian Creed;[109] and though he was himself for a short time a Catholic convert he was reluctant to take Anglican orders because that would mean subscribing to the Thirty-Nine Articles. The Bible itself, he told his Catholic opponent Father Knott, could it speak would say to Catholics: 'Cast away the vain and arrogant pretence of infallibility, which makes your errors incurable.'[110] Similarly, he had nothing but ironical contempt for the doctrinal rigors of extreme Puritanism: a truly moral life is impossible for those who 'lay their sins upon Divine prescience, and predestination, saying with their tongues, O what wretched sinners have we been! but in their hearts, How could we help it! We are predestinate to it, we could not do otherwise'.[111]

In the beautiful sermons of John Hales we find the moral applications of Chillingworth's theology. His plea for simple Christian virtue, like Whichcote's and John Smith's, should have fallen gratefully on the ears of those accustomed to the tirades of Prynne and the rancor of religious controversy. Hales' great sermon on 'Christian Omnipotency', a challenge flung in the teeth of the Presbyterians, defends regenerated human nature against the dreadful Puritan consciousness of sin. *Felix culpa*: 'it hurts not us that Adam fell; nay, our strength and glory is much improved, that by Christ we are redeemed.'[112] We have a clear mandate, through both grace and reason, to lead a good life; when 'through sloth and idleness, luxury and distemper', we attribute our faults to original sin we evade our personal responsibility for living a life of reason and piety.[113] Faith alone is not enough for such a life, for we are tested by our works. The best way to learn if one is favorable to God is to scrutinize his daily acts.

> Many deceive themselves, whilst they argue from their Faith to their Works, whereas they ought out of their Works to conclude their Faith; whilst presuming they have Faith, and the Gifts of Sanctification, they think all their Actions warrantable: whereas we ought first thoroughly

---

[109] So did Jeremy Taylor, and for the same reason: in it there is nothing 'but damnation and perishing everlastingly' (*The Liberty of Prophesying*, II, 36 [*Works*, V, 405]).
[110] *Works*, I, 198. [111] Sermon I, *Works*, III, 20.
[112] *Golden Remains*, p. 148. [113] *Ibid.*, p. 158.

ANGLICAN RATIONALISM

to sift all our actions, to examine them at the Touch of God's Commandments, and if indeed we find them currant [sic], then to conclude that they come from the sanctifying Graces of the Holy Spirit. It is Faith indeed that gives the Tincture, the Die, the Relish unto our Actions; yet, the only means to examine our Faith, is by our Works.[114]

Lucius Cary, Viscount Falkland, was another, like Chillingworth and Hales, whom it is still tonic to read. From his seat in Parliament he argued on the very eve of rebellion that it was yet possible for the established church and the Puritans to come to terms. As for Rome, its absolutist claims made rational argument impossible and conciliation futile. Even though it is unlikely that all those damned by the Catholics are really damned, there could be no doubt that those killed by them are really dead.[115] Even granting that the Roman church is infallible, 'he that denies it and imployes his reason to seeke if it be true, should be in as good case as he that believes it and searches not at all the truth of the proposition he receives'.[116] Even toward the establishment which he hoped to save, his attitude was, for his day, wonderfully realistic. Even though it has in 'recrimination' erred 'a little (which is a little too much)', it is not positively committed to a foolish claim of infallibility, and so there is hope for it.[117] The bishops admittedly strain a good man's patience: in urging a divine and exclusive franchise for the establishment some of them are 'so absolutely directly and cordially Papist, that it is all, that fifteene hundred pounds a yeare can doe to keepe them from confessing it'.[118] But such men can be removed, and the establishment itself, as a national church defensible in Hookerian terms, is too organic a part of the commonwealth to be summarily destroyed. 'Wee should not roote up this ancient tree as dead as it appeares, till wee have tried whether by this or the like lopping of the branches, the sappe which was unable to feed the whole, may not serve to make what is left both to grow and flourish.'[119]

The amiable and attractive Anglicans would agree, then, that man's prerogative of seeking the truth was essential for a life of dignity, reason, and self-respect. No church that usurped the prerogative was worth a good man's respect. No authoritarian claims

[114] Ibid., pp. 132-3.
[115] Of the Infallibilitie of the Church of Rome, p. 9.
[116] Ibid., p. 12.   [117] Ibid., p. 10.
[118] A Speech Made to the House of Commons Concerning Episcopacy, p. 7.
[119] Ibid., p. 15.

that denied man's sacred right of assent could long sustain its own pretensions. For as Chillingworth says, in a crucial passage, the assent to truth is as important as truth itself.[120] It is little wonder that he was cordially detested by Jesuit and Presbyterian alike. His extension of the claims of human reason was, in a sense, the logical development of Hooker's defense of the establishment; in another sense it was a threat to any ecclesiastical organization whatever. As he lay dying after the siege of Colchester, Francis Cheynell, his Presbyterian custodian, tried vainly to force from him an admission of Socinianism; and when he failed he hurled into his open grave a copy of *The Religion of Protestants* with the hope that its monstrous errors would 'rot with the author and see corruption'.[121] In an age of such violent partisan strife we should expect no less; and yet it is depressing that men of moderation and reason like Chillingworth and Hales and Falkland, even though they spoke for the purest and strongest element in Protestant thought, seemed to their fellows at best anachronistic and futile, at worst unspeakably blasphemous. Clarendon's noble words about his friend Falkland may stand as an epitaph for all these brave and hopeless men: his death was so great a blow to England that 'if there were no other brand upon this odious and accursed civil war, than that single loss, it must be most infamous, and execrable to all posterity'.[122]

VI. THE FLIGHT FROM REASON

Though in the main stream of Anglican rationalism, the latitudinarians may be said to have widened the gap between faith and reason, and thus to have contributed to the secularization of truth. In the work of Jeremy Taylor, who lived on into the Restoration and attained the dignity of a bishopric, the Hookerian fusion of truth and piety crumbles still more. Taylor's incomparably beautiful exposition of those great ideals of reason, freedom, and toleration still stands as the literary consummation of Anglicanism, but philosophically it brought him to the verge of nominalism. Thus like the natural philosophy preached by Bacon and the mechanism preached by Hobbes, his theology points to the terminus of that Christian humanism which could not long

---
[120] *Works*, I, 157.
[121] Gardiner, *History of the Great Civil War*, I, 282–4.
[122] *The History of the Rebellion*, II, 465.

THE FLIGHT FROM REASON

survive the assaults of sectarian struggle, Protestant individualism, and science.

Curiously enough, it is possible to discern the same tendencies in the meager writings of Lord Brooke, a man whose strong Puritanism makes him in other respects antipodal to Taylor. Certainly his attacks upon the episcopacy must have horrified Taylor, as they horrified all Anglicans. Denouncing the bishops as 'superstitious Formalists, Arminians, Socinians, Papists, or Atheists',[123] he urged that complete separation of church and state which, as we shall see in the next chapter, was one of the first results of alienating nature from grace.

> If the Church swallow up the State, as it is in Popery, and Episcopacy, the issue will be slavish, grosse superstition, and stockish Idolatry. If the State overtop the Church, there will be ignorance and atheisme: but give to God that which is Gods, and to Caesar that which is Caesars: and both Church and State will fare the better.[124]

More ominous, however, was his attack on the Anglican concept of things indifferent, a concept indispensable to the defense of the *via media*. As a Puritan, a Platonist, and an idealist, Lord Brooke has affinities with such men as Sebastian Franck, Sébastien Castellio, and Jacobus Acontius; that is, he was fundamentally opposed to those broadly Aristotelian principles of reason and causality which informed the best Anglican thought.

For the Anglican church – that is, the 'Bishops (and their Creatures)'[125] – to determine the truth of things indifferent raised in a man of Lord Brooke's philosophical mind the gravest epistemological questions. Like Bacon, whom he often professed to admire, he was profoundly skeptical of the scholastic claims for natural reason. To search for first causes ('*doctrinam phantasticam, litigiosam, fucatam, & mollem;* a nice, unnecessary, prying into those things which profit not')[126] is to presume too much. Just as the new science teaches us that 'sense hath done as sense will doe, misguided our Reason',[127] so the most casual reflection will teach us that the reason abstracted from sense is false. We can know the names of things, never the things themselves; and what wisdom we acquire must be through intuition, not through the specious instruments of our understanding. Such intuition teaches

---

[123] *A Discourse opening the Nature of Episcopacy*, II.vi (Haller, II, 136).
[124] *Ibid.*, I.ix (Haller, II, 92).   [125] *Ibid.*, I.iv (Haller, II, 55).
[126] *The Nature of Truth*, p. 142.   [127] *Ibid.*, p. 106.

us that truth must be a unity, emanating from its source in God:

> The very knowledge of the Being of things, is more than we are capable of. And as yet that is necessary, so we keepe our selves still to this principle, that those things are all of one nature, variegated only in our apprehension: and this knowledge I must consent to.[128]

To realize this fact is to realize that there are no things indifferent. Just as the limitations of discursive reason require that 'Causes we cannot, neither shall ever finde out',[129] so also they make obvious our need for 'some spiritual light' by which the soul 'might soare and raise it selfe up to Universall Being, bathe it selfe in those stately, deep, and glorious streames of Unity, see God in Jesus Christ, the first, chief, and sole cause of all Being'.[130] This aspiration is the key to moral conduct, and the answer to the foolish prelates.

> Thus we could lay aside all foolish questions, could we seek into our hearts, according to the Poets advice, *Ne te quaesiveris extra*, and not into the causes, and the Being of causes, things too high for us; We might have an Heaven here, we might see how Christ is one with GOD, and wee one with Christ; so wee in Christ, one with GOD.[131]

Truth, then, passes the comprehension of man and the limits of his shaky natural reason. It is divine, and akin to grace; and therefore we can know it in only two ways: by examining the Scripture and by yielding to the intuitive persuasions of right reason. Things are either right or wrong, good or bad; and there is not, as the bishops tell us, a class of things indifferent. 'There is no One thing, no One Act, in all the World, That I may doe, or not doe, *ad placitum*, at my pleasure, all Circumstances considered.'[132] If things seem to be indifferent, then we may be sure that our understanding is dark. 'Nothing is Indifferent *in Re, in Se*; but to our Understanding some things seem so, for want of Good light.'[133] Needless to say, that good light cannot be equated with the prelatical establishment. To argue otherwise is to say that

> when ever Reason doth happen to dictate Right, it is but by chance, or some fancy of its owne; not by any certaine constant Rule, taken from the Nature of Things, rightly stated in such and such circumstances; For

---

[128] *Ibid.*, pp. 131–2.
[129] *Ibid.*, p. 127.
[130] *Ibid.*, pp. 143–5.
[131] *Ibid.*, pp. 169–70.
[132] *A Discourse opening the Nature of Episcopacy*, I.v (Haller, II, 69).
[133] *Ibid.*, I.v (Haller, II, 71).

THE FLIGHT FROM REASON

if so it must still judge *eodem modo*, after the same manner, of That which is so circumstantiated. And, if it once vary from this Rule, it will seeme to have no Rule, but its owne fancy. And in this Case, we shall be under Reason, as under a most corrupt Judge, that will follow no constant Rule (founded on the Nature of Things) but onely his owne humor.[134]

Such a passage shows us many things: Lord Brooke's characteristic Puritan subjectivism and individualism, his Puritan compulsion to judge all things by the highest possible standard, his Puritan contempt for the quasi-rational, expedient, and political elements in Anglican thought. Also it shows us with what subtlety and high seriousness the whole tradition of Renaissance rationalism was being attacked, not only by atheists and 'meer naturalists', but by men of the most passionate religious convictions.

This glance at the anti-intellectualism of a Puritan nobleman may serve to introduce us to the anti-intellectualism of a high Anglican divine. On occasion, at least, Taylor seems as liberal as it is possible for a man to be and retain his commitments to organized religion. To the dismay of his nineteenth-century editor he denied the doctrine of original sin, he made explicit Hooker's rather cautious defense of free will, he maintained the great Protestant principle of religious individualism, he defended the Anglican *via media* – and yet, paradoxically enough, his final position was probably closer to Ockham than to Aquinas.

'Original sin is not our sin properly, not inherent in us, but is only imputed to us, so as to bring evil effects upon us.'[135] Adam had 'liberty of choice and chose ill, and so do we'. It is impious to think that we, unlike Adam before the Fall, are incapable of choosing good, for 'we can choose good, and as naturally love good as evil, and in some instances more'. A man cannot naturally hate God, or his parents, or cleanliness. In fact, our nature is not congenitally perverted but merely 'defective' in one respect only: 'we do not naturally know, nor yet naturally love those supernatural excellencies which are appointed and commanded by God as the means of bringing us to a supernatural condition. That is, without God's grace, and the supernatural work of grace, we cannot be saved.'[136] But since we have this supernatural aid, and since we have the capacity for virtuous natural knowledge, we

---
[134] *Ibid.*, I.v (Haller, II, 66–7).
[135] *Unum Necessarium*, VII.ii.10 (*Works*, VII, 309).
[136] *Ibid.*, VI.iv.67 (VII, 275–6).

lack nothing. Men are prone to error, of course: they have different faculties that pull them different ways,[137] and from Adam they have inherited if not sin at least a 'natural necessity of sinning'.[138]

But all men do not choose the same sin, nor for the same cause, nor invariably; it is clear, then, that 'choice and election still remains [sic] to a man, and that he is not naturally sinful, as he is naturally heavy, or upright, apt to laugh, or weep. For these he is always, and unavoidably'.[139] To deny these facts, and to affirm that man is incapable of any good action, or any sound natural knowledge through the exercise of his native faculties, is to undermine all morality: 'precepts of holiness might as well be preached to a wolf as to a man, if man were naturally and inevitably wicked'.[140]

So much for the doctrine of total depravity. Taylor goes on, in his unread masterpiece *Ductor Dubitantium*, to seek sanctions for moral conduct outside the discipline of the church or the precepts of the Scripture. As a Protestant he took the obvious course: his *magnum opus*, like the other major casuistical treatises of the century, can only proceed on the assumption that the dictates of the human conscience are compatible with those of revealed truth.

> When God sent the blessed Jesus into the world to perfect all righteousness, and to teach the world all His Father's will, it was said and done, 'I will give My laws in your hearts, and in your minds will I write them'; that is, you shall be governed by the law of natural and essential equity and reason, by that law which is put into every man's nature; and besides this, whatsoever else shall be superinduced shall be written in your minds by the Spirit, who shall write all the laws of Christianity in the tables of your consciences.[141]

For man's conscience, which is his natural knowledge of good and evil, is his unique glory, and when he loses it he loses also his reason, and so his title to human dignity. As an integral factor in God's great design, it rests on many props: a good will, a clear heart, a free spirit, a devout mind, and so on;[142] but mainly

---

[137] *Ibid.*, VI.iv.68–70.
[138] *Ibid.*, VII.v.18 (VIII, 319–20); cf. *Sermons*, p. 76.
[139] *Unum Necessarium*, VI.v.71 (*Works*, VII, 279).
[140] *Ibid.*, VI.v.72 (VII, 279).
[141] *Ductor Dubitantium*, I.i.7 (*Works*, IX, 6).
[142] *Ibid.*, I.i.11–21.

THE FLIGHT FROM REASON

it rests on an enlightened natural reason. By our reason we realize that moral conduct is 'principled by creation' and 'instructed or illuminated in the regeneration' of man.[143] Prudence alone suffices for things of this world ('particular and circumstantiate actions'), but conscience demands the criteria of morality; it is concerned not with expediency but with truth, and truth is laid up in the bosom of God. 'Prudence intends to do actions dexterously and prosperously; conscience is to conduct them justly and according to the commandment.'[144] Conscience thus acquires the highest epistemological function of making available to man the dictates of the divine will, and when it speaks clearly it carries the highest authority possible.

From this typically Protestant (almost Augustinian) defense of religious subjectivism Taylor derives his doctrine of toleration. For him as for Chillingworth, morality supersedes dogma; all the exfoliations of doctrine cannot obscure the unique sufficiency of the Apostles' Creed,[145] and all the essentials of a good life are comprised in a few articles of faith and in the dictates of a clear conscience.

> How many volumes have been writ about angels, about immaculate conception, about original sin, when that all that is solid reason or clear revelation in all these three articles may be reasonably enough comprised in forty lines?[146]

On many matters the Scripture is obscure. There are many corrupt and uncertain readings, many 'tropes, metonymies, ironies, hyperboles, proprieties and improprieties of language', many 'mysteries' incapable of clear statement, many methods of exegesis and searching.[147] Therefore the truly wise and pious man 'will be very far from confidence' in his own interpretation and very loath to impose his upon other men.[148] God gave man reason, and the morality of reason is conscience; with its help each man may reach his own decision concerning the multitude of things indifferent. 'God will have no man pressed with another's inconveniences in matters spiritual and intellectual, no man's salvation to depend on another's: and every tooth that eats sour

---
[143] Ibid., I.i.20 (IX, 12).
[144] Ibid., I.i.26 (IX, 15).
[145] The Liberty of Prophesying, I.7.
[146] Ibid., 'The Epistle Dedicatory' (Works, V, 361-2).
[147] Ibid., III.1-9 (V, 409-21).
[148] Ibid., IV.8 (V, 427-8).

grapes shall be set on edge for itself, and for none else.'[149]

There is much talk of reason, of course, but those who talk most tend to forget that it is not

> a distinct topic, but a transcendent that runs through all topics: for reason, like logic, is instrument of all things else; and when revelation, and philosophy, and public experience, and all other grounds of probability or demonstration, have supplied us with matter, then reason does but make use of them.[150]

To escape the wicked jars of sectarian controversy, then, Taylor prescribes the Christian virtues of meekness, charity, and toleration. 'That faith which is a worthy preparatory to the holy communion must be the actual principle and effective of a good life.'[151] If only, he sighs wearily, 'men would not call all opinions by the name of religion, and superstructures by the name of fundamental articles, and all fancies by the glorious appellative of faith'.[152] Since in Taylor's significant assumption faith is an act of the understanding and heresy of the will, religious error can come only from a perversion of our faculties by bad education, by weakness, by 'mistaken piety'. This kind of error, merely an 'invincible and harmless prejudice', has in its 'heartiness' no sin. But genuine heresy involves the 'obstinacy of the will and choice', and 'the adequate perfect formality of heresy is whatsoever makes the error voluntary and vicious'.[153] No man is a heretic against his will; therefore a 'wicked person in his error becomes heretic, when a good man in the same error shall have all the rewards of faith'.[154]

In view of all this it is 'unnatural and unreasonable' to persecute any religious opinion held on rational grounds. No man should with impunity deny an article of the Apostles' Creed or preach a wicked life, but all propositions 'extrinsical to these two considerations, be they true or be they false, make not heresy, nor the man a heretic'.[155] Since the understanding is 'a thing wholly spiritual', it cannot be punished corporally. 'You may as well cure the colic by brushing a man's clothes, or fill a man's belly

---

[149] Ibid., X.3 (V, 496).
[150] Ibid., X.5 (V, 498).
[151] The Worthy Communicant, III.4 (Works, VIII, 101).
[152] The Liberty of Prophesying, 'The Epistle Dedicatory' (Works, V, 348).
[153] Ibid., II.10 (V, 384–85).
[154] Ibid., II.22 (V, 397).
[155] Ibid., II.41 (V, 409).

with a syllogism.'¹⁵⁶ The main thing, then, is not the belief – erroneous or otherwise – but the spirit in which it is held. If a good man believes, 'according to his light, and upon the use of moral industry', what seems to him true, his belief is acceptable to God 'whether he hits upon the right or no'.¹⁵⁷

As a plea for toleration in an age of brutal intolerance *The Liberty of Prophesying* is a noble testament of Protestant individualism. Its value as a defense of natural theology is, however, more dubious. From Taylor's argument for private conscience as an instrument of moral and even religious truth, and from his identification of conscience with reason, we might infer that he had restated that fusion of knowledge and faith, truth and goodness, which was Hooker's *summum bonum*. Actually, he did nothing of the sort. His plea for toleration is built on essentially antirationalistic assumptions which, made explicit in the *Ductor Dubitantium*, constitute a powerful attack on the Renaissance tradition.

Like all Protestants committed to combating Catholic authoritarianism, Taylor was forced to elevate private conscience above the demands – either dogmatic or ostensibly rational – of any church discipline, and the intuitive conviction of faith above the inferential proofs of natural reason. Caught between uncongenial dogma (he obviously recoiled from the doctrine of innate depravity, for example) and a secularism that would give only the most perfunctory allegiance to supernatural truth, Taylor represents the dilemma of his age. His liberalism seems to cloak an essential skepticism that was forced by the logic of his position, and the cost of his toleration was intellectual certainty.

> In this world we believe in part, and prophesy in part, and this imperfection shall never be done away with till we be translated to a more glorious state: either then we must throw our chances and get truth by accident or predestination, or else must lie safe in a mutual toleration and private liberty of persuasion, unless some other anchor be thought upon where we may fasten our floating vessels and ride safely.¹⁵⁸

Almost, this is the skeptic's *cul de sac*, and the irony of it is that Taylor was an Anglican of the Anglicans, a man dedicated to

---

¹⁵⁶ *Ibid.*, XIII.10 (V, 522). A test-case for Taylor's theory of toleration was provided by the Anabaptists, perhaps the most detested of contemporary sects. After an agonizingly long analysis of their views concerning baptism and civil disobedience (*ibid.*, ch. xviii) Taylor concludes that their doctrine 'is wholly to be reproved and disavowed'; but he urges that the erring zealots 'be treated with the usages of a Christian; strike them not as an enemy, but exhort them as brethren' (XVIII.33 [V, 589]).
¹⁵⁷ *Ibid.*, II.22 (V, 397).   ¹⁵⁸ *Ibid.*, VII.19 (V, 483).

maintaining the status of the establishment, combating Puritan separatism and voluntarism, and perpetuating the *via media* between faith and reason. Yet he moved from the tranquillity of Lord Carbery's Golden Grove to that harsh oppression of the Irish Catholics in his last years, and from the spacious rationalism of Hookerian theology to something very like fideism and nominalism.

This movement becomes very clear in the *Ductor Dubitantium*. In that endless, and endlessly interesting, book we learn that there are three kinds of reason. The first is *noesis*, 'or the first notions of things abstract, of principles and the *primo intelligibilia*: such as are, the whole is greater than half the whole; good is to be chosen; God is to be loved; ... for these are objects of the simple understanding, congenite notices, concreated with the understanding'. The second is *dianoesis*, 'or "discourse", that is, such consequents and emanations which the understanding draws from her first principles' – in other words, inferential knowledge. The third is *pistis*, 'that is, such things which the understanding assents to upon the report, testimony and affirmation of others, viz., by arguments extrinsecal [sic] to the nature of the thing, and by collateral and indirect principles'.[159]

It is clear that all three kinds of reason are applicable to religious as well as secular knowledge. For example, by *noesis* we know that God is good; by *dianoesis* we know through inference or illation that nothing but good is to be spoken of God; by *pistis* we know that God is triune. These commonplaces are obviously in the best tradition of Renaissance optimism: they would seem to secure the prerogatives of natural knowledge and to save the sanctity of faith. However, as Taylor pushes on with his analysis of the morality of knowledge he so steadily constricts the area of natural knowledge while augmenting that of faith that he, like certain Puritans, is forced to segregate reason and goodness altogether. This is an astonishing and hitherto little-noticed performance for such a panjandrum of the Anglican church in its golden age.

We must expect Taylor to keep reason well below faith. By His mysteries 'God hath confounded reason, that faith may come in her place'. Where the mystery is impenetrable – as in the Incarnation or the Resurrection – 'reason must put on her muffler,

[159] *Ductor Dubitantium*, I.ii.2 (*Works*, IX, 59–60).

THE FLIGHT FROM REASON   235

and we must be wholly conducted by revelation'. Since human reason cannot penetrate the ultimate mysteries of God, until He chooses to reveal them to our faith, 'we are to be still and silent, admiring the secret, and adoring the wisdom, and expecting till the curtain be drawn, or till Elias come and tell us all things'.[160] Such limitations of the efficacy of natural reason had been canonical ever since St Paul spoke to the men of Athens on the Areopagus, and Taylor is, of course, uttering a pious platitude when he says 'we must believe what we cannot understand'.[161]

But what is extraordinary – and especially in that tradition of post-Thomistic rationalism to which Taylor ostensibly belongs – is the effort to demolish the claims of natural reason within its own legitimate sphere. One of the main props of Renaissance optimism had been the principle of right reason, that epistemological and moral absolute which unites truth and goodness, which defines the essence of God, and which constituted man's highest faculty. God employs it, so generations of moralists had believed, as the principle of moral causality governing the sequence of natural events, man as an innate cognitive faculty by which he learns the truth in order to do the good. As the Christian equivalent of Socrates' equation of virtue and knowledge, or of the Stoic principle of cosmic reason, it was a basic ingredient of Renaissance optimism. Through it every event assumed a moral dimension, and the most fundamental operations of the universe were brought within the scope of man's rational and moral comprehension. Yet Taylor systematically demolishes it.

He does so through his denial of natural law, and he centers his attack there because he regards natural law as the most sinister threat to religious truth. Hooker had been able to construe nature in sacramental terms, and align all events along a moral axis. By the middle of the seventeenth century it was apparently no longer possible to do so. At least so Taylor must have thought, for he, a rational theologian, is compelled to deny the central axiom of rational theology. Thanks to the Protestant bifurcation of nature and grace, and to the Baconian segregation of secular and religious knowledge, by Taylor's time natural truth was being cut loose from morality. Only with the utmost difficulty (as Descartes

[160] *Ibid.*, I.ii.3 (IX, 56, 57, 62).
[161] *Ibid.*, I.ii.3 (IX, 64).

makes painfully clear) could mechanical causality still be adjusted to the demands of theology, and the chasm between truth and goodness was becoming too wide to bridge. Caught in this dilemma, Taylor unhesitatingly denies the validity of natural truth.

In an age when men were all too willing to find the allegedly moral sanctions for their conduct in those processes from which might be inferred the 'laws' of nature, Taylor once more advances the claims of supernatural truth not available to reason, not implicit in the very structure of the universe, but contingent wholly on the will of a sovereign and inscrutable God. There is, he admits (probably with a nod toward Hobbes), a *jus naturae* by which the 'natural, wild, or untutored' man does what seems proper to preserve himself; but he insists that we must distinguish this *jus naturae* from the *lex naturae*, which is nothing less than the revealed will of God. *Justum nihil est non constituta lege*.[162] Taylor can find no basis for this *lex naturae* in the commonly cited arguments of universal natural instincts of 'consent of nations'. Examination shows that there is no such universal moral code, and Ulpian's pronouncement – *Jus Naturale est quod natura omnia animalia docuit* – contradicts the observed facts. As certain researches of 'this last age' have shown, the *jus gentium* of the Roman Stoic lawyers is a fiction and 'an uncertain thing, variable and by chance, growing by accidents, and introduced by violence, and therefore [it] could not be the measure of the law of nature'.[163] By *jus naturae* man is free, by *lex naturae* he is bound. 'Right is liberty, but law is a fetter.'[164]

If, then, *lex naturae* is a fiction contrived by self-seeking politicians, and not an organic function of natural processes inferred by reason and therefore honored with universal assent, where may man find his moral sanctions? Obviously in the fiat of God alone. *Lex naturae*, therefore, is

> nothing but the law of God given to mankind for the conservation of his nature and the promotion of his perfective end: a law for which man sees a reason and feels a necessity. God is the law-giver, practical reason or conscience is the record; but revelation and express declaring it was the first publication and emission of it, and till then it had not at all the solemnities of law, though it was passed in the court, and decreed and recorded.[165]

[162] *Ibid.*, II.i.14 (IX, 279–81).
[164] *Ibid.*, II.i.34 (IX, 295).
[163] *Ibid.*, II.i.20 (IX, 287–8).
[165] *Ibid.*, II.i.35 (IX, 296).

THE FLIGHT FROM REASON

Since the necessary ingredient of law is compulsion, not rationality,[166] reason cannot be the criterion of *lex naturae*, for it is too unstable –

> such a box of quicksilver that it abides no where; it dwells in no settled mansion; it is like a dove's neck, or a changeable taffeta; it looks to me otherwise than to you who do not stand in the same light as I do; and if we enquire after the law of nature by the rules of our reason, we shall be uncertain as the discourses of the people, or the dreams of disturbed fancies.[167]

It is patently absurd to say that right reason is both the law of nature and the cognitive faculty for recognizing that law. Right reason, stripped of its spurious metaphysical absolutes, is merely an instrument – like conscience, 'which is also reason' – for 'using the law of nature' and for 'obeying the obliging power'.[168] Thus it is a faculty, not a moral absolute; and *lex naturae* is God's commandment and therefore wholly dependent on His will, not on an intrinsically rational principle operative in the whole universe and determining its processes. Man's capacity for inferring underlying principles from the data of sensation, at best a twisted path to natural truth, can tell us nothing of the moral obligations which God has prescribed for us. By using his reason alone no man can be 'sure that any thing is a law of nature, because it seems to him hugely reasonable, neither if it be so indeed, is it therefore a law'. A law is binding, the dictates of reason are not. 'For reason can demonstrate, and it can persuade and invite, but not compel any thing, but assent, not obedience, and therefore it is no law.'[169]

As a moral creature in need of salvation, then, man must forego an impious reliance upon his reason, and fall back on faith and conscience. 'Faith contains all the treasures of divine knowledge and speculation. Conscience is the treasury of divine commandments and rules in practical things. Faith tells us why, conscience tells us what we are to do. Faith is the measure of our persuasions, conscience is the measure of our actions.'[170] Reason thus stripped of any moral efficacy, there remains for man only the obedience to the Bible and to those supra-rational, intuitive dictates of his conscience. The chief of God's attributes is His sovereignty, and

[166] *Ibid.*, II.i.40.
[168] *Ibid.*, II.i.30 (IX, 293).
[170] *Ibid.*, I.i.10 (IX, 8).

[167] *Ibid.*, II.i.31 (IX, 293).
[169] *Ibid.*, II.i.30 (IX, 293).

He compels assent to those commands which yield to no understanding. Bound to neither truth nor reason, what He wills is right because He wills it, and man has only to obey.[171]

It is no wonder that Taylor ends his discussion by citing Ockham: he has pushed his nominalism to its source. 'But whatsoever is a sin, is so because it is forbidden, and without such a prohibition, although it might be unreasonable, yet it cannot be criminal or unjust.'[172] The conclusion shows how far a man had to go in resisting that secularism which threatened to reduce both God and goodness to the level of man's natural understanding:

> The purpose of this discourse is this, that we look no further for tables of the law of nature, but take in only those precepts which bind us Christians under Christ our lawgiver who hath revealed to us all His Father's will.[173]

VII. HOBBES: THE SECULAR ARGUMENT

Taylor's retreat to voluntarism – a complicated development which we have merely sketched in its broadest outlines – may be regarded as his reaction to the burgeoning contemporary theories of natural reason, natural law, natural rights, all of them powerful weapons for those attacking the *de jure divino* and therefore inviolable pretensions of the Stuarts and their Erastian establishment. In denying the allegedly rational, natural, and *a priori* sanctions for (subversive) political and religious conduct, Taylor no doubt thought to preserve intact the anachronistic values of a hierarchal society, a hierarchal church, and a social structure erected on the concept of divinely ordained status. These were values which the House of Stuart and the Anglican establishment had come to symbolize, and for Taylor to defend them as he did was to assume the paradoxical position of defending an allegedly rational church on irrational or supra-rational grounds. Caught between the tradition of Anglican rationalism of the right and the new naturalism of the Puritan left (which we shall examine in the next chapter) he was forced into a repudiation of reason that would have appalled Hooker. But history repeats itself in ways not always discernible to its protagonists, and the progress from

---

[171] *Ibid.*, II.i.52 (IX, 304–5).
[172] *Ibid.*, II.i.58 (IX, 307).
[173] *Ibid.*, II.i.59 (IX, 307). Since this chapter was written there has appeared a very able article on Taylor's voluntarism. See Robert Hoopes, 'Voluntarism in Jeremy Taylor and the Platonic Tradition', *The Huntington Library Quarterly*, XIII (1950), 341–54.

Hooker to Taylor is uncommonly like that from St Thomas to Ockham. To all those who based their heresies – political and religious – on the prerogatives of man's natural reason and natural rights Taylor replied with an uncompromising voluntarism and nominalism, and denied to that reason any object other than God's revealed will. It is ironical that he should have done so, and the irony becomes poignant when we realize that he, who sought so desperately to preserve the *status quo*, was in a sense of the devil's party without knowing it. For theologically he advocated, as a voluntarist and a nominalist, virtually the same values that Hobbes was advocating ethically and politically – and of all men he must have hated Hobbes the most. In a curious way, then, both Taylor and Hobbes jeopardized the tradition of moral and rational truth in their flight from reason; and as royalists and Erastians – for Hobbes was nominally one and emphatically the other – both defended the Anglican establishment for reasons which contravened the whole course of rational theology. Each in his own way denied the ancient conviction that law depends on morality, and Hobbes very systematically developed the counter-claim that morality depends on law.

Taylor construes reason as an 'instrument' rather than a ground or object of knowledge, a method for organizing experience and (within sharp limits) deriving inferences rather than for apprehending those immutably 'rational' principles which define both truth and goodness. Thus, in spite of the ostensibly rational latitudinarianism of *The Liberty of Prophesying* his rationalism is a hobbled thing compared to Hooker's. He cannot regard it as a metaphysical and moral absolute that manifests itself both in that eternal law laid up in the bosom of God and in those positive laws which derive their sanction from their great prototype. If there are such absolutes, man – *qua* man – has no access to them, and therefore he must base his notions of truth and goodness on the supra-rational fiat of God. Man's 'conscience' is a rational faculty for obeying such laws, but not for comprehending them. The essence of law is compulsion, and the most awful of God's attributes is sovereignty; therefore His laws require not comprehension but obedience to 'the obliging power'. Merely through the exercise of his natural reason no man can know that 'anything is a law of nature, because it seems to him hugely reasonable, neither if it be so indeed, is it therefore a law'.

It may seem curious that in all of this Taylor, the Anglican bishop, more sharply repudiates rationalism than Hobbes, the mechanical philosopher; and yet the reason is not far to seek. It is questionable that Taylor had any consistent metaphysic at all, but Hobbes was committed without reservation to the proposition that only bodies in motion are real: he was convinced that the end of human knowledge is the geometrical description of the displacement of bodies, and with a philosopher's compulsion for consistency he sought to derive all parts of his system – psychological, ethical, political – from this cardinal premise of mechanism. If every event is essentially a body's change of location, then even the most complicated events are merely aggregates of such changes. Therefore a consistent philosophy would proceed on the sound geometrical principle (which Descartes enshrined in the *Discours*) of moving from the simplest and most basic principles to those increasingly complex principles which depend upon them. Such a method, which Hobbes shared with some of the best minds of his century, led him to begin with an analysis of bodies in motion (i.e. of mechanics), then to apply his findings to human conduct in terms of psychology and physiology, and to conclude with a study of communal human conduct in corporations like the state and the church. But because his system was so geometrical and mechanistic, it was also rational, in the seventeenth-century sense of the term: he thought that rationally apprehended, *a priori* principles and axioms were necessary for the construction of any system, and that the basic principles of mechanics, as of politics, were conceived in the mind rather than snatched from the swarming presentations of sensory experience. In spite of his icy contempt for Aristotle and for notional philosophy he did not resort to pure empiricism; and his massive system is built, piece by piece, on a few rationally conceived propositions.

It is extremely important, however, that although Hobbes derived his political and ecclesiastical views – with which we are here primarily concerned – from such 'rational' hypostases as natural law and the social contract, he refused to invest such principles with any moral significance. The seventeenth century was incorrigibly given to glib and facile arguments from natural law, but it was a major event of European intellectual history when this law came to be conceived as mechanical rather than

HOBBES: THE SECULAR ARGUMENT 241

moral. By the law of nature, Hooker had argued, man knows not only that the soul should rule the body, but that the essence of the soul is its sovereign reason;[174] the first command of that reason is the Golden Rule,[175] and therefore truth and goodness coalesce, not only in the conduct of each man's daily life, but in the very fabric of his social institutions.[176] By the middle of the seventeenth century, however, there was a sharp declension from this high position (which was really archaic when Hooker advanced it). Bacon would deny it, and so, probably, would Milton. Richard Baxter, though a Puritan rationalist, specifically repudiates it, as does Taylor: natural law is nothing but the 'signification of God's governing will ... in which God declareth to man his duty, and his reward or punishment'.[177] Inevitably Hobbes denied it too. His thinking was uncompromisingly secular, and when he posited a law of nature he did so without any moral commitments whatever. Yet this law of nature became the base of his ethical and political theory. If Taylor converts natural law into a body of supra-rational precepts whose sanctity depends only on God's declared will, Hobbes converts it into a set of amoral – but utilitarian – principles conceived through the processes of natural reason to be essential for social intercourse. For very different reasons, then, both alienate from it that fusion of moral and therefore rational truth which St Thomas and Hooker had made its content.

It is a basic fact, says Hobbes, that although as corpuscular individuals men are motivated by 'a perpetuall and restlesse desire of Power after power, that ceaseth onely in Death',[178] this very fact – which, of course, contravenes many centuries of pious fictions about man's dignity, nobility, and rationality – is a corollary of the instinct for self-preservation. This instinct is formulated in the law of nature, and this law with all its varieties and derivatives is contained in 'this one Sentence, approved by all the world, Do not that to another, which thou thinkest unreasonable to be done by another to thy selfe'.[179] It is significant but essential that

---

[174] *Laws*, I.viii.6.
[175] *Laws*, I.viii.7.
[176] *Laws*, I.x.1. For two influential ancient statements of this moral natural law, see Cicero, *De re publica*, III.xxii; Lactantius, *Divine Institutes*, VI.viii.
[177] *The Catechizing of Families*, ch. v (*Works*, XIX, 22); cf. *The Reasons of the Christian Religion*, I.x (*Works*, XXI, 5–17).
[178] *Leviathan*, ch. xi (p. 49).
[179] *Ibid.*, ch. xxvi (p. 144).

Hobbes thus states the Golden Rule negatively, for in his view each man's internal economy consists of pursuing those 'motions' (or sensations) that aid and avoiding those that hinder the 'vital motion' of his heart. When life is thus reduced to manipulating antithetical impulses of desire and aversion, it is clear that good and evil become of utilitarian rather than of moral concern; and furthermore that in the ceaseless struggle for supremacy which is man's natural (or pre-social) condition each man's hand is raised against his fellow's in the race for survival. Consequently, the first necessity for achieving and maintaining communal life is that law of nature ('nature' being here shifted to mean organized society) which checks mutually destructive impulses. The law of nature, then, is a naturally and rationally conceived inhibitory device for attaining large, desirable ends even at the cost of immediate, personal gains.[180]

Whereas each man has a *jus naturale* by which he is at liberty 'to use his own power, as he will himselfe, for the preservation of his own Nature', this right is superseded by that *lex naturalis* 'found out by Reason, by which a man is forbidden to do, that, which is destructive of his life, or taketh away the means of preserving the same'.[181] In the primordial and intolerable state of nature every man

> has a Right to every thing; even to one anothers body. And therefore, as long as this naturall Right of every man to every thing endureth, there can be no security to any man (how strong or wise soever he be,) of living out the time, which Nature ordinarily alloweth men to live, And consequently it is a precept, or generall rule of Reason, That every man, ought to endeavour Peace, as farre as he has hope of obtaining it; and when he cannot obtain it, that he may seek, and use, all helps, and advantages of Warre. The first branch of which Rule, containeth the first, and Fundamentall Law of Nature; which is, to seek Peace, and follow it. The Second, the summe of the Right of Nature; which is, By all means we can, to defend our selves.[182]

Such a passage – which is central to Hobbes' theory – helps us understand Cudworth's denunciation of those 'atheistic politi-

---

[180] Hobbes defines the law of nature variously in various places – in *Elements of Law Natural and Politic*, in *De cive*, and in the *Leviathan* – but all his accounts are essentially the same. In *De cive* (II.i [*English Works*, II, 16]) he speaks of it as a 'dictate of right reason'. It is unlikely that a man of his wit and malice should not have smiled at so ironical a perversion of that venerable term.

[181] *Leviathan*, ch. xiv (pp. 66–7).

[182] *Ibid.*, ch. xiv (p. 67). See ch. xv (pp. 82–3), ch. xxvi (p. 142).

cians' who 'make a villain' of human nature and debase human reason and justice to 'ignoble and bastardly' brats of fear.[183] To all such objections, however, Hobbes could answer blandly that 'as to the whole Doctrine, I see not yet, but the Principles of it are true and proper; and the Ratiocination solid'.[184]

In setting up the simple proposition that the great goal of self-preservation is better attained by peace and concord than by violence and enmity, Hobbes secularized and naturalized the law of nature. In his system it becomes a supremely useful device for achieving an end that is desirable not because it is moral, but because it is necessary for preserving life. It is an end which should determine not only the 'morality' of each man's life, but also the structure of his social institutions; hence the necessity of the social contract – that covenant by which men agree to submit their private wills to a sovereign will in the interests of preserving peace. The 'only way' for a group of individuals, each with presumably clashing and destructive desires,[185] to attain general concord is 'to conferre all their power and strength upon one Man, or upon one Assembly of men, that may reduce all their Wills, by plurality of voices, unto one Will'. By the social contract each man is bound to obey unquestioningly the sovereign who himself is bound to obey no one because his will must be supreme – otherwise he is not a sovereign. Only by submitting their wills to a supreme will can men alleviate their desperate natural condition, which is 'solitary, poore, nasty, brutish, and short'.[186] When this is done, under the sanction of natural law, then 'the Multitude so united in one Person, is called a COMMON-WEALTH, in latine CIVITAS. This is the Generation of that great LEVIATHAN, or rather (to speak more reverently) of that Mortall God, to which wee owe under the Immortall God, our peace and defence'.[187]

From this notion of illimitable and indivisible sovereignty conferred by contract Hobbes derives his notorious absolutism. It is,

---

[183] *The True Intellectual System*, IV, 198. Alexander Ross' first reaction to reading the *Leviathan* was compounded of anger and anguish: 'Me thinks I see Religion and learning, Divinity and true Philosophy, devotion and piety, for which this Islaud [*sic*] hath been glorious for many generations, saying in the voice that the Christians heard in Jerusalem immediately before the destruction thereof, *Migremus hinc*' (*Leviathan Drawn out with a Hook*, sig. A3ᵛ-A[4]ʳ).
[184] *Leviathan*, 'Review and Conclusion' (p. 390).
[185] *Ibid.*, ch. xiii (p. 64).
[186] *Ibid.*, ch. xvii (p. 89).
[187] *Ibid.*, ch. xvii (p. 89).

in a manner, the secular version of Taylor's theological absolutism, and it owes as little to the traditions of Christian humanism. Indeed, Hobbes is not only one of the most relentless critics of Aristotle, scholasticism, and rational theology; he goes out of his way to denounce the whole corpus of ancient moral philosophy: all foolish fictions about man's rights to freedom and reason and individual responsibility show nothing but the danger of reading too many classic writers; and the evil fruits of their seditious doctrines make clear that 'there was never any thing so deerly bought, as these Western parts have bought the learning of the Greek and Latine tongues'.[188] Since the price of security is the loss of natural liberty, to secure its social ends sovereignty must be absolute and indivisible. Therefore 'nothing the Soveraign Representative can doe to a Subject, on what pretence soever, can properly be called Injustice, or Injury; because every Subject is Author of every act the Soveraign doth'.[189] So long as the sovereign commands nothing counter to the law of self-preservation he requires unquestioning allegiance, for that is his very *raison d'être*.[190]

The laws that he promulgates are as binding as those laws of nature from which he derives his sanction. Therefore against the compulsions of the civil or statute law those natural rights embodied in the common law are as nothing. Such rights, 'that is, the naturall Liberty of man, may by the Civill Law be abridged, and restrained: nay, the end of making Lawes, is no other, but such Restraint; without the which there cannot possibly be any Peace'.[191] And if common law is thus superseded by civil statutes, so are the 'ghostly' rights of any ecclesiastical corporation. If sovereignty is indivisible, it is intolerable that civil and religious power each be autonomous – for where would sovereignty reside? Just as the sovereign has in his disposal those civil 'Rules' which require obedience for the general good, so he has in his disposal those ecclesiastical 'Rules' for governing the state church. Law to be law must be compulsory, and as the church is a corporation established for the ends of social conformity, its laws admit no

---

[188] *Ibid.*, ch. xxi (pp. 113–4); cf. ch. xxix (p. 174).
[189] *Ibid.*, ch. xxi (p. 112).
[190] *Ibid.*, 'Review and Conclusion' (pp. 386–7). This defense of *de facto* government – Stuart, Cromwellian or other – of course gave offense to royalists, for in making naked force rather than legitimacy the basis of sovereignty, Hobbes, as Clarendon pointed out angrily, could argue for the Protectorate as well as for the Stuart dynasty.
[191] *Leviathan*, ch. xxvi (p. 142).

HOBBES: THE SECULAR ARGUMENT

dispute. If any 'Ghostly Authority' coexists with the secular sovereign and has the power to declare what is sin, it has also the power to declare what is law, sin and law being synonymous.[192]

Hobbes is a complete Erastian. His defense of a compulsory national church represents the furthest extension of the Stuarts' common argument against Puritan dissidents, with the significant difference that it has a secular rather than a *de jure divino* base. Never has the matter been put more bluntly: to his thinking a church is a 'Company of men professing Christian Religion, united in the person of one Soveraign: at whose command they ought to assemble, and without whose authority they ought not to assemble'.[193] To argue liberty of conscience from natural rights – which have been abridged by the social contract – is ridiculous, for properly speaking religion 'is a law of the kingdom, and ought not to be disputed'.[194] Only two things are essential for salvation, faith in Christ and obedience to laws. The kingdom of heaven is shut to none but sinners, and sinners are those who refuse to obey laws.[195] A church is a real church only when it has the coercive power of compelling 'due obedience'; otherwise 'it is a multitude, and persons in the plural, howsoever agreeing in opinions'. No questions about 'spiritual' matters are admissible, for every church should appoint 'some canonical interpreter, whose legitimate office it is to end controversies begun ... and whose authority therefore must be no less obeyed, than theirs who first recommended the Scripture itself to us for a canon of faith'.[196] Beyond this, Erastianism could hardly go, nor even the Laudian church seek a more undisguised *de facto* sanction.

[192] *Ibid.*, ch. xxix (p. 175).
[193] *Ibid.*, ch. xl (p. 252).
[194] *Behemoth*, pt. II (*English Works*, VI, 276); cf. *Philosophical Rudiments*, XVII.18 (*English Works*, II, 275), XVII.27 (*English Works*, II, 292–5).
[195] *Ibid.*, XVIII.3 (*English Works*, II, 302); cf. XVIII.13 (*English Works*, II, 314–5).
[196] *Ibid.*, XVIII.18 (*English Works*, II, 275).

VI

CHURCH AND STATE

1. *JUS DIVINUM*

The essential fact about Stuart religious controversy was its crucial political implications, for in the seventeenth century men had not yet lost the long habit of seeking theological sanctions for their secular activities. Indeed, the irony of the age, as we shall see, was that the segregation of politics and theology was urged on theological grounds, so that the secularization of political theory was in itself a corollary of theological presuppositions.

The sixteenth century had been an age of nationalism and absolutism, reciprocal forces made necessary to fill the vacuum left by the decline of Rome. Although the Tudors, like their mighty rivals the Valois and the Hapsburgs, could not afford such luxuries as religious toleration and democracy, their absolutism none the less rested on broad popular support; otherwise it could not have been so successful. Moreover, Tudor political theory – fairly represented by Sir Thomas Smith's *De republica Anglorum* and Bacon's essays – made large allowances for the harmony and balance of the crown and the courts (with Parliament considered as the highest court) exercising their respective powers under the constitution.

Although Bacon, as an ambitious politician, made extravagant claims for the royal prerogative and fulsomely flattered his monarch in the dedication to *The Advancement of Learning*, his political ideal seems to have been essentially Tudor: 'Of the True Greatness of Kingdoms and Estates' advocates a militant Protestantism under the guidance of a monarch strong in his prerogatives and clearly superior to both Parliament and the nobility; 'Of Seditions' prescribes for poverty and discontent conventional mercantilist expansion; 'Of Judicature' denies to the courts the liberty of meddling in questions of state and royal prerogatives, but it regards the king's judges as lions under the throne. Certainly Bacon, as a good Elizabethan, never raised the question of supremacy, nor did he feel the necessity of locating the seat of sovereignty in either crown or Parliament. The harmony of powers made that an idle question. As Lancelot Andrewes had said, preaching before Elizabeth, the monarch is a 'nail driven into a wall', and he prayed to God that the nail be never loosened: 'for if it should, all our cups would batter with the fall, and all the music of our choir be marred; that is, both Church and country be put in danger.'[1]

With their astonishing capacity for blundering the Stuarts rejected this doctrine of balance. So did their opponents. Sir Edward Coke cared nothing for democracy, but he insisted, against the extravagant demands of James, that the king enjoyed his prerogatives under, not above, the law; and so he was logically compelled to advance the pregnant proposition that all political power was derived from the common law. This notion, as developed by Parliamentarians like Eliot and Hampden, sharply posed the question of sovereignty from the political side; the Presbyterian demands for their reformed church discipline posed it just as sharply from the ecclesiastical side. In broadest terms, the Stuarts' rebuttal, and claim for royal supremacy, took the form of *jus divinum* and Erastianism.

The divine right of kings, a theory obsolete when the Stuarts advanced it and radically incompatible with the temper of the English people, was used to justify a political and religious policy which never had much popular support and which steadily lost ground as the century wore on. The 'fundamental' law, James told Parliament in 1607, is *jus regis*;[2] all others may be abrogated at will by the king, for he alone 'is above the law, as both the author and giver of strength thereto'.[3] Even a wicked king must be regarded as sent by God for a curse to his people and a plague for their sins;[4] a king's limitless power is determined by status, not by a fictitious contract or legal bond between him and his people, and since that status is fixed by God, to God alone is he responsible.[5]

> Kings are justly called Gods, for that they exercise a manner or resemblance of Divine power upon earth: For if you wil consider the Attributes to God, you shall see how they agree in the person of a King. GOD hath power to create, or destroy, make, or unmake at his pleasure, to give life, or send death, to judge all, and to be judged nor acomptable to none:

[1] *Ninety-Six Sermons*, II, 10.   [2] *Political Works*, p. 300.
[3] Ibid., p. 63.   [4] Ibid., p. 67.
[5] Ibid., p. 68.

To raise low things, and to make high things low at his pleasure, to God are both soule and body due. And the like power have kings.⁶

As the embittered protests of Coke and the tumultuous history of Stuart Parliaments show, this kind of talk could in the nature of things arouse no genuine popular support. When James summarily ordered a pickpocket to be hanged without trial on his first progress from Edinburgh to London,⁷ he profoundly shocked his new subjects: "'tis strangely done,' muttered Sir John Harington.⁸ But James could never learn better, nor could his son. Sir Robert Berkeley, speaking for the prosecution at Hampden's trial over the ship money, bluntly stated the Stuart concept of law: 'I never read nor heard, that lex was rex; but it is common and most true, that rex is lex, for he is "rex loquens", a living, a speaking, an acting law.'⁹

This obsolete but sinister notion of supremacy and the Erastian policy inherited from the Tudors were reciprocally useful. If the king, the Lord's anointed, was the head of both church and state, it followed that all vexing questions of discipline and nonconformity should evaporate. At least, such was the theory studiously developed to counter the Presbyterian demands for an autonomous discipline.¹⁰ Thus Erastianism, a policy first advanced to arouse young national states against the Catholic threat, came to be the defense of a shaky theory of royal supremacy against internal religious dissent. Though no Erastian, in his flaming

---

⁶ Ibid., pp. 307–8. For a list of the customarily quoted Biblical texts supporting *jus divinum*, see Ralegh, *History*, I.ix.1. One of the most notorious systematic defenses of divine right was Henry Ferne's *Resolving of Conscience*; its date – 1642 – is an ironical clue to its relevancy.
⁷ *The True Narration of the Entertainment of His Royal Majesty*, p. 35.
⁸ *Nugae Antiquae*, II, 226.
⁹ Quoted by Davies, *The Early Stuarts*, p. 83.
¹⁰ Thomas Erastus was a Swiss Protestant who, serving in the court of Frederick III at Heidelberg, had been drawn into a bitter controversy with Beza over the Prince Elector's proposed introduction of Calvinism. His two famous works – not published in his lifetime – were the *Theses* and *Confirmatio Thesium* (1589), written to contest the rigid Calvinist position that only the presbyters could properly determine who should or should not receive the sacrament. The ninth thesis states the crucial problem: 'Whether any person ought, because of his having a sin, or of living an impure life, to be prohibited from the use and participation of the sacraments with his fellow-Christians, provided he wishes to partake with them.' Using Scriptural citation, Erastus argued that nothing justifies such usurpation of power by the clergy. In the seventy-fourth thesis he proposed that 'if that Church and State were most wisely founded, arranged, and appointed' the godly Christian magistrate should have the authority claimed by the (Calvinist) theocrats. This was a restatement of the notion, common in the Hildebrantine controversies, that if a church is granted powers of excommunication, etc., it constitutes a power in the state greater than the state itself. See Henson, *Studies in English Religion in the Seventeenth Century*, pp. 126–36.

Appeal to the German Nobility Luther had construed the emergent nationalism of the German people as one of the 'walls' against papal arrogance and iniquity. 'Therefore I say, Forasmuch as the temporal power has been ordained by God for the punishment of the bad and the protection of the good, we must let it do its duty throughout the whole Christian body, without respect of persons, whether it strike popes, bishops, priests, monks, nuns, or whoever it may be.'[11]

In the early seventeenth century the Catholics – and especially the Jesuits – were still a danger, of course. As Selden said, 'the papists where ere they live have another King att Rome'.[12] The novel element in the Jacobean situation was that an Erastian church under a *jus divinum* monarch was needed also against domestic malcontents who, blocked in their efforts to secure disciplinary reforms with the Anglican establishment, were turning to political action.

The shifting thus of ecclesiastical demands from Convocation to Parliament was the most momentous event in Stuart history, for it reflected that fundamental shift in political theory from government by status to government by contract. When the Presbyterians began to think of the king as exercising only delegated authority and therefore as answerable to Parliament – and yet more when the Independents ignored Parliament to appeal directly to the people – a new epoch was opening. That Elizabethan (and medieval) reliance on order and degree which informs the politics of *Gorboduc* no less than of *Coriolanus* and *Troilus and Cressida*, and which had implications for every aspect of sixteenth-century thought, had nearly finished its long career. Even when Ralegh repeated the ancient commonplaces in the preface to his *History* they were obsolescent.

> For that infinite wisdom of God, which hath distinguished his angels by degress; which hath given greater and less light and beauty to heavenly bodies; which hath made differences between beasts and birds; created the eagle and the fly, the cedar and the shrub; and among stones, given the fairest tincture to the ruby, and the quickest light to the diamond; hath also ordained kings, dukes, or leaders of the people, magistrates, judges, and other degrees among men.[13]

---

[11] Bettenson, *Documents of the Christian Church*, p. 276.
[12] *Table Talk*, p. 98.
[13] p. xxxvi.

When the Puritans and the lawyers raised the question of Parliamentary as opposed to royal supremacy they sharpened the crown's counter-measure of *jus divinum*, and thus were sowed the seeds for the Great Rebellion and the modern conception of constitutional monarchy. No English king since Charles II has been in any doubt that he held his place through the good offices of Parliament, and the Revolution of 1688 made it painfully clear, even to the last and weakest of the Stuarts, that no pretensions of *jus divinum* could weigh against the delegated sovereignty of the people's representatives. It is quite likely that James recognized the gravity of the Puritan demands, and that he opposed them precisely because they did imply the relocation of political sovereignty. At any rate, he contemptuously rejected the modest proposals of the Millenary Petition (1603) which a wiser monarch would have granted so as not to raise any embarrassing questions of the supremacy; and the following year, at the Hampton Court Conference, he made his own arrogant claims for royal supremacy unequivocally clear. No bishop, no king. Against the Puritan ministers, as the gossipy Harington reported, he 'rather usede upbraidinges than argumente'. When he told them they wanted to strip Christ again, that he tired of their 'snivellinge', that he wished those who would take away the surplice 'mighte want for their own breech', then his bishops seemed mightily pleased, 'and said his Majestie spoke by the power of inspiration'.[14]

The Puritans, recognizing that from such a monarch they could expect nothing, were compelled to seek their reforms from Parliament. It was a slow business, of course. Not until the Long Parliament summoned the Westminster Assembly in 1643 did they have a chance to effect those Presbyterian reforms for which they had been agitating ever since the days of Cartwright, and when they finally got the chance they did not quite know what to do with it. For by then the Independents were on the scene, and the Presbyterians in Parliament found themselves defending the sacramental power of the church, established *de jure divino* and finally reformed by the Presbyterian discipline, against those who refused the state any voice whatever in matters of conscience and religion.

But this is to anticipate. Until the 'forties the Presbyterians had to press their demands as best they could against a crown that claimed divine sanction and against an episcopacy named by that

[14] *Nugae Antiquae*, II, 228. See Fuller, X.i.21-6.

crown. Consequently the Stuarts were convinced that the Puritans and the Catholics represented the same kind of danger to the body politic as disgruntled minorities. Both would deny to the civil government any legitimate control over religion, and both contended that civil power in religion was an invasion of spiritual autonomy – as indeed it was. As Samuel Butler, who to his sorrow knew a good deal about Puritanism, wittily said,

> Presbytery does but translate
> The papacy to a free state:
> A commonwealth of Popery,
> Where ev'ry village is a See
> As well as Rome, and must maintain
> A title-pig metropolitan;
> Where ev'ry Presbyter and Deacon
> Commands the keys for cheese and bacon,
> And ev'ry hamlet's governed
> By's Holiness, the Church's head,
> More haughty and severe in's place
> Than Gregory and Boniface.[15]

Defending the Catholic cause, Cardinal Bellarmine had argued that 'potestas ecclesiastica, quae spiritualis est, praeest potestati politicae temporali, & eam dirigere debet ad finem supremum aeternae vitae'. Oddly enough, the Puritans were almost compelled to agree. In trying to separate ecclesiastical and political power they made their greatest contribution to political theory. It was not that the Presbyterians were interested in toleration: when they came to power they substituted a religious for the Stuarts' political persecution; but in order to dress the balance of state over church they were forced to challenge the Erastian policy of the Stuarts. 'Noe man fashioneth his house to his hangings', said John Cotton, 'but his hangings to his house. It is better that the commonwealth be fashioned to the setting forth of God's house, which is his church: than to accommodate the church frame to the civill state.'[16] Against both Catholics and Puritans, however, the Stuarts used the same strategy. They arrogated to themselves a divine mandate for governing both church and state, and they chose to believe that the prelatical discipline of the established church enjoyed a divine sanction.

[15] *Hudibras*, I.iii.1201–12.
[16] 'Copy of a Letter from Mr Cotton to Lord Say and Seal in the Year 1636', Miller-Johnson, p. 209.

Although Hooker had lent the weight of his learning to defending an Erastian church, it cannot be said that he would have approved all the policies of Charles and Archbishop Laud. Hooker's view was, not unnaturally, Elizabethan. In that dubious eighth book of the *Laws* he proposed an intimate state-church relationship on analogy of the Old Testament. The monarch is bound by the Gospel, of course, but his power is not merely temporal; thus his right to be regarded as governor of the church, his right to appoint bishops, and his appellant jurisdiction over ecclesiastical courts. However, at the base of Hooker's religious thinking lay the concept of the king's power as representative and constitutional – and this the Stuarts were loath to accept. Hooker thought of church discipline as only one phase of civil society; and civil society, like the dictates of reason which should inform it, must command common consent. 'Laws they are not therefore which public approbation hath not made so.'[17] Since both Catholics and Presbyterians would deny allegiance to ecclesiastical law they jeopardized the entire social order, for a society without religion is unthinkable: 'all true virtues are to honour true religion as their parent, and all well-ordered commonweals to love her as their chiefest stay'.[18] Equally unthinkable is the notion that this chiefest stay should be deprived of the beauty, order, and reason of law, or that such law should not derive its strength from broad popular support.

Thus a social contract is clearly implied[19] that men might live together at all, and another contract that they might live under a certain kind of government. For men knew that

> strifes and troubles would be endless, except they gave their common consent all to be ordered by some whom they should agree upon: without which consent there were no reason that one man should take upon him to be lord or judge over another; because, although there be according to the opinion of some very great and judicious men a kind of natural right in the noble, wise, and virtuous, to govern them which are of servile disposition; nevertheless for manifestation of this their right, and men's more peaceable contentment on both sides, the assent of them who are to be governed seemeth necessary.[20]

---

[17] I.x.8.   [18] V.i.5.   [19] I.x.1.
[20] I.x.iv. Hooker goes on to say that for a man to exercise absolute power without either an 'express commission immediately and personally received from God' or else by the consent of his subjects 'is no better than mere tyranny' (I.x.8). And again in the second book (II.vii.6): 'For men to be tied and led by authority, as it were with a kind

JUS DIVINUM   253

Although the Stuarts and their prelates were glad to have Hooker's defense of the Erastian establishment, they could obviously not reconcile his theory of government by consent with *jus divinum*. If they had, many men who spilled their blood in battle might have died in bed. 'Consider that all authority descends from God,' cautioned Jeremy Taylor, 'and our superiors bear the image of the divine power.'[21] The practical consequences of this proposition are most conveniently seen in the work of Archbishop Laud, whose *Relation of the Conference between William Laud . . . and Mr. Fisher the Jesuite* illustrates both his Hookerian rationalism and his ecclesiastical absolutism, and thus symbolizes the dilemma of the Stuarts.

Essentially an analysis of the uses and limitations of human reason in religious matters, the *Relation* takes the Hookerian position of tolerance within Erastian and doctrinal limits. Only the articles of the Creed and the belief in the absolute infallibility of the Bible are essential for salvation,[22] and thus even those who are misled by fomenters of heresy may be in a 'state of salvation'.[23] There is no one true church, argues Laud against his Catholic opponent.[24] All churches are true so long as they are based on the Bible and on man's rationally acknowledged need for salvation through Christ; and yet some uniformity is a social and political necessity. Although it is obvious that faith is a higher kind of knowledge than reason, the articles of faith may be confirmed or supplemented in various ways: by the traditions of the church, by the testimony of the Scripture, by the dictates of the Holy Ghost, and by natural reason (available to all 'that have not imbrutished themselves, and sunk below their species, and order of nature').[25]

In the government of a church all these methods of attaining truth should be used. Thus even though reason cannot establish

---

of captivity of judgment, and though there be reason to the contrary not to listen unto it, but to follow like beasts the first in the herd, they know not nor care not whither, this were brutish.' Cudworth (*The True Intellectual System*, IV, 206) speaks of the 'bond or vinculum' which holds civil society together as rationally apprehended natural justice – 'something of a common and public, or of a cementing and conglutinating nature'.
[21] *Holy Living*, III.i.
[22] *Works*, II, 32–3, 48–50.
[23] *Ibid.*, II, 350–1.
[24] *Ibid.*, II, 143, 218; cf. Donne's desire to find religion 'not from corners, nor Conventicles, nor schismatical singularities; but from the association, and communion of thy Catholique Church' – that is, from the all-inclusive body of believers (*Devotions*, p. 40).
[25] *Works*, II, 71.

an article of faith, it can demonstrate such an article as too elevated for either proof or refutation;[26] moreover, it can operate powerfully in that large area of things indifferent in determining such practices as are compatible with both piety and expediency. In his toleration of things not fundamental Laud (like Taylor in *The Liberty of Prophesying*) seems to veer close to Arminianism, and he is broadly latitudinarian in spiritual matters; but his Erastianism is pronounced: the established church must have the power to prescribe the rites and disciplines thought necessary for social and political unity. The inner sanctity that comes from grace is our greatest service to God, but this sanctity is best revealed by the external worship of God in His church.[27] The pretensions of private conscience – which would set this or that vagary or this or that zealot against the accumulated wisdom of centuries and against the health of the body politic – are obviously intolerable. The impious notion that it was mere 'superstition' for 'any man to come with more reverence into a church, than a tinker and his bitch come into an ale-house'[28] is the most monstrous evil and the most sinister threat to the established church. If government and religion are to endure, it may not be condoned.

Thus to check the Catholics Laud provides for some measure of religious individualism; to check the Puritans he prescribes for some measure of unity and conformity. In view of his own ecclesiastical and political career it cannot be said that he carried out either prescription with success. In his view the established church was an instrument of the state; and since the state itself rested on *jus divinum*, the prelatical establishment could be said to enjoy both an Erastian and a divine sanction. This is not to say that the Stuart church had abandoned the theology of Parker, Jewel, and Hooker. But although Calvinism was still the dominant belief of most Englishmen at James's death, doctrinal matters came to be subordinated to the needs of a militant Erastianism. As Henson has said, 'the royal prerogative was frankly placed at the service of a religious faction'.[29] The primate was Charles's chief minister, another bishop was his lord treasurer, and the clergy were generally bound fast to the support of a political policy that was forcing the Puritans to civil disobedience.

---

[26] *Works*, II, 88–9.   [27] *Ibid.*, II, xvi.
[28] *Ibid.*, VI, 57.
[29] *Studies in English Religion in the Seventeenth Century*, p. 30.

JUS DIVINUM

As Laud said in a sermon before his king, by the law of nature the commonwealth 'goes first; first men, before religious and faithful men; and the Church can have no being but in the Commonwealth'.[30] Upon such a principle, Hooker's broadly rational accommodation of the traditional rites so odious to the Puritans could become an excuse for the most savage persecution. It is true that the ordinances and discipline of the established church are things indifferent, but if such things indifferent are left to each man's private judgment the very power of the state is jeopardized. By the Stuarts' doctrine of divine right the monarch was the Lord's anointed; also he was the supreme head of the church, and therefore any attack on that church was an attack on his sacred person. Given a dynasty built on such principles, and a primate of Laud's intensely Erastian convictions, the calamities of the early seventeenth century were inevitable. As Mr Gooch has pointed out, there were some very good reasons for the increasing unpopularity of the Anglican church: it was Anglo-Catholic, politically reactionary, and tainted by a servile and time-serving clergy.[31] Moreover, its program and interests ran counter to the most powerful movements of popular thought. In a century when there was rising among the Puritan small landowners and merchants a steady demand for social and economic leveling, for relocating political sovereignty in the people, for secularizing political sanctions in the natural law, the crown and Convocation attempted to make compulsory a set of political and ecclesiastical principles basically antagonistic to the national conscience. The Canons of 1603, codifying the Anglican triumph at the Hampton Court Conference, laid down the basis of that Laudian absolutism which finally received its *coup de grâce* in the Toleration Act of 1689; but between those terminal dates lay nearly a century of violence, compulsion, and terror – the price of a dynasty that sought to check the main current of English political thought.

James had early scented the danger in the Puritans' program for disciplinary reform. 'They cry, "Wee are all but vile wormes",' he warned his son, 'and yet, will judge and give law to their King, but will be judged nor controlled by none.'[32] James's own notions

---
[30] *Works*, I, 6; cf. II, 223, 228–9.
[31] For a good Anglican's testimony on this obvious weakness, see Burton, *Anatomy*, I, 378.
[32] *Political Works*, p. 38.

of sovereignty were of a different sort. Keep your hands off all questions of prerogative, he told his judiciary in 1616. 'If there fall out a question that concerns my Prerogative or mystery of State, deale not with it: . . . for they are transcendent matters.'[33] To such principles Laud gave the support of his towering ambition, his learning, and his fierce loyalty. The way to 'keep unity', he preached before Charles's third Parliament in 1628, 'both in Church and State, is for the governors to carry a watchful eye over all such as are discovered, or feared, to have private ends'.[34] Private ends were those not consonant with the prescribed conformity in things indifferent; and so in spite of his theoretical tolerance he regarded it as his episcopal function to spearhead the oppressive conformity which bears his name. For his pains he became the most cordially detested man since Thomas Cromwell. And yet his motives, like those of most men, were capable of the most pious rationalization. Speaking before the Star Chamber in 1637 at the trial of Bastwick, Burton, and Prynne, he pictured himself as one vilified for doing his duty:

> For my care of this Church, the reducing of it into order, the upholding of the external worship of God in it, and the settling of it to the rules of its first reformation, are the causes (and the sole causes, whatever are pretended) of all this malicious storm, which hath lowered so black upon me, and some of my brethren.[35]

The care of the church meant a program of calculated repression. Laud's metropolitan visitations and the various ecclesiastical courts – archdiaconal, diocesan, provincial, and the dread High Commission – might alarm legalists like Coke in assuming judicial power, but in Laud's view they were essential in compelling that religious conformity without which the state would be chaos, and each man's determination of things indifferent as valid as his betters'. Caught between the aggressive Jesuits and the fanatical Puritans, as Laud told his royal master, the establishment would be 'ground to powder' unless strong measures were taken.[36] Charles thoroughly agreed; in fact, he thought that some of the Sectarians 'seem to have learned and to practice the worst Principles of the worst Papists'.[37] And so Laud cropped ears, slit noses,

---

[33] *Political Works*, p. 32. [34] *Works*, I, 167.
[35] *Works*, VI, 42. [36] *Ibid*., II, xiii.
[37] *Political Works*, p. 85. An example of the Stuarts' stubborn refusal to make really popular concessions is suggested by the complicated Sabbatarian controversy. In his *Doctrine of the Sabbath* (1595) Nicholas Bound (or Bownde) had called for a rigid observ-

branded foreheads, suppressed popular preaching, destroyed conventicles, and harried dissenters out of the land with the best will in the world.[38]

ation of the Sabbath on the model of Hebraic austerity from which, he charged, the bishops had fallen away. This was answered by Thomas Rogers in the preface to his treatise on the Thirty-Nine Articles (*Faith, Doctrine, and Religion . . . in England*, 1607); he saw the Sabbatarian demands as merely one more token of Presbyterian disaffection. Taking the line that the Sabbatarian policy of the Puritans challenged the right of the established church to order the holy days and their observation, James went out of his way to deny the Presbyterians their request. In 1617 he decreed that once a man had attended services he could lawfully disport himself innocently the rest of the day, and a year later his so-called *Book of Sports* codified the lawful Sabbath amusements possible for his subjects. This book, odious to the Puritans, was reissued in 1633. Hence Milton's complaint (*Of Reformation in England*, bk. II [*PW*, II, 401–2]) that on the Sabbath godly, sober men should be 'plucked from their soberest and saddest thoughts, and by bishops, the pretended fathers of the church, instigated, by public edict, and with earnest endeavour pushed forward to gaming, jigging, wassailing, and mixed dancing, is a horror to think!' But the tide turned, of course: the Parliament in 1644 decreed that December 25th should be a fast-day for the remembrance of sins in making it formerly a day of revelry; and in 1647 the observation of Easter, Whitsuntide, and other ancient festivals was likewise forbidden by law. See Fuller, XI.ii.33; XI.iv.55–61. The Sabbatarian controversy reminds one of Macaulay's inspired quip: that the Puritans hated bearbaiting not because it gave pain to the bear but because it gave pleasure to the spectators. He is ironically amusing, also, on the abolition of Christmas by the Long Parliament: 'The Long Parliament gave orders, in 1644, that the twenty-fifth of December should be strictly observed as a fast, and that all men should pass it in humbly bemoaning the great national sin which they and their fathers had so often committed on that day by romping under the mistletoe, eating boar's head, and drinking ale flavoured with roasted apples' (*History*, I, 143).

[38] The most famous of Laud's persecutions was that of Burton, Bastwick, and Prynne – 'three persons most notorious for their declared malice against the government of the Church by Bishops', as Clarendon said (*History*, I, 155). Prynne, that most unlovely of all the unlovely Presbyterians, had long been a thorn in Laud's side. In 1636 he published his *News from Ipswich*, which not only contained a bitter personal attack on the primate but also urged, among other things, that all bishops be summarily hanged for suppressing the truth. He was haled before the Star Chamber along with Burton and Bastwick: the former had been twice before the privy council in the 'twenties for writing seditious pamphlets and in 1636 had been arrested for preaching two subversive sermons on Guy Fawkes' day; the latter, a Puritan physician, had been languishing in prison since 1633 for writing against the prelates, but he had put his time to good use by composing his famous *Letany*, which young John Lilburne had smuggled to Holland to be published. All three, arraigned for writing scandalous and libelous books against the establishment, were sentenced to be fined, pilloried, have their ears cropped, and be imprisoned for life. A huge mob witnessed the execution of this barbarous sentence, and their persecution became a *cause célèbre*. Three inflammatory and influential books appeared as a result: Bastwick's *Letany*, Prynne's *New Discovery of the Prelates' Tyranny*, and the anonymous *Brief Relation of Certain special and most material passages, and Speeches in the Star Chamber*. See Gardiner, *History of the Great Civil War*, VIII, 226–34; Haller, *The Rise of Puritanism*, pp. 250 f.; Fuller, XI.ii.56–75.

On a slightly higher and more theoretical plane the bishops' case was formally stated by Joseph Hall's *Episcopacy by Divine Right Asserted* (1640), which Laud himself scrutinized sheet by sheet before it appeared; it advanced the same thesis as Hall's *Humble Remonstrance to the High Court of Parliament* (1640) – that to overthrow episcopacy would destroy society. Of course, there were many Presbyterian rebuttals: Alexander Henderson's *Unlawfulness and Danger of Limited Prelacy* (1641) was echoed by Robert Baillie's *Unlawfulness and Danger of Limited Episcopacy* in the same year; in February of 1642 five Puritan ministers, who called themselves Smectymnuus, issued their *Answer to . . . An Humble Remonstrance*; this led to a *Defence* by Hall, then a *Vindication* by the five brethren, then

If his predecessor, Archbishop Abbot, had been suspiciously sympathetic with the Puritans,[39] he himself was determined to set matters right. In doing so he had to forget those broad Hookerian principles of reason and toleration. Coleridge speaks somewhere of the meek deliverances to God's mercy with which Laud accompanied his votes for the tortures and mutilations of Leighton and other Presbyterians.[40] The irony is not misplaced, for Laud was in the supremely ironical position of professing a set of values radically incompatible with his actual administration of ecclesiastical affairs. Perhaps Clarendon is right in saying his basic error was his belief that 'innocence of heart, and integrity of manners, was a guard strong enough to secure any man in his voyage through this world';[41] at any rate, he was caught in a position from which there could be neither retreat nor advance, and he came to realize it.

His reports to the king between 1633 and 1639 became increasingly bitter and hopeless, and he at last confessed, on the eve of the Great Rebellion, that the 'stiffness' of certain dissenters was incorrigible. He had long been aware of the Puritans' strategy: they clamor from both press and pulpit to 'make a heat among the people; and so by mutiny to effect that which by law they cannot; and by false and most unjust calumnies to defame both our callings and persons'.[42] But he was unable to turn back the clock as he and his master wished. And so he was at last brought to the block, praying that his enemies might repent, but if not that their wicked designs might fail as being counter to the glory of God, the stability of the crown, the honor of Parliament, and the safety of the church.[43] 'We have lost of the substance of Religion by changing it into opinion', he told his executioners[44] – and those words might stand as the monument to his futile and misdirected effort to stem the tide of the English Reformation.

a *Short Answer* by Hall, then another rejoinder by the five, then Milton's *Animadversions* against Hall, then the *Modest Confutation* to which Milton replied in his famous *Apology for Smectymnuus* (May 1642). See Haller, *Tracts on Liberty*, I, 16; Masson, *Life of Milton*, II, 237-69 (for a full account of the controversy).

[39] See Clarendon, *History*, I, 148. See Fuller, X.v.12-7.
[40] See Jeremy Taylor, *Works*, I, cccxxx.
[41] *History*, I, 149.
[42] *Works*, VI, 44. In the *Eikon Basilikon* (p. 11) Charles himself meditates on the popular 'Tumults' following the opening of the Long Parliament: they were 'like an Earthquake, shaking the very foundations of all; then which nothing in the world hath more of horrour'.
[43] Gardiner, *History of the Great Civil War*, II, 107.
[44] Walton, *Lives*, II, 276.

II. CIVIL DISOBEDIENCE

While the Stuarts, virtually ignoring the liberal wing of the Anglican establishment, were enforcing a suicidal policy of divine right and Erastianism, the opposition became steadily broader and more complex in its motives. We have thus far spoken of Puritans more or less generically, as if all Puritans were at all times committed to the same principles and striving to achieve the same ends. This was by no means the case, and we must now discriminate the main offshoots of Elizabethan Puritanism as they entered the political arena toward the fourth decade of the seventeenth century.

Although Calvin realized the danger of proliferating sects and tried to guard against them, the danger was implicit in reformed theology. His test for certainty of religious truth – the internal knowledge of the 'spirit' – raised a question which he could never answer: why is not one man's religious certainty as convincing as another's? The history of the Sectarians of the seventeenth century, all so rigorously opposed by the Presbyterians, show how real this difficulty became. A born bigot, Calvin anticipated it,[45] and charged it to inexact knowledge of the Scripture, lashing out at those who, with inadequate knowledge of God's word, imagining

> to themselves some other way of approaching to God, must be considered as not so much misled by error as actuated by frenzy. For there have lately arisen some unsteady men, who, haughtily pretending to be taught by the Spirit, reject all reading themselves, and deride the simplicity of those who still attend to (what they style) the dead and killing letter.[46]

The threat of schism persisted and increased, however, until in England it finally destroyed the chance for a completed reformation made possible by the Great Rebellion.

Cartwright's *Book of Discipline* had by no means established uniformity of dissent for Englishmen. There was a large and increasingly important group of orthodox Calvinists who wished merely to get control of the establishment and reform its discipline on the Genevan model. These were the Presbyterians. The Congregationalists, on the other hand, sought to limit church membership to a smaller body of the elect and permit more individual freedom of discipline to preachers and their congregations. These

---

[45] *Institutes*, I.ix. [46] *Ibid.*, I.ix.1.

became the Independents of Milton's age. More or less beyond the pale were the Separatists – led by Browne and Barrow – who sought reformation without tarrying by breaking completely from the establishment and setting up autonomous 'holy communities'.[47] And in time there were those Seekers, Ranters, Muggletonians, Quakers, and the like who pushed the prerogatives of Protestant individualism so far they could hardly be defined as organized groups at all. Burton's attitude toward such schismatics and enthusiasts would be shared by even the Presbyterians. As examples of religious melancholics there were

> Hacket that said he was Christ, Coppinger and Arthington, his disciples: Burchet and Hovatus, burned at Norwich. We are never likely seven years together without some such new Prophets, that have several inspirations, some to convert the Jews, some fast forty days, [some] go with Daniel to the Lion's den; some foretell strange things, some for one thing, some for another. Great Precisians of mean conditions and very illiterate, most part by a preposterous zeal, fasting, meditation, melancholy, are brought into these gross errors and inconveniences.[48]

As the civil crisis in England came to a head in the 'forties and 'fifties, these various kinds of dissidents drew their theological and political lines more sharply. An unregenerate royalist like Hobbes professed himself unable to tell one from another: Milton's *Second Defense* and Salmasius' *Defensio regia*, though 'very good Latin both', were so equally bad that it is 'hardly to be judged which is worse ... so like is a Presbyterian to an Independent'.[49] But there were real differences, and no one living in the mid-seventeenth century could ignore them. The Presbyterians who under Cartwright had initiated the Puritan attempt to reform the establishment remained the conservative party. They advocated Parliamentary supremacy, but only to attain their own *de jure divino* discipline; and once they thought they had attained it they jealously guarded their and the king's pre-

---

[47] John Smyth had by 1606 gathered a flock of Separatists at Gainsborough; he led them to Holland the next year and there they were joined by John Robinson's congregation from Scrooby. But Smyth, losing control of his followers, drifted off to the Mennonites. Some of his flock followed Thomas Helwys back to England about 1612; others went over to Robinson. In 1609 this very able man led them to Leyden (where they prospered mightily) and eventually to Plymouth in New England.

[48] *Anatomy*, III, 426. For Hobbes' analysis of the cranks, false prophets, and 'fanaticks' of the early 'forties, see *Behemoth*, pt. I (*English Works*, VI, 167–8); for those of the Protectorate, *ibid.*, pt. IV (VI, 397–8). On the notorious Hacket ('that said he was Christ'), see Fuller, IX.vii.32–7.

[49] *Behemoth*, pt. IV (*English Works*, VI, 368).

rogatives and were deaf to any plea for toleration or civil liberty. Such intransigence inevitably brought them into conflict with the Independents of the center, the heirs of earlier Congregationalists. This loosely defined group, whose strength lay in the army and outside of Parliament, insisted on the principle of congregational autonomy. Significantly, their religious liberalism quickly fanned out into political liberalism. Some of them were not adverse to a state-controlled Presbyterian establishment, but all wanted toleration – both civil and religious – for dissenting groups. Although few would go as far as Roger Williams and William Walwyn in demanding complete freedom from civil or ecclesiastical control, they were all compelled to advocate some degree of toleration for others in order to get it for themselves. 'If sects and schisms be turbulent in the unsettled estate of a church, while it lies under the amending hand,' said a notable Independent, 'it best beseems our Christian courage to think they are but as the throes and pangs that go before the birth of reformation, and that the work itself is now in doing.'[50]

As the army gained power while the timid Presbyterians were backing and filling with the captured king, the Independents developed such extremists as the Levelers and the Diggers. Under the leadership of Lilburne and Winstanley respectively, these groups – which in time were easily suppressed by Cromwell's conservative policy – went ahead to demand first civil and then economic equalitarianism as natural rights. Thus they emancipated political theory from theology and pushed the latent individualism of the Protestant ethos to extremes which the seventeenth century was by no means ready to accept. Finally, to the far left lay such Sectarians as the Baptists, Quakers, Millenarians, Fifth Monarchy Men, and assorted fanatics who lost all concept of church discipline in their search for personal illumination and mystical rapture. The fact that all these were for various reasons opposed to the episcopal establishment and sought various reforms permits us to call them Puritans, but it also suggests how little meaning that term came to have.[51]

Theologically and politically, the Presbyterians represented the extreme right wing of Puritanism. From the time of Cartwright

[50] *The Reason of Church Government*, I.vii (*PW*, II, 469).
[51] For a good contemporary analysis of the Puritan sects, see John Saltmarsh, *The Smoke in the Temple*, pp. 9–24; for the Presbyterian view, see Baxter, *Autobiography*, pp. 73–4, and the hysterical denunciation of Edwards and Pagitt noted below.

they had been reformist, not separatist, and, although they were eventually forced to advocate Parliamentary sovereignty to achieve their disciplinary reforms, they generally maintained Calvin's own very cautious view of civil disobedience. The royalists commonly traced the Puritans' political subversion back to Calvin, and it is true that such great Reformation principles as the rightful duty of free inquiry and the priesthood of all believers contained the seeds of liberty and equality; but both Calvin and Luther took a very dim view of political insubordination.[52] Calvin, the main force behind English Puritanism, had only one basic conviction about politics – that under no circumstances should the independence of spiritual authority be subordinated to the secular power. As the history of his Genevan tyranny makes clear, he had no such scruples about the integrity and independence of the civil power, and neither did those Presbyterians who gained control of the Long Parliament and convoked the Westminster Assembly. In the famous last chapter of the *Institutes*, however, Calvin did make the necessary allowance for passive obedience. If a ruler is good, he commands allegiance because his power, like all power, is derived from God; if bad, he must be endured as God's agent for punishing sins. The only loophole for a theory of justifiable insubordination is Calvin's provision for those 'inferior magistrates'[53] who may properly resist tyranny and ungodliness for the protection of the holy community. The right of resistance is in no sense a general right, however, and as a born autocrat Calvin specifically repudiated such political extremists as Knox, who defended resistance as a popular right to achieve political reform.

As developments in both France and England showed, however, Calvinistic political theory could not be contained within the narrow limits of the *Institutes*. Following the obscenity of St Bartholomew's Day, 1572, the Huguenots were compelled to push beyond mere passive obedience, and to defend their intransi-

---

[52] 'Tria sunt genera vitae', said Luther; 'Laborandum est, bellandum, guberandum' (*Tischreden*, no. 3993 [IV, 62]; cf. no. 6942 [VI, 284]). The rulers who rule by virtue of their 'natural reason' which God has given them are aided by laws written for the guidance of the common man (*ibid.*, no. 6955, [VI, 290–1]). As Troeltsch has said, this irrational natural law implies not the theory of contract by the governed but rather the medieval notion of status. Force is imperative if status is to be preserved as God gave it. 'No one need think that the world can be ruled without blood', warned Luther. 'The civil sword shall and must be red and bloody' (quoted by Tawney, *Religion and the Rise of Capitalism*, p. 87).
[53] IV.xx.3.

gence. One way of defending popular resistance and combating Catholic tyranny was that employed by François Hotman in his *Franco-Gallia* (1573). There monarchy itself is depicted as an unwelcome and unjustified innovation in the constitutional history of France, a modern corruption without the mandate of popular consent necessary to any form of government. Although this same argument turns up occasionally among English Puritans of the mid-seventeenth century, a more common defense of resistance was that based on those philosophical principles influentially advanced by the famous and anonymous *Vindiciae contra tyrannos* (1579).

The *Vindiciae*, written to protect religious minorities from *de facto* political power, derives government from a double contract – one between God and a people (like that made by the Jews when they became a chosen people), the other between a people thus obligated to God and their king. That the author (perhaps Languet) felt it necessary to provide for the first contract suggests the obvious fact that in the late sixteenth century men still sought sanctions in theology; that he provided for the second, which is central in his defense of resistance, suggests that political theory was on its way to becoming secularized. What is more immediately important, however, is that by both contracts the king's sovereignty is limited: by the first it is delegated from God, by the second from the people, and it follows, therefore, that a king who violates either has lost the right of obedience. Since a king's relation to God is like a vassal's to his liege, the king 'looseth his Right, and many times his Realm also, if he despise God, if he Complot with his Enemies, and if he Commit Fellony against that Royal Majesty'.[54] God demands holiness and the people demand justice (the 'vertue that gives to every one that which is his own');[55] if a king uses his delegated authority to subvert either demand 'he is not more a king, but a Tyrant; no longer a Judge, but a Malefactor'.[56] Resistance is not only a right against such a monster; it is a duty. The first item in the law of nature is self-defense, not only of our lives but of those 'liberties, without which life is scant worth enjoying, against all injury and violence'.[57] The people, as the ultimate repository of political sovereignty under God's covenant, thus have the moral obligation

---

[54] *Vindiciae*, p. 8.
[56] *Ibid.*, p. 91.
[55] *Ibid.*, pp. 43–4.
[57] *Ibid.*, p. 128.

to resist and even to destroy, through their accredited leaders and magistrates, a godless tyrant. If his assaults are verbal, then a people's rebuttal may be verbal; 'if the Sword be drawn against them, they may also take Arms, and fight either with tongue or hand, as occasion is'. All is fair – even ambushes and surprises may be met in kind – so long as 'the people' do not deteriorate into that horror, a headless rabble. The author of the *Vindiciae* was no more interested than Calvin in really popular sovereignty, nor did he allow to each man the right to take action against a disqualified ruler. God has ordained 'magistrates' through whom the people must act; it is their function 'to restrain the encroachments of Sovereignty, and to represent the whole body of the People'.[58]

No notable advance from this cautious theory of contract toward general popular rights can be claimed for the English Presbyterians. They wanted a disciplinary monopoly and in order to get it they had to oppose the Stuarts' absolutist claims; but toleration and civil liberties could, in the nature of things, find no place in their program, and they were much more intent on freeing the church from politics than in freeing politics from the church. Moreover, they, unlike the author of the *Vindiciae*, never sanctioned rebellion. They were quite content to keep the crown so long as they could attain their goal of a Presbyterian discipline. Drawing their main strength from the aristocrats and the wealthy London merchants, they sought not popular but Parliamentary sovereignty; and they would use Parliamentary sovereignty as an adjunct of a national church set up along Genevan lines. When the king, playing both ends against the middle and trying to outmaneuver both the Independent army and the Presbyterian Parliament, refused their terms, they were terrified and impotent. Confronted with the Independents' demands for toleration, popular rights, and complete separation of church and state, they at last realized that things had got disastrously out of hand.

For the limit of their ambition was a strict adherence to the Covenant and a national church as prescribed by the Westminster Assembly. To get this they were willing to challenge Stuart absolutism with Parliamentary supremacy, but they were emphatically not willing to infer from this Parliamentary supremacy any broad theory of natural rights, civil or religious. As Charles

[58] *Vindiciae*, p. 34.

said, their abortive alliance with the Scots was accompanied with 'common and vulgar flourishes for Religion and Liberty', but their real desire was to destroy the episcopacy and to substitute a Presbyterian monopoly.[59] Denouncing demands for toleration and civil liberties, John Winthrop told the General Court in Boston that men in society should not expect to enjoy that natural liberty which is 'incompatible and inconsistent with authority'. Civil liberty leaves men free to pursue what is 'good, just, and honest', but it by no means gives them license to urge their private religious convictions against a theocratic church.[60]

Thus, though the Presbyterians centered their attack on the prelatical discipline as contrary to God's word, they had no patience with more extreme demands for religious individualism or democracy. 'Against this Hierarchie,' said Alexander Leighton in denouncing the episcopacy, 'we do not commence, but renew our suite, for the recovery of the Keyes of Christ, and the veyle of his Spouse.... So hate them with a perfect hatred.'[61]

> Can Christ endure in stead of the Sacrament of his body and blood, according to his own Institution, a Popish Altar to be erected? Coaps, Cloaths, and Lights befitting the same Wafers, Wine mixt with Water, and the Crucifix upon the Altar? with this rotten staffe, and stifeling Leiturgie hath that corrupt Crew pranct up their Masse.[62]

The Episcopacy is unchristian, inimical to sound doctrine and the safety of the kingdom, a slander to God, a danger to the very institution of monarchy, and the direct cause of England's 'bloody Troubles, Devastations, Desolations, Persecutions of the Truth, from Forraines or Domestiks'.[63] The remedy is obvious: let the Parliament remain sitting 'till the tenets of the Hierarchie be tryed, by God and the countrie; that is, by the Lawes of God, and the Land'.[64]

[59] *Eikon Basilikon*, p. 66.
[60] Miller-Johnson, pp. 206-7. In a lay sermon to his fellows on the voyage to New England, Winthrop had earlier spoken out against unbridled religious individualism: 'for the worke wee have in hand, it is by a mutuall consent through a speciall over-ruleing providence, and a more than ordinary approbation of the Churches of Christ to seeke out a place of Cohabitation and Consortshipp under a due forme of Government both civill and ecclesiasticall' (*ibid.*, p. 197). In his account of the Antinomian controversy which threatened to wreck the Boston experiment, William Bradford recalled that Thomas Shepard, as a leader of the orthodox, had denounced in Mrs Hutchinson and his misguided followers no less than eighty intolerable positions – 'some blasphemous, others erroneous, and all unsafe' (*ibid.*, pp. 133-4).
[61] *An Appeal to the Parliament*, 'The Epistle to the Reader', sig. **v.
[62] *Ibid.*, pp. 97-8.
[63] *Ibid.*, pp. 3-4.   [64] *Ibid.*, p. 175.

All the classical Presbyterian demands for redress of religious grievances through Parliamentary action take the same line. The king is contractually committed to preserving the moral health of the state, and (in terms of the Presbyterian equation of moral health with Genevan discipline) he must be checked by the higher power of Parliament when he fails to do so. As Rutherford and Prynne agreed, since the king is an agent of the people and is therefore answerable to the Parliament of the people, his pretensions to supremacy are absurd. Government itself is sanctioned by the law of nature, but the form of government has no such sanction: *in radice* government is prescribed, *in modo* it is voluntary; for 'the scripture cleareth to us that a king is made by the free consent of the people (Deut. 17: 15) and so not by nature'.[65]

Ironically enough, while the Presbyterians were thus evolving their theory of Parliamentary supremacy during the 'thirties, Charles, relying on the 'thorough' policy of Wentworth and Laud, was governing England without any Parliament at all. At last, however, the Lord delivered the king into the hands of his enemies. With unthinkable obtuseness Charles did what his father would never have done: in 1638 he tried to impose Laud's Prayer Book on the Scottish Kirk. Since the Presbyterian Kirk, ever since the days of Knox, had been the only real governing body of Scotland, the reaction was prompt and sharp. The Church Assembly at Glasgow continued its sittings even though the king had formally abolished it, enlisted the powerful support of the Earl of Argyle, promulgated its Covenant, raised an army under the command of Alexander Leslie, and prepared to defy the king and the dreaded Wentworth (whom Charles had summoned from Ireland to deal with them). To fight a war, however, Charles had to get money, and to get money he had to call Parliament for the first time since he had angrily prorogued it eleven years before. This so-called Short Parliament (April 13th–May 5th, 1640) did little but reveal the extent to which Commons would oppose the king's absolutist intentions, but when the Scots, having crossed the Tweed, demanded money to evacuate Northumberland and Durham, Charles was fairly over the barrel. Having been forced to call the Short Parliament to levy taxes for fighting the Scots, he was then forced to call the Long Parliament to raise

---

[65] Rutherford, *Lex Rex*, p. 207. An equally influential statement of the same proposition is Prynne's *Sovereign Power of Parliaments* (1643).

NATURAL SANCTIONS

their blackmail (November 1640). Baxter's account of this crisis in English history is wonderfully laconic: 'The Scots came with an army, and the king's army met them near Newcastle; but the Scots came on till an agreement was made, and a parliament called; and the Scots went home again.'[66]

At last it seemed that the rule of the saints was at hand. But while visionaries like Hanserd Knollys were lost in their Utopian raptures – with the 'wonderful confluence' of the faithful 'Holiness shall be written upon their pots, and upon their bridles: upon every thing their graces shall shine forth exceedingly to the glory of God'[67] – such sober statesmen as Pym and Hampden, Hyde and Falkland, tried to forge a working alliance of Presbyterians and moderate Episcopalians to meet the problems of England. They worked swiftly, and extremely well. Having unanimously impeached Laud and passed a bill of attainder against Wentworth (now Earl of Strafford), they abolished by statute such absolutist iniquities as the Star Chamber, the High Commission, and the Prerogative Courts; and they decisively repudiated Charles's extra-Parliamentary devices of illegal taxation. Then, inevitably, they split on ecclesiastical policy. In 1641 the Puritans in Commons mustered a small majority to pass the Root and Branch bill abolishing episcopacy and to adopt the Grand Remonstrance (giving to Parliament control over the king's ministers and over the reformation of the state-church along Presbyterian lines). Such measures wrecked their coalition with the Episcopalians. Then when Commons went further and demanded control over the army for quelling the Catholic revolt in Ireland, Charles made his foolish attempt to seize the five members on the floor of the House. In this dramatic effort to reassert his royal supremacy he failed, and with his flight to the north it was clear that war was inevitable. The question of sovereignty was now to be resolved with steel.

III. NATURAL SANCTIONS

With the actual outbreak of fighting, Parliament was quickly put on the spot by the Scots' demand for enforced Presbyterian discipline as the price of military aid. All that Parliament was willing to do was to affirm its wish for the abolition of the episcopacy,

[66] *Autobiography*, p. 20.
[67] *A Glimpse of Sions Glory*, Woodhouse, pp. 237–9.

but Charles's early successes so strengthened the Presbyterians' position that they were able to push through the convocation of the Westminster Assembly. That body, summoned to examine questions of liturgy, discipline, and the like, was to be represented by both Houses of Parliament, English divines, and eight Scottish commissioners. The Scottish-Presbyterian coalition followed this by promulgating the Solemn League and Covenant by which England, Scotland, and Ireland were pledged to preserve the church of Scotland and to reform discipline south of the Tweed, to bring the churches of the three kingdoms into the closest conformity, and to abolish popery and prelacy forever. Whatever the Presbyterians in Parliament might do – and they did a good deal in replacing the Prayer Book with their own *Directory*, as well as in the reorganization of all London churches on Genevan discipline – any permanent national success would depend on the army. The army, however, was becoming increasingly Independent.

The subsequent struggle between a Presbyterian Parliament, an Independent army, and the Episcopalian royalists – a struggle recorded in the sessions of Parliament and the Westminster Assembly, in the army debates at Putney, in the thousands of pamphlets now preserved in the Thomason collection – represented for the first time in European history the public discussion of large public issues.

This great struggle for Puritanism and liberty, the clearest challenge to royal supremacy in a century that was becoming steadily more absolutist on the Continent, seemed to confirm the most advanced contemporary political theory. Apologists of Parliamentary supremacy, moreover, were quick to draw on that theory in defending their own seditious conduct against the Lord's anointed. As we have seen, the author of the *Vindiciae contra tyrannos* had adumbrated a theory of social contract in justifying civil disobedience. About the same time, George Buchanan – writing for the future James I, of all people – had advanced a notorious argument for civil disobedience in his *De jure regni*. With remarkable freedom from theological considerations Buchanan construed government as a purely secular and contractual relation between a community and its king; when the king fails in his obligations or ignores the terms of his contract as properly prescribed by the community, tyrannicide becomes not only expedient but desirable. Such Jesuits as Suarez and Bellarmine had regarded government as a purely secular and purely human institution in order to check any *de jure divino* pretensions that might collide with those of the papacy. Even Hooker, the greatest of the Anglican apologists, had gone so far as to decree that 'Laws they are not . . . which public approbation hath not made so'.

More systematically, Johannes Althusius, in his *Politica methodice digesta* (1603), had sought to emancipate political theory from theology. As a good Calvinist he had identified natural law with the second table of the Decalogue, but, having made that concession to his times, he proceeded to develop a remarkably naturalistic theory of government. Starting from the Aristotelian and Stoic proposition that social life is natural to man, Althusius derived all government, association, or *consociatio* from a double contract. By the first men agree to live together for the common good, by the second to live together under this or that form of authority, be it the family, a voluntary corporation (*collegium*), the local community, the province, or the state. In the most complex of all such associations, the state, sovereignty necessarily resides in the people whose consent is essential to its very being. Although the people, by contract, delegate their sovereignty to such magistrates and administrators as they might agree upon, it is only delegated, and it reverts to the people if the administrative officials – which, be it noted, would include kings – forfeit their contract to manage the state for the public good.

Much more influential than Althusius, but comparable to him in releasing government from religious sanctions, was Hugo Grotius. This great Dutch jurist, himself the victim of religious and civil disorder, was more concerned with deriving on rational grounds a code of international law than with adjudicating questions of sovereignty within states. Although he locates sovereign power (acts 'not subject to the law of another, so that they can be rendered void by the act of any other human will')[68] within the state, he denies that it always resides in the people of that state. A nation 'may choose what form of government it will',[69] but as history shows, once they have reposed sovereignty in a particular set of officials there it usually stays: 'And here we must first reject the opinion of those who say that sovereignty every-

[68] *De jure belli ac pacis*, I.iii.7 (Coker, *Readings*, p. 413).
[69] *Ibid.*, I.iii.8 (p. 414).

where and without exception belongs to the people, so that the people have authority to coerce and punish kings when they abuse their power. What evil this opinion has caused, and may yet cause, no wise man can fail to see.'[70]

Grotius' contribution to political theory lay, then, not in a defense of popular rights, but rather in the establishment of international law on grounds that were *a priori*, rational, and untheological. With the collapse of a central ecclesiastical power at the Reformation and the subsequent atrocities committed in the name of religion, it was clear that international morality needed a firmer basis than this or that competing theology.

> For I saw prevailing throughout the Christian world a license in making war of which even barbarous nations would have been ashamed, recourse being had to arms for slight reasons or for no reason; and when arms were once taken up, all reverence for divine and human law was lost, just as if men were henceforth authorized to commit all crimes without restraint.[71]

In the powerful *Prolegomena* Grotius first attacks the notion – advanced by the skeptic Carneades but more immediately derived from Machiavelli – that 'there is no natural law, since all men, as well as other animals, are impelled by nature to seek their own advantage; and that either there is no justice, or if it exist, it is the highest folly, since through it one harms oneself in consulting the interests of others'.[72] Man is a unique animal for many reasons, but perhaps the first of them is his desire for society and a corresponding concern for the common good. No appeal to utility, like Carneades', can obscure the fact that all men, at all times, have shown the urge to maintain social order; social order demands law, and law requires that 'each should leave to another what is his and give to him what is his due'.[73]

This, then, is the 'natural source' of moral conduct as codified by law. Although God clearly approves of the status that law has always held among all men, that status depends on nothing but human nature and the universal principles of right reason. Natural law, made manifest by man's natural concern for society, is the source of all lesser kinds of law – civil and international – which impose order and morality on man's conduct as a social animal.

[70] *De jure belli ac pacis*, I.iii.7 (p. 414).
[71] *Ibid.*, Prolegomena, sect. 28 (p. 409).
[72] *Ibid.*, sect. 5 (p. 404).
[73] *Ibid.*, sect. 9 (p. 406).

For the mother of natural law is human nature itself, which would lead us to desire mutual society even though we were not driven thereto by other wants. The mother of civil law is obligation by compact; and since compacts derive their force from natural law, nature may be said to be the great-grandmother of civil law.[74]

In short, although the dictates of natural law coincide with the commands of God, 'the author of nature', it needs no other sanction than that of reason. 'Natural law is the dictate of right reason, indicating that any act, from its agreement or disagreement with the rational nature, has in it moral necessity or moral turpitude.'[75] Not only would men rationally infer the principles of natural law even if God did not concur in them, God Himself cannot change these principles.

> The law of nature is so immutable that it cannot be changed even by God himself. For though the power of God be immense, there are some things to which it does not extend; because if we speak of such things being done, our words are mere words and have no meaning, being self-contradictory. Thus God himself cannot make twice two not to be four; and in like manner He cannot make that which, according to reason, is intrinsically bad, not be bad. For as the essence of things, by virtue of which they exist, does not depend on anything else, so it is with the properties which follow necessarily that essence; such a property is the baseness of certain actions, as compared with the nature of a being enjoying sound reason. So God himself allows himself to be judged by this rule.[76]

Thus for several generations had Continental theorists slowly developed a set of secular and naturalistic sanctions for those varieties of political conduct intolerable to the Stuarts and their *jus divinum*. We have seen how a notable Anglican reacted to this secularized political theory, but in this respect Jeremy Taylor, like the dynasty he supported, was something of an anachronism. The Presbyterians did not scruple to borrow such elements of the new political naturalism as were useful to them, and the Independents, with more courage than success, went far beyond them in completely segregating the religious and political activities of the human animal.

Although such Presbyterians as Leighton and Rutherford had long advocated, for reasons not necessarily connected with popular rights, a doctrine of Parliamentary supremacy, the cataclysmic events of the early 'forties demanded fresh justification. Of the

---
[74] *De jure belli ac pacis*, sect. 16 (p. 407).
[75] *Ibid.*, I.i.10 (p. 411).
[76] *Ibid.*, I.i.10 (p. 412).

spate of Parliamentary defenses one of the most important was Henry Parker's *Observations upon some of his Majesty's Late Answers and Expresses* (1642). Though expertly tailored to accommodate the Puritan view of fallen man, it shows the lengths to which a theory of popular sovereignty, based on purely secular considerations, had gone by the eve of the Great Rebellion. Before the Fall, argues Parker, no government was necessary because Adam had imprinted in his heart and in his conscience the law of nature. After the Fall, however, some sort of government became imperative; hence the evolution, by contract and agreement, of those institutions whose main function is to maintain common welfare and to insure social amity. Now in England this supreme mandate for preserving the common good is invested in Parliament – of which 'the whole Kingdome is not so properly the Author as the essence it selfe'.[77] The impious myth that a king's prerogatives come from God by a special ordinance is, therefore, an insubstantial basis for government. 'It can be nothing else amongst Christians but the Pactions and agreements of such and such politique corporations.'[78]

In kings, it must follow, power 'is but secondary and derivative', for its 'fountaine and efficient cause is the people'.[79] The transcendent principle of all government is *salus populi*. 'The Charter of nature intitles all Subjects of all Countries whatsoever to safetie by its supreame Law';[80] and when a people's safety is jeopardized by an overvaulting prince then the law of nature must be invoked to check this violation of the social contract. Hence the justification of Parliamentary action against the king's prerogative. Parliament exists as the voice of the people to express their sovereign will. Parker's long and legally very penetrating analysis of Parliamentary supremacy is finally summarized in seven headings. Parliament has 'an absolute indisputable power of declaring Law'; it is bound by no precedent; it may exercise its functions without the crown; its members cannot be charged with treason 'without leave'; its sovereign power is lodged in both houses, 'the King having no negative voyce'; it can levy forces against the personal command of the king for the *salus populi*; and finally it may depose the king.[81]

[77] Haller, II, 171.
[79] *Ibid.*, II, 170.
[81] *Ibid.*, II, 211–2.
[78] *Ibid.*, II, 167.
[80] *Ibid.*, II, 170.

In Parker's famous pamphlet we may see to what good use the Puritans could put the myth of the social contract – a myth owing nothing to theological sanctions but powerfully subversive to any absolutism based on *jus divinum*. The medieval concept of status, governmental and other, could have no meaning for the Parliamentarians whose demands were steadily eating away the prerogatives of an obdurate king. Thus Milton's attack on *de jure divino* sanctions is emphatically Puritan, even though as a Christian humanist his political thinking was essentially aristocratic and conservative. He found the current notions of contract and legality supremely useful for his onslaughts on the crown and the episcopacy, and these onslaughts were generated by an optimistic and reformist zeal that still burns with a fiery rhetoric. It is the very 'property' of truth, he argues in that flaming 'Conclusion' to *The Reason of Church Government*, that 'all honest and legal freedom of civil life cannot be long absent' once the people are freed from the 'thraldom of sin and superstition'.[82] And even though the optimism of such early pamphlets as the *Apology for Smectymnuus* and *Areopagitica* (which viewed man as a rational creature capable of rational well-being in the glorious dawn of a completed Reformation) gradually gives way to a darker view in the divorce tracts, even as late as *The Tenure of Kings and Magistrates* (1649) he insists that the people retain ultimate sovereignty, and that they suffer their rulers only through the social contract contrived for the rationally conceived general good. 'No man, who knows aught, can be so stupid to deny, that all men naturally were born free, being the image and resemblance of God himself, and were, by privilege above all the creatures, born to command, and not to obey.' However, with Adam's Fall dissent and deceit arose, so that men 'agreed by common league to bind each other from mutual injury. . . . Hence came cities, towns, and commonwealths'. Since some superior authority was clearly called for in complicated social structures, kings and magistrates were ordained as 'deputies and commissioners, to execute, by virtue of their intrusted power', the people's sovereign will. When the first bad king showed the necessity of inhibitory laws restricting his authority, it became clear that although 'the magistrate was set above the people, so the law was set above the magistrate'. A magistrate who ignores this basic principle has

[82] *PW*, II, 503.

broken his tacit contract with the people, who then are 'disengaged' from their allegiance to him.[83]

The Tenure of Kings and Magistrates, written to justify the execution of Charles, had to seek its thesis in those same assumptions of popular sovereignty and government by contract that had been written into *The Remonstrance of the Army* (October 1648), the document that had precipitated his trial and judgment.[84] That an intransigent individualist like Milton – whom it is sentimental to call democratic – could rattle off such glib commonplaces shows us how radically the basis of political thinking had changed since the days of Tudor absolutism. Although it is disheartening to follow the downward course of Milton's political thought to its *cul de sac* in *The Ready and Easy Way*, the fact is that his early pamphlets drew heavily on contemporary theories of contract, and were, therefore, notably liberal. Actually, he was incapable of practical and sustained political thinking. While the Levelers were drawing up specific plans for implementing those principles which Milton at least temporarily held, he was dreaming of a completed Reformation in which political controls would be supererogatory. He defended in turn the Long Parliament, the Rump, the Protectorate; and at last, on the very eve of the Restoration, he bravely but foolishly advanced the bizarre proposals of *The Ready and Easy Way*. As the humanized Christ of *Paradise Regained* suggests, Milton never lost his faith in the personal integrity of the individual man, but his confidence in mankind steadily deteriorated. He could never reconcile his own individualism, and his belief in that 'strenuous liberty' which derived from both the aristocratic traditions of Renaissance humanism and the inwardness of his Puritan ethos, with the democratic and leveling forces of his age. Even *The Tenure of Kings and Magistrates* reveals a callous indifference to democracy, for it defends a *fait accompli* to which the people had obviously not been a party; in it, Milton clearly assumes that the mass of men are through sloth and sin incapable of self-government. The success of *Eikon Basilikon* (John Gauden's pious fiction) confirmed his rapidly darkening estimate of popular opinion, so that in *Eikonoklastes* we have the sorry spectacle of his undisciplined fury and contempt for the *mobile vulgus*.

[83] *PW*, II, 8–11.
[84] See Gardiner, *History of the Great Civil War*, IV, 233–6.

NATURAL SANCTIONS

And what the people but a herd confus'd,
A miscellaneous rabble, who extol
Things vulgar, and well weigh'd, scarce worth the praise?[85]

If the Presbyterians had enjoyed a fair measure of political success at the beginning of the war, they sadly failed otherwise. While Parliament, following the indecisive encounter with the royalists at Edgehill, at last succeeded in turning Charles back at Newbury, and thus saved London, the godly divines gathered at the Westminster Assembly (1643-48) were meeting rough weather in their effort to impose Presbyterian discipline on England. Clarendon, hardly an unbiased reporter, said that the Assembly was so stacked with Presbyterians that there were no more than twenty of the whole body who were 'not declared and avowed enemies to the doctrine or discipline of the Church of England; some of them infamous in their lives and conversations; and most of them of very mean parts in learning, if not of scandalous ignorance; and of no other reputation, that of malice to the Church of England'.[86] On the other hand, Baxter, writing after his Utopian dreams had faded away in the Restoration, thought that had the Assembly succeeded, 'England had been like in a quarter of an age to have become a land of saints and a pattern of holiness to all the world, and the unmatchable paradise of the earth'.[87]

Neither view may stand without qualification, of course, but actually the Assembly accomplished a good deal by its Presbyterian lights. Among other things it revised the Thirty-Nine Articles, it went far toward establishing the Presbyterian discipline as official, it tried to protect that discipline by the same *jus divinum* sanction which the hated prelates had used for episcopacy, it substituted its own *Directory* for the Book of Common Prayer, it promulgated the larger and smaller catechisms. The trouble was that owing to the increasing weight and opposition of the Independents it was able to make none of these alleged reforms stick. Only in London and Lancashire were they formally adopted, and even there they were strongly challenged. As Henson has said, the Presbyterian experiment failed almost as soon as it was seriously tried. In their unfortunate union of obsoleteness and arrogance the divines who haggled so interminably at Westminster could hope to please neither the Anglicans 'under a sad and

---
[85] *PR*, III.49-51; cf. *PL*, VII.171-81, XII.90-101; *PR*, II.463-72.
[86] *History*, II, 424.   [87] *Autobiography*, p. 84.

daily apprehension of expulsion'[88] nor the Independents clamoring for more liberty and toleration than any Presbyterian would grant.

Inevitably, the Presbyterians in Parliament came to be identified with the glacial progress and reaction of the Assembly,[89] and against the mounting demands of the Independents in the army they could hurl only groans and denunciations. Such grotesque works as Prynne's furious pamphlets or Edwards' *Gangraena* or Pagitt's *Heresiography* tell us a good deal of the temper of the Presbyterians, but they were worth nothing against an army that had beaten the king in battle and would presently bring him to the block. Milton's account of Presbyterian perfidy in *The Tenure of Kings and Magistrates* is perhaps not wholly fair, but it is fair enough to make us glad that the Presbyterian experiment failed.

IV. PURITANISM AND LIBERTY

'The Bishops being put out of ye house,' asked Selden, 'whome will they lay ye ffault upon now: when ye Dog is beat out of ye Roome where will they lay the stinke?'[90] The stunning Par-

---

[88] Walton, *Lives*, II, 261.

[89] In its early years the Long Parliament was fairly well united against the king and the bishops, but once the army flexed its muscles and the Independents became a real threat to the Presbyterians, Parliament directed a good deal of its legislation against Puritan liberalism. Its ordinance for the ordination of the clergy (1644, and again in 1646) was designed to stop lay preaching among the sects; and although not until 1648 did it adopt the Presbyterian *Directory* which the Westminster Assembly had framed in 1645, its ordinance of September 2nd, 1646, against all blasphemy and heresy carried the threat of corporal punishment for those who dared to oppose the Presbyterians. See Haller, I, 77.

[90] *Table Talk*, p. 18. Selden's political position is usually described as Erastian. He was a legalist, and as such a thorn in the flesh to both the bishops and the Presbyterians. When the Westminster Assembly proceeded to act as if the Presbyterian discipline were to be a government *de jure divino* – thus reviving the old Stuart danger in a new form – Selden was one of the most effective members of the Parliamentary opposition. In his *History of Tithes* he had already shown that any *jus divinum* claim was historically and constitutionally unsound, and, as Fuller records, the divines at Westminster complained that with his prodigious learning he had an unfair advantage over them all. The bishops erred in trying to compel 'blind obedience' on freeborn Englishmen, thought Selden: 'I were these gloves; but perhaps if an Alderman should command me; I should think much to doe it' (*Table Talk*, p. 14). Equally foolish is the Presbyterian device of forcing the most unwanted reforms by arguments drawn from 'Religion & the Law of God'. Thus any bigot 'getts a Text & interpretts it as hee pleases, & soe thinkes to gett loose' (*ibid.*, p. 121). Government can only be by law and contract – 'A King is a thing men have made for their owne sakes for quietness sake' (*ibid.*, p. 61) – and law must mean the law of the realm, not a hypostatized law of nature or an alleged law of God. 'If you should say you held your Land by Moses or Gods Law; and would trye it by that you may p[er]haps loose it; but by ye Law of ye Kingdome you are sure to carry it: soe may ye Bi[sho]pps by this plea of Jure Divino loose all. The Pope had as good a Tytle by the Law of England as could be had; had he not left that; and claimed by power from God' (*ibid.*, p. 20).

PURITANISM AND LIBERTY

liamentary victory at Naseby (June 14th, 1645) and the capitulation of Oxford a year later brought peace, of a sort; it also brought to the Puritans their new responsibilities of governing England. No longer a dissenting minority, they were now forced to conduct the affairs of state – and until Cromwell at last sickened of their conduct and established his own form of dictatorship they made a sorry mess of it. The Laudian terror of the 'thirties (culminating in the atrocities on Burton, Bastwick, and Prynne) had solidified the Puritan defiance and made possible the early successes of the Long Parliament. The Presbyterian and theocratic designs of that Parliament, though ably defended by Parker and others, at last roused the Independent and Sectarian protests of Goodwin, Walwyn, and Williams; and then the arguments for popular, as opposed to Parliamentary, supremacy were pushed by Lilburne and Overton to that democratic extreme memorialized by the Large Petition of 1647. When this petition was ordered burned by the common hangman in May 1647, it meant that Parliament had repudiated democracy and that the Protectorate lay ahead.

The conclusion that emerges from these tangled events is that although the Puritans had sought certain reforms since the time of Cartwright, between 1643 and 1660 they could not unite long enough to make those reforms stick. Indeed, they could not even agree about what reforms were needed, or how far they should go. The Presbyterians were content merely with reform, and once church discipline was purified they drew back in alarm from the more drastic civil demands of the Independents. To achieve both reformation and liberty proved impossible. 'The liberty demanded by the left destroyed the reformation desired by the right, and the reformation desired by the right denied the liberty demanded by the left.'[91] The bishops were sequestrated, the episcopacy was demolished, the divines were sitting sagely at Westminster – and yet England was far from peaceful and godly. As Lilburne wrote in 1645, just as the watermen used to cry 'Westward ho',

> so according to the present current of the times, most honest men have more then cause to cry in the Water-mens language, Aegypt hough, hough, the house of Bondage, slavery, oppression, taxation, heavy and cruell, heavy and cruell, wee can no longer beare it, wee can no longer beare it, wee can no longer beare it.[92]

[91] Barker, *Milton and the Puritan Dilemma*, p. 20.
[92] *Englands Birthright Justified*, Haller, III, 301.

The fact is that with the defeat of Charles the Puritan revolution got quickly beyond the control of the Presbyterians. The emergence of Cromwell and the successes of the New Model Army – where Independent and Sectarian sympathies were very strong – had pushed both political conduct and political theory to limits from which every good conservative recoiled in horror. Although we need not retrace the tumultuous and exciting history of the 'forties, we can see that the Independents, in spite of their eventual failure in the Protectorate, struck a genuinely new note in English political theory. Starting from the conventional Presbyterian notions of contract and consent they went ahead to develop current doctrines of natural right, and thus to achieve a thoroughly naturalistic rationale of political conduct. When men like Lilburne and Overton, and the army agitators who stated their case at the Putney debates, dared to dispense with all theological sanctions for government, it meant that the theocratic political theory which had carried over from the Middle Ages to the Renaissance had at last spent its force. In thus emancipating politics from theology the Independents inevitably argued from the postulates of natural law and natural rights. While the Presbyterians still clung – with a tenacity born of desperation – to the Calvinistic view of nature as corrupt and man as vile, the Independents were finding in an alleged natural law new anchors of man's dignity, rights, and secular obligations. Although without immediate practical consequences (for by the 'fifties the Independents had ceased to count politically), the agitation of the Independents, Levelers, and Sectarians marked a significant new departure in the history of modern political theory.

As we have seen, the conflict between Presbyterians and Independents had begun almost as soon as the Long Parliament addressed itself to the grim business of waging war against the king. In a sense it had begun long before, when those Presbyterians insisting on a Genevan reform of the Elizabethan establishment had been opposed by those Separatists and Congregationalists who regarded the autonomous holy community as the goal of church discipline. But with the outbreak of the war, differences over discipline rapidly fanned out into much larger differences over the basic questions of church and state, and over the kinds of liberty appropriate to man as both Christian and citizen. Although in a sketch like this we cannot hope to treat adequately the innumerable forays and rebuttals that constituted this controversy during the 'forties, perhaps we can suggest the development of Independent political theory by treating *seriatim* some of the principal episodes.

In the beginning there was a common resentment at the crown and its episcopacy. Whatever the purity of his motives and the precise quality of his religious emotion, it is obvious that John Lilburne was a born propagandist, a man who could whip up public opinion and mold it to his purposes. As Clarendon wryly said, 'he raised in himself a marvellous inclination and appetite to suffer in the defence or for the vindication of any oppressed truth'.[93] When he entered the stage of history with his punishment for defending Burton, Bastwick, and Prynne, he seized the occasion to inflame popular sentiment against Laud and his bishops. *A Work of the Beast* was a heady stimulus to that resentment that was gathering against Laud and his agents. If we may believe Lilburne's own account of the affair, no martyr was ever more articulate. As he was tied to the cart's tail and stripped for the whip he prayed to God for fortitude:

> When the first stripe was given I felt not the least paine but said, Blessed be thy name O Lord my God that hast counted mee worthy to suffer for thy glorious names sake; And at the giving of the second, I cried out with a loud voice Hallelujah, Hallelujah, Glory, Honour, and Praise, bee given to thee O Lord forever, and to the Lambe that sitts upon the Throne. Soe wee went up Fleetstreete.[94]

In the stocks his tirade against the bishops was so rousing the onlookers that a warden (not knowing the kind of man he was dealing with) suggested that he suffer more decorously. 'Whom I bidd meddle with his owne businesse, for I would speake come what would, for my cause was good for which I suffered, and here I was ready to sheb [*sic*] my dearest blood for it.'[95] What could Laud do with a man like this?

The common animus against the bishops presently lost its butt, however, and Puritans of all stripes and colors were left free to wrangle with each other. The interminable arguments over discipline need not detain us, however fascinating they were to the

---
[93] *History*, III, 670.
[94] *A Worke of the Beast*, Haller, II, 7-8.
[95] *Ibid.*, II, 9.

participants. Even Bastwick, a popular martyr, was enthusiastically attacked when he wrote his *Independency not God's Ordinance* in support of the Presbyterian program. 'It was far better with you when you suffered for Presbyterie in opposition to Prelaticall tyranny', said one of his antagonists, 'then now, if you would make others suffer by Presbytery, in opposition to the Congregationall government.'[96] The inevitable splintering tendency of Puritan individualism which the Presbyterians were vainly trying to check came to a head, however, with the publication (January 1644) of the famous *Apologetical Narration*, the work of 'five dissenting brethren' who joined with Thomas Goodwin in petitioning Parliament to curb the sinister Presbyterian aims of the recently convened Westminster Assembly. The temperate request of these Independents for freedom in matters of church discipline was received with rage and derision. Within a month Adam Steuart, a Presbyterian stalwart, retaliated in angry, anguished tones with *Some Observations and Annotations*, and so was joined the fray that was presently to produce Milton's *Areopagitica*, the one literary monument of the often dreary controversy.[97]

The *Apologetical Narration* proved to be the catalyst that dissolved the queasy peace between the Puritan right and center. Without reference to the specific requests of the five dissenting brethren the question quickly broadened to a general discussion of toleration – of 'liberty of conscience' – that was to burn angrily for a whole decade. Notable among the defenses of toleration that resulted were Henry Robinson's *Liberty of Conscience* (March 1644) and Roger Williams' *The Bloody Tenent* (July 1644), but in the swarm of pamphlets from both sides the argument usually raged with more heat than light. However, certain principles emerged and certain results were anticipated, and these we must try to untangle.

The five brethren had, accurately enough, declared their goal to be the 'very middle way' between Separatists and Presbyterians, between those who would drown the voice of the elders by putting church government in the hands of the people and

---

[96] J. S., *Flagellum Flagelli*, p. 3.
[97] The presses groaned with attacks on Independency: in the summer of 1644, for example, there appeared in quick succession Alexander Forbes' *Anatomy of Independency*, Thomas Edwards' *Antapologia*, and the indefatigable Prynne's *Twelve Questions* – all violently denouncing the toleration requested by the Independents. On the five dissenting brethren, see Fuller, XI.v.48-50.

those who would 'swallow up' the interests and wants of the people in a Genevan state church.[98] The Independents, of whom Milton was the greatest though by no means the most influential in his own day, were puzzled and alarmed by the course of recent events. During all those years when the Presbyterians were evolving their own defense of civil disobedience through lawful 'magistrates' they had advanced theories of contract and Parliamentary supremacy as a needed check to the *de jure* claims of the crown and the bishops. Yet in the early 'forties emerged the paradox that by some strange metathesis Parliamentary sovereignty meant Presbyterian sovereignty, and that the erstwhile champions of popular government had themselves become the most intolerable tyrants.

To exchange Laud for Prynne was to exchange one form of absolutism for another. It is curious that this Presbyterian duplicity was not discerned sooner than it was; but when it became apparent, the Independents rose as one man. They felt, with certain justification, that the long-delayed Reformation was being delayed by a new set of tyrants. Does Presbyterian arrogance admit no limits, asked Thomas Goodwin. Does it have a '*non esse errare* settled by God, as an inheritance upon it?'[99] If a 'complete Nationall Reformation be indeed the Garland or Crown that is contended for', then let the Presbyterians, like the Independents, stay within their 'Jurisdiction'; after that 'there will not be the least occasion to feare, but that the whole and entire body of the Nation will shine with the beauty and lustre of a perfect Reformation'.[100] As things now stand, he warns, the policy that 'conjures all mens gifts, parts, and industrie into a synodicall circle, and suffers them onely to dance there' raises the danger of preserving 'errors and heresies' and of 'Shutting the doore' upon truth.[101]

In Milton's angry view such Presbyterians as Baillie, Rutherford, and Edwards (of the notorious *Gangraena*) were no better than traitors to the Reformation.

---

[98] See John Cotton, *The Keyes of the Kingdom*, Woodhouse, p. 296.
[99] *The Danger of Fighting against God*, Haller, III, 30.
[100] *Ibid.*, III, 29.
[101] *Ibid.*, III, 39; cf. *The Ancient Bounds, or Liberty of Conscience*, Woodhouse, pp. 253-4.

> Because you have thrown off your Prelate Lord,
> And with stiff Vows renounc'd his Liturgy
> To seize the widow'd whore Plurality
> From them whose sin ye envied, not abhorr'd,
> Dare ye for this adjure the Civil Sword
> To force our Consciences that Christ set free,
> And ride us with a classic Hierarchy
> Taught ye by mere A.S. and Rotherford?
> Men whose Life, Learning, Faith and pure intent
> Would have been held in high esteem with Paul
> Must now be nam'd and printed Heretics
> By shallow Edwards and Scotch what d'ye call:
> But we do hope to find out all your tricks,
> Your plots and packing worse than those of Trent,
>   That so the Parliament
> May with their wholesome and preventive Shears
> Clip your Phylacteries, though baulk your Ears,
>   And succour our just Fears,
> When they shall read this clearly in your charge:
> New Presbyter is but Old Priest writ Large.

The Independents' anger against obdurate Presbyterians in Parliament, and then against Parliament itself, mounted steadily during the mid-'forties. For example, Overton's wrath against the divines at Westminster reaches wonderful heights of invective. They do not scruple, he charges,

> to guzle up and devoure dayly more at an ordinary meale, then would make a Feast for Bell and the Dragon, for besides all their fat Benefices, forsooth they must have their foure shillings a peece by the day, for sitting in constollidation; and poore men when they had fil'd all Benefices with good Trencher-men of their owne Presbyterian Tribe, they move your Lordship, that all Ministers may be wholy freed from all manner of Taxations, that now the Trade of a Presbyter is the best Trade in England.[102]

Walwyn declared that Edwards' vituperation against pious dissenters derived not from any 'true zeal to any thing you apprehend as truth' but from his fear for the financial and political perquisites that his party enjoyed.[103] The 'passion, sweat, and labour' of Presbyterian sermons against Independents are expended not to win souls to Christ, but 'to revile and reproach, and make

---

[102] *The Araignement of Mr Persecution*, Haller, III, 246.
[103] *A Whisper in the Eare of Mr Thomas Edwards Minister*, Haller, III, 321-2.

odious conscientious well affected people, because of difference in judgment'.¹⁰⁴

Yet Walwyn, a remarkably clear thinker, was able to see the underlying issues beneath the wordy violence of the pamphlet warfare. As late as 1645 he still hoped that Parliament could be saved from the Presbyterian hegemony so that they could legislate properly for the church in such sore travail – 'a thing of a very nice and dainty nature, especially being undertaken in a time of a home-bred Warre'.¹⁰⁵ Such legislation, he thought, should be based on the premise that no man can delegate to another the right and duty of determining his religious convictions, or to

> binde himselfe to doe any thing therein contrary to his understanding and conscience: nor to forbeare to doe that which his understanding and conscience bindes him to performe: therefore no man can refer matters of Religion to any others regulation.¹⁰⁶

Behind this passage lies the significant assumption that the law of nature provided sanction not only for civil disobedience (as the Presbyterians urged) but also for those rights of conscience which no government could abrogate. The assumption was a milestone in the increasingly secular political theory which the Independents had begun to advance. To rise up against unlawful authority 'in your owne defence, in the defence of your lives, your estates, your liberties, your wives, your children, your friends, your lawes, your religion', John Goodwin told the embattled Londoners, is a duty made imperative by the law of nature, and consequently 'no wayes offensive either in the sight of God, or reasonable men'.¹⁰⁷ This was the law that Lilburne had cited against the Star Chamber ('for nature is alwaies a preserver of it selfe and not a distroyer'),¹⁰⁸ that Milton thought remained even in fallen man to be renewed to its 'primitive brightness' through the process of regeneration,¹⁰⁹ that John Cook (as chief prosecutor at the legally dubious trial of King Charles) urged as sanction for the court's sending the Lord's anointed to the scaffold. As a

---
¹⁰⁴ *Ibid.*, III, 328.
¹⁰⁵ *A Helpe to the Right Understanding of a Discourse Concerning Independency*, Haller, III, 195.
¹⁰⁶ *Ibid.*, III, 196.
¹⁰⁷ *Anti-Cavlierisme*, Haller, II, 252.
¹⁰⁸ *A Worke of the Beast*, Haller, II, 14–5.
¹⁰⁹ *De doctrina*, I.xxvi (*PW*, IV, 378).

law 'impressed' on all men 'by the light of Nature, principles suckt in by education, or a light from God upon their spirits',[110] it came to enjoy the same status as those natural and inviolable laws which the seventeenth century believed to govern the mechanical processes of nature. Implicit as it was in the very fabric of God's creation, and available to all men through the processes of natural reason, it could be cited as the court of last appeal against all forms of tyranny or political folly. It was as useful to Overton and Lilburne as to Hobbes and Filmer, and its wide prestige among men of the most radically different convictions underscores one of the chief developments of seventeenth-century political theory: the urge to find natural and secular rather than Scriptural sanctions for men's social behavior.

Early in the war, when Parliament's cause was so shaky that Charles was marching virtually unresisted to reclaim his capital, it was John Goodwin, an Independent minister, whose eloquence roused 24,000 Londoners to stream down the Western Road and turn back the king at Turnham Green (November 13th, 1642). The words that Goodwin used in denouncing that 'bloody and butcherly Generation, commonly knowne by the name of Cavaliers', he could almost as easily hurl against the Presbyterians in Parliament. They are 'ready in a posture of hatred,' he thundered, 'and malice, and revenge, with other preparations answerable hereunto, to fall upon us, and our lives and liberties, both spirituall and civill, upon our estates, our Gospell and Religion, and all that is, or ought to be deare and precious unto us.'[111] This suggests Lilburne's tone three years later when he shrilly denounced the Presbyterians' effort to compel both a political and a religious conformity. 'You spend a great deale of paines in citing old rusty Authors,' he tells Prynne, 'to prove that Kings, Councels, Synods and States have for so many hundred years medled with matters of Religion, I grant you they have; but I demaund of you, by what Right, or by what Authority out of the Word of God they have so done?'[112] In Henry Robinson's notable plea for Independency, *Liberty of Conscience* (1644), the issue is put squarely up to the Presbyterians and the Parliament which they then controlled: 'Persecution is a sinne, a signe of the Church malignant', whether

---

[110] Webster, *The Saints Guide*, p. 28.
[111] *Anti-Cavalierisme*, Haller, II, 220-1.
[112] *A Copie of a Letter*, Haller, III, 184.

it be practiced by pope, bishops, or Presbyters. There can be no middle ground:

> Either a Liberty of Conscience must be permitted to us to enjoy our owne opinions in matters of Religion, or else there is a necessity of being liable and subject against Conscience, whensoever the civill powers which surely are no more infallible then Ecclesiasticall, shall happen to enact or stablish any thing else, lesse consonant and agreeing to the world of God.[113]

But perhaps the most forcible, if not the most subtly argued, attack on Presbyterian tyranny was Overton's *Arraignment of Mr Persecution* (1645). There the irony, vividly projected in allegory, mounts to something very like art in spite of – or perhaps because of – the heaving, undisciplined prose. Mr Persecution, the villain of the piece, having first hidden among the papists and then the prelates, at last finds refuge with the Presbyterians. He changes his name to 'Classical Presbyterie (a new cheat to cosen the world)', comes down from Scotland to England, puts on a 'Sylogisticall pair of Britches' with a 'Rhetoricall Cassok' and a 'Sophisticall Girdle'. Then he runs into a 'wildernesse of Trophes, and Figures' where his pursuers – Mr God's Vengeance, Mr Long-Sufferance, Mr Peace-with-all-men, and the rest – would have lost him

> had it not been for the Spirits Teaching, by whose direction they trac'd him through the various windings, subtile by-Pathes, secret tracts, and cunning Meanders the evening wolves, wild Boares and Beasts of the Forrest in the briery thickes of Rhetoricall Glosses, Sophistications, and scholastick Interpretations had made, but being fit to lay hands on him, the cunning Hocus Pocus vanish'd out of their sight, and presently takes Sanctuary, for looking about for him, Behold, he was doing his business (Sr. Reverence) in the Pulpit, thumping it devoutly, and most furiously like the Son of Thunder he ratld the Anabaptists, Brownists, &c. letting his bolts (which according to the Proverbe were soon shot) fly at randome against them.[114]

The angry, earnest pamphlets – and they were almost without number – show clearly the mounting discontent that was presently to erupt against the Presbyterians after the king had been fairly beaten in the field by an army of Independents. More importantly, they show that, at least for a vocal and insistent segment of English Puritans, political theory could no longer be contained within merely theological limits. As Mr Haller has said, for the

[113] Haller, III, 160.   [114] Haller, III, 211-2.

ancient notion of a supernatural law protecting certain divinely sanctional institutions (like kingship or a hierarchical social structure) there was being substituted the notion of an allegedly rational law of nature and of natural rights protecting the individual's liberty of conscience.

When the surrender of Essex at Lostwithiel had deprived the Presbyterians of their champion in the army high command, the issues between Parliament and army became even more urgent, for then they bore upon questions of both religion and military strategy. The Presbyterians in Westminster were content to come to terms with Charles so that they could be free for the serious work of suppressing the sects; but the Independents in the field were determined, especially after Manchester had permitted the king to escape from the second battle of Newbury (October 27th, 1644), that Charles must be brought to his knees. With the formation of the New Model Army (1645) and its subsequent successes under Fairfax and Cromwell the war sped swiftly to its end. When he lost the battle of Naseby (June 14th, 1645) Charles actually lost his crown too, and the setbacks of his arms thereafter – Langport, Sherborne, Bristol (with the loss of Rupert), Philiphaugh (with the loss of Montrose) – led inevitably to his desperate gamble of fleeing to the Scots (May 5th, 1646). A month later Oxford capitulated.

But though the war was over, the troubles of the victors were not. Since an army largely Sectarian had beaten the Lord's anointed into submission, it expected – not unnaturally – to enjoy some of the fruits of its victory. Such fruits would consist primarily of enabling legislation for civil and religious liberties that no Presbyterian Parliament would willingly grant. The significance of this stage of the controversy (between the end of the first war and the execution of the king) lay in the increasingly secular nature of the army's demands. The energies that had gone into waging war were now diverted into formulating and then arguing for a set of political principles that went far beyond the earlier haggling over matters of discipline.

As Overton, speaking for the Levelers, said in his famous *Remonstrance* to Commons, the laws sustained by Parliament 'are unworthy a Free-People, and deserve from first to last, to be considered, and seriously debated, and reduced to an agreement with common equity, and right reason, which ought to be the Forme and Life of every Government'.[115] Instead, Parliament set about enthusiastically to persecute both Anglicans and Sectarians, and even to disband the New Model Army without providing for its pay so sadly in arrears. The army itself began to press systematically its claims for toleration (and even democracy of a sort); and the king, as usual playing one side against the other, hoped somehow to save himself in their inevitable collision.

In the summer of 1646 Parliament, backed by the Scots, offered its versions of peace: a Presbyterian monopoly in England, a strict enforcement of the old anti-Catholic penalties, and a militia to be controlled by Parliament for twenty years. When Charles temporized, the impatient Scots turned him over to Parliament. It was then that the angry army seized the initiative by its abduction of his royal person at Holmby House (June 3rd, 1647) and by its abortive attempt to exclude the eleven chief Presbyterians from Commons. Meanwhile Cromwell, in the name of the army, relayed to Charles 'The Heads of the Proposals' which his son-in-law Ireton had drawn up. Although foolishly rejected by both king and Parliament, these were the best and most moderate terms yet proposed. They provided for biennial Parliaments (with strengthened appointive powers), religious toleration for all but Catholics, and an army under the control of a new Parliament to be elected on a broadened popular franchise.

These terms refused, the more radical elements in the army, hitherto restrained and represented by Cromwell and Ireton, threatened to get beyond their officers' control. Led by their 'agitators' (or agents), they proceeded, with what seemed both natural and theological sanctions, to advance their own proposals in 'The Agreement of the People', the most famous statement of the Levelers' demands. These included the abolition of the monarchy, a popular referendum for setting the peace, a unicameral Parliament (with strictly delegated powers) to be elected through a reformed and broadened franchise, and civil and religious liberties for all but Catholics.

These Levelers – first appearing in the army as a determined, articulate, and well-organized minority sparked by Lilburne and Overton – came to nothing politically in the final settlement, but they are important in the history of political theory. Their day of glory was in the army debates held at Putney in the summer of

[115] Haller, III, 365.

1647, when, as they thought, Cromwell seemed to be playing into the Presbyterians' hands by his cautious policy of waiting for the cat to jump. The shorthand record of these debates, an extraordinary glimpse into the political forces at work in the late 'forties, shows us clearly the growing cleavage between such conservatives as Cromwell and Ireton and the advocates of something approaching genuine democracy.[116] As John Goodwin, a leading spokesman for the Independents out of the army, put it, the doctrine of natural rights could no longer be safely denied. 'Every man esteemeth it as properly his own, as any immunity contained in Magna Carta, to use his conscience without control.'[117] It was when the Levelers sought to extend natural rights to such purely secular considerations as the franchise that they encountered the unyielding opposition of Cromwell and Ireton.

We can feel the tension rising as the debates proceed to such charged questions. Rainborough, ably supported by Petty, argued that since 'the poorest he that is in England hath a life to live, as the greatest he', an honest government could rest only on the sanction of really popular elections.[118] To this Ireton answered that the franchise must be restricted to those with a 'permanent fixed interest in this kingdom', that is, to holders of property. It was a view which to the more advanced Levelers seemed in violation of man's natural right for government by consent. 'I do not find anything in the Law of God, that a lord shall chose twenty burgesses, and a gentleman but two, or a poor man shall choose none.'[119] Though probably less conservative than his gifted son-in-law, Cromwell agreed with Ireton that Rainborough's policy 'must end in anarchy'.[120] But in the plain, blunt words of Rainborough and Wildman we can detect the same principles that Lilburne had been advocating in his pamphlets. 'And unnatural, irrational, sinful, wicked, unjust, devilish, and tyrannical, it is for any man whatsoever, spiritual or temporal, clergyman or layman, to appropriate and assume unto himself a power, authority and jurisdiction, to rule, govern or reign over

---

[116] The army debates are available either as *The Clarke Papers* (ed. C. H. Firth, 4 vols., 1891-2) or as *Puritanism and Liberty* (ed. A. S. P. Woodhouse, 1938), the latter with a long and brilliant introduction.
[117] *Independency Gods Verity*, Woodhouse, p. 186.
[118] Woodhouse, p. 53.
[119] Woodhouse, p. 56.
[120] Woodhouse, p. 59.

any sort of men in the world without their free consent.'[121]

Wildman formulated the shocking demands more gravely and succinctly: 'Every person in England hath as clear a right to elect his representative as the greatest person in England. I conceive that's the undeniable maxim of government: that all government is in the free consent of the people.'[122] The most that Ireton would concede, however, was that if any person is reluctant to pay allegiance to a government for which his consent is not solicited, then 'he may go to another kingdom'.[123] It is a retort we have heard many times since. The Levelers were seeking political, not economic, leveling, but when Rainborough suggested that the 'chief end of this government is to preserve persons as well as estates', he was introducing a concept that Ireton simply could not grasp.[124] Sexby pointed out to Ireton that of the many thousands of soldiers who had suffered to redeem their country from prelatical despotism, few had much property, even though they all had a birthright. 'But it seems now, except a man hath a fixed estate in this kingdom, he hath no right in this kingdom. I wonder we were so much deceived.'[125]

To all such sentimental and unallowable arguments Ireton – 'the Army's Alpha and Omega', as Lilburne sneeringly called him[126] – made stalwart resistance. To change the 'fundamental constitution' was to open the gate to a flood of unknown evils. The foolish doctrine of natural rights is unrealistic: property does not come to a man either through the law of God or a law of nature, but through his own endeavors and his inheritance. The thought of all men repudiating their 'engagements' or obligations from some wild notion of what is just or unjust made him tremble. Rights are conferred by the law of the land, and since men are by nature corrupt and will ever be so, law cannot be built on the silly assumption that every man is as good as every other man. Such dangerous equalitarianism would mean the end of all government, and thus of all society.

This clash – and there were many such clashes in the course of the Putney debates – prefigures with sufficient clarity the course of the Puritan revolution that, having generated such soaring hopes for democracy and freedom, was to end in the Caesarism

---

[121] *The Free-mans Freedome Vindicated*, Woodhouse, p. 317.
[122] Woodhouse, p. 66.   [123] Woodhouse, p. 67.
[124] Woodhouse, p. 67.   [125] Woodhouse, p. 69.
[126] Woodhouse, p. 345.

of Cromwell.[127] Those Leveler principles of natural rights, government by consent, and individual liberty of conscience, though consonant with many of the reforms intended by 'The Heads of Proposals', were extended to limits which the dominant minds of the age could and would not tolerate. The army debates having ended in a stalemate, as it were, Cromwell regained much of his waning prestige with his troops by resolving to negotiate no further with the treacherous king. But the Levelers were not content. The following year they sought to become a civil party with their petition to Commons (September 11th, 1648), a sort of party platform which Parliament declared to be harmful in intent and destructive of both Parliament itself and civil society.[128] Truly, as John Goodwin remarked in 1649, persecution is never so bitter as when the oppressors flatter themselves that they act with God's sanction. 'When conscience and concupiscence meet (as oft they do in religious men) the conjunction is very fiery.'[129]

[127] At the first Parliament of the Protectorate, Cromwell, though bent on a policy of 'healing and settling', attacked the Levelers in language calculated to please his audience (the franchise having been limited to a two-hundred pound qualification for county votes): he denounced them as men who would abolish the immemorial and time-tested rankings of society, and therefore as enemies to the state. See Davies, *The Early Stuarts*, p. 175.
[128] See Gooch, *Democratic Ideas in the Seventeenth Century*, pp. 150–2.
[129] *Right and Might Well Met*, Woodhouse, p. 218. Under the leadership of the strange and able Gerald Winstanley the Diggers (or 'True Levellers', as they called themselves) became briefly notorious in 1649. An astonishing by-product of Sectarian political theory, the Diggers pushed beyond merely political to economic reforms that constituted an incipient communism. Like the Levelers finding their sanction in the law of nature, the Diggers proposed nothing less than a sweeping agrarian reform. Although God made the world a 'common treasury', the first evil result of man's fall was that acquisitive instinct through which he has enslaved his fellows and prostituted his reason: 'we see proud imaginary flesh, which is the wise serpent, rises up in flesh and gets dominion in some to rule over others, and so forces one part of the creation, man to be a slave to another' (*The True Levelers Standard Advanced*, Woodhouse, p. 379). The law of nature teaches us that each man should, as a natural right, enjoy the means of self-subsistence; therefore the current inequitable distribution of such means must be corrected.
The remedy is to revert to the primitive purity of common property, for when the prophecies of Scripture are fullfilled man will have the law of righteousness once more written in his heart, brotherhood rather than competition will govern economic conduct, and 'then this enmity in all lands will cease' (*ibid.*, p. 380). Thus the Diggers' program: 'The work we are going about is this: to dig up George's Hill and the waste ground thereabouts, and to sow corn, and to eat our bread together by the sweat of our brows' (*ibid.*, p. 381). The Diggers' naive efforts on George's Hill were quickly and easily suppressed, of course, but Winstanley persisted in his convictions long enough to address his *Law of Freedom* to Cromwell in 1652. This remarkable book – which had no effect whatever on the legislation enacted by Protectorate Parliaments – was built on the proposition that poverty is the greatest threat to civil peace and even personal virtue. The proletarian and Utopian program that Winstanley advocated – which was, quite simply, that all land be held in common – could not, in the nature of things, gain much support in the seventeenth century; but it is useful in reminding us how far Sectarian thought could go in liberating politics and morality from their theological bases.

V. THE TWO COVENANTS

Although the pressure of events and the swirling currents of day-to-day decisions tended to confuse motives and blur the outlines of the Puritans' liberal political theory, it is possible to trace the main movements in its developments. In spite of its naturalistic implications it had a theological foundation. The chief difference between Presbyterians and Independents, as we have seen, lay in their notions of church discipline, but that difference was enough to generate all their other differences. Hanserd Knollys defined an Independent church as one with 'A Presbyterian-Government, which hath not Dependencie upon any in matters meerly Ecclesiasticall (but upon the Lord Jesus Christ, Who is the Head of the Church)'.[130] Although not all Independents would subscribe to a strict Presbyterian discipline, they would all agree that a congregation of worshipers constituted an autonomous church, and that it should neither consent to nor indulge in any effort, by ecclesiastical or civil officers, to enforce national conformity. Since they demanded toleration for themselves, they could hardly do less than request it for others. Such ecclesiastical liberalism derived ultimately from a new conception of Christian liberty, and this in itself was a notable modification of those doctrinal rigors which had conferred upon early Reformation theology its terror and its strength.

Luther's pietistic conception of Christian liberty had certainly contained no threat to the powers that be. By the illumination of grace, and emphatically not by his own exertions or works or reason, man attains the imputed righteousness of Christ; this places him, as it were, beyond the law of the Old Testament and liberates him from those dread monsters of 'his sin, his blindness, his misery, his impiety, ignorance, hatred, and contempt of God, death, hell, the judgment and deserved wrath of God' of which it was the function of the law to make him mindful.[131] The new law of the Gospel, on the other hand, assures him 'that liberty whereby Christ hath made us free: not from an earthly bondage ... but from God's everlasting wrath'.[132] The freedom of the Christian man, then, is heavenly, not earthly; and its franchise is

---
[130] *A Moderate Answer unto Dr Bastwick's Book*, p. 2.
[131] *A Commentarie of Master Doctor Martin Luther upon the Epistle of S. Paul to the Galathians*, Woodhouse, pp. 223–4.
[132] *Ibid.*, p. 225.

for a supernaturally induced peace of soul rather than unseemly and subversive political agitation.

Calvin, too, could find no sanction for civil disobedience or toleration in the doctrine of Christian liberty. In his view, the old law of the Mosaic code was prohibitory 'because it produces fear in the mind', but the new law of the Gospel, a 'covenant of liberty', confirms that 'confidence and security' which distinguishes the elect.[133] And the elect, as the *Institutes* makes all too clear, are not prone to err in the direction of political or ecclesiastical liberalism. The effects of the 'liberty' that they enjoy are various: through it they cast off the 'yoke' of the old law so that they may 'yield voluntary obedience to the will of God'; moreover they are exempt from those dietary and other restrictions concerning things indifferent because the certainty of salvation and the perfect acquiescence in God's sovereignty induces a spiritual intensity that makes dietary or other prohibitions unnecessary.[134]

But the seventeenth century had more to worry about than dietary restrictions. No theology that failed to answer new needs and give hope to new aspirations could long sustain its appeal. The Elizabethan Presbyterians had labored valiantly by their lights, but as the shabby history of such reactionaries as Prynne and Rutherford shows, the extreme right wing of Calvinism was radically antagonistic to the forces of a new age. The emergence in the seventeenth century of the covenantal version of Calvinism is a clear sign that assumptions that might loosely be called rational, humanistic, and liberal were forcing fundamental revisions of the Calvinistic ethos.[135] The political implications of such assumptions are seen at once in the demands of the Independents as they were voiced in the army debates, in the Levelers' petitions, in those remarkable pamphlets of the 'forties. These demands, however, rested on a theological base which it is needful to sketch before we leave the vexed problems of Puritanism and liberty.

For all its early successes Calvinism raised many more questions than it answered. How was a moral life possible under the dread decree of predestination? How could man come to terms with

[133] *Institutes*, II.xi.9.
[134] *Ibid.*, III.xix.2–8.
[135] As so often when writing of Puritanism, one has gratefully to acknowledge that Perry Miller has made this subject his own. See especially, 'The Marrow of Puritan Divinity', *Transactions*, 1933–7 of the Colonial Society of Massachusetts, pp. 247–300.

THE TWO COVENANTS

so inscrutable and awful a despot as the one revealed in the *Institutes*? How could a good man feel sure he was of the elect? How could he assume any degree of responsibility for his conduct without jeopardizing the absolute sovereignty of God? How could the ways of that God be brought within the scope of man's limited comprehension? Arminianism had advanced one solution to this central dilemma of Calvinism, but it elevated man at the expense of God, and at the Synod of Dort it was firmly repudiated. Another solution, one more compatible with historic Calvinism and with the facts of sacred history, was that covenantal theory adumbrated by William Perkins and systematically developed by William Ames, John Preston, and Richard Sibbes.

At the heart of the new theology lay the doctrine of the double covenant, a doctrine that preserved God as creator and master, man as creature and subject, but that none the less enriched the relationship between God and man with rational and legalistic implications very congenial to certain seventeenth-century Calvinists. When God made Adam He entered into an agreement with him, committing Himself to certain rewards if Adam would fulfil certain obligations. These obligations constituted that moral law of nature which God implanted in Adam's very heart, so that obedience to it would be natural and instinctive. Even though Adam failed and fell, God in His infinite mercy tried again, this time with Abraham. 'And I will establish my covenant between me and thee and thy seed after thee in their generations for an everlasting covenant, to be a God unto thee, and to thy seed after thee.'[136] This was the covenant of works, made explicit and in the fulness of time, as Perkins said, formulated in the Ten Commandments.[137] By it God undertook to confer certain benefits on man in return for man's worship and obedience. But God's benevolence did not end there: in His mighty plan for the salvation of fallen humanity He sent His Son that He might atone for the sins of the race, and with the promulgation of the Gospel a new covenant became necessary.

This second covenant was of grace, not works. By it man promises faith in the miraculous Incarnation, Atonement, and Resurrection of Christ in order to assure himself of eternal life. It is that covenant 'whereby God freely promising Christ, and

---

[136] Genesis xvii:7.
[137] *A Golden Chaine*, pp. 119–20.

his benefites, exacteth againe of man, that hee would by faith receive Christ, and repent him of his sinnes'.[138] Signalizing as it did an agreement between God and His elect, it marked an immense advance over the covenant of works. As Winthrop told the saints on their voyage to New England, the bond between God and them was clear: 'wee have taken out a Commission, the Lord hath given us leave to drawe our owne Articles wee have professed to enterprise these Accions upon these and these ends', and if God brings them to their haven, then their obligation is binding. They will be obliged to fulfil their contract with Him with a 'strickt performance' of love and piety. But if they turn away and neglect their 'Articles' to 'prosecute our carnall intencions' then the Lord will surely 'breake out in wrathe against us be revenged of such a perjured people and make us knowe the price of the breache of such a Covenant'.[139]

Thus, as Preston said, by the covenant of grace God made enormous concessions to His creatures, reducing His operations to their comprehension and delimiting His infinite sovereignty for their benefit.

> I will not onely tell thee what I am able to doe, I will not onely expresse to thee in generall, that I will deale well with thee, that I have a willingnesse and ability to recompence thee, if thou walke before mee and serve mee, and bee perfect; but I am willing to enter into Covenant with thee, that is, I will binde my selfe, I will ingage my selfe, I will enter into bond, as it were, I will not bee at liberty any more, but I am willing even to make a Covenant, a compact and agreement with thee.[140]

On the basis of this second covenant the seventeenth-century divines – who yielded to no man in logical refinement and theological hair-splitting – constructed a theology that would have astonished Calvin. By injecting reason into Calvinism they subverted it. The supra-rational God who in His awful majesty was hidden behind a veil came forth as an amiable, even accommodating deity, eager to compound with His children, and setting terms so favorable that one could not without folly resist them. His price for an eternity of bliss was light, his demands perfectly congruous with natural reason, and reducible to such clear and natural propositions that they could be met by anyone. As Mr

[138] *Ibid.*, pp. 325–6.
[139] *A Model of Christian Charity*, Miller-Johnson, p. 198.
[140] Quoted by Miller, 'The Marrow of Puritan Divinity', p. 263.

THE TWO COVENANTS

Miller has said, even if this theology was not strictly rational, it was very reasonable, and as such it was a typical product of seventeenth-century thought. The clear, self-evident articles of agreement between God and man at once suggest the simplicities of Ramean logic, the scientific quest for axioms, the effort to reduce natural theology to such self-evident propositions that one need only look about him to see that the heavens declare the glory of God.

As an effort to inject reasonableness into Calvinism, covenantal theology had consequences that were immediately apparent. It made possible the development of a moral and ethical code, thus tacitly conferring on man a certain responsibility for his own spiritual well-being. By the use of his reason man is permitted, as Milton said, to repair the ruins of his first foundation, and to enkindle those remaining sparks of natural virtue which even the Fall had not wholly obliterated. Thus the need for grace – made possible by the second covenant – becomes intellectually recognized, and by taking thought of his needs man is in some measure equipped to satisfy them. No one escapes the onus of original sin, but that sin, conceived as an imputed obligation to seek atonement, loses much of its Calvinistic terror and hopelessness. Since he could rationally comprehend God's plan for his salvation, and since he could hope for release from the burden of his sin, man by taking advantage of the second covenant could infer that works are, if not the cause, at least an accompaniment of regeneration. The great doctrine of justification by faith alone was, in the nature of things, inadequate for the seventeenth century; and by the doctrine of the double covenant man was permitted to hope that by God's grace he could live well, and by living well testify to the fact of his salvation.

But the most significant consequences of covenantal theology derived from the ecclesiastical and political individualism that it sanctioned. By the covenant of grace the elect are granted exemption, as it were, from the compulsions and restraints of the old law; and since the old law was made necessary by the iniquities and impotence of fallen man in a state of nature it was inoperative on those regenerated into a state of grace. For if the old law was designed to confirm man's conviction of guilt and teach him the need of a divine mediator, then it was fulfilled and transcended by the new law. By the Gospel man is raised to be a joint-heir with Christ; and so love and not fear, freedom and not restraint, become the keys to Christian virtue. Thus Christian liberty could be defined as a release from the rigors of the Mosaic code through faith in Christ. The typical Puritan individualism of which Milton, after his fashion, made literature rests upon the assumption that the new law of the Gospel abrogates the old law of the Mosaic code. The written, ceremonial, and external law of the Old Testament is canceled by the sanctions for grace and love and freedom in the New Testament; thus the proposition that 'liberty is the best school of virtue' is central in the ethical thought of Milton and many other Puritans.[141]

This 'liberty' could be extended to man's social responsibilities. As some Puritans went ahead to argue, the prohibitions of 'magistrates' – conceived as any temporal superiors sanctioned by God for the governing of sinful man – could mean nothing to the elect who are not liable to the restraints imposed on the reprobate. In terms of that fundamental individualism which had made the Reformation possible, those happy few assured of eternal bliss in the presence of God were obviously far beyond the discipline of any national church or state.

> The old Covenant was over the Old man, and its Condemnation or punishment was over the Old man, to wit, this corruptable fallen State of Mortality, and therefore they executed death upon the transgressors thereof. The New Covenant is over the New man, to wit, the Spirit that shall be raised out of this corruptable at the Resurrection; therefore hath it the promise of forgivenesse of sins, and eternall life.[142]

Thus those irradiated by the grace of God had achieved that Christian liberty to which the restraints and humiliations proper to man's natural state are unthinkable. They have attained that sublime condition in which the bondage of the flesh or the claims and pretensions of the natural man or of natural reason are annihilated by the ineffable knowledge of God. In a sense they have lost a life, but also they have gained a life, and their sublimation of self gives rise to an arrogance possible only for the saints of God.

---

[141] *The Second Defence*, PW, I, 294. In *The Doctrine and Discipline of Divorce* (esp. II.viii), as in *Tetrachordon*, Milton advances the argument obliquely to support the doctrine of Christian liberty: Christ's attack on divorce (Matthew v:32) cannot impose a restraint not formulated by the ceremonial law (Deuteronomy xxiv: 1-2) which had been abrogated by the Gospel. For Milton's conception of the liberty – not license – of marriage, see *The Doctrine and Discipline of Divorce*, I.ix; cf. PL, IV.743-57.
[142] *The Araignement of Mr Persecution*, Haller, III, 237.

THE TWO COVENANTS

As John Webster, whose antirationalism we have glanced at already, explained this Puritan paradox, to attain his regeneration man must 'be brought to the full, and absolute abnegation of all his wit, reason, will, desires, strength, wisdome, righteousness, and all humane glory and excellencies whatsoever';[143] and yet this loss of selfhood makes possible the most poignant subjectivism and sense of separateness.

For between the works of the flesh and those of the spirit no compromise is possible; between the reprobate and the elect the chasm is unbridgeable. The world hates Christ for many reasons, said William Dell, but chiefly because His word of faith is wholly spiritual 'and hath nothing in it that is sutable to flesh and blood; Nothing in it, that pleaseth the Fancy, or Reason, or Understanding of man; it hath nothing in it wherein a Naturall or Carnal heart can take pleasure, but is throughout a Word of Faith'.[144] What this amounts to is a vigorous restatement of that ancient dualism that has taken so many forms in Western thought: Plato's of permanence and change, St Paul's of the carnal and the spiritual man, Augustine's of the celestial and terrestrial cities, Calvin's of grace and nature. 'For these are two distinct seeds and sorts of people; the one from beneath, the other from above; the one the seed of woman, the other the seed of the serpent; and between these God hath put such an enmity that no man can take away.'[145]

The immediate practical corollary of this Puritan subjectivism was, of course, certain Sectarians' refusal to tailor their spiritual life to the needs of any secular authority. For a state or commonwealth to 'set up, and appoint a National Ministry' or to compel conformity on those sanctified with the seal of the spirit 'is to take unto themselves the power, wisdom, and right of the Almighty'.[146] As Milton said, in his maturest theological conviction, it is not 'within the province of any visible church, much less of the civil magistrates, to impose their own interpretations [of the Scripture] on us as laws, or as binding on the conscience'.[147] By their faith the elect are knit together into a 'spiritual society'

---

[143] *Academiarum Examen*, p. 16. Significantly, Webster closes this chapter (no. ii) concerning Christian humility with a quotation (p. 17) from Bacon to the effect that theological truth must be drawn 'ex verbo, & oraculis Dei, non ex lumine naturæ, aut rationis dictamimei'.
[144] Dell, *The Stumbling-Stone*, p. 15.
[145] Dell, *The Way of True Peace and Unity*, Woodhouse, p. 303.
[146] Webster, *The Saints Guide*, p. 21.
[147] *De doctrina*, I.xxx (*PW*, IV, 444).

more binding than any conceivable human institution, a society whose powers are, of course, irrelevant to those outside its limits. What connection can exist between those saints who preach only the regeneration of the spirit and those worldlings who 'chiefly teach the Law, and Morall Doctrine, and Workes, or the Philosophy, and Philosophicall subtilties and speculations, which yet the Apostle hath expressly forbidden, Col. 2.8'?[148] To ask the question is to answer it.

'For what hath the Church to do with those that are not of the Church? ... For church-power, which is spiritual, is no more suitable to the world than worldly power, which is fleshly, is suitable to the Church.'[149] A strong mystical Puritan like John Saltmarsh thought we know salvation only by its own 'pure, spirituall, and glorious assurance', not by any 'Demonstrations of Salvation' based on rational or argumentative grounds, nor by any ecclesiastical tradition, nor by any legislation in the interests of a national church.[150]

> What is man that he should conceive that God is only in a place, or Temple, or form of Worship, or Systeme of Doctrine of his forme or making, since the time is come, that we do no longer worship in this Temple, nor at Jerusalem; but they that worship, must worship in spirit and truth; which truth, is he only who is the truth.[151]

How far from real piety are those who use the 'Civill power to make peace' among the jarring sects, 'reckoning a compulsive Uniformity, for Unity, Peace, and Truth. This is one way to deal with the body indeed but not with the soul, to make the outward man but not the inward'.[152]

To certain Sectarians, then, the claims – Presbyterian or Anglican – for conformity constituted an affront to the liberty of a Christian man. Some Puritans (including young Milton)[153] had hoped that, once the Reformation hindered by the prelates was completed, such consequences as civil liberty and universal civic virtue would come of themselves; but when it became clear that the Presbyterians intended to compel conformity to their own

---

[148] Dell, *The Tryal of Spirits*, pp. 27–8.
[149] Dell, *The Way of True Peace and Unity*, Woodhouse, p. 308.
[150] *Sparkles of Glory*, pp. 274–5.
[151] *Ibid.*, sig. A3ᵛ.
[152] Saltmarsh, *Smoke in the Temple*, p. 8.
[153] For a convenient catena of Scriptural citations on freedom of conscience, see *A Treatise of Civil Power in Ecclesiastical Causes*, PW, II, 539–42.

THE TWO COVENANTS 299

questionable reforms such Independents as Robinson, Walwyn, and Williams began to speak of liberty of conscience, and then of civil liberty, as corollaries of Christian liberty. 'To compell me against my conscience, is to compell me against what I beleive [sic] to be true,' said Walwyn, 'and so against my faith; now whatsoever is not of faith is sin; To compell me therefore against my conscience, is to compell me to doe that which is sinfull.'[154]

The only power that 'magistrates' can exert over the saints, said Dell, is merely 'negative and permissive, that they should not forbid & hinder them to declare the things that God hath revealed in them, and commanded them to utter, nor prohibite them the way of their worship and serving of God'.[155] They are members of Christ's kingdom, and so the 'Civill Power or Authority of the world' can have no meaning for them.[156] The final inference is momentous for the history of Protestantism: 'it is not the way of peace to mingle the Church and the world, but to separate them, and to keep them distinct; that those that are of one nature and spirit may be of one communion among themselves'.[157] The conviction so widely held by the Sectarians and Independents that, as Lilburne put it, 'it is the incommunicable Prerogative of Jesus Christ alone to be King of his Saints, and Law-giver to his Church and people' was one whose practical consequences serve to distinguish modern from Renaissance political theory. Though its implications were perhaps not fully realized, except perhaps by hardheaded realists like Lilburne and Overton, they were the most pregnant products of Puritan political thought. 'There is no foundation so sure and precious to build the honour, peace and safety of Cesar upon, as a stone duly pitched for a land-mark between God and him.'[158]

The man who worked out this bifurcation of spiritual and secular to its furthest limits – and so became a monster to some of his contemporaries – was Roger Williams. In trying to protect completely the spiritual autonomy of the elect, he denied to the civil power any spiritual or religious adjuncts whatever. To save religion, that is, he secularized politics. In his view of Christian

---

[154] *The Compassionate Samaritane*, Haller, III, 86.
[155] *The Saints Guide*, p. 37.
[156] *Ibid.*, p. 33.
[157] Dell, *The Way of True Peace and Unity*, Woodhouse, p. 311. See *The Ancient Bounds*, Woodhouse, pp. 256–7.
[158] Thomas Goodwin, *The Danger of Fighting Against God*, Haller, III, 57.

liberty the ceremonial law of the Old Testament is a type prefiguring the antitype of the Gospel; and so that Presbyterian uniformity argued from the Old Testament must yield to the law of love and freedom announced in the Gospel. One is of the flesh, the other of the spirit, and to compel the law of the flesh upon those liberated by the spirit is impious folly. Therefore liberty of conscience – and the toleration it implies – is the immediate consequence of regeneration.

In the notorious *Bloody Tenent of Persecution* (1644) the latent secularism of Independent political theory attained its first full expression. 'An enforced uniformity of religion throughout a nation or civil state confounds the civil and religious, denies the principles of Christianity and civility, and that Jesus Christ is come in the flesh.'[159] To keep clearly distinguished the 'principles of Christianity and civility' we must remember that the church (which Williams, as an Independent, defines as a 'company of worshippers, whether true or false') is as autonomous a corporation as a college of physicians or a company of 'Turkey merchants' operating in London. Its internal affairs are its own, and may be conducted without the peace of the city, or the commonwealth, being 'in the least measure impaired or disturbed'.[160] Between the world and the true church is a bottomless gulf: 'the world lies in wickedness, is like a wilderness, or a sea of wild beasts innumerable, fornicators, covetous, idolaters, &c.'; but the elect must none the less live in the world without being a part of it, and Christ Himself 'commands a permission of them in the world, until the time of the end of the world, when the goats and sheep, the tares and wheat, shall be eternally separated each from other'.[161]

This essential duality between the world and the spirit is the most potent argument against confusing the reprobate with the elect, or smiting with the civil sword those saints whom no magistrate can compel against their consciences. As we learn from II Corinthians x: 4, there is

> a twofold state, a civil state and a spiritual, civil officers and spiritual, civil weapons and spiritual weapons, civil vengeance and punishment and a spiritual vengeance and punishment – although the Spirit speaks not here expressly of civil magistrates and their civil weapons – yet, these states

[159] *The Bloody Tenent*, Woodhouse, p. 266.
[160] *Ibid.*, p. 267.   [161] *Ibid.*, pp. 268–9.

THE TWO COVENANTS

being of different natures and considerations, as far differing as spirit from flesh, I ... observe that the civil weapons are most improper and unfitting in matters of the spiritual state and kingdom, though in the civil state most proper and suitable.[162]

The function of the civil sword is to defend 'persons, estates, families, liberties of a city or civil state', but in the nature of things it cannot 'extend to spiritual and soul-causes, spiritual and soul-punishment, which belongs to that spiritual sword with two edges, the soul-piercing (in soul-saving, or soul-killing), the word of God'.[163] How blind the folly of those Presbyterians – 'Mr Cotton and others' – who, although themselves formerly 'under hatches', now force others against their conscience in order to attain an impious conformity.[164]

Hence I argue, if the civil magistrate have no power to restrain or constrain his subjects in things in their own nature indifferent, as in eating of meats, wearing this or that garment, using this or that gesture, but that they are bound to try and examine his commands, and satisfy their own reason, conscience, and judgment before the Lord, and that they shall sin if they follow the magistrate's command, not being persuaded in their own soul and conscience that his commands are according to God: it will be much more unlawful and heinous in the magistrate to compel the subjects unto that which according to their consciences' persuasion is simply unlawful, as unto a falsely constituted church, ministry, worship, administration, and they shall not escape the ditch by being led blindfold by the magistrate.[165]

Such pronouncements reveal that the most seminal results of left-wing Puritan agitation derived from the desire to save the individual's or the holy community's religious conscience from the needs of civil or ecclesiastical conformity. This conviction led inevitably to that separation of the elect and reprobate, religious and secular, church and state which is perhaps the most significant achievement of Protestantism. What had started as a theologically argued counterclaim to Presbyterian demands for a national church became a thoroughly secular conception of the function of the state. In order to protect themselves from a compulsive Presbyterian discipline allegedly authorized by the Old Testament the Independents invoked the sanctions of the new law of the Gospel. In resisting ecclesiastical conformity they were compelled to resist (on sound Presbyterian principles) civil tyranny

---

[162] *The Bloody Tenent*, Woodhouse, p. 274.
[163] Ibid., p. 276.
[164] Ibid., pp. 280–1.   [165] Ibid., p. 286.

– a resistance which in the diastole and systole of events fanned into a political theory disassociated from theology. Hence their demands for freedom of conscience, and for the autonomy of the holy community, led to a repudiation of civil power in religious matters which loosed political theory from its ancient theological moorings. This emancipation, in turn, permitted the development of those new civil freedoms, conceived as merely natural rights, which have been indispensable to the growth of democracy.

VII

THE CONQUEST OF NATURE

I. THE RECONSTRUCTION OF KNOWLEDGE

It now remains, in this final chapter, to trace not the history of scientific thought in the seventeenth century but some of the ways in which men sought to reconstruct their knowledge of a 'nature' being steadily loosened from theological and even moral presuppositions. Since the main movement of late Renaissance thought – political, theological, and philosophical – had been in the direction of such an emancipation, it remained for the seventeenth century not only to push it forward, but also to devise new tools and methods proper for its uses. The widely felt compulsion to evolve new methodologies for dealing with new kinds of knowledge was the most generative factor in the thought of the century; for in spite of the immense prestige that certain traditional attitudes and assumptions retained, it was becoming increasingly evident, at least in certain quarters, that nothing less than a radically new departure was needed if man was to exploit his new franchise for mastering the processes and prerogatives of nature.

Broadly speaking, the seminal minds of the seventeenth century evolved two strategies for the pursuit of natural knowledge, the rationalistic and the empirical. The great Continental rationalists best represented by Galileo, Descartes, and Spinoza generally conceived of reality in terms of mathematical relationships subsuming the fluctuations and deceptions of sensory appearance – relationships that could, under proper conditions, be intuited directly by the mind of man and then for purposes of description and explanation applied mathematically to the data of sensation. Their methodology, in short, was essentially deductive and essentially Platonic, for they hypostatized a fundamentally rational structure in the universe which the human mind, by rigorous and systematic intellection, could isolate and comprehend. On the other hand, such English empiricists as Bacon, Hobbes, and Locke sought not to transcend sense by a process of pure deduction and intuition, but by purifying and correcting the processes of sensation to find in the systematic observation of natural processes ('bodies in motion') the key to the understanding and thus to the control of nature. Their method, then, was essentially inductive.

There was much overlapping. Both great schools agreed in rejecting the inherited assumption that things are characterized by qualities, for both came to realize the extraordinary utility of geometry as a tool for measuring quantitative relationships but powerless for measuring qualitative relationships. Both agreed in rejecting the common-sense notion that the world is pretty much as it seems to be, and thus in construing reality as something beneath the falsity of appearances. Both agreed in rejecting the concept of substance and in replacing it with the concept of structure as the ultimate object of intellection. Both agreed – significantly, in view of certain skeptical elements in late Renaissance thought – that the world was intelligible through and through, if only a proper methodology could be substituted for the messy accumulation of custom, error, and superstition that they had inherited. Finally, both agreed that teleology, however useful to post-Socratic philosophy and to Christianity, had no relevance in natural philosophy: in rejecting quality they also rejected (moral) purpose, and in seeking to know the how rather than the why of natural processes they directed their attention to efficient rather than final causes.

In spite of their obvious but perhaps unconscious obligations to the past – we do not proceed far in Bacon or Descartes before we realize that they owed more to the odious Schoolmen than they would care to admit – the great minds of the century of genius succeeded, in a couple of generations, in giving a new movement to European thought. Their enterprise was daring, and they knew it. As they stood on the edge of a brave new world their hopes soared like eagles. They had no doubt, apparently, that the conquest of nature was possible if only, stripped of the heavy and useless baggage of the past, they could start afresh. On the large assumption that the conquest of nature was possible, they needed only to proceed warily and systematically, to formulate and follow a proper methodology. The only course for the reconstruction of knowledge – and nothing less is needed, says Bacon – is 'that the entire work of the understanding be com-

THE RECONSTRUCTION OF KNOWLEDGE

menced afresh, and the mind itself be from the very outset not left to take its own course, but guided at every step; and the business be done as if by machinery'.[1]

Thus *The Advancement of Learning* – prophetic title – sets the tone. As Descartes said, 'it were far better never to think of investigating truth at all, than to do so without a method';[2] and his *Discourse on Method* consequently lies at the base of his system: to take nothing as true which he did not clearly recognize to be so, to divide each problem into its small constituent parts, to proceed in a strict order from the simplest and easiest to the increasingly complex, and to make enumerations 'so complete and reviews so general that I should be certain of having omitted nothing'.[3] Spinoza in general concurred. He thought it possible for man to train his mind that it may, 'by a given standard, comprehend whatsoever is intelligible, by laying down certain rules as aids, and by avoiding useless mental exertion'.[4] For doubt derives not from the inaccessibility of knowledge, but from poor procedure – 'from want of due order in investigation'.[5] For that chesty generation of Restoration Baconians who formed the Royal Society Sprat's views are almost official. The Schoolmen are not wholly despicable, he admitted, for at least by their horrible example we may learn 'how farre more important a good Method of Thinking, and a right course of apprehending things, does contribute towards the attaining of perfection in true knowledge, then the strongest, and most vigorous wit in the World, can do without them'.[6]

The pressure for the formulation of a new methodology was, of course, cognate with the mounting revolt against scholasticism – loosely conceived as the traditional instrument of knowledge that bore the double face of truth and piety. The iconoclasts of the seventeenth century in both theology and science had come to believe that truth and piety referred to quite different orders of reality which permitted no interaction, that a theology and a natural philosophy both deriving from a common set of 'notional', mythopoetic, or *a priori* assumptions could yield no proper know-

---
[1] *NO*, 'Preface' (*Works*, VIII, 60–1).
[2] *Rules*, no. IV (*Works*, I, 9).
[3] *Discourse*, pt. II (*Works*, I, 92).
[4] *On the Improvement of the Understanding*, Wild, p. 13.
[5] *Ibid.*, Wild, p. 32.
[6] *The History of the Royal-Society*, p. 15.

ledge of either religion or nature, and consequently that the most compelling demand of the age was for a new method directed toward new objects of natural knowledge. It had been the great effort of the Reformation to reconstruct the basis of religious knowledge, and the subsequent elevation of grace above nature, faith above reason, had incidentally made it possible to regard nature and reason as segregated from grace and faith. The result for the seventeenth century was a view of nature freed from its traditionally intimate correspondence with theology, with the resulting compulsion to seek out a new kind of truth about that nature and to employ that truth for man's secular advantage.

One of the first fruits of this segregation – which we have already examined in other connections – was the refusal of certain *avant garde* thinkers to concern themselves with final causes. Such a refusal, usually argued in the most pious terms, was a necessary protective device for those seeking a sanction for mere natural truth. Bacon had decreed only two limits for the aggressive human intellect: the truths of revealed religion and the necessities of 'use and action'. Because the Fall of Adam was the dreadful consequence of 'approaching and intruding into God's secrets and mysteries',[7] his posterity should take care that in exercising their divine mandate for knowledge they should not repeat that primal sin.

> For if any man shall think by view and inquiry into these sensible and material things, to attain to any light for the revealing of the nature or will of God, he shall dangerously abuse himself. It is true that the contemplation of the creatures of God hath for end (as to the natures of the creatures themselves) knowledge, but as to the nature of God, no knowledge, but wonder; which is nothing but contemplation broken off, or losing itself.[8]

The immense 'prejudice' that both divine and human knowledge have suffered by 'the intermingling and tempering of the one with the other' should check our aspirations. Religion has been larded with heresy and natural knowledge with 'speculative fictions and vanities'.[9] Although that part of truth which 'defineth of good and evil' is not available to man's scrutiny save in the revealed word of God, 'use and action' remain to fix the goals and determine the course of his natural intellection. The end of proper

---
[7] *Valerius Terminus*, *Works*, VI, 28.
[8] *Ibid.*, *Works*, VI, 29.
[9] *Ibid.*, *Works*, VI, 29.

knowledge is the 'benefit and relief of the state and society of man; for otherwise all manner of knowledge becometh malign and serpentine'.[10]

Although Descartes, as the *pontifex maximus* of Continental rationalists, could not share Bacon's utilitarianism, he explicitly sanctioned the segregation of religious and natural truth (indeed, he erected his metaphysic on it). In a significant distinction he announced that belief is a function of will, knowledge of intelligence,[11] and his statement of the case, though without Bacon's gorgeous rhetoric, was vastly more influential:

> Knowing that my nature is extremely feeble and limited, and that the nature of God is on the contrary immense, incomprehensible, and infinite, I have no further difficulty in recognizing that there is an infinitude of matters in His power, the causes of which transcend my knowledge; and this reason suffices to convince me that the species of cause termed final, finds no useful employment in physical [or natural] things; for it does not appear to me that I can without temerity seek to investigate the [inscrutable] ends of God.[12]

Descartes' position is clear: he is neither so foolish nor impious as to seek rational knowledge of such mysteries as the Trinity or the Incarnation,[13] nor even to 'seek for the reason of natural things from the end which God or nature has set before him in their creation'. It is presumptuous to assume that 'God could take us into His counsels', or to believe that by investigating effects we could reach back to that inaccessible first cause.

> But regarding Him as the efficient cause of all things, we shall merely try to discover by the light of nature that He has placed in us, applied to those attributes of which He has been willing we should have some knowledge, what must be concluded regarding the effects that we perceive by the senses; but we must keep in mind what has been said, that we must trust to this natural light only so long as nothing contrary to it is revealed by God Himself.[14]

If Descartes was at least ostensibly a good Christian and Catholic, Spinoza was neither, and the *Ethics* is a mighty proof of that danger which lesser men had feared and sought to evade. Like the new philosophers he refused to recognize final causes, or moral

[10] *Valerius Terminus, Works*, VI, 33-4.
[11] *Rules*, no. III (*Works*, I, 8).
[12] *Meditation IV* (*Works*, I, 173).
[13] *Principles*, I.xxv.
[14] *Ibid.*, I.xxviii (*Works*, I, 230-1).

causality, as a proper object of human intellection; but unlike them he refused to isolate such concepts within the sacrosanct area of revealed religion. As a result he drained religion, as customarily conceived, of moral purpose and anthropomorphic warmth, and so for his pains was excoriated by all men of good will as an atheistical monster. A stone falls on a man's head. Why? Because the wind blew hard. The wind blew hard because there was a storm at sea, and the man, having an invitation to dinner, happened to be passing. The piously foolish, says Spinoza, will ask further. 'But why was the sea agitated? why was the man invited at that time? And so they will not cease from asking the causes of causes, until at last you fly to the will of God, the refuge for ignorance.'[15] Why will men not realize that in seeking such final causes (which are nothing but 'human fictions') they are blaspheming the God whom they profess to adore? 'For if God works to obtain an end, He necessarily seeks something for which He stands in need.'[16]

> The reason or cause, therefore, why God or nature acts and the reason why He exists are one and the same. Since, therefore, He exists for no end, He acts for no end; and since He has no principle or end of existence, He has no principle or end of action. A final cause, as it is called, is nothing, therefore, but human desire, in so far as this is considered as the principle or primary cause of anything.[17]

In Spinoza religion and naturalism perhaps coalesced, after a fashion, but at a price to religion too great to be endured. Spinoza would not resort to Bacon's and Descartes' polite evasions in barricading religion behind a wall of revelation, nor would he admit that varieties of truth, natural or religious, yield only to their proper instruments; but in seeking to reunite religion and reason he achieved a monument of pure intellection hardly recognizable as religion at all. He pushed to its limits that imperial extension of natural knowledge that, in spite of Bacon's disclaimers, is radically incompatible with revealed religion. It should not surprise us that the deistic progress of seventeenth-century thought led only to the eruption of long-suppressed anti-intellectual forces in many varieties of pietism, mysticism, Methodism, and assorted religious enthusiasms. The emergence of Jonathan

---

[15] *Ethics*, pt. I, appendix (*Wild*, p. 139).
[16] *Ibid.*, pt. I, appendix (Wild, pp. 137–8).
[17] *Ibid.*, bk. IV, preface (Wild, p. 284).

THE KNOWLEDGE OF NATURE 309

Edwards and John Wesley from the theological climate that produced Tindal and Chubb is no more surprising than the wide following which theologians like Barth and Niebuhr command in our own day.

II. THE KNOWLEDGE OF NATURE

Needless to say, in the late Renaissance the auguries of change from a generally theistic to a generally naturalistic view of secular knowledge were greeted with very mixed emotions. As we have seen, the radical split between those realms which the late Middle Ages and the Renaissance had generally thought to be united or at least to be intimately and reciprocally related resulted in a dislocation of every aspect of European thought. The dislocation was *au fond* epistemological. In the traditional view represented by St Thomas, epistemology had begun with phenomenology – the data of sensation – and proceeded analogically from known to unknown through some inferred degree of correspondence toward the double goal of truth and piety. The method could be reversed, working from unknown to known, but the strategy of analogy or correspondence remained operative. The assumption of correspondence involved the further assumption that the essentially quantitative knowledge yielded by sensation – this color, that color, another color – induced a higher qualitative knowledge: from the data of sense could be inferred another kind of data relating to value and thus productive of moral truth. As men tried to understand the physical they were driven beyond surfaces to the supersensible reality of spirit. The two halves of experience were fused, and natural philosophy, the legitimate domain of secular intellection, proved to be an avenue to the metaphysical.

Consequently, much Renaissance 'philosophy' is theosophical. Perhaps, as Mr Burtt has argued (and Mr Strong denied) the motor force behind the rise of modern science was Neo-Platonism. Certainly Ficino and Pico (and, across the Alps, Reuchlin) came to employ an erudite and fantastic numerology to demonstrate the correspondence between nature and spirit; and Bembo, in Castiglione's beautiful fourth book, described the facile progress from the experience of physical beauty to a rapturously mystical absorption into the Godhead. The temporal microcosm reflected the (mathematical) harmony and beauty of the spiritual macrocosm, and all experience merged into a continuum. Mystic and naturalist alike had learned to reverse the Nicene formula: they approached God through nature rather than nature through God. 'O admirable impartiality of Thine, thou first Mover,' breathes Leonardo (than whom no man was ever less mystical). 'Thou hast not permitted that any force should ever fail of the order of quality of its necessary effects.'[18]

Inevitably, however, this delicate – uncritical? – compromise between sense and spirit yielded to insistent new pressures, both theological and scientific. Some day, perhaps, a proper history of Renaissance scientific thought will be written, and when it is it will have to take into account many things not necessarily scientific that suggest the running of the tide. Leonardo's casual remark that 'all our knowledge has its origins in our perceptions',[19] even though at least partially compatible with the Thomistic theory of cognition, is as profoundly suggestive of the future as many other of his insights. Although we have learned to discount the raptures of Burckhardt and Symonds, and so tend to deny the *sui generis* aspects of Renaissance culture, we can hardly fail to recognize the shift in men's interests after the fourteenth century. Many things mark this shift: Petrarch's daring and typical desire for personal fame in the *Secretum* (a desire which would have been alien to St Thomas, just as Cellini's would have been to the nameless architects of Chartres); the new pictorial realism that showed comely persons standing out in bold relief from a fair and smiling landscape; the shameless luxury for which a worldly papacy set the model; the unclerical psychology of Pomponazzi and the unclerical metaphysics of Telesio; the growth of something very much like scientific naturalism in the university of Padua.[20] Artists, popes, princes, even speculative thinkers were turning more and more to the concrete, the natural, and the

---

[18] *The Literary Works*, art. 1134 (II, 237). For the importance of Nicholas Cusanus, and especially of his *De docta ignorantia* in this connexion ('In omnibus partibus relucet totum'), see Cassirer, *Die Philosophie der Renaissance*, pp. 55–9.

[19] *The Literary Works*, art. 1147 (II, 239).

[20] As Mr Randall has pointed out in a notable article ('The Development of Scientific Method in the School of Padua', *JHI*, I [1940], 177–206), the application of Aristotelian logic to actual medical problems led, between Pietro d'Abano and Zabarella, to the development of that methodology with which Galileo had such astonishing success in the early seventeenth century. Some of those contemporaries of Descartes who most lustily vilified Aristotle were more indebted to him, and to the 'notional' way of thought, than they themselves realized.

THE KNOWLEDGE OF NATURE

physical as areas of human experience available for scrutiny, exploitation, and present pleasure.

In this regard no man is more revealing than Leonardo. His life was dedicated to inquiry and experiment, and nothing subject to empirical investigation was alien to him. His soulful injunction, 'O wretched mortals, open your eyes',[21] epitomizes his own quest for knowledge, a quest partially but wonderfully memorialized in those jottings now enshrined in the notebooks. Nothing – color, perspective, architecture, anatomy, politics, geology, astronomy, æsthetics – lay beyond his notice, and what he noticed he tried to account for in natural terms. 'But first I shall test by experiment before I proceed further, because my intention is to consult experience first and then with reasoning show why such experience is bound to operate in such a way.'[22] When God and religion do turn up – infrequently – in Leonardo's scribblings, they are perfunctorily dismissed as sacrosanct, supernatural, and therefore closed to critical scrutiny.

There were more systematic threats to tradition, however. About the same time that Calvin and Luther were challenging conventional epistemology in their effort to protect theology from the pollution of that discursive reason which inferred general, even religious, truth from sensory data, Copernicus was fracturing the realms of nature and spirit in another way. He was tentatively advancing a new concept of natural knowledge conceived and describable in mathematical terms – which is to say, he was anticipating that segregation of quality and quantity which has become a distinguishing feature of modern thought.

It is true that in his famous letter to Paul III Copernicus professed to bring the observable facts of astronomy into a more harmonious system for the greater glory of that supreme architect who is God.[23] But his method had momentous results: he used

---

[21] *The Literary Works*, art. 1182 (II, 245).
[22] *Ibid.*, art. 1148A (II, 239).
[23] Ptolemy's barbarous mumbo-jumbo was, in Copernicus' view, a blasphemous mockery of God's mechanical prowess. As he said in the *Commentariolus*, it was 'neither sufficiently absolute nor sufficiently pleasing to the mind' (*Three Copernican Treatises*, p. 57). Note the remark of Copernicus' pupil Rheticus (*ibid.*, p. 132) that recent observations 'and mathematical reasoning convince us that Ptolemy's hypotheses and those commonly accepted do not suffice to establish the perpetual and consistent connection and harmony of celestial phenomena and to formulate that harmony in tables and rules. It was therefore necessary for my teacher [i.e. Copernicus] to devise new hypotheses, by the assumption of which he might geometrically and arithmetically deduce with sound logic systems of motions like those which the ancients and Ptolemy, raised on high, once "perceived with the divine eye of the soul"'

the data of sensation, but he sought to systematize these data mathematically, and to solve problems presented by sensation in terms of certain mathematical principles or symbols derived from relationships existing in the mind *a priori*. This effort resulted in the ontological separation of reality and appearance, a separation best known in later philosophy by Locke's segregation of primary and secondary qualities. Copernicus inevitably faced the difficulties engendered by isolating these merely useful (and perhaps even true) mathematical principles from moral or theological presuppositions. Even though the assumption of a mobile earth in a heliocentric universe might seem absurd in the light of revealed truth, he contended, it at least 'saved the phenomena' by permitting certain celestial movements to be described more accurately than before. But his explanations did not assuage the angry suspicions of the church, for his hypothesis raised questions most offensive to the custodians of divine truth. Was the universe perhaps fundamentally mathematical in structure, rather than moral? Was the allegedly rational and logical relationship existing between things (as Aristotle and St Thomas had seemed to show) less basically 'true' than the mathematical relationships suggested by Plato? And, if so, do mathematical relationships imply any necessary morality? Indeed, are they even compatible with the kind of religious truth made compulsory for the salvation of fallen man?

Like most men of their age (notably Bruno), Copernicus and Kepler retained strong elements of anthropomorphism and allegory in a metaphysic that seemed to demand the rigorous elimination of moral causality and purpose. For example, both sang paens to the deific architecture of the heavens,[24] and Kepler even went so far as to identify the sun with God the Father, the sphere of the fixed stars with God the Son, and the etherial medium by which the heat of the sun impels the planets in their courses as God the Holy Ghost. 'Curvum autem rectissime Deo, rectum creaturae comparatur. In globo igitur est trinitas, sphaericum, centrum, capacitas. Sic in mundo quieto, Fixae, Sol, aura sive aethra intermedia: et in Trinitate Filius, Pater, Spiritus.'[25] This

[24] See *De revolutionibus*, I.10.
[25] Kepler, *Mysterium cosmographicum*, 'Prooemium' (*Opera*, I, 11). And again: 'Propositum est mihi, lector, hoc libello demonstrare, quod Creator Optimus Maximus, in creatione mundi hujus mobilis et dispositione coelorum ad illa quinque regularia corpora, inde a Phythagora et Platone ad nos usque celebratissima, respexerit, atque ad illorum naturam coelorum numerum, proportiones, et motuum rationem accomodaverit' (*ibid.*, 'Praefatio ad Lectorum' [*Opera*, I, 106]).

THE KNOWLEDGE OF NATURE

sort of thing suggests strongly the commonplaces of natural theology – the melancholy Jacques' talk of sermons in stones, Hamlet's of the majestical roof fretted with golden fire, John Swan's of the heavens as 'bedecking that vaulted roof with shining lights and beauteous starres: which like glittering saphires, or golden spangles, in a well wrought canopie, do show the admired work of the worlds brave palace'.[26] For such habits of thought Jeremy Taylor's remark is almost a cenotaph: 'he disparages the beauty of the sun, who enquires for a rule to know when the sun shines, or the light breaks forth from the chambers of the east'.[27]

The accelerating progress of natural science, no longer the handmaiden of its queen theology, could not for long be contained within Neo-Platonic and Neo-Pythagorean formulas. Kepler was fortunate in having at his disposal the uncommonly accurate experimental data of Tycho Brahe which, since they were only with forcing compatible with his early myth-making, led him to the formulation of his three 'laws'. These laws, in turn, showed his contemporaries how a brilliant hypothesis – for example, that of elliptical cycles of planetary motion – might be verified through empirical data. In spite of his persistent interest in astrology, these laws, as mathematical descriptions of certain natural processes, owe nothing to moral or religious presuppositions. The propositions that the orbit of a planet around the sun is an ellipse with the sun in one of the foci, that the vector from the sun to a planet describes equal areas in equal times, that the periodic times of any two planets' revolution squared are in the ratio of cubes of their mean distance from the sun, tell us a great deal about planetary motions, but nothing whatever about the Trinity or even about natural morality.[28] But, as Kepler said, one considers the weight of authority in theology, of reason in philosophy.[29]

As monuments of observation and mensuration, these laws were gravid with implications for that approach to the kind of truth thought to derive from a close and systematic scrutiny of

[26] *Speculum Mundi*, VII.i.
[27] *Sermons*, p. 11.
[28] On the three laws, see Dampier, *A History of Science*, p. 140; Dreyer, *History of the Planetary Systems*, pp. 382 f.
[29] See Campanella, *The Defense of Galileo*, p. xxvi. Note Cardan's distinction of three kinds of truth: reason for the sages, authority for the vulgar, and experience for those who really want to understand. 'Quae [i.e. experientia] tamen si recta sit apud omnes omnibus potior erit.' See Busson, *Les Sources et le développement du rationalisme*, p. 233, n. 1.

natural events: causality is seen to lie in the inherent mathematic harmony of the universe, a harmony that both describes the way things are and the reason they are that way; moreover, this harmony – the term itself is a Pythagorean relic – is most succinctly and inclusively stated in mathematical symbols expressing quantitative, not qualitative, relationships.[30] For in Kepler's view, quantity was the object of the faculty of cognition just as sound is of hearing and color of sight. Man's mind, he said, 'perceives any given thing more clearly in proportion as that thing is close to bare quantities as to its origin, and the further a thing recedes from quantities, the more darkness and error inheres in it'.[31] The disenchantment at the end of the Renaissance was poignant, as many varieties of skeptics show. Sense might be frail and prone to error; reason might convince us only of man's incorrigible tendency to hide his ignorance in untested and untestable systems. But to men of Kepler's persuasion – Galileo, Descartes, young Pascal, Hobbes, Newton, and many others – mathematics seemed to offer a certain path to knowledge. As Dilthey has said, they saw opening before them 'eine grenzenlose Zukunft', and their elation was contagious. Kepler himself, announcing his third law in a dedication to James VI of Scotland, speaks like Dante, who had seen the Godhead:

> It is now eighteen months since I got the first glimpse of light, three months since the dawn; a very few days since the unveiled sun, most admirable to gaze on, burst out upon me. . . . The die is cast – the book is written, to be read either now or by posterity, I care not which. It may well wait a century for a reader, as God has waited six thousand years for an interpreter of his works.[32]

The first great hero of the new science was Galileo. Bacon, like Moses, could only reach the borders of the promised land, promising that when induction should become the key to truth 'then at last we shall see the dawn of a solid hope'.[33] But Galileo went further: he both formulated a methodology of induction and also gave spectacular proof of its validity. As both a speculative thinker and a technologist he was the first truly representative man of modern science. Newton dazzled the eighteenth century like a

---

[30] See Burtt, *Metaphysical Foundations*, ch. i, *passim*.
[31] Quoted by Smith, *A History of Modern Culture*, I, 156.
[32] Quoted by Brewster, *Newton*, I, 234.
[33] *NO*, I.cvi (*Works*, VIII, 139).

meteor, but without Galileo's dynamics would Newton have published the *Principia* so soon?[34]

At every point Galileo's modernity stands out against Bacon's anachronisms. Where Bacon preached and orated, lingering in the shadow of scholasticism and using his induction to search out the forms of reality, Galileo experimented and observed. He, unlike Bacon, recognized the essentially mathematical basis of the new science hidden under Kepler's Neo-Pythagoreanism and he shaped his methodology toward the discovery and formulation of those mathematical relationships that to him constituted reality. 'Since many years', he wrote in 1597, he had been 'a follower of the Copernican theory',[35] and in his own original work on mechanics and dynamics he showed mathematics to be of supreme utility both in acquiring new knowledge and in describing his results. 'The force of rigid demonstrations such as occur only in mathematics', he has Salgredo say in the *Two New Sciences*, 'fills me with wonder and delight.'[36] The whole book, in fact, bursts with the optimism of wide-eyed discovery: 'the common opinion is here absolutely wrong'; 'a very clever and elegant demonstration'; 'a remarkable statement'; 'the demonstration is ingenious and the inferences drawn from it are remarkable'.[37] When even the stupid and reactionary Aristotelian Simplicio begins to acknowledge the power of mathematics in understanding the great book of nature the victory is won.

> *Salgredo*: What shall we say, Simplicio? Must we not confess that geometry is the most powerful of all instruments for sharpening the wit and training the mind to think correctly . . . ?
> *Simplicio*: Indeed I begin to understand that while logic is an excellent guide in discourse, it does not, as regards stimulation to discovery, compare with the power of sharp distinction which belongs to geometry.[38]

Like Kepler, Galileo viewed nature as orderly, deterministic, and mathematical; and, like most other scientists of his century, he seized on mathematics as the symbol for best understanding and describing the simplicity of nature. The book of nature, he

---

[34] It has been suggested by J. J. Fahie ('The Scientific Work of Galileo', *Studies in the History and Method of Science*, II, 278–80) that Newton's three laws of motion are all implicit in Galileo's conclusions: the first in his theory of uniform motion, the second in his theory of projectiles, the third in his theory of the inclined plane and in his definition of momentum. On Galileo's dynamics, see H. T. Pledge, *Science since 1500*, pp. 60–1.
[35] Quoted by Wolf, *A History of Science*, p. 29.
[36] *Dialogues Concerning Two New Sciences*, p. 276.
[37] *Ibid.*, pp. 2, 60, 72, 30.   [38] *Ibid.*, p. 137.

contended, 'is written in the mathematical language, and the symbols are triangles, circles, and other geometrical figures, without whose help it is impossible to comprehend a single word of it; without which one wanders in vain through a dark labyrinth'.[39] Galileo might observe and wonder about the oscillations of the lamps in the Pisan cathedral – unlike Bacon, he always began with observation – but he could not claim understanding until he had reduced the isochronism of the pendulum to mathematical statement.

Indeed, his reliance on mathematics determined both his methodology and his metaphysics. In place of Bacon's three tables of instances he employs mathematics at every stage of his induction. Having observed the phenomenon – the swinging lamps, the falling bodies – he begins with a hypothetical assumption mathematically derived from the mathematical relations pertaining to a given effect. Next he deduces the necessary properties derived from the assumption. Finally, these deduced properties are checked against the actually observed phenomenon.[40] It is in this use of hypotheses, subject to verification or alteration in the face of facts, that Galileo anticipated the most fruitful methodology of modern science.

Galileo's metaphysics (and he was not a metaphysician) are similarly mathematical. For him the universe is made up of bodies in motion, and therefore capable of mathematical statement, in space and time; consequently, whatever we know of things in nature we must learn through their motions. The motion of objects in space, if traced to a cause, will reveal a motion; if followed to an effect, it will reveal another motion. Philosophy then becomes the science of dynamics, the mathematical statement of the motion of bodies. Galileo, like his contemporaries, paid lip-service to God as the ultimate source of motion, but of all men he was the least interested in final causes. In nothing is the revolt against scholasticism better illustrated than in his disregard for the Aristotelian principle of causality. The venerable four causes (which even Bacon did not hesitate to invoke) and the long dominion of teleology faded before Galileo's principle of force as alone responsible for the movement of bodies in space.

[39] Quoted by Burtt, *Metaphysical Foundations*, p. 64. See P. P. Wiener, 'The Tradition behind Galileo's Methodology', *Osiris*, I (1930), 732–46, and Randall's article cited in n. 20 above.
[40] See Burtt, pp. 70 f.

THE KNOWLEDGE OF NATURE 317

Thus his concept of inertia – that a body maintains its state, either of rest or uniform motion in a straight line – makes Aristotle's principle of continued force absurd: the action of force is required not in motion, but only in a change of velocity or direction.[41]

Implicit in such doctrines as these lay the scientific, mechanistic threat to a Christian tradition of fifteen centuries. For its purposes, the Inquisition acted wisely in forcing Galileo to recant his heresies. If, as he said, 'there can be but one true and primary cause of the effects that are of the same kind',[42] then what seemed to the church the horror of a mechanistic cause and effect cosmology was at hand. The universe could no longer be viewed as the handiwork of an anthropomorphic God who noted the fall of the sparrow, who manipulated events at His pleasure, and who lay beyond contingency. Instead, it appeared to be the perfect machine of the deists and the agnostics where cause inevitably produced an ascertainable effect, and where mathematical formulas supplanted the Nicene Creed. Teleology and morality would presently become quaint words rather than religio-metaphysical principles; and 'reality' would reduce itself to bodies acting on bodies in accordance with the 'laws' of dynamics.

Though no one of the early seventeenth century would have dared put it in these terms, it is possible for us to infer from the scattered evidence that by the time of Kepler and Galileo a major change was occurring in European thought. The realm of nature, stripped of its theological opprobrium, was being conceived as an object for secular scrutiny and comprehension rather than a symbol of moral value; moreover, to expedite such scrutiny men were devising in mathematics a tool that, though worthless for purposes of morality or for all but the most desiccated natural theology, was proving to be a dazzling success in quantitative analysis. Whatever our deceiving senses or our wish-projections may tell us to the contrary, warned Descartes, there is only 'one matter in the whole universe', all of whose properties may be reduced to 'the one, viz. that it can be divided, or moved according to its parts, and consequently is capable of all these affections which we perceive can arise from the motion of its parts'.[42] We can measure extension and we can gauge motion, but anything

---

[41] See Dampier, 'From Aristotle to Galileo', *Background to Modern Science*, p. 37.
[42] *Principles*, II.xxiii (*Works*, I, 265).

beyond that bears no reference to certain knowledge. Similarly, Hobbes contrasts rational and geometrical knowledge – the one riddled with error resulting from 'want of method', the other so firm and safe that its conclusions are 'indisputable'.[43] Questions of law, morals, and justice are 'perpetually disputed' because when men's passions are involved their appeal is always to such frail criteria as 'reason' and 'custome'. 'Whereas the doctrine of Lines, and Figures, is not so; because men care not, in that subject what be truth, as a thing that crosses no mans ambition, profit, or lust.'[44] It was a dire omen for religion when a secular saint like Spinoza could soberly and systematically undertake to reduce God and nature, good and evil, to the demonstrations of geometry.

The slow acceptance of the Copernican hypothesis – surely the most dramatic example and symbol of the new knowledge of nature – is a well-known story. Copernicus himself was formally condemned twice by no less eminent a body than the Council of Cardinals; and at the very end of the sixteenth century Bruno, who seems to have understood the metaphysical implications of the Copernican hypothesis, died a fiery death to memorialize the collision between a theistic and a secular view of nature.[45] Du Bartas pronounced the conservatives' decree on such iconoclasts:

> You have mis-cast in your Arithmetike,
> Mis-laid your Counters, groapingly you seeke
> In nights black darkness for the sacred things
> Seal'd in the Casket of the King of Kings.[46]

Whatever his virtues, Du Bartas is not remembered for his originality, and his distrust of the new astronomy merely versified the commonplace. Years before, Luther had dismissed Copernicus ('a certain new astronomer') as one seeking notoriety rather than truth. Since the sun stood still for Joshua, said Luther (and how many times was the argument repeated), the Ptolemaic system was good enough for him.[47] Even Tycho Brahe rejected the Copernican hypothesis, at least in part for religious reasons;[48]

---

[43] *Leviathan*, ch. iv (p. 20).   [44] *Ibid.*, ch. xi (pp. 52–3).
[45] For the sordid details of Bruno's trial before the Venetian Inquisition, see Boulting, *Giordano Bruno*, pp. 267 ff.
[46] *Divine Weekes*, p. 15; cf. pp. 120–1; for Du Bartas' eulogy of Ptolemaic astronomy, see pp. 128, 133 f., 489 f. Sir John Davies' view in *Nosce Teipsum* (*Complete Poems*, I, 25) is comparable.
[47] See Smith, *The Age of the Reformation*, p. 621.
[48] See Wolf, *A History of Science*, p. 125.

THE KNOWLEDGE OF NATURE 319

and Donne who mocked it in his youth[49] lived to lament it in his age.[50]

None the less, the Copernican heresy, and the new view of nature which it symbolized, was slowly making its way against the most formidable opposition. A milestone in its progress was Galileo's great letter to the Duchess of Tuscany – a letter which, though ostensibly an effort to reconcile Scriptural and Copernican astronomy, is actually a notable declaration of independence for natural knowledge. Galileo is careful to make the customary disclaimers – 'I do neither intend, nor pretend to gain to my self any fruit from my writings, that is not Pious and Catholick'[51] – but his real purpose is to discountenance those zealots and obscurantists who, seeking to preserve tradition at any cost whatever to intellectual integrity, utter the most cynical slanders on the plain and mathematically demonstrable facts of natural knowledge. What this comes to, of course, is a defense of empirical fact against Scriptural revelation – a defense that restated, in slightly different terms, the separation of natural and religious truth.

The issue is fairly joined: since no proposition can be at once true and false, those addlepated literalists who run 'to the Scriptures for a Cloak to their inability to comprehend' should properly address themselves to demonstrating Copernicus' alleged lies rather than smothering truth with spurious authority.[52] It is not that the Bible lies, explains Galileo; it only seems to do so when imperfectly understood. When we remember that the Scripture, if taken literally, can be made to support heresy (by showing God with hands and feet, as being wrathful and forgetful, and ignorant of the future), we should realize that it must be interpreted. In His infinite mercy and wisdom God has 'accommodated' the difficulties of revelation to the 'Capacity of the Vulgar, who are very rude and unlearned'; to arrive at its 'true senses', however, we need 'grave and skilful expositors' to penetrate its crude fables and myths.[53] In terms of this theory of accommodation (which was destined to a fertile history in the seventeenth century)[54] we

[49] *Ignatius His Conclave* is typical of young Donne's breezy and sardonic skepticism.
[50] See *LXXX Sermons*, p. 823.
[51] Salusbury, *Mathematical Collections and Translations*, I, 432.
[52] Ibid., I, 455. In a marginal note Salusbury, the translator, remarks: 'If this passage seem harsh, the Reader must remember that I do but Translate.'
[53] Ibid., I, 432.
[54] For example, Edward Wright, in his 'Laudatory Address' prefixed to Gilbert's *Of the Loadstone*, had blandly pointed out that we are not to reject the theory of diurnal

should seek to understand 'Natural Problemes' through 'Sensible Experiments and Necessary Demonstrations' rather than through the muddy allegory of certain obscure passages in the Bible.

Both Scripture and nature proceed from the Divine Word, but with the significant difference that, while one is shaped to man's rude comprehension, the other is 'inexorable and immutable, and never passing the bounds of the Laws assigned her, as one that nothing careth whether her abstruse reasons and methods of operating be, or be not exposed to the Capacity of Men'. Whatever its uses for salvation – and all agree that it is indispensable – the Bible is but little concerned with astronomy. In that science, as in others like it, it were impious not to use the sense, discourse, and understanding granted us by a benevolent God. For as Cardinal Baronius has said, the intention of the Holy Ghost is to teach us how to get to heaven, 'not how Heaven goeth'.[55] We are enjoined to neglect no part of God's truth, and if the Copernican hypothesis were silenced by those who feared its theory of diurnal revolution, the suppression would be nothing less than 'an open contempt for a hundred Texts of the Holy Scriptures, which teach us, that the Glory, and the Greatnesse of Almighty God is admirably discerned in all his Works, and divinely read in the Open Book of Heaven'.[56]

As Campanella – who had known torture from the Inquisition for his Copernican heresies – said in defense of Galileo himself, the book of nature is vast and a 'tiny glimmer is all we know'. Since no philosopher or no theologian has yet advanced a wholly satisfactory hypothesis to account for the 'nature, order, situation, quantity, motion, and configuration of the heavens', it remains a religious duty to seek out the glory of God in His handiwork.[57] Those who deny that duty are bad Christians. They declare the words of God are superior to the testimony of nature, the book of God, and they torture the meaning of Scripture to fit their limited interpretations. The wisdom of God is exceeding vast and is not confined to the narrow wit of one man.[58]

Galileo's own prodigious gains in technology and methodology

motion from Scriptural evidence alone. 'It does not seem to have been the intention of Moses or the prophets to promulgate nice mathematical or physical distinctions: they rather adapt themselves to the understanding of the common people and to the current fashion of speech, as nurses do in dealing with babes; they do not attend to unessential minutiae' (p. xlii).

[55] Salusbury, I, 436.
[56] Ibid., I, 444.
[57] The Defense of Galileo, p. 30.
[58] Ibid., p. 21.

THE KNOWLEDGE OF NATURE 321

sent a wave of excitement over all Europe, and, though traditionalists like Burton and Milton suspended judgment, their less cautious contemporaries hailed it. Joseph Glanvill, ignoring the 'hoot of the Rabble', claimed for it the support of all 'great Wits'.[59] Among them must be numbered Christopher Wren, who warmly defended it in his installation lecture at Gresham College.[60] Of course, the Royal Society and its historian Thomas Sprat declared their allegiance; and when young Richard Bentley made the town ring with his Boyle Sermons (1692) he could blandly – and truthfully – say that 'we do now generally believe the Copernican system'.[61] As a man who could instruct a princess of the blood in Greek letters, Roger Ascham had contemptuously dismissed 'mathematicall heades' as 'solitarie' and 'unfit to live with others'.[62] Bentley, scarcely more than a century later and a far more eminent teacher of classic letters, could announce with italics that God *always acts geometrically*. It is not our task to trace the history of science between Copernicus and Newton, but even these scattered quotations will suggest its progress. By Bentley's day the event was clear: the mathematicians and experimental philosophers had at last succeeded in laying their impious hands on the ark of the covenant.

In this, as in so many other things, it was Descartes who spoke for his age, even for his posterity. His account of the impact that mathematics had upon his thinking and his imagination is one of the great passages of European philosophy. On that memorable night of November 10th, 1619, when he first fully realized that mathematics was a superb instrument of natural knowledge, his career, and the career of modern thought, gained a new impetus. Mathematical relationships acquired almost the sanctity of Platonic ideas.

> For example, when I imagine a triangle, although there be nowhere in the world be such a figure outside my thought, or ever have been, there is nevertheless in this figure a certain determinate nature, form, or essence, which is immutable and eternal, which I have not invented, and which in no wise depends on my mind, as appears from the fact that diverse properties of that triangle can be demonstrated, viz. that its three angles are equal to two right angles, that the greatest side is subtended by the greatest angle, and the like.[63]

[59] *The Vanity of Dogmatizing*, pp. 76–7.
[60] *Parentalia*, pp. 204 ff.
[62] *The Scholemaster*, p. 34.
[61] *Works*, III, 92.
[63] *Meditation V* (*Works*, I, 180).

The inference is clear: such relationships have a timeless and immutable validity in the very nature of things, and the human mind is equipped through mathematics to understand them. As Descartes wrote to Mersenne, the laws of mathematics, having been laid down by God, are eternal and compulsory; moreover, they lie open to man's scrutiny and comprehension, for they are as innate in his mind as they are fundamental to the outer universe which they inform.

> Or il n'y aucune en particulier que nous ne poissions comprendre se nostre esprit se porte a la consyderer, & elles sont toutes *mentibus nostris ingenitae*, ainsy qu'un Roy imprimeroit ses lois dans le coeur de tous ses sujects, s'il en avoit aussy bien le pouvoir.[64]

Man is able to penetrate beneath the blooming welter of sense and through the fables and lies of authoritarians to the reality which has hitherto been concealed. For the lesson of geometry is for all to read:

> Provided only that we abstain from receiving anything as true which is not so, and always retain the order which is necessary in order to deduce the one conclusion from the other, there can be nothing so remote that we cannot reach to it, nor so recondite that we cannot discover it.[65]

Whatever yields to measurement – 'numbers, figures, stars, sounds or any other object' – is the proper object of mathematical knowledge, which means that the whole realm of *res extensa* is available for man's comprehension.[66]

Descartes' conviction was endemic. To list only a few among numberless testimonials, John Webster (whose interests were generally antithetical to Descartes') spoke breathlessly of 'the superlative excellency' by which mathematical science transcends 'the most of all other Sciences, in their perspicuity, veritude and certitude, and also in their uses and manifold benefits';[67] Isaac Barrow cited in praise of geometrical knowledge its clearness of conceptions, easy definitions, obvious truth of axioms, clear derivation of postulates and hypotheses, order of demonstrations, and the like;[68] and Joseph Glanvill, though an Anglican clergyman, was certain that 'Geometry is so fundamentally useful a Science, that without it we cannot in any good degree understand the

---

[64] *Œuvres*, I, 145.
[65] *Discourse*, pt. II (*Works*, I, 92).
[66] *Rules*, no. IV (*Works*, I, 13).
[67] *Academiarum Examen*, p. 40.
[68] See Burtt, *Metaphysical Foundations*, pp. 146–7.

artifice of the Omniscient Architect in the composure of the great world, and our selves'.[69] As usual, Hobbes reduced his contemporaries' verbiage to the bluntness of art: pre-mathematical natural philosophy was rather a dream than a science. 'For Nature worketh by Motion; the Wayes, and Degrees whereof cannot be known, without the knowledge of the Proportions and Properties of Lines, and Figures.'[70] Is it any wonder that Spinoza should at last attempt to geometrize philosophy, and even to reduce the conditions of human bondage to axioms and postulates, treating 'human actions and appetites just as if I were considering lines, planes, or bodies'?[71]

III. THE BACONIAN LEGACY

Kepler and Galileo, then, bring us well into the seventeenth-century development of a metaphysic conceived and describable in terms of mathematics, a typically Continental metaphysic that, within a few decades, was to produce the great rationalistic systems of Descartes, Spinoza, and Leibnitz. English philosophy of the same period, however, was mainly empirical and utilitarian, and to understand its origins we must turn to Galileo's contemporary, Francis Bacon.

Like most men of his time, and in spite of his reputation as the prophet of the modern age, Bacon was a transitional figure between the medieval and the modern world. He himself would deny his allegiance to the past. He was the new John the Baptist, superbly scornful of the Aristotelianism that made philosophy and science subservient to logic; and therefore 'sophistical and inactive'.[72] He was even contemptuous of classical skepticism, really more pernicious than the fallacies of Plato and Aristotle because

> when the human mind has once despaired of finding truth, its interest in all things grows fainter; and the result is that men turn aside to pleasant disputations and discourses and roam as it were from object to object, rather than keep on a course of severe inquisition.[73]

---

[69] *Plus Ultra*, p. 25. For a notable statement of the same view, see Boyle, *Of the Usefulness of Mathematicks to Natural Philosophy*, Works, III, 156–66.
[70] *Leviathan*, ch. xlvi (p. 366).
[71] *Ethics*, bk. III, introduction (Wild, p. 206).
[72] *NO*, I.liv (*Works*, VIII, 86).
[73] *Ibid.*, I.lxvii (*Works*, VIII, 98).

In the metaphor of the four idols he dismissed all the previous achievements of the human race, and wiping the slate clean he urged men to reconstruct *ab ovo* their thinking and their knowledge. He exhorted and cajoled; he insisted that only man's 'despair' at finally attaining truth after so many centuries of error could delay the great instauration.[74] 'We must begin anew from the very foundations, unless we would revolve for ever in a circle with mean and contemptible progress.'[75] Like Columbus, we must strike out bravely, ignoring the fallacies of the past and confident of the glory that awaits.[76]

These are stirring words, but we must remember that for all his vaulting ambition Bacon was not the complete 'new man' whom he celebrated. For one thing, he failed to comprehend the significance of the Copernican revolution, or even of the experimental science which Leonardo had hailed with the intuition of genius. He thought the concept of the diurnal motion of the earth 'most false';[77] he had no patience with Harvey's anatomical experiments; he was astonishingly unsympathetic with mathematics – a tool which Cusanus and Leonardo had worshiped, and which Galileo and Newton were to employ in building their new world of materialism and positivism. A really fundamental inquiry of astronomical phenomena was still needed, he declared, for

> all the labour is spent in mathematical observations and demonstrations. Such demonstrations however only show how all these things may be ingeniously made out and disentangled, not how they may truly subsist in nature; and indicate the apparent motions only, and a system of machinery arbitrarily devised and arranged to produce them, – not the very causes and truth of things.[78]

This, from a contemporary of Kepler and Galileo, is astonishing; and in spite of Bacon's golden fame in England some of the best minds of the Continent could neither forgive nor forget.[79]

---

[74] *NO*, I.xcii (*Works*, VIII, 128).   [75] *Ibid.*, I.xxxi (*Works*, VIII, 74).
[76] *Ibid.*, I.xcii (*Works*, VIII, 129).
[77] *De augmentis*, III.iv (*Works*, VIII, 487–8).
[78] *Ibid.*, III.iv (*Works*, VIII, 488).
[79] As Huygens wrote to Boyle (*Œuvres Complètes*, X, 404), many of the 'new men' of the late Renaissance such as Telesio, Campanella, and Gilbert were less emancipated than they had thought: they retained from their Aristotelian legacy 'plusieurs qualitez occultes' because they lacked the mathematics 'pour faire un systeme entier'. Specifically, Bacon had recognized the weakness of the Aristotelians and had even adumbrated a promising methodology, but he was blocked by his ignorance of mathematics. 'Mais au reste il n'ententoit point les Mathematiques et manquoit de penetration pour les chose de physique.'

THE BACONIAN LEGACY 325

The remark about the 'very causes and truth of things' suggests the Baconian metaphysics of form – a metaphysics derived from that very scholasticism which Bacon boasted to have exorcised from European thought, and for which of all intellectual disciplines he professed the most contempt. Actually, as a metaphysical realist Bacon hypostatized a rationally comprehensible permanence beneath the fluctuations of sensory data which links him with the Schoolmen. This permanence he called form, and in denouncing, against all varieties of skeptics and obscurantists, the fallacy that forms 'are past finding out and beyond the reach of man',[80] he made the knowledge of forms the crown of his natural philosophy.

> For the Form of a nature is such, that given the Form the nature infallibly follows. Therefore it is always present when the nature is present, and universally implies it, and is constantly inherent in it.[81]

Bacon's conception of form is, though basic, very obscure. At times he speaks of form as the cause of things,[82] at others as the 'law' which determines their operations. 'For though in nature nothing really exists beside individual bodies, performing pure individual acts according to a fixed law, yet in philosophy this very law, and the investigation, discovery, and explanation of it, is the foundation of knowledge as well as of operation. And it is this law, with its clauses, that I mean when I speak of Forms; a name which I the rather adopt because it is grown into use and become familiar.'[83] But whether this function was normative or formative or both, Bacon regarded the knowledge of forms as the very seamark of human intellection; and his stirring call to trace out their reality behind the deceits and errors of appearances, though couched in philosophical terms, approaches the limits of art.

> Of a given nature to discover the form, or true specific difference, or nature-engendering nature, or source of emanation (for these are the terms which come nearest to a description of the thing), is the work and aim of Human Knowledge.[84]

[80] *NO*, I.lxxv (*Works*, VIII, 107).   [81] *Ibid.*, II.iv (*Works*, VIII, 170).
[82] *Ibid.*, II.i.   [83] *Ibid.*, II.ii (*Works*, VIII, 168).
[84] *Ibid.*, II.i (*Works*, VIII, 167). Bacon is careful to distinguish his concept of form from Plato's. His forms are 'upheld by matter' (*AL*, bk. II [*Works*, VI, 220]), but Plato lost 'the real fruit of his opinion, by considering of forms as absolutely abstracted from matter, and not confined and determined by matter; and so turning his opinion upon Theology, wherewith all his natural philosophy is infected' (*ibid.*, bk. II [*Works*, VI, 219-20]). In

Bacon was, as he thought, nothing if not practical. By making a distinction between natural science (the discovery of causes) and natural prudence (the production of effects) he reversed the typical Greek (and, *mutatis mutandis*, Christian) notion that the highest wisdom is contemplation. The Greeks had thought of nature as fixed and finite, but Bacon thought of it as plastic and malleable; and therefore he based his methodology on his metaphysics of forms. Under proper procedure, man may ascertain the forms of nature, and when he has done so he may manipulate nature to his own ends. Thus Bacon's cardinal principle, so antithetical to Socrates', that knowledge is power. The 'transformation of bodies', either simple or multiple, made possible for man through his knowledge of forms, 'opens broad roads to human power, such as (in the present state of things) human thought can scarcely comprehend or anticipate'.[85]

In developing his methodology for comprehending the forms of nature, then, Bacon was extremely careful, as he thought, to avoid the errors of his predecessors. A major impediment to learning was man's supine habit of relying on the constructs of his own mind rather than on the facts of nature available to his observation. Since extreme rationalism can lead only to the fabrication of systems, reason must be constantly checked and controlled by the senses. We must never forget the concrete fact, for even though the senses can lead to error, the hazard can be minimized by controlled experiment. Hence the acid warning against excessive and fruitless investigation in the 'first principles of things and the highest generalities of nature', for 'utility and the means of working result entirely from things intermediate'.[86] Therefore, utility and the means of working were always the objects of Bacon's methodology.

> Hence it is that men cease not from abstracting nature till they come to potential and uninformed matter, nor on the other hand from dissecting nature till they reach the atom; things which, even if true, can hardly do but little for the welfare of mankind.[87]

his apparent rejection of antiquity Bacon dismissed both Plato and Aristotle because both, as he thought, missed the significance of form: one 'made over the world to thoughts' and the other 'made over thoughts to words' (*Of the Principles and Origins of Nature, Works*, X, 352).
[85] *NO*, II.v (*Works*, VIII, 172).
[86] *Ibid.*, I.lxvi (*Works*, VIII, 97).
[87] *Ibid.*, I.lxvi (*Works*, VIII, 97).

Conversely, he warns against the bleak empiricism of simple enumeration, by which one merely records the data of sense; for through mere description man can never reach the non-sensible reality of forms. The pure rationalist is condemned because he ignores sensation and particulars, the pure empiricist because he never rises above them. By avoiding such extremes, Bacon seeks to combine the best features of each.

> I propose to establish progressive stages of certainty. The evidence of the sense, helped and guarded by a certain process of correction, I retain. But the mental operation which follows the act of sense I for the most part reject; and instead of it I open and lay out a new and certain path for the mind to proceed in, starting directly from the simple sensuous perception.[88]

What, then, was the methodology through which Bacon promised a glorious future for the human race? It was that by which one passed inductively from the analysis of sensation to the ultimate truth of form.

> There are and can be only two ways of searching into and discovering truth. The one flies from the senses and particulars to the most general axioms, and from these principles, the truth of which it takes for settled and immoveable, proceeds to judgment and to the discovery of middle axioms. And this way is now in fashion. The other derives axioms from the senses and particulars, rising by a gradual and unbroken ascent, so that it arrives at the most general axioms last of all. This is the true way, but as yet untried.[89]

'Simple sensuous perception' – the phrase not only suggests the empiricism at the center of Bacon's system, but also anticipates the dominant preoccupation of English philosophy for the next century. In his apparent revolt against the 'notional' and *a priori* rationalism of the Schoolmen Bacon conceived it his function to restore simple perception as the beginning of knowledge. Not that he was unaware of the immense opprobrium – both theological and epistemological – that generations of European thinkers had heaped upon mere sensory cognition. Man's sense is liable to a double indictment, as he admits. Either it gives no information or it gives false information. Moreover, since the 'testimony and information of the sense has reference always to man, not to the universe' – that is, since the data of sensation have no necessary correspondence with their objects out in nature – 'it is

[88] *Ibid.*, 'Preface' (*Works*, VIII, 60).
[89] *Ibid.*, I.xix (*Works*, VIII, 71).

a great error to assert that the sense is the measure of things'. None the less, the sense is man's most certain instrument of cognition, and no philosophy that ignores it can claim respect. What is needed, then, is not a skepticism that denies the possibility of human knowledge, nor a scholastic rationalism that flees sense to seek refuge in the untested constructs of the human mind, but a genuine reconstruction that by disciplining the vagaries of sense to the rigors of a sound method will lead to valid knowledge of at least a limited area of experience. 'I have sought on all sides diligently and faithfully to provide helps for the sense – substitutes to supply its failures, rectifications to correct its errors.' Controlled experiments are the keys to knowledge, and as he announces that cardinal fact Bacon's voice takes on a hierophantic tone:

> And thus I conceive that I perform the office of a true priest of the sense (from which all knowledge in nature must be sought, unless men mean to go mad) and a not unskilful interpreter of its oracles; and that while others only profess to uphold and cultivate the sense I do so in fact. Such then are the provisions I make for finding the genuine light of nature and kindling and bringing it to bear.[90]

In his famous metaphor Bacon construes the human mind as 'an enchanted glass, full of superstition and imposture, if it be not delivered and reduced'.[91] But he never doubted its deliverance, and his surging – sometimes offensive – confidence is the most distinctive feature of his efforts to reconstruct human knowledge.[92]

If, therefore, man would hope for truth so that he might control and not merely contemplate nature, he must rise above his errors and discipline his instrument of knowledge. Bacon never poses the question as sharply as one might wish, but in his intermittent critique of sensation and of the validity of what Locke was to call the secondary qualities of matter he suggests a fundamental difference between the scientific and the pre-scientific evaluation of man's estate. The implication is clear that what certain uncritical thinkers had erroneously considered knowledge was no more than the fallacious appearances that things had for them; or, as A. E. Taylor has said, that what they thought to be the properties of things must have been 'simply unreal, fabricated by the mind as an unauthorized comment on nature's text'.[93] Consequently,

[90] *Instauratio magna*, 'The Plan of the Work' (*Works*, VIII, 43–5).
[91] *AL*, bk. II (*Works*, VI, 276).
[92] See ch. iv, sect. v above.
[93] 'Francis Bacon', *Philosophical Studies*, p. 275.

man's vaunted preëminence, conferred upon him by his godlike reason, is an empty honor. His real dignity can be secured only by a true knowledge of things 'according to the measure of the universe', and that knowledge is possible only through a reconstructed epistemology.

Beginning with the equipment that he has, bad as it is, he must learn to pass from the particulars of sensation to that knowledge of forms which is power. 'The human senses and understanding, weak as they are, are not to be deprived of their authority, but to be supplied with helps.'[94] These helps are Bacon's rules for induction, which comprise the three stages of the *gradus ad Parnassum*.[95] First, we must 'prepare a Natural and Experimental History, sufficient and good; and this is the foundation of all'. This typically Baconian project – which fertilized so many other projects, notably that of the Royal Society – would, properly subsidized by the crown, eventuate in a universal history of natural phenomena. Proceeding by observation and experiment, it would regard nothing as alien to its purposes: cookery, chemistry, glassmaking, physiology, and all other processes, however vulgar and 'mechanic', would fall within its net; and through both its speculative and its operative phases – that is, both through its search for causes and its scrutiny of effects – it would make possible man's dominion of nature.

Next, because natural and experimental history is so various and diffuse, it must be 'ranged and presented to view in a suitable order. We must therefore form Tables and Arrangements of Instances, in such a method and order that the understanding may be able to deal with them'. But even with such preparation the human understanding is prone to err and 'unfit to form axioms, unless it be directed and guarded. Therefore in the third place we must use Induction, true and legitimate induction, which is the very key of interpretation'.[96] In such 'true' induction we rise, by a 'just scale of ascent, and by successive steps not inter-

---

[94] *NO*, I.lxvii (*Works*, VIII, 98); cf.I.xxxvii.
[95] *Ibid.*, II.x (*Works*, VIII, 178–9).
[96] There is, of course, such a thing as faulty induction. That which proceeds by simple enumeration is 'childish': 'its conclusions are precarious, and exposed to peril from a contradictory instance; and it generally decides on too small a number of facts, and on those only which are at hand. But the induction which is to be available for the discovery and demonstration of sciences and arts, must analyse nature by proper rejections and exclusions; and then, after sufficient number of negatives, come to a conclusion on the affirmative instances' (*ibid.*, I.cv [*Works*, VIII, 138–9]).

rupted or broken', from the less to the more abstract – 'from particulars to lesser axioms; and then to middle axioms one above the other; and last of all to the most general'. The lowest axioms are virtually indistinguishable from 'bare experience' while the highest are 'notional and abstract and without solidity'. Therefore we should rest in the middle, which are 'the true and solid and living axioms, on which depend the affairs and fortunes of men'.[97]

The end of induction is the knowledge of those forms which will enable man both to comprehend and control the processes of nature. The search of such forms must not be confused with the simple observation of nature. To inquire the forms of a lion, an oak, gold, water, air is 'vain'; but to inquire the forms of sense, voluntary motion, vegetation, color, gravity, levity, heat, cold, and similarly fundamental processes is to seek out the very alphabet of nature. These 'essences (upheld by matter)', as the objects of man's highest natural cognition, constitute that 'Metaphysic' which crown Bacon's reconstruction of knowledge.[98]

Bacon himself illustrates this cumbersome method by analyzing a proper investigation of heat.[99] He first collects a table of positive instances – all the occurrences of the phenomenon as noted in the rays of the sun, in meteors, in flame, in acids, and the like. Then he collects a table of negative instances, where the phenomenon is absent although other similar circumstances are present (as in the rays of the moon, the action of quicklime, and the like). Finally, he collects a table of degrees or comparisons, which records the grades and variations of the phenomenon. At last, then, on the basis of such tables, true induction is possible, for 'the first work . . . of true induction (as far as regards the discovery of Forms) is the rejection or exclusion of the several natures which are not found in some instance where the given nature is present, or are found in some instance where the given nature is absent, or are found to increase in some instance when the given nature decreases, or to decrease when the given nature increases'.

> Then indeed after the rejection and exclusion has been duly made, there will remain at the bottom, all light opinion vanishing into smoke, a Form affirmative, solid and true and well defined.[100]

The form affirmative of heat thus proves to be that most general

---

[97] *NO*, I.civ (*Works*, VIII, 137–8). [98] *AL*, bk. II (*Works*, VI, 220–1).
[99] *NO*, II.xi ff. [100] *Ibid.*, II.xvi (*Works*, VIII, 205).

axiom which is the object of Bacon's quest: 'Heat itself, its essence and quiddity, is Motion and nothing else.'[101]

It should be clear that Bacon's importance lies not in his achievements but in his aspirations. In spite of his rhetoric, his boasting, his sinuous character, he did have a vision of a new kind of knowledge. In an age still largely dominated by inherited patterns of thought and emotion, when most men still had good reason to fear the weight of traditional authority, he dared to propose a new conception of human dignity. Because he failed to realize that mathematics was indispensable for describing those natural processes which he sought to bring under man's dominion, and because he failed to realize the crucial role that hypothesis should occupy in any strategy of natural knowledge,[102] his methodology could really lead no further than the virtuosos of the Royal Society whom Butler and Shadwell caricatured. None the less, Bacon's fame is secure. His thought is a curious medley of anticipations and survivals, but for all his obligations to the past he strikes the genuine seventeenth-century note against a sickly *fin de siècle* despair of the late Renaissance. He reaffirmed, in a way to suit the coming age, the immemorial axiom of human dignity. In asserting that to know was to fulfil man's highest function Bacon carried on a central theme of European thought. That the great theme, which has supported so many variations, could also support his secularism and utilitarianism and empiricism offended and still offends many; but it explains why his figure looms so large in seventeenth-century thought, and why the gentlemen of the Royal Society admired, just this side of idolatry, King James's Lord Chancellor.

IV. NATURE AS MECHANISM

At one end of the seventeenth century Bacon said his intention was to provide 'helps for the sense'; at the other Spinoza assured Simon de Vries that mere observation of 'experience' could never 'teach us the essence of things'.[103] These two remarks, one by an empiricist (of sorts) and the other by an uncompromising rationalist, suggest one of the major revolutions in modern thought: the conviction that the world is not as it seems, and that

---
[101] *NO*, II.xx (*Works*, VIII, 211).
[102] Note the specific attack on 'Anticipations' in *Valerius Terminus*, *Works*, VI, 65–6.
[103] *Letters*, no. X (Wild, p. 409).

'truth' lies buried somewhere beneath the swarming, misunderstood presentations of sense. When Boileau remarked that Descartes had cut the throat of poetry he was acknowledging the success of this revolution, for in alienating *res cogitans* from *res extensa* – the realm of spirit, thought, value, purpose, morality, and aspiration from that of matter, motion, mechanism, and geometry – Descartes had influentially set his seal on one of the main developments of the new natural philosophy. It was that the colors, textures, sounds, smells, and tastes of 'simple sensuous perception' bear no necessary relation to those things out there in nature which seem to stimulate them, and that therefore mere sensation or mere phenomenology cannot give us truth.

It is all too easy, says Descartes wryly, to 'allow ourselves to fall into the error' of believing that what we perceive as color represents color in the object of perception, 'and then supposing that we have a clear perception of what we do not perceive at all'.[104] The result was that man with his vivid but unreliable impressions of things in nature – those impressions which St Thomas had contended were the very grounds of knowledge – was cut off from that reality conceived as mathematical relationships or as forms or as invisible particles of matter or as an unknowable substance. Thus, as Mr Willey has said, after Descartes it was generally thought that poetry could not deal with truth, but only with fictions and appearances. The warm and sensuous components of poetry were stripped of meaning. Dehumanized, secularized, and drained of its rich anthropomorphic content, nature came to be regarded, concluded Mr Whitehead, as 'soundless, scentless, colourless; merely the hurrying of material, endlessly, meaninglessly'. Montaigne's early recognition of this fact is one reason for the greatness of his *Apology for Raymond Sebond*:

> Our ideas are not due to direct contact with outside things, but are formed through the mediation of the Senses; and the senses do not take in the outside objects, but only their own impressions. So the idea and image we form is not that of the object, but only of the impression and the feeling

---

[104] *Principles*, I.lxx (*Works*, I, 249). In *Meditation III* Descartes dramatically presents the processes through which, by examining a piece of wax, he reached this conclusion. As we learn from *Meditation IV*, Descartes often reminds us of Augustine in more than his general epistemology of intuition. Not only does knowledge begin with *cogito ergo sum*, but error is conceived as *privatio boni* – not 'a real thing depending on God, but simply a defect'.

made by it on the senses; which impression and the object are different things. Wherefore whoever judges by appearances, judges by something other than the object.'[105]

As we have had occasion to see in the course of these studies, it was not always thus. St Thomas had no doubt that what Locke would call secondary qualities had objective existence which it was the function of sense to apprehend: sense, he said, 'has no false knowledge about its proper objects, except accidentally and rarely, and then because of an indisposition in the organ it does not receive the sensible form rightly'.[106] This perhaps naive conviction had underlain most varieties of Renaissance epistemology. Whether Thomistic, Neo-Platonic, Stoic, or other these epistemologies had generally and tacitly followed the Aristotelian assumption that there is a fixed relationship between substances and their qualities, and that the qualities available to sense are necessarily the ground of all higher forms of inferred or generalized 'truth'.

Thus in his frigidly Aristotelian *Rule of Reason* Thomas Wilson argued that it is sheer folly to try 'to reason of those thinges, whiche our senses judge to be true. As to knowe by reason, whether fire be hote, or no, the whiche were madnesse to aske, and surelie, if any one should so reason with me, I would bid him, putte his finger in it'.[107] As a good Ramean, Abraham Fraunce regarded the sense as a 'most upright judge of suche thinges as are properly under his jurisdiction, as the sight of colours, the hearing of soundes, the smelling of smelles'.[108] Gabriel Harvey called sense the basis of all knowledge: 'Experientia, anima animae, firmissima demonstratio, et irrefutabile kriterion.'[109] Sir John Davies, in a rather more systematic approach to the problems of epistemology, advanced the proposition that secondary qualities, inherent in objects, are the invulnerable data of cognition:

> The colour, taste, and touch, and sent, and sound;
> The quantitie, and shape of every thing
> Within th' Earth's center, or Heaven's circle found.

Our senses record not things but the 'forms of things',

> As when a seale in waxe impression makes,
> The print therein, but not it selfe it leaves.

[105] *Essays*, II, 49. [106] *ST*, I.xvii.3. [107] Folio 89r.
[108] *The Lawiers Logike*, sig. B4r. [109] *Marginalia*, p. 212.

In short, the senses are 'the windows' through which the soul views 'The light of knowledge, which is life's lodestar'.[110]

To mark the 'advance' in seventeenth-century thought against these very typical expressions of confidence in sensory cognition we may put Hobbes's blunt dictum: 'Whatsoever accidents or qualities our senses make us think there be in the world, they be not there, but are seeming and apparitions only: the things that really are in the world without us, are those motions by which these seemings are caused.'[111]

In general, the rationalists of the seventeenth century tried to penetrate the 'apparitions' of sense by intuiting the rationally conceived and mathematically described principles – Descartes' 'clear and distinct ideas' are typical – which determine the pattern of bodies in motion, and then through deduction explaining the processes of nature with only a supplementary use of observation. In demonstrating the kind of success possible with this methodology, as Mr Burtt has said, Kepler and Galileo had incidentally made possible the inference that man is 'an irrelevant spectator and insignificant effect of the great mathematical system which is the substance of reality'.[112] It is not that corporeal objects do not exist in nature, admits Descartes, for it is unthinkable that God should deceive us in our strong inclination to believe that they do exist. But we must not believe that we can know them other than through such properties as extension, length, breadth, and motion which yield to mathematical analysis. 'As to other things such as light, colours, sounds, scents, tastes, heat, cold and the other tactile qualities, they are thought by me with so much obscurity and confusion that I do not even know if they are true or false.'[113] Mathematics is our only path to knowledge, and only such things as are 'comprehended in the objects of pure mathematics, are truly to be recognised as external objects'.[114]

---

[110] *Nosce Teipsum, Complete Poems*, I, 64-5.
[111] *Treatise of Human Nature*, II.10 (*English Works*, IV, 8). See *Elements of Philosophy*, IV.xxv.2.
[112] Burtt, *Metaphysical Foundations*, p. 80. Note Descartes' opinion (*Principles*, III.iii [*Works*, I, 271]) that though it may be 'a pious thought, as far as Morals are concerned', to believe that God created all things for man's use and knowledge, yet 'such a supposition would be certainly ridiculous and inept in reference to questions of Physics, for we cannot doubt that an infinitude of things exist, or did exist, though now they have ceased to exist, which have never been beheld or comprehended by man and which have never been of any use to him'.
[113] *Meditation III* (*Works*, I, 164).
[114] *Meditation VI* (*Works*, I, 191).

Although this sort of uncompromising rationalism was never popular in England, Bacon taught his posterity to be deeply skeptical of mere sensory knowledge. Apart from Bacon, moreover, there was that very ancient Christian suspicion of the perishable body and its faculties. Just as we can know little of the soul that is incarcerated in the flesh, warns Jeremy Taylor, so we can know little of the external objects which deceive the senses. Although our eyes

> can behold a staff thrust into the waters of a troubled river, the very water makes a refraction, and the storm doubles the refraction, and the water of the eye doubles the species, and there is nothing right in the thing: the object is out of its just place, and the medium is troubled, and the organ is impotent.[115]

The history of seventeenth-century empiricism is a history of the suggested methods by which man may learn to discipline and rectify the processes of that enchanted glass which is his mind. Thus although Browne acknowledged the fallacies of sense, he contended that they might be transcended by passing from observation of things to a reasoning on the 'causes which determine their verities'. When we fail to seek general principles through experience, and rely on sense alone, we live and die in a species of error which is 'derogatory unto God, and the wisdom of the Creation'.[116] Even if he did not share Browne's Anglican bent toward rational and natural theology, John Webster was similarly convinced, like all good Baconians, of the dangers of undisciplined sensation. Reason is based on sense, since it 'doth but compound, divide, and compare the several species that are received by the senses, and make Deduction, and draw Conclusions from them'. None the less, man will wander in scholastic ignorance until some 'prevalent way' be discovered for rectifying the fallacies of sensation so that 'the fountain may be made cleer at the head, and rise of it'.[117]

However, most of those who advanced under Bacon's banners, whether Anglican virtuosos like Browne or Puritan utilitarians like Webster, were emotionally incapable of completing that conquest of nature which their master had announced. They were under commitments, theological or otherwise, that made a pro-

---

[115] *Sermons*, p. 495.
[116] *Pseudodoxia Epidemica*, I.iii.
[117] *Academiarum Examen*, pp. 101–2.

perly philosophical reconstruction of natural knowledge difficult if not impossible. The *Pseudodoxia Epidemica* and *The Saint's Guide* still survive as reasons for their failure.

Not so with Thomas Hobbes – 'of Malmesbury', as he was fond of styling himself. That curious and fear-racked man, who seems to have been born old and to have lived on forever as the Nestor of his age, at last faced squarely the issues which the hastening secularization of thought had made urgent. With an intellectual vigor unmatched in earlier English philosophy he brought out into open statement all those naturalistic movements of the late Renaissance which we have examined, and for better or worse he made it impossible for subsequent English thinkers to revert to the old evasions and the fragile compromises. If nature, as Hobbes said, is an inclusive mechanical system, then the human mind, with all its aspirations, wish-projections, self-deceits, and moral fantasies, must be regarded as a part of that system, subservient to those general laws of dynamics which Galileo had demonstrated and in no way a separate 'soul-substance' set above *res extensa*.

Refusing the gambit of Bacon's forms or of Descartes' dualism, Hobbes came forward as an uncompromising nominalist, and from the simple proposition that reality consists of nothing but bodies in motion he evolved a psychology and a political theory that make him loom, to borrow Baxter's words about Cromwell, as a monitory monument to posterity. Climaxing the nascent Renaissance naturalism in science and metaphysics, Hobbes systematically exploited the Machiavellian fracture of morality and political conduct. Though an execrable mathematician,[118] he accepted with delight the notion that nature is knowable as a mechanism measurable in mathematical terms, and thus he completed the abolition of moral purpose as a formative natural principle. He demonstrated once and for all – or so his terrified antagonists feared – that to know anything we must reduce it to its simplest parts and then seek out the efficient cause of their motions. The result, as Mr John Dewey has said, was that at last

---

[118] Hobbes' ineptness at mathematics was fabulous. He tried to square the circle, he challenged Boyle's theory of the vacuum, he acrimoniously contested the achievements of such of his betters as Wallis and Ward. Huygens' opinion (quoted by Louis I. Bredvold, 'Dryden, Hobbes, and the Royal Society', *MP*, XXV [1927–28], 425, n. 1) was not without justice: he said that in Hobbes he found 'rien de solide, mais seulement de pures visions'.

NATURE AS MECHANISM

politics and morality were loosened from divinity and made a branch of natural science. For philosophy, announced Hobbes with crushing finality, can properly concern itself only with

> the Knowledge acquired by Reasoning, from the Manner of the Generation of any thing, to the Properties: or from the Properties, to some possible Way of Generation of the same: to the end to bee able to produce, as far as matter, and humane force permit, such Effects, as humane life requireth.[119]

Although we have already glanced at Hobbes' political theory, we should remember that any system derived from a view of man's life in his natural state as solitary, poor, nasty, brutish, and short marked a startling innovation in seventeenth-century thought. Yet far more startling was the relentless logic with which Hobbes derived that view from a set of more or less current metaphysical assumptions. If he was absolutist in his politics, he was equally so in his materialism:

> The World, (I mean not the Earth onely, that denominates the Lovers of it Worldly men, but the Universe, that is, the whole masse of all things that are) is Corporeall, that is to say, Body; and hath the dimensions of Magnitude, namely, Length, Bredth, and Depth: also every part of Body, is likewise Body, and hath the like dimensions; and consequently every part of the Universe, is Body; and that which is not Body, is no part of the Universe.[120]

This materialism could yield only the most mechanistic psychology. As Descartes' thought led him toward such a view of human processes he drew back into that dualism which, even if it failed to explain satisfactorily any connection between *res extensa* and *res cogitans*,[121] at least reserved *res cogitans* as a special category exempt from mechanics.[122] Hobbes, however, did not scruple to reduce man to the all-inclusive category of matter in motion. The opening sentences of his introduction to the *Leviathan*

---

[119] *Leviathan*, ch. xlvi (p. 363).
[120] *Ibid.*, ch. xliv (p. 367).
[121] See *The Passions of the Soul*, I.xxxi, for Descartes' account of a 'certain very small gland' (the pituitary) that serves as the point of contact between man's soul and body. The metaphysical difficulties of Cartesian dualism resulted, of course, in the most extreme occasionalism, in which the principle of *concursus Dei* became virtually a metaphysical absolute.
[122] Descartes would go no further than to construe man's involuntary activities (that is, those not dependent on his absolutely free will) as following their courses 'just as the movements of a watch are produced simply by the strength of the springs and the form of the wheels' (*The Passions of the Soul*, I.xvi [*Works*, I, 340]).

are sufficiently clear: if nature is the art 'whereby God hath made and governes the World', then why may not man himself be regarded as a part of that nature? 'For seeing life is but a motion of Limbs, the beginning whereof is in some principall part within; why may we not say, that all *Automata* (Engines that move themselves by springs and wheeles as doth a watch) have an artificiall life? For what is the Heart, but a Spring; and the Nerves, but so many Strings; and the Joynts, but so many Wheeles, giving motion to the whole Body, such as was intended by the Artificer?'[123]

The psychology and the ethics derived from this mechanistic assumption show us how far Hobbes pushed forward the naturalistic view of man that made untenable the orthodox optimism based on the belief in reason and free will. As usual, the most trenchant statement of Hobbes's position is his own: because man is a body continually being acted upon by other bodies we must first of all realize that he can entertain no 'conception' in his mind 'which hath not at first, totally, or by parts, been begotten upon the organs of Sense'.

> The Cause of Sense, is the External Body, or Object, which presseth the organ proper to each Sense, either immediatly, as in the Tast and Touch; or mediately, as in Seeing, Hearing, and Smelling: which pressure, by the mediation of Nerves, and other strings, and membranes of the body, continued inwards to the Brain, and Heart, causeth there a resistance, or counter pressure, or endeavour of the Heart, to deliver it self: which endeavour because Outward, seemeth to be some matter without. And this seeming, or fancy, is that which men call Sense; and consisteth, as to the Eye, in a Light, or Colour figured; To the Eare, in a Sound; To the Nostrill, in an Odour: To the Tongue and Palat, in a Savour; And to the rest of the body, in Heat, Cold, Hardnesse, Softenesse, and such other qualities, as we discern by Feeling. All which qualities called Sensible, are in the object that causeth them, but so many several motions of the matter, by which it presseth our organs diversely. Neither in us that are pressed, are they any thing else, but divers motions; (for motion, produceth nothing but motion).[124]

It is not that such a psychology had no precedent – the Galenic faculty psychology made popular by Elyot and Bright and many others was, of course, basically mechanistic – but that Hobbes so unflinchingly pushes home its epistemological implications. Even though those 'qualities called Sensibles' are somehow in the object,

---

[123] 'The Introduction' (p. [1]).   [124] *Leviathan*, ch. i (p. 3).

NATURE AS MECHANISM

we can know them only as motions, not as objects: when we say we see a red horse we can mean only that 'the said image or colour is but an apparition unto us of the motion, agitation, or alteration, which the object worketh in the brain, or spirits, or some internal substance of the head'.[125] At the very base of his epistemology Hobbes puts a gulf between the real things in nature and the perceptions of those things. 'And though at some certain distance, the reale, and very object seem invested with the fancy it begets in us; Yet still the object is one thing, the image or fancy is another.'[126] The Aristotelian jargon of 'Philosophy-schooles' notwithstanding, we must not delude ourselves that an object of vision emits a 'visable species', of hearing an 'audible species', of understanding an 'intelligible species'. Such terms are merely verbal, and prime examples of that 'insignificant Speech' which is a major cause of error.[127]

The data of cognition, then, are merely 'fancies'. All that the mind can derive from the motions of sense are apparitions which, remembered, constitute our imagination – a faculty that 'is nothing but decaying sense; and is found in men, and many other living Creatures, as well sleeping, as waking'. 'Much memory' is experience; and as for 'Understanding', it is a species of 'Imagination that is raysed ... by words, or other voluntary signes; ... and is common to Man and Beast. For a dogge by custome will understand the call or the rating of his Master; and so will many other Beasts'. Man's understanding is special only in so far as it deals with his own 'conceptions and thoughts, by the sequel and contexture of the names of things into Affirmations, Negations, and other formes of Speech'. Mental discourse consists of a 'Trayne of Thoughts' (which may or may not be 'without Designe' or directed to some end), and reason – that faculty which sixteen centuries of Christian thinkers had agreed linked man to God – is the capacity for dealing with many thoughts in relation to one another. 'When a man Reasoneth, hee does nothing else but conceive a summe totall, from Addition of parcels; or conceive a Remainder, from Substraction of one summe from another.'[128] Error, in this arithmetical system, can mean nothing but wrong conclusions as a result of faulty additions or subtrac-

[125] *Human Nature*, II, 4 (*English Works*, IV, 4).
[126] *Leviathan*, ch. i (p. 4).
[127] Ibid., ch. i (p. 4).
[128] Ibid., ch. v (p. 18).

tions; and although such inaccuracies have many causes – 'want of Method', a loose use of language through improper definitions, semantic shifts, reliance on metaphor – it can be eliminated by an 'apt imposing of Names' and by a 'good and orderly Method'. Thus when reason is properly conducted it ends in science, 'the knowledge of Consequences, and dependance of one fact upon another'.[129]

In such an epistemology language is obviously of crucial importance. Through it we verbalize 'Mental Discourse', and when we err, it is usually because we misuse those counters which are the feeble surrogates of reality. Words may be either 'Markes, or Notes of remembrance' when they serve the 'Registering of the Consequences of our Thoughts', or 'Signes' when many use them 'to signifie (by their connexion and order,) one to another, what they conceive, or think of each matter; and also what they desire, feare, or have any other passion for'.[130] But since the only truth we have is the truth of our 'affirmations' – there being no necessary connection between a thing and what we call it – the abuse of language is the most fertile source of error.

> Seeing then, that truth consisteth in the right ordering of names in our affirmations, a man that seeketh precise truth, had need to remember what every name he uses stands for; and to place it accordingly; or else he will find himselfe entangled in words, as a bird in limetwiggs; the more he struggles, the more belimed. And therefore in Geometry, (which is the onely Science that it hath pleased God hitherto to bestow on mankind,) men begin at settling the significations of their words; which settling of significations, they call Definitions; and place them in the beginning of their reckoning.[131]

All of which enables us to conclude, if we grant Hobbes's premises, that if man cannot attain truth he can at least attain consistency in verbalizing his reactions to the motions of bodies.

> The Light of humane minds is Perspicuous Words, but by exact definitions first snuffed, and purged free from ambiguity; Reason is the pace; Encrease of Science, the way; and the Benefit of man-kind, the end. And on the contrary, Metaphors, and senseless and ambiguous words, are like *ignes fatui*; and reasoning upon them, is wandering amongst innumerable absurdities; and their end, contention, and sedition, or contempt.[132]

---

[129] *Leviathan*, ch. v (pp. 19–21). [130] *Ibid.*, ch. iv (p. 13).
[131] *Ibid.*, ch. iv (p. 15). [132] *Ibid.*, ch. v (p. 22).

A digression is perhaps justified at this point. Hobbes's concern with language and his general distrust of metaphor and rhetoric places him in that general seventeenth-century reaction to the verbal elegance of Renaissance humanism. In a famous series of articles the late Morris Croll explained the displacement of the Ciceronian by the Attic style – the *genus grande* by the *genus humile* – toward which Lipsius, Montaigne, and Bacon exerted such influence by the increasing popularity of plain language ('curt' or 'loose') as a vehicle of truth and mental activity rather than a device for manipulating sensuous rhythms. But there was more than anti-Ciceronianism at work. As we have seen, the movement of scientific thought and the development of the special language of mathematics for conveying scientific truth cast severe doubts on the validity of all merely verbal symbols, and particularly upon those employing the traditional aids of metaphor, rhetoric, and rhythm. John Webster's ferocious attack on scholastic logic and university training also involved an attack on sloppy writing, and the *Academiarum Examen* marks a milestone in the rejection of that Renaissance humanism which Bacon had already denounced because it led men to 'study words and not matter'.[133]

Bacon's distrust of poetry was a natural consequence of his empirical and utilitarian program for the advancement of learning. He had notoriously described poetry as the typical product of the imagination, and therefore epistemologically invalid because it is 'not tied to the laws of matter' and 'may at pleasure join that which nature hath severed, and sever that which nature hath joined, and so make unlawful matches and divorces of things'. It is, in his contemptuous phrase, 'Feigned History', and however great the solace of its deceits to 'magnanimity, morality, and to delectation', it can give us no truth about things in nature: 'it doth raise and erect the mind, by submitting the shews of things to the desires of the mind; whereas reason doth buckle and bow the mind unto the nature of things'.[134]

Not unnaturally, the Puritans, who for different reasons put a low value on the sensuous delights of poetry, developed a comparable obscurantism and utilitarianism. Since the aim of the Puritan sermon was instruction and its subject truth, preachers generally agreed that on grounds of neither morality nor utility could they indulge in mere literary elegance. 'If I had gone about

[133] *AL*, bk. I (*Works*, VI, 120).   [134] *Ibid.*, bk. II (*Works*, VI, 202-3).

to effect writing in a high strain,' explained Sibbes, 'I should have missed of my end, and crossed the argument in hand.'[135] Similarly, Baxter apologized for his youthful interest in the flowers of rhetoric, and defended that plain style where 'the apprehensions of present usefulness or necessity prevailed against all other motives'.[136] When one deals with truth one cannot dally with 'ornaments or accidents', but only 'naked evidence'.[137] When Fuller eulogized William Perkins as a preacher who had reduced scholastic jargon and abstruse theology to 'plain and wholesome meat for his people',[138] he was acknowledging the wide movement toward simplicity and utility which even men like Hooker and Taylor could not always resist.[139]

That Thomas Nashe had loftily derogated this kind of writing as the work of 'sectaries' who preach their bald, bare sermons 'in ditches, and other Conventicles, when they leape from the Coblers stal to their pulpits'[140] suggests the obvious fact that social forces also were at work in the emerging theory of plain style. Thomas Deloney, who was certainly a popular writer in both senses of the word, made it clear that his books were addressed to an unpretentious, almost unliterary, class of readers. He promises to treat of John Winchcomb 'in a plaine and humble manner, that it may be the better understood of these for whose sake I took pains to compile it, that is, for the well minded Clothiers'.[141] And those 'Courteous Readers' of *The Gentle Craft* are enjoined not to expect to find 'any matter of light value, curiously pen'd with pickt words, or choise phrases, but a quaint and plaine discourse best fitting matters of merriment, seeing we have herein no cause to talke of Courtiers or Scholars'.[142]

Although we can do no more than glance at these complicated developments here, we can perhaps understand the importance which Hobbes ascribed to language when we recall that in his

[135] *Works*, I, 41. [136] *Autobiography*, p. 102.
[137] *Ibid.*, p. 115. [138] *The Holy State*, II.10.
[139] Walton records (*Lives*, II, 82-3) that Hooker preached to his 'unlearned hearers' by using 'familiar examples' and 'convincing applications; never labouring by hard words, and then by heedless distinctions and sub-distinctions, to amuse his hearers, and get glory to himself; but glory only to God'. And Taylor, dedicating *The Worthy Communicant* to Princess Mary, promised that its style would be 'fit for closets, plain and useful' (*Works*, VIII, 4).
[140] *Pierce Pennilesse*, *Works*, I, 192.
[141] *Works*, p. [2].
[142] *Ibid.*, p. [140]. For an example of Deloney's realism – which was only sporadic, of course – note the remarks of the master's wife to Crispine on the fiscal hazards of raising a family (*The Gentle Craft*, *Works*, p. 103).

NATURE AS MECHANISM

day religious, social, and philosophical forces were all converging on the conviction that the semantic line between the word and the thing, always liable to deflection and error, must be rigorously disciplined. At its best the movement away from the baroque and florid rhetoric of Donne and Browne and Taylor led to the admirable 'loose' style of Dryden's prefaces and to Bunyan's incomparable effects in the splendor of simplicity.

> My sword I give to him that shall succeed me in my pilgrimage, and my courage and skill to him that can get it. My marks and scars I carry with me, to be a witness for me, that I have fought his battles who now will be my rewarder. When the day that he must go hence was come, many accompanied him to the river side, into which as he went he said, 'Death, where is thy sting?' And as he went down deeper, he said, 'Grave, where is thy victory?' So he passed over, and all the trumpets sounded for him on the other side.[143]

At its worst it led to the lifeless and dusty aridities of much Restoration pulpit oratory.[144] But we must remember that Sprat made a chastened style *de rigueur* for the gentlemen of the Royal Society, that John Wilkins's famous *Essay towards a Real Character and a Philosophic Language* (which appeared under the auspices of the Society in 1668) demanded an exact and orthographically fantastic correspondence between words and things, and that John Locke lent his great influence to the agitation for a language stripped of messy and poetical connotations. The function of wit, said Locke, is to make facile if specious correspondences, that of judgment to make scrupulous discriminations. 'This is a way of proceeding quite contrary to metaphor and allusion; wherein for the most part lies that entertainment and pleasantry of wit, which strikes so lively on the fancy, and therefore is so acceptable to all people, because its beauty appears at first sight, and there is required no labour of thought to examine what truth or reason there is in it.'[145] It is no wonder, then, that Locke gravely urged those unfortunate parents whose children had a taste for poetry to have it 'stifled and suppressed as much as may be'.[146]

But to return to Hobbes's epistemology, we must note his

---

[143] *The Pilgrim's Progress*, p. 375.
[144] For example, see John Wilkins' seventh sermon, on wisdom (*Sermons*, pp. 197 ff.) – the sort of discourse that prompted his editor and son-in-law, the great Tillotson, to commend his style as one of 'clearness and closeness and strength' (*ibid.*, sig. A2ᵛ). And, according to Congreve, Dryden claimed to have built his style on Tillotson's.
[145] *Essay*, II.xi.2 (Fraser, I, 203).
[146] *Some Thoughts Concerning Education*, sect. 174 (*Works*, IX, 167).

important distinction between those mental operations that result either in 'power cognitive, or conceptive' (consisting of sense, imagination, discussion, ratiocination, and knowledge) or in 'power motive'. The former – called 'animal' or 'voluntary' – gives motion to other bodies, the latter to the body wherein it exists, finding expression in 'affections and passions'. Both kinds of power have as their goal the acquisition and continuance of domination: this, to anticipate the eighteenth century, is man's ruling passion that 'ceaseth only in death'. Since conceptions and apparitions 'are nothing really, but motion in some internal substance of the head', they affect us either there or, by a curious deflection, in the heart. Once arrived at the heart the conception either helps or hinders its 'vital motion' or respiration, pulse, digestion; and thus arises passion. If the 'apparitions' of the outer world help man's vital motion the result is pleasure, 'which is nothing really but motion of the heart, as conception is nothing but motion in the head'. When they hinder vital motion, the result is pain. All conduct, therefore, reduces itself to our reaction to externals, and such reaction must be a variety of either appetite or aversion.[147]

Just as this physiology is linked to its psychology, so it in turn leads to its ethics. Pleasure and pain are physiological facts which result in action, for appetite and aversion are the grounds of good and evil ('Nor is there any such thing as absolute goodness, considered without relation'). Since appetite demands satisfaction, *bonum* and *finis* are different names for the same thing. As for felicity – the 'utmost end' – 'there is no such thing in this world, nor way to it, more than to Utopia: for while we live, we have desires, and desire presupposeth a further end'.[148] The master keys of appetite and aversion permit Hobbes 'to search out and declare' from what conceptions proceed the passions. The catalogue is justly famous. Glory comes from the conception of 'our own power above the power of him that contendeth with us'; humility results from 'the apprehension of our own infirmity, dejection and poorness'; anger is 'nothing but the appetite or desire of overcoming present opposition'; and laughter is 'sudden glory arising from some sudden conception of some eminency in ourselves, by comparison with the infirmity of others, or with

---

[147] *Human Nature*, VI.9 (*English Works*, IV, 30).
[148] *Ibid.*, VII.5 (*English Works*, IV, 33).

our own formerly'. And so the list proceeds: shame, courage, hope, pity, envy, and all the rest stalk by like figures in a pageant. The sum of Hobbes's wisdom as a moralist – a term he would angrily reject – is contained in his final analogy: life is a race which has 'no other goal; nor other garland, but being foremost'. To turn back is repentance, to be weary is despair, to 'hold fast by another' is love, 'continually to be out-gone' is misery, 'continually to out-go the next before' is felicity, and to forsake the course is to die.[149]

Such a synoptic treatment of one of the most powerful intellects of European thought cannot do justice, but it can perhaps help us to understand the peculiar force of Hobbes's impact on his contemporaries. More drastically than any other man of his age he who opened his career with a translation of Thucydides and closed it with one of Homer cut his links with the past. Taking his stand on those naturalistic assumptions which had run through the late Renaissance only in a furtive and subterranean fashion, he painted a portrait of the natural man that his more timid fellows regarded as a sight to dream of, not to tell. At almost every point he contravened the cherished Christian and humanistic values of two millennia. Even though his bleak pronouncement that the life of man is 'a perpetual and restless desire of power after power that ceaseth only in death' constituted the secular version of Calvin's theological voluntarism, his insistence that problems of ethics and morality cannot, like mathematical problems, be treated rationally because they engage man's fiercest passions did violence to the cardinal principle of Christian humanism: the conviction that the *summum bonum* is a life of piety and reason attainable through education and self-discipline. As a nominalist he of course refused to concede the possibility of moral absolutes, and in the wonderfully ironic fourth book of the *Leviathan* he barely concealed beneath his attack on the Catholic church his inveterate hatred of all forms of supernaturalism.

> And in these foure things, Opinion of Ghosts, Ignorance of second causes, Devotion towards what men fear, and Taking of things Casuall for Prognostiques, consisteth the Naturall seed of Religion; which by reason of the different Fancies, Judgements, and Passions of severall men, hath grown up into ceremonies so different, that those which are used by one man, are for the most part ridiculous to another.[150]

[149] Ibid., VIII.1–IX.21 (*English Works*, IV, 34–53).
[150] *Leviathan*, ch. xii (p. 56).

If everything is corporeal, the soul, too, is corporeal, a body acted upon by the motions of other bodies and therefore determined; for though man, motivated by appetite and aversion, seems to have the power of choice, the power is illusory because the choice is merely the 'last appetite' of will; and because the will cannot originate its choices it is not free.

> As in the water, that hath not only liberty, but a necessity of descending by the Channel; so likewise in the Actions which men voluntarily doe: which, because they proceed from their will, proceed from liberty; and yet, because every act of mans will, and every desire, and inclination proceedeth from some cause, and that from another cause, in a continuall chaine, (whose first link is in the hand of God the first of all causes,) they proceed from necessity.[151]

The vehement and tediously articulate antagonism which such heresy stimulated in Bramhall, More, Cudworth, and many others symbolizes the ferocity of the reaction to Hobbes. Descartes, more moderately than most, perhaps isolated the basic cause of that reaction when he remarked that Hobbes's principles are 'tres-mauuaises & tres-dangereuses, en ce qu'il suppose tous les hommes méchans, ou qu'il donne suiet de l'estre'.[152] And yet, paradoxically, Hobbes's main concern was probably to achieve a rationale of human conduct conceived, as he thought, in terms that would not affront the modern intelligence. Although he insisted on a naturalistic analysis of human nature, based on the coldest of materialism, his absorbing interest was not man in the purity and isolation of a clinical specimen but man in society, and in the fiercely competitive environment of his fellows. Everywhere in the opening chapters of his masterpiece we hear those tones of unquiet anticipation of the *de cive* part of the discussion: his metaphysics, his psychology, and his ethics are the anchors of his political theory; and politics, or sociological complications, interest him chiefly. Though the method is naturalistic, the tone is social. Hobbes importantly anticipates the eighteenth century in his concern with man as a creature among his fellows rather than as a lonely soul beset by sin and saved by grace in a lonely cosmos inhabited only by him and his God. Though his view of man is, in Christian terms, intolerably pessimistic, he does arrive at a program by which passion and error may be disciplined to the uses of society. Because he refused to consider man

[151] *Ibid.*, ch. xxi (p. 111). [152] *Œuvres*, IV, 67.

in other than natural terms he was able to achieve a form of secular morality; and both his naturalism and secularism make him one of the founding fathers of modern thought.

V. THE RESTORATION DILEMMA

It is perhaps fair to say that none of Hobbes's detractors were worthy of their antagonist. Certainly none of them successfully faced the problems that they had to answer if they were to evade his nominalism and mechanism. If that generation of experimental philosophers who established and carried forward the Royal Society may be cited as typical, then it is clear that none of Hobbes's English contemporaries offered a genuine alternative to his system. For the most part they were good Baconians committed to the compilation of that natural history which their master had declared to be the first step toward the reconstruction of knowledge. Some of them, of course, were more, and a few of them – notably Boyle and Newton – were actually men of science; but the philosophers like More and Glanvill maintained propositions, such as the existence of witches and demons, that protected religious orthodoxy only at the most dreadful cost to the consistency of their secular views; and the scientists like Boyle and Newton either slid easily into a trite natural theology or, refusing even to attempt an integration of natural and religious truth, sought a sanction for their refusal in that positivism which itself was made possible by the rejection of authority.

This positivism was one of the most notable developments of Restoration thought. When Samuel Parker exhorted the Royal Society to proceed speedily with its natural history, he took care to point out that the forming of hypotheses 'must be the work of future Ages'. The immediate utility of experiments is obvious, 'yet their Application to any Hypotheses is doubtful and uncertain'. The great work of the century, he contended, was to compile 'true and exact Histories of Nature for use and practice'; but if men went further to attempt hypotheses it should be only for 'delight and Ornament'.[153] Since the validity of hypothesis depended on epistemology, the distrust of hypothesis marked an epistemological uncertainty that Newton, at least, never surmounted.

[153] *A Free and Impartial Censure of the Platonick Philosophie*, pp. 45-6.

In publishing his astonishing work on the microscope – by which a whole new world was opened to the experimental philosophers – Robert Hooke refused to go beyond the mere recording of details; in his fear of 'notional' and unfounded explanations of natural phenomena he explicitly denied any desire to 'bind' his reader's 'understanding to an implicit consent'.[154] Such caution would seem to suggest genuine positivism, even skepticism, yet Hooke's brief excursion into epistemology, in the preface of his *Micrographia*, exhibits a surprising naiveté. He readily points out the dangers of sensory cognition in the 'disproportion of the Object to the Organ' and the 'error in the Perception'; and he proceeds to a conventional attack on the 'rational' truths abstracted from sensation. But his remedy, like Bacon's, is to strengthen the senses – a remedy that 'can only proceed from the real, the mechanical, the experimental Philosophy'. This circular argument is anything but acute, yet the Restoration rarely advanced beyond it. Although the senses are admittedly prone to err, if we expect to attain truth we must use experiment and devise instruments (such as 'Optical Glasses') to learn the ways of nature. If only 'reason' is scrupulously based on observation, so 'that there remain no room for doubt or instability', then all will be well:

> If once this method were followed with diligence and attention, there is nothing that lyes within the power of human Wit (or which is far more effectual) of human Industry, which we might not compass.[155]

Although Hooke insists that 'the Science of Nature' has been too much regarded as 'only a work of the Brain and the Fancy', and although he prescribes a 'return to the plainness and soundness of Observations on material and obvious things',[156] he ignores the possibility that if vision errs when a man looks at a distant steeple it might also err when he looks at a hair under a microscope, or at the sun through a telescope.

Joseph Glanvill expresses the same unconscious confusion more urbanely. The opening chapters of *The Vanity of Dogmatizing* (which are vastly indebted to Descartes' *Mediations*) are a witty survey of man's capacity for error. 'The tumultuary disorders of our passions', the fallacies of our prejudicial education, the in-

---

[154] *Micrographia*, sig. b1r.
[155] *Ibid.*, sig. a1v–b2r.   [156] *Ibid.*, sig. b1r.

THE RESTORATION DILEMMA 349

tolerable presumption of scholastic self-deceit, should all teach us that we can know nothing with certainty. The most rudimentary questions about man – how his soul can animate his body – is so baffling that 'to hang weights on the wings of the winde seems far more intelligible'.[157] Even our cognitive faculties are incorrigibly corrupt. We can never be sure that our sensory reports of external objects bear any real relation to those objects. When the ear tingles we really hear a sound, but if we infer that the sound actually exists in nature then 'it's the fallacy of our Judgments. The apparitions of our frighted Phancies are real sensibles: But if we translate them without the compass of our Brains, and apprehend them as external objects; it's the unwary rashness of our Understanding deludes us'.[158] Obviously, then, the first step to philosophy and 'grounded Science' is to destroy 'the confidence of Assertions, and to establish a prudent reservedness and modesty in Opinions'.[159]

And yet genuine skepticism is not the conclusion of this very skeptical attitude. In Glanvill's view, imagination is the villain of the faculties,[160] and knowledge is possible if we discipline that rebel to good sense. Glanvill lays it down as axiomatic that our 'Faculties are true, viz. That what our understandings declare of things clearly and distinctly perceiv'd by us, is truly so, and agreeing with the realities of things themselves. This is a Principle that we believe firmly; but cannot prove, for all proof, and reasoning supposeth it'.[161] If such a solution seems too easy we must recall that some such rationalization was absolutely necessary for the very existence of that experimental philosophy to which Glanvill was committed. If knowledge hangs on experiment, and experiment on sensory cognition, then sensory cognition must be valid, no matter what the skeptics say.

> But when the Senses are exercised about their right Objects, and have the other Circumstances that are requisite, we then assent without doubting. And this fullness of assent is all the certainty we have, or can pretend to; for after all, 'tis possible our Senses may be so contriv'd, that things may not appear to us as they are: But we fear not this, and the bare possibility doth not move us.[162]

[157] p. 20. [158] p. 93.
[159] 'Against Confidence in Philosophy', *Essays*, p. 1.
[160] Note the elaborate analysis of imagination in *The Vanity of Dogmatizing*, pp. 96–8.
[161] 'Of Scepticism and Certainty', *Essays*, p. 48.
[162] *Ibid.*, p. 49.

Not only did such evasions serve Glanvill and Sprat;[163] even real scientists did not scruple to use them. Both Boyle and Newton, the proudest exhibits of the experimental philosophy in England, were intensely religious men and one of them at least an authentic scientific genius; yet neither could resolve the epistemological problems of that philosophy. In spite of Boyle's prolix and full-breathed, or Newton's more cryptic and parenthetical, efforts to reconcile natural and supernatural truth, neither could rejoin those two realms which Descartes had declared to be separate, and one of which Hobbes had seemed to demolish. Their best efforts could merely hasten the advent of deism, not produce that alleged fusion of religious and secular knowledge which was crumbling away.

Their failure was certainly not for want of trying. The sheer bulk of Boyle's work, embalmed in the five stately folios assembled by Thomas Birch, is appalling. And yet, apart from his strictly scientific papers, how little it all comes to. The old, old arguments are gravely refurbished and brought forth; the old, old disclaimers for merely natural knowledge are marshaled against the mechanists; and it is an open question whether there is one original idea in morals or religion in all those thousands of pages.

> That the consideration of the vastness, beauty, and regular motions, of the heavenly bodies; the excellent structure of animals and plants; besides a multitude of other phaenomena of nature, and the subserviency of most of these to man; may justly induce him, as a rational creature, to conclude, that this vast, beautiful, orderly, and (in a word) many ways admirable system of things, that we call the world, was framed by an author supremely powerful, wise, and good can scarce be denied by an intelligent and unprejudiced observer.[164]

Mere mechanism and materialism is a heinous affront to God, but experimental philosophy – as Bacon had long before said – excites and cherishes our devotion while it instructs our understanding and gratifies our curiosity. For through its discipline we

---

[163] And for others, too. For example, Richard Baxter defends the validity of sensory cognition (*Christian Directory*, I.xiii.10) on the grounds that God would not conceivably deceive us in so fundamental a way. See *The Catechizing of Families*, ch. ii (*Works*, XIX, 13): if our senses are unreliable, then 'God is our deceiver, and we are remediless'.

[164] *The Christian Virtuoso*, *Works*, V, 42. The affinity between this ancient attitude and outright deism is sufficiently clear. For example, Boyle himself argues (*Of the Usefulness of Natural Philosophy*, I.iv [*Works*, I, 446]) that since God arranged His creation 'into an innumerable multitude of very variously figured corpuscles' whose structures and processes He sustains by His 'ordinary preserving concourse', His role was not unlike the maker's of the great clock at Strasbourg.

THE RESTORATION DILEMMA 351

learn that to know God only in His works is to know Him from afar, so that we are forced to acknowledge the desperate limitations of our natural faculties, and thus lie prostrated before those mysteries – natural as well as theological – which teach us humility. Because His power and His wisdom are the most awful of God's attributes, 'how unfit must such imperfect creatures, as we are, to talk hastily and confidently of God, as an object, that our contracted understandings grasp, as they are able (or pretend to be so) to do other objects!' Both through our sinful natures and our feeble natural faculties we are 'infinitely beneath' Him; therefore it is clear

> how unable, as well as unworthy, we are to penetrate the recesses of that inscrutable, as well as adorable nature; and how much better it would become us, when we speak of objects so much above us, to imitate the just humility of that inspired poet, that said Such knowledge is too wonderful for me; it is high, I cannot attain unto it.[165]

Such conventional and traditional piety is probably the germ of Boyle's secular positivism. As a Christian he had to believe what he could not understand; as a scientist he had to acknowledge the narrow reach of natural knowledge; and so, paradoxically, he argued the case for experimental philosophy while admitting its radical inadequacies. The 'most towering and subtle of speculators, metaphysicians, and mathematicians' must all confess that they are baffled by 'unconquerable difficulties'. They are sharply checked by those 'priviledged things' which demonstrate even to 'this inquisitive age we live in' that the really fundamental questions of metaphysics and epistemology, to say nothing of 'that infinite and most monadical being (if I may so speak) that we call God' are hopelessly beyond our comprehension.[166] Thus, having forced our natural faculties to their limits, we must conclude that the body-soul relationship is 'a thing so unexampled in nature, and so difficult to comprehend, that I somewhat question, whether the profound secrets of theology, not to say the adorable mystery itself of the incarnation, be more abstruse

---

[165] *Of the High Veneration Man's Intellect owes to God, Works,* V, 156–7.
[166] *A Discourse of things above Reason, Works,* IV, 42–3. Thus Boyle thinks it 'probable' that God seldom disrupts the 'merely corporeal' part of the universe or 'the most catholic laws of motion'; but miracles are not impossible, and it is quite likely that He – 'perhaps oftener than mere philosophers imagine' – works directly through psychological and physiological channels to guide the affairs of men. See *A Free Inquiry into the received Notion of Nature,* sect. VI (*Works,* IV, 398).

than this'.¹⁶⁷ Boyle refuses even to speculate on the true nature of sound or color, or on the other elements of sensation which would seem to be man's only media of contact with the outer world. A secondary quality is what it is – whatever it is – because it pleased God to have it so. It is man's duty to learn what he can about God's creation, of course, for thus he deepens his sense of inadequacy. 'For admiration (I do not say astonishment or surprize) being an acknowledgment of the objects transcending our knowledge, the learneder the transcendent faculty is, the greater is the admired object's transcendency acknowledged.' Truly, a little learning is a dangerous thing. The 'vulgar astonishment of an unlettered starer' is as nothing compared to that 'prostrate veneration' which is the last and finest reward of 'industrious curiosity'.¹⁶⁸

And so, ironically, a notable advocate of experimental philosophy is inexorably forced to celebrate that 'broken knowledge' which Bacon had declared incompatible with and subversive to natural knowledge. Boyle was better equipped than such popularizers as Glanvill and Sprat to argue the claims of the new philosophy, but because he knew more than they he was less cocksure. Their facile claims for the compatibility of natural and religious truth were after all inadequate; and the man who wrote *The Christian Virtuoso* also wrote *A Discourse of Things above Reason* – an anguished, penetrating statement of that dilemma which perhaps only evasions could resolve. To preserve the sovereignty and mystery of God is a challenge to the naturalist, as Boyle admits; and yet it is 'a sad thing' when men 'grudge to spend now and then a few hours in the contemplation and internal worship of that most glorious and perfect being, that continually employs the devotion of Angels themselves'.¹⁶⁹

This is essentially the view held by Newton. As a scientist he enlisted the aid of God to prevent the fixed stars from collapsing and crashing together in space, but he also posited Him as the 'Author' of the whole majestic structure whose laws, if not whose basic substance, are the object of human intellection. Newton's

---

¹⁶⁷ *Of the Excellency of Theology*, sect. III (*Works*, III, 433). See *Occasional Reflections*, sect. IV (*Works*, II, 190); *Of the Usefulness of Natural Philosophy*, I.v (*Works*, I, 460).
¹⁶⁸ *Of the Usefulness of Natural Philosophy*, I.v (*Works*, I, 462).
¹⁶⁹ *Of the High Veneration Man's Intellect owes to God*, *Works*, IV, 354. Boyle was widely regarded – for example, by Stillingfleet, Peter du Moulin, and Cudworth – as the champion of theism against Hobbes. See Louis I. Bredvold, *The Intellectual Milieu of John Dryden*, p. 58, n. 30.

positivism is gravid with implications for modern science: unlike Galileo or Descartes he made no use of *a priori* ideas, mathematical or other; the most he would say is that a mathematical procedure is useful for certain kinds of investigation, even though we dare not claim for it universal validity in explaining all phenomena. He regarded man's soul, or mind, as confined in his body with no immediate contact with the world outside. It is located within that *sensorium* which receives 'motions' from externals and then relays such motions to the muscles by means of the animal spirits. But we are not to confuse these motions with reality: 'In bodies, we see only their figures and colors, we hear only the sounds, we touch only their outward surfaces, we smell only the smells, and taste the savors; but their inward substances are not to be known either by our senses, or by any reflex act of our minds.'[170] Being an experimental philosopher he rejected hypotheses as inadmissible, like everything not immediately derived from experiment. Writing to young Bentley, who was delivering the Boyle Sermons, Newton carefully disengaged himself from Bentley's unwarranted assumptions. 'You sometimes speak of gravity as essential and inherent in matter,' he tells him. 'Pray, do not ascribe that notion to me; for the cause of gravity is what I do not pretend to know, and therefore would take more time to consider of it.'[171]

For Newton science was nothing more or less than a body of mathematically formulated laws describing the behavior of things in nature, and such laws can be predicated solely on experimental data.[172] He insists that only 'the ideas and will of a Being necessarily existing' can account for the 'diversity' and intricately adjusted relationships of 'natural things',[173] but beyond that he refuses to go. In reply to some theological questions of Thomas Burnet he remarked characteristically:

> You ask what was that light created the first day? Of what extent was the Mosaical chaos? Was ye firmament, if taken for ye atmosphere so considerable a thing as to take up one day's work?... To answer these things fully, would require comment upon Moses whom I dare not pretend to understand: Yet to say something by way of conjecture, one may suppose that all ye planets about o[u]r sun were created together.[174]

[170] *Principia*, 'General Scolium' (p. 546).
[171] Bentley, *Works*, III, 210.
[172] See Burtt, *Metaphysical Foundations*, pp. 221–3.
[173] *Principia*, 'General Scolium' (p. 546). [174] Brewster, *Newton*, II, 360.

Newton's theological interests were, to say the least, quaint. His favorite study was the Book of Daniel and Revelation, whose allegorical possibilities fascinated him endlessly. The man who wrote the *Principia* also wrote widely on theology; but he refused to employ the instruments of natural knowledge on the arcana of revealed truth, and most of us would probably agree with Coleridge's blunt opinion that his religious 'lucubrations' seem 'little less than mere raving'.[175]

VI. MECHANISM VS. EXPERIMENT

For reasons which should now be sufficiently clear Hobbes is the watershed of seventeenth-century English thought. He did what Montaigne had tried to do in a less orderly way: he stripped man, not to his shirt, but completely naked, and thus posed the most formidable threat of his century to those values, true or false, upon which had been erected the theistic optimism of the Renaissance.

In spite of his deficiencies as a mathematician – the work of Galileo, Pascal, Gassendi, Boyle, Descartes, Wallis, Ward, Huygens, Newton, and many others make Hobbes's own mathematical efforts ludicrous – his achievement was to restate the basic problems of metaphysics, psychology, and political morality in terms applicable to the new philosophy. Therefore we can ignore him no more than his contemporaries could. This new philosophy was a vague thing, deriving from various motives, coalescing various traditions, and encrusted with various inherited and ill-assimilated values. But one assumption loomed large: that all physical phenomena are reducible to matter and motion, and that matter consists of minute or corpuscular bodies. In the late seventeenth century this assumption, and the systems built upon it, was variously called atomical, corpuscularian, Cartesian, mechanical, or even Epicurean; but all may be taken as varieties of naturalism as the term has been used in this book. Generally speaking, there was a recognized cleavage between its two main forms, that experimental philosophy built on the tradition of Baconian empiricism and the mechanical philosophy that carried the great prestige of Descartes.[176] As strategies for interpreting

---

[175] *Table Talk*, p. 115.
[176] Boyle (*The Christian Virtuoso, Works*, V, 41) discriminates and evaluates the varieties of the new science very carefully. See Jones, *Ancients and Moderns*, p. 193 f. For a typical

nature and man's place in nature both were radically incompatible with the sacramental view of nature which the Renaissance had inherited from the Middle Ages, and both resulted from the fracturing of that uneasy synthesis which had subsumed the tradition of Christian humanism.

Commonly denounced as the *bête noire* of mechanical philosophy, Hobbes made explicit the atheistical implications and possibilities of this new complex of naturalism; consequently he also jeopardized all those values – moral, literary, and cultural if not specifically theological – which had been embedded in the sacramental view of nature. Justly or not, he came to be identified as the evil genius of the new philosophy, and that philosophy to be regarded as atheistic naturalism. In Hooker's palmy days, only a couple of generations earlier, an atheist could be dismissed as a monster dedicated to 'sensual profit or pleasure',[177] but by the middle of the seventeenth century atheism had a new rationale and presented a more present danger to the orthodox.

Thus the atheistical elements in the new philosophy stimulated the fiercest reaction, and in many quarters. Unregenerate traditionalists like Alexander Ross and Henry Stubbe, who gloried in their defense of Aristotle and cordially damned all varieties of the new philosophy, experimental or mechanical, execrated it as a threat to what they fondly hoped was the *status quo*. Seeking to protect themselves from the charge of impiety, the experimental philosophers proper, like Glanvill and Sprat and More and Boyle, argued that a methodical observation of nature could either uncover new truths compatible with revealed theology or else establish as facts those beliefs now held only by faith. Savants and scholars like Méric Casaubon attacked the new philosophy on the ground that it would demolish all the rich fruits of learning and history and reason that constituted the strength of the humanistic tradition. A sampling of each type of reaction will suggest the involvement in which men of the most varied intellectual hues found themselves in the middle of the seventeenth century.

For the first class Alexander Ross may stand as a fair specimen. That curious man, whom Mr Bush has described as the Aristo-

---

Restoration opinion of 'the illustrious Des-Cartes', see Glanvill, *The Vanity of Dogmatizing*, pp. 48, 108–9.
[177] *Laws*, V.ii.1; cf. Nashe's denunciation of learned atheists and 'Mathematitions' (*Pierce Pennilesse*, *Works*, I, 172), which more properly anticipates the seventeenth-century view.

telian fundamentalist of his age, did valiant if ineffectual battle against all forms of *avant garde* thought. He wrote vehemently against Bacon, Browne, Wilkins, Hobbes, and many others, including the fabulous Sir Kenelm Digby. Since, as a buccaneer, courtier, astrologer, medical quack, botanist, Catholic apologist, and virtuoso general of his age, Digby touched most aspects of early seventeenth-century thought, it was inevitable that he should have been, among other things, a sort of Cartesian. Indeed, as early as 1637 he sent Hobbes a copy of the *Discours* from Paris, and seven years later he published his *Two Treatises* on the nature of bodies and the nature of the soul – a partly Cartesian, partly Aristotelian set of speculations that prompted Ross's angry rebuttal in *The Philosophical Touchstone*.

Against Digby's alleged atomism and materialism Ross hurls a point-by-point denunciation, all enveloped in a heroic defense of Aristotle against his modern rivals and detractors. Happily, we need not follow it in detail, but merely note the tone and motive. In Ross's view Digby's recourse to the new philosophy is an offense against God, Aristotle, and the very foundations of social amity. In 'these sad times', he charges, Digby is amusing himself with his 'owne shadow and conceipts, playing with these, as a Cat doth with her owne taile'. But it is dangerous play: 'You make the Aristotelians speak absurdities of your owne invention, and of which they never dreamed, and then you laught at them, comparing them to a body, that, by adding *Bus*, turned all English words into Latine.'[178] Ross was habitually an angry man, but he was made especially angry by Digby's secularism. His implication that man can subsist very comfortably on this planet by a Baconian exploitation of his native resources struck Ross as little less than atheistic.

> We shall make but a sorry account, if wee follow such guides as our owne nature, reason, and knowledge: These are blind guides, which will lead us into the ditch. The Scripture tells us, that the natural man comprehendeth not the things of Gods Spirit, neither can he; . . . until Christ both spiritually quickend us, our reason and nature will little availe us.[179]

Digby's secularism, however, goes hand in hand with his materialistic psychology, which Ross, in his really stirring peroration, cries out against in horror as an attack on the immortality of the soul.

[178] pp. 62–3.   [179] pp. 104–5.

MECHANISM VS. EXPERIMENT

We must bid adieu to vertuous actions, and to all spirituall comforts. Christ died, the Apostles laboured, the Martyrs suffered, but all in vaine, if the soule be mortall. Our faith, our hope, our preaching and reading, our restraint from pleasures, our sorrowing for sins, our taking up of our crosse, and following of Christ, is all in vaine, if the soul be mortall: And, in a word, wee Christians are of all men the most miserable, if the soule be mortall... Admit but such Lucretian doctrine, you may as well shake hands with heaven and hell.[180]

A generation later, in rebuttal to Glanvill's *Plus Ultra*, Méric Casaubon presented the humanist's case against experimental philosophy. As was proper for the son of the great scholar whom James I had fetched over to England, he wrote in grave and temperate fashion, but his aversion to the dominant course of English thought was as great as Ross's had been. His great fear is that the new philosophy, 'of late years much cried up in London and elsewhere', will prove to be injurious if not 'destructive' to 'good learning'.[181] Fundamental to that learning, as he understands it, is the currently despised 'notional' philosophy which informs Aristotle's 'incomparable' ethics and is the life-blood of literary art and moral knowledge. Would Joseph Glanvill 'have all ancient Poets, Greek and Latin, turned out of doors' because they are by his criteria 'useless'? 'Can such a thing enter into the heart of men, that pretend to the improvement of learning?'[182] Since there is strong evidence that Glanvill would like to sympathize with Lord Herbert's kind of deism (as an antidote to the 'controversies' of the Schoolmen), Casaubon is baffled to read his ill-argued defense of Christian revelation, where he shows himself 'much abhorring, or professing to abhor all innovations in it, or that it should suffer any thing by experimental Philosophie'.[183] Although Casaubon is willing to grant the ancient truism that a study of the book of nature confirms the glory of God, he fears those who 'magnifie this study' as though 'there were no other wisdom in the world to be thought of, or pursued after'.[184] By their devotion to only 'useful, true, solid learning' – the shibboleth of Bacon's utilitarianism – they approach the 'great precipice' in forgetting the superior importance of spiritual values.[185] The virtuosos who ignore the intellectual and moral legacy of

---

[180] p. 123.
[181] *A Letter of Meric Casaubon D. D. &c. to Peter du Moulin*, p. 17.
[182] *Ibid.*, p. 15.   [183] *Ibid.*, pp. 18–9.
[184] *Ibid.*, p. 24.   [185] *Ibid.*, p. 30.

CC

the past, and for the accumulated wisdom of the race substitute the chimera of mere utility, seem to envisage an infinite progress toward the 'commodity' of mere secular well-being. But, ends Casaubon with delicate irony, 'may not a man go too far in this study, and overvalue his progress so far, as to think nothing out of his reach?'[186]

As we have already seen, however, Glanvill would not have conceded the possibility. Though by no means an original thinker, he was the most graceful and articulate publicist for the new philosophy in England. Like Sprat, whose *History of the Royal Society* was virtually canonical, he was also an Anglican clergyman. Both were confronted with the double task of stating the case of the new philosophy while defending it against the common charges of impiety, naturalism, and even atheism. Committed as they were to the most vehement anti-Aristotelianism, to the emerging idea of progress, to the advance of man's natural knowledge and secular well-being through experimental philosophy, they were also committed to the anomolous duty of defending revealed religion.

Bringing to a close his long and sinuous attack on antiquity, the habit of authority, and the dogmatic natural philosophy of the Aristotelians, Glanvill makes a scrupulous exception for the verity of Christian revelation, which obviously owes nothing to observation and experiment. He lays it down as axiomatic that 'as far as the operation of nature reacheth, it worketh by corporeal instruments', but he makes it emphatically clear that mysteries like the Trinity and the Incarnation reach far beyond nature.[187] He favors no 'new-broach'd conceit in Divinity; For I own no Opinion there, which cannot plead the prescription of above sixteen hundred years'. A skeptic in philosophy need not be a rebel to religion, for the Gospel light began in its zenith while philosophy began in 'Crepusculous obscurity; and it's yet scarse past the Dawn'. The revelation of Christian mystery came all at once, and perfectly, whereas the natural arts and sciences are still embryos that can be matured only by 'Times gradual accomplishments'.[188] In short, the great doctrine of the uniformity of nature, the necessary ground of modern science and the most

---
[186] *Ibid.*, p. 34.
[187] *The Vanity of Dogmatizing*, pp. 7-8.
[188] *Ibid.*, pp. 186-7.

MECHANISM VS. EXPERIMENT

significant product of seventeenth-century thought, was by Glanvill and like-minded men sharply checked at the threshold of the supernatural. Only thus could revealed religion be saved.

Sprat, who in the fulness of time became Dean of Westminster, Bishop of Rochester, and a member of James's notorious Ecclesiastical Commission of 1686, demanded a similarly conventional segregation of natural and supernatural truth, yet only with the most extreme reluctance does he fence off God and the soul as subjects exempt from the critical scrutiny of the 'free, and unconfin'd' gentlemen of the Royal Society. They 'meddle' with sacred truth 'onely as the Power, and Wisdom, and Goodness of the Creator, is display'd in the admirable order, and workmanship of the Creatures'. This kind of religious truth, virtually indistinguishable from the conclusions of natural cognition, is, of course, unable to fill the mind 'with such tender, and powerful contemplations' as do the supra-rational mysteries of Christianity, yet none the less it is not without utility: it may very well 'serve in respect to Christianity, as Solomon's Porch to the Temple'.[189]

Indeed, it is hard for Sprat to delimit properly the area of natural knowledge. Because the faculties of his soul are 'hard to be reduc'd to any certain observation of the senses' and because his soul and body 'are not onely one natural engine (as some have thought)', it would seem that man may claim a special status. Yet it is easily possible that the prodigious advance of techniques and instruments will soon make possible an astonishing analysis of his spirits, natural functions, and diseases. 'There may, without question, be very neer ghesses made, even at the more exalted, and immediate Actions of the Soul; and that too, without destroying its Spiritual and Immortal Being.' Certainly, the reconstruction of knowledge on sound Baconian principles must result in the steady decline of ignorance and superstition. Already the experimental philosopher has learned that he

> cannot suddenly conclude all extraordinary events to be the immediate Finger of God, because he familiarly beholds the inward workings of things: and thence perceives that many effects, which use to affright the Ignorant, are brought forth by the common Instruments of Nature. . . .

[189] *The History of the Royal-Society*, pp. 82–3. Sprat's career as an ecclesiastical politician led him to that bitter day when, officiating as dean in Westminster Abbey, he read James' declaration of indulgence to a congregation that first murmured and then noisily departed, leaving him with the paper trembling in his hand. See Macaulay, *History*, II, 1001.

He cannot be forward to assent to Spiritual Raptures, and Revelations: because he is truly acquainted with the Tempers of mens Bodies, the Composition of their Blood, and the power of Fancy: and so better understands the difference, between Diseases, and Inspiration.[190]

For the nonce, however, Sprat concedes sanctity to two things only, God and the human soul. Otherwise the gentlemen of the Royal Society take the whole creation to be their province, and there

> they wander, at their pleasure: In the frame of Mens bodies, the ways for strong, healthful, and long life: In the Arts of mens Hands, those that either necessity, convenience, or delight have produc'd: In the works of Nature, their helps, their varieties, redundencies, and defects: and in bringing all these to the uses of humane Society.[191]

Could Bacon have asked for more?

By the time Sprat published his *History* in 1667, what Glanvill had called time's gradual accomplishment seemed to be proceeding apace. In only a few years, boasted Glanvill, the Royal Society had done more for the advancement of learning and felicity 'than all the Philosophers of the Notional way, since Aristotle opened his Shop in Greece'.[192] And yet in that dawn when it was bliss to be alive such propagandists as Glanvill and Sprat were faced with a vexing dilemma. However eagerly they propagated the new gospel of man's secular improvement, they had to be most careful in maintaining the special sanctity of that other Gospel. In them the bifurcation of those two orders of truth came to that poignant crisis which we, three centuries later, can comprehend all too well.

Natural religion inevitably became the bulwark of their defense against pious detractors; and in restating its ancient claims they sought to evade the dilemma that their secularism had forced on them. However shaky their position was metaphysically, it proved to be the least unsatisfactory solution to a problem which actually could yield no solution. The data of observation can only confirm the glory of God, argued Glanvill: one can no more look at a watch without assuming it had a maker than study the processes of nature without assuming they are controlled by God. 'I say therefore, that if we do but consider this Fabrick with minds

[190] *The History of the Royal-Society*, p. 340.
[191] *Ibid.*, p. 83.
[192] 'Of the Modern Improvements of Useful Knowledge', *Essays*, p. 37.

unpossest of an affect[ed] madness; we will easily grant, that it was some skilful Archeus who delineated those comely proportions, and hath exprest such exactly Geometrical elegancies in its compositions. But what this hidden Architect should be, and by what instruments and art this frame erected; is as unknown to us, as our Embryo-thoughts.'[193] Experimental philosophy is only a search for causes, and, properly conducted, the search not only leads us to the first cause but also to the conviction that the relatedness and cohesion of natural processes is made possible only by that sustaining power of a God who somehow keeps his geometrical elegancies in order. 'For unless there be something, upon which all the rest may depend for their cohesion; the hanging of one by another, will signifie no more then the mutual dependence of causes and effects in an infinite Series, without a First: the admission of which, Atheism would applaud.'[194] 'O truly Royal', sang Dryden in celebrating the virtuosos of Gresham College,

> who behold the law
> And rule of beings in your Maker's mind;
> And thence, like limbecs, rich ideas draw,
> To fit the level'd use of mankind.[195]

It is true, Glanvill admitted on second thought, that mere mechanical philosophy is a real danger to religion. To a world grown weary 'of Qualities and Formes, and declaring in favour of the Mechanical Hypothesis', those 'brisker Geniuses, who desire rather to be accounted Witts, then endeavour to be so', were at first beguiling, even though they advocated 'Mechanism upon Hobbian conditions'. With the establishment of the Royal Society, however, the danger was averted, for that august body had made it clear that 'Mechanick Philosophy yields no security to irreligion, and that those that would be gentilely learned and ingenious, need not purchase it, at the dear rate of being Atheists'.[196] Not only does experimental philosophy confirm the verities of religion; it also contributes to man's intellectual emancipa-

---

[193] *The Vanity of Dogmatizing*, p. 43.
[194] *Ibid.*, pp. 50–1.
[195] 'Annus Mirabilis', ll. 661–4.
[196] *Scepsis Scientifica*, 'Address to the Royal Society', sig. A4r-B1v. The first edition of *The Vanity of Dogmatizing* was, in effect, a defense of Cartesianism, but the long preface to the second edition (i.e. *Scepsis Scientifica*) marks an abrupt shift from mechanic to experimental philosophy, from the 'dogmatism' of the Cartesian hypothesis to the skepticism and empiricism of Bacon and Boyle and Newton.

tion from the errors of the past in bringing order to the 'shifts, windings and unexpected Caprichios of distressed Nature, when pursued by a close and well managed Experiment'. In short, it provides for both the immortal and the temporal felicity of man; and when through its benefits the 'frugaller Sons of fortune' come to enjoy the 'accelerating and bettering of Fruits, emptying Mines, drayning Fens and Marshes', they will realize that God is best served by mastering those processes of nature which demonstrate His power. To understand the 'Art whereby the Almighty Wisdom governs the Motions of the great Automaton, and to know the wayes of captivating Nature, and making her subserve our purposes and designments' is, far beyond political or military renown, the true dignity of man.[197]

Although this kind of talk met prompt and angry opposition – Thomas White's *Scire sive sceptices et scepticorum a jure disputationis exclusio* attacked Glanvill as early as 1663 – the most persistent, if not the most subtle, of the outraged traditionalists was Dr Henry Stubbe. Against the secularism, utilitarianism, and imputed atheism of the new philosophy he fired a salvo of angry pamphlets. He countered Glanvill's *Plus Ultra* with *The Plus Ultra reduced to a Non Plus* (1670), and on the theory that the best defense is a vigorous offense he wrote three more attacks in the same year: *Campanella Revived* construes the Royal Society as a sinister plot to introduce popery into England; *Legends no Histories* is a grim catalogue of Sprat's scientific and theological errors; *A Censure upon Certain Passages Contained in The History of the Royal Society, As being Destructive to the Established Religion and the Church of England* is an atrabiliar rebuttal to Sprat's new *History*. Stubbe was duly dusted off by Glanvill in *A Prefatory Answer* the next year ('In these worthy workes I cannot tell which I shall admire most, his impudence or his impertinence'),[198] but he promptly replied in the second edition of his *Censure*; Glanvill rejoined the fray in 1671 with *A Further Discovery of M. Stubbe*, alleging a sanction for the labors of the works of Bacon, whereupon Stubbe turned his attack on Bacon with a devastating analysis of his comments on sweating sickness in *The History of Henry VII*.

And so the controversy sputtered on, tediously, wordily, tritely. Certainly it produced no original thought on either side: everything that could have been said on the subject, given the historical

[197] Ibid., sig. B2ʳ-B4ʳ.   [198] *A Praefatory Answer*, p. [193].

MECHANISM VS. EXPERIMENT

situation of science and philosophy in the early 'seventies, had already been said. None the less, the vehemence of Stubbe's restating an essentially anachronistic position tends to confirm one of the basic propositions of this book – that the complex of traditional notions which had been central to Renaissance thought retained their vitality far into the seventeenth century. *The Plus Ultra reduced* is, for Stubbe, a fairly temperate exposition of the rooted antagonism to the new philosophy. It is not only an effort to minimize the strictly scientific achievements of that philosophy but also an attack on the utilitarian rationale of the movement as represented by the Royal Society. Why, asks Stubbe, concern ourselves with the diurnal motion of the earth or the possible inhabitants of other worlds? Why such a pother about perfecting the telescope? The world will wag on much as before, diurnal motion or not, and the natives of Venus – if there are any – can have no relevance for our temporal or eternal well being:

> In case all our other trading should be lost, we shall not finde out any gainful commerce with them; nor need we dread that they will piss out our Eyes as we look up. So that let their telescopes be brought to that unimaginable perfection, whereby to discover the inhabitants of the Planets as plainly as mites in Cheese, and let the Conclusion fall which way it will, things will fall out no otherwise than they do.[199]

The fact of the matter is, argues Stubbe, that the vaunted utility of the new philosophy is a hoax that conceals a sinister attack upon the ancient union of (Aristotelian) reason and religion. Glanvill libels the dead and affronts the living in deprecating the uses of traditional reason – that reason which has protected Christianity from Arians, Jews, Mohammedans, papists, and Socinians, and without which the 'Christian Religion must inevitably fall without the aid of a Miracle. It is a kind of Apostasy from the Niecene and Athanasian Creeds to slight Metaphysicks'.[200]

Stubbe could not have been a very lovable man, and as his attacks grew sharper in his later pamphlets the seamier side of his antagonisms became apparent. From a defense of religion he passed to one of Christianity, and specifically of the Anglican establishment; and the broad philosophical issue at stake deteriorated to polemics in bigotry and vituperation. The refusal to deal

---

[199] *The Plus Ultra reduced*, p. 10. Butler's 'Elephant in the Moon' is a more delectable statement of the same proposition; cf. *Hudibras*, II.iii.745-50.
[200] Ibid, p. 1.

firmly with doctrinal questions, he charges, shows the ominous intent of those who profess the new philosophy of experiment and utility. 'Adiew to all the Sermons of Bishop Andrews [sic] upon the fifth of November: all that King James writ against the Papacy, and to prove the Pope to be Antichrist: farewell to a great part of our Homilies, to part of the thirty nine Articles.'[201] In Stubbe's sinuous dialectic the aims of the Royal Society somehow became identical with the Catholic threat, its interest in natural history with sedition. Sprat's *History* had shamelessly laid bare the real designs of the virtuosos – not only to remove the 'Rubbish' of the ancients' moral philosophy, but also to demolish the whole literary tradition of Western Europe.[202] Sprat's audacious dedication of his work to King Charles, and the king's too generous patronage of the Society, could only raise the gravest doubts of that monarch's place in history.[203] For Sprat's own blasphemous essays in theology are enough to damn the philosophy which he defends. Stubbe denounces in the bitterest terms Sprat's urbane assumption that between the Roman and the reformed churches there are, for men of breeding and intelligence, no great barriers in doctrine, so that a wise man may entertain a proper respect for 'so ancient and famous' a church as the Catholic.[204] He objects to Sprat's remark that before the Fall a natural religion was the only religion, and that even today a knowledge of natural processes will induce more piety than all the superstitions of the ignorant.[205] And he especially objects to Sprat's cavalier citation of Biblical 'wit' in secular writing as a piece of impiety that, like Cowley's, could undermine the very structure of the Anglican establishment.[206] But what could be expected, he demands in anguish, of a man who called miracles God's divine experiments, or of the 'philosophy' that, however camouflaged, was the most horrible blasphemy?

Henry More, among others, resented Stubbe's aspersions. As he wrote to Glanvill, he was appalled at so foolish a man charging the Royal Society with impiety, especially since that Society repudiated mere 'Mechanick Philosophy' with all its atheistic implications. What it does aim at, instead, 'is a more perfect

---

[201] *Campanella Revived*, pp. 2–3.
[202] *Legends no Histories*, sig. A1r.
[203] *Ibid.*, sig. B1r.
[204] *A Censure upon Certaine Passages Contained in the History of the Royal Society*, p. 4.
[205] *Ibid.*, pp. 36 f.   [206] *Ibid.*, p. 62.

MECHANISM VS. EXPERIMENT

Philosophy, as yet to be raised out of faithful and skilful Experiments in Nature, which is so far from tending to Atheism, that I am confident, it will utterly rout it and the Mechanical Philosophy at once'.[207] Stubbe, however, refused to grant the distinction between 'mechanical' and 'experimental', and his wrath was not assuaged. The result of all these experiments and observations, however speciously they might be rationalized, is to construe God as an efficient cause operating within a mechanistic system.

> For if it be not granted, that every part of the Corporeal Universe, or this great Aggregate of Bodies, do move in certain Lines, according to the determinate Figures thereof, and that without the Particular Concourse of an Immaterial Incorporeal Being, putting such Corpuscles into this or that Particular Motion, and continuing it therein Mechanically, then doth the whole Systeme of the Mechanical Philosophy fall to the ground; and the Demonstrations cease to be any longer such.[208]

It was a telling point, and we are astonished to find Stubbe putting his finger on that crucial inconsistency which the philosophical acumen of Descartes, the wit of Glanvill, the desperate fundamentalism of Newton could not explain away.

Perhaps it seems perverse or ironical to end this book with the egregious Henry Stubbe, so that his hoarse voice has the last word for the old order whose decline he resisted so stoutly. Of course, that irascible and unlovely conservative was by no means the only man of his time seeking to check the tide of science and 'progress'; none the less, in the losing cause for which he fought the rearguard action it was mainly little men like him who still clung, with anger or resignation, to those moral and rational and aristocratic values which were crumbling. Apart from Milton there were no big men left to carry on, and even Milton, isolated among the sons of Belial, seemed to realize his isolation,

> fall'n on evil days,
> On evil days though fall'n, and evil tongues;
> In darkness, and with dangers compast round,
> And solitude.

For as the seventeenth century came to its triumphant close under the aegis of Locke and Newton it was along the procedural lines

---

[207] Glanvill, *A Praefatory Answer*, p. 155.
[208] *A Reply to a Letter of Dr Henry More*, pp. 65–6.

which Glanvill had defended. For reasons which this book has tried to suggest, that complex of values which we call Christian humanism was losing its formative functions for morality and literature, and an era of utility, natural religion, progress, and social commentary was at hand. Swift, for one, recognized the change and after his fashion resisted it; but most of his contemporaries were more complaisant. Pope and Addison, Mandeville and Bolingbroke, Tindal and Toland, Leibnitz and Voltaire were the new voices in the land, and it goes without saying that they raised a new song. Not that everyone was at ease in Sion: as Berkeley and finally Hume made painfully clear, Locke's magisterial summary of the new philosophy raised more questions than it answered, and neither Glanvill nor his immediate posterity lived to glory in the noontide splendor of the new dispensation.

None the less, as such things go it was new. It might be said of an old man dying toward the end of the seventeenth century that he had seen the end of the Middle Ages, the beginnings of the modern world; in the long sweep of intellectual history he had lived through what Browne had called one of the great mutations of time. Between his birth and his death the educated person's conception of nature, and of man's place in nature had undergone changes which to St Thomas would be incredible, even to Hooker grossly improbable. To suggest the manifold consequences of the transition from a sacramental to a secular view of nature lies beyond the reach of this book, or of a whole shelf of books; but to unsnarl some of the tangled forces behind the transition is to realize that the seventeenth century is one of the pivotal epochs of Western thought. With the close of the Renaissance the ancient tradition of human dignity, as conceived in terms of Hellenic and Christian humanism, entered its long decline.

BIBLIOGRAPHY

THIS BIBLIOGRAPHY INCLUDES the primary sources quoted in the text and only the most important of the secondary materials cited in the notes.

Treatises quoted from Haller, Miller and Johnson, and Woodhouse (for example, John Cotton's *Keyes of the Kingdom of Heaven* and Lord Brooke's *Discourse Opening the Nature of Episcopacy*) are not listed separately.

Addison, Joseph, Richard Steele, and others, *The Spectator*, 4 vols., Everyman's Library, n.d.
Agrippa, Henry Cornelius, *The Vanity of Arts and Sciences*, trans. J[ames] San[ford], 1694 (First published 1569).
Ames, William, *English Puritanisme. Containing the main Opinions of the rigidest sort of those that are called Puritanes in the Realme of England*, 1640.
Andrewes, Lancelot, *Ninety-Six Sermons*, 5 vols., 1841.
———, *A Pattern of Catechistical Doctrine and Other Minor Works*, 1846.
Aquinas, St Thomas, *The Summa contra Gentiles*, trans. The English Dominican Friars, 4 vols., 1924-1929.
———, *Summa Theologica*, trans. The Fathers of the English Dominican Friars, 2d ed., 22 vols., [1920?]-1925.
Ascham, Roger, *The Scholemaster* (1570), ed. Edward Arber, 1927.
Aubrey, John, *Brief Lives*, ed. Oliver Lawson Dick, 1949.
Augustine, Bishop of Hippo, *The City of God*, trans. Marcus Dod, 2 vols., 1872-1884.
———, *The Confessions*, trans. E. B. Pusey, Everyman's Library, 1924.

Bacon, Francis, first Baron Verulam and Viscount St. Albans, *The Works*, ed. James Spedding, Robert Leslie Ellis, Douglas Denon Heath, 14 vols., 1857-1874.
Barker, Arthur, *Milton and the Puritan Dilemma 1641-1660*, 1942.
Baxter, Richard, *The Autobiography: Being the Reliquiae Baxterianae Abridged from the Folio* (1696), ed. J. M. Lloyd Thomas, 1925.
———, *The Practical Works*, 23 vols., 1830.
———, *The Saints' Everlasting Rest*, abridged by Benjamin Fawcett, 1833.
Bentley, Richard, *Works*, ed. Alexander Dyce, 3 vols., 1838.
Bettenson, Henry (ed.), *Documents of the Christian Church*, 1947.
Boswell, James, *Life of Johnson*, Oxford Standard Authors, 2 vols., 1927.
Boulting, William, *Giordano Bruno: His Life, Thought, and Martyrdom*, 1914.
Boyle, Robert, *The Works*, ed. Thomas Birch, 5 vols., 1744.

Bradford, William, *History of Plymouth Plantation 1606-1646*, ed. William T. Davis, 1908.
Bredvold, Louis I., *The Intellectual Milieu of John Dryden: Studies in Some Aspects of Seventeenth-Century Thought*, University of Michigan Publications Language and Literature, vol. XII, 1934.
———, "Dryden, Hobbes, and the Royal Society", *MP*, XXV (1928), 417-438.
Breton, Nicholas, *Melancholike Humours*, ed. with an essay on Elizabethan melancholy by G. B. Harrison, 1929.
Brewster, Sir David, *Memoirs of the Life, Writings, and Discoveries of Sir Isaac Newton*, 2d ed., 2 vols, 1860.
Brooke, first and second Barons, see Greville, Fulke and Robert.
Browne, Sir Thomas, *The Religio Medici & Other Writings*, Everyman's Library, 1931.
———, *The Works*, ed. Geoffrey Keynes, 6 vols., 1928.
Bruno, Giordano, see Jordani Bruni Nolani.
Bunyan, John, *The Pilgrim's Progress from This World to That Which Is to Come*, Everyman's Library, 1913.
Burton, Robert, *The Anatomy of Melancholy*, ed. A. R. Shilleto, Bohn's Standard Library, 3 vols., 1896.
Burtt, E. A., *The Metaphysical Foundations of Modern Physical Science*, 1925.
Busson, Henri, *Les Sources et le développement du rationalisme dans la littérature française de la renaissance (1553-1601)*, 1922.
Butler, Samuel, *The Poetical Works*, The Aldine Edition of the British Poets, 2 vols., n.d.

Calvin, John, *Institutes of the Christian Religion*, trans. John Allen, 7th American ed., 2 vols., n.d.
Campanella, Thomas, *The Defense of Galileo*, trans. and ed. Grant McColley, Smith College Studies in History, vol. XXII, 1927.
Carpenter, Nathanael, *Philosophia libera, triplici: exercitationum decade proposita*, 2d ed., 1622.
Cartwright, Thomas, *A Directory of Church-government*, 1644.
Cary, Lucius, second Viscount Falkland, *Of the Infallibilitie of the Church of Rome*, 1645.
———, *A Speech Made to the House of Commons Concerning Episcopacy*, 1641.
Casaubon, Méric, *A Letter of Meric Casaubon D. D. &c. to Peter du Moulin D. D. and Prebendarie of the same Church: Concerning Natural experimental Philosophie, and some books lately set out about it*, 1669.
Cassirer, Ernst, Paul Oskar Kristeller, John Herman Randall, Jr. (edd.), *The Renaissance Philosophy of Man*, 1948.
Chapman, George (trans.), *The Iliads of Homer, Prince of Poets*, ed. Richard Hooper, 2 vols., 1857.
———, *The Poems*, ed. Phyllis B. Bartlett, 1941.
———, *The Tragedies*, ed. Thomas Marc Parrott, 1910.
Charles I of England, see *Eikon Basilike*.
Chillingworth, William, *The Works*, 3 vols., 1820.
Clarendon, first Earl of, see Hyde, Edward.
Clark, G. N., *The Seventeenth Century*, 1929.

Cochrane, Charles Norris, *Christianity and Classical Culture: A Study of Thought and Action from Augustus to Augustine*, 1940.
Coker, Francis William (ed.), *Readings in Political Philosophy*, 1947.
Coleridge, Samuel Taylor, *The Table Talk and Omniana*, ed. T. Ashe, Bohn's Standard Library, 1884.
Copernicus, Nicolaus, *De revolutionibus orbium caelestium libri VI*, 1873.
Cornwallis, Sir William, the younger, *Essayes*, ed. Don Cameron Allen, 1946.
Craig, Hardin, *The Enchanted Glass: The Elizabethan Mind in Literature*, 1936.
Crane, Ronald S., "Anglican Apologetics and the Idea of Progress, 1699-1745", *MP*, XXXI (1933-1934), 273-306, 349-382.
Cudworth, Ralph, *The Rrue Intellectual System of the Universe*, ed. Thomas Birch, 4 vols., 1820.

Dampier, Sir William Cecil, *A History of Science and Its Relations with Philosophy and Religion*, 3d ed., 1946.
Dante Alighieri, *The Divine Comedy*, trans. Charles Eliot Norton, 3 vols., 1902.
Davies, Godfrey, 'Arminian versus Puritan in England, ca. 1620-1640', *The Huntington Library Bulletin*, no. 5 (1934), 157-179.
———, *The Early Stuarts 1603-1660*, 1937.
Davies, Sir John, *Complete Poems*, ed. Alexander B. Grosart, 2 vols., 1876.
Da Vinci, Leonardo, *The Literary Works*, ed. Jean Paul Richter, 2d ed., 2 vols., 1939.
Dekker, Thomas, *The Guls Hornbook and the Belman of London*, The Temple Classics, 1941.
———, *Thomas Dekker*, ed. Ernest Rhys, The Mermaid Series, n.d.
Dell, William, *A Plain and Necessary Confutation of divers gross and Antichristian Errors, Delivered . . . By Mr. Sydrach Simpson, Master of Pembroke*, 1654.
———, *The Stumbling-Stone, or, A Discourse touching that offence which the World and Worldly Church do take against 1. Christ Himself. 2. His true Word*, 1653.
———, *A Testimony from the Word Against Divinity-Degrees in the University*, n.d.
———, *The Tryal of Spirits Both in Teachers & Hearers. Wherein is held forth the clear Discovery, and certain Downfal of the Carnal and Antichristian Clergie of these Nations*, 1653.
———, *The Way of True Peace and Unity among the Faithful and Churches of Christ, in all Humility and Bowells of Love Presented to them*, 1654.
Deloney, Thomas, *The Works*, ed. Francis Oscar Mann, 1912.
Descartes, René, *Oeuvres*, ed. Charles Adam and Paul Tannery, 12 vols., 1897-1910.
———, *The Philosophical Works*, trans. Elizabeth S. Haldane and G. R. T. Ross, 2 vols., 1911-1912.
De Wulf, Maurice, *History of Mediæval Philosophy*, trans. Ernest C. Messenger, 2 vols., 1926.
Digges, Thomas, see Johnson Francis R. and Sanford V. Larkey.
Donne, John, *Complete Poetry and Selected Prose*, ed. John Hayward, 1929.
———, *Devotions upon Emergent Occasions*, ed. John Sparrow, 1923.
———, *Fifty Sermons*, 1649.
———, *Ignatius His Conclave; or, His Inthronisation in a late Election in Hell*, 1635.

BIBLIOGRAPHY

Donne, John, *LXXX Sermons*, 1640.
———, *The Poems*, ed. H. J. C. Grierson, 1933.
———, *The Works*, ed. Henry Alford, 6 vols., 1839.
Downame, George, see Ramus, Peter.
Drayton, Michael, *Minor Poems*, ed. Cyril Brett, 1907.
Dreyer, J. L. E., *History of the Planetary Systems from Thales to Kepler*, 1906.
Dryden, John, *Essays*, ed. W. P. Ker, 2 vols., 1900.
———, *The Poetical Works*, ed. George R. Noyes, 1909.
Du Bartas, Guillaume de Salluste, *Divine Weekes & Workes*, trans. Joshua Sylvester, 1605.

Earle, John, *Microcosmography or A Piece of the World Discovered in Essays and Characters*, The Temple Classics, 1934.
Eikon Basilike or the King's Book, ed. Edward Almack, 1903.
Elizabethan Critical Essays, ed. G. Gregory Smith, 2 vols., 1904.
Erdmann, Johann Eduard, *A History of Philosophy*, trans. Williston S. Hough, 4th ed., 3 vols., 1910.

Fahie, J. J., "The Scientific Work of Galileo", *Studies in the History and Method of Science*, ed. Charles Singer, 2 vols., 1921.
Falkland, second Viscount, see Cary, Lucius.
Fenn, William W., "The Marrow of Calvin's Theology", *Harvard Theological Review*, II (1909), 323-339.
Firth, C. H. (ed.), *Stuart Tracts 1603-1693*, An English Garner, n.d.
Fischer, Kuno, *History of Modern Philosophy. Descartes and His School*, trans. J. P. Gordy, ed. Noah Porter, 1887.
Fraunce, Abraham, *The Lawiers Logike, exemplifying the praecepts of Logike, by the practise of the common Lawe*, 1588.
Fuller, Thomas, *The Church History of Britain* (1655), 3 vols., 1837.
———, *The Holy State and the Profane State* (1642), ed. Maximilian Graff Walten, 2 vols., 1938.

Galileo Galilei, *Dialogues Concerning Two New Sciences*, trans. Henry Crew and Alfonso de Salvio, 1939.
Gardiner, Samuel R., *The History of England from the Accession of James I. to the Outbreak of the Civil War 1603-1642*, 10 vols., 1884.
———, *History of the Great Civil War 1642-1649*, 4 vols., 1893.
Gee, Henry and William John Hardy (edd.), *Documents Illustrative of English Church History*, 1921.
Gilbert, William, *On the Loadstone and Magnetic Bodies, and on the Great Magnet the Earth*, trans. P. Fleury Mottelay, 1893.
Glanvill, Joseph, *Essays on Several Important Subjects in Philosophy and Religion*, 1676.
———, *A Praefatory Answer to Mr. Henry Stubbe, the Doctor of Warwick*, 1671.
———, *Scepsis Scientifica: or, Confest Ignorance, the way to Science; In an Essay of the Vanity of Dogmatizing*, 1665.
———, *The Vanity of Dogmatizing*, Reproduced from the Edition of 1661, with a Bibliographical Note by Moody E. Prior, The Facsimile Text Society, 1931.

BIBLIOGRAPHY 371

Gooch, G. P., *English Democratic Ideas in the Seventeenth Century*, 2d ed., 1927.
Greene, Robert, *Robert Greene*, ed. Thomas H. Dickinson, The Mermaid Series, n.d.
Greville, Fulke, first Baron Booke, *Poems and Dramas*, ed. Geoffrey Bullough, 2 vols., n.d.
Greville, Robert, second Baron Brooke, *The Nature of Truth Its Unity and Union with the Soule, Which is One in its Essence, Faculties, Arts; One with Truth*, 1640.
Grierson, Sir Herbert J. C., *Cross Currents in English Literature of the XVIIth Century*, 1929.

Hakewill, George, *An Apologie or Declaration of the Power and Providence of God in the Government of the World*, 2d ed., 1630.
Hales, John, *Golden Remains, of the ever Memorable Mr. John Hales, of Eaton-Colledge, &c.*, 1688.
H[all], J[ohn], *An Humble Motion to the Parliament of England Concerning the Advancement of Learning: And Reformation of the Universities*, 1649.
Hall, Joseph, *Works*, ed. Philip Wynter, 10 vols., 1863.
Haller, William, *The Rise of Puritanism*, 1938.
——— (ed.), *Tracts on Liberty in the Puritan Revolution 1638-1647*, 3 vols., 1934.
[Harington, Sir John], *A New Discoverie of a Stale Subject, called the Metamorphosis of Ajax*, 1596.
———, *Nugae Antiquae: Being a Miscellaneous Collection of Original Papers in Prose and Verse*, 3 vols., 1779.
Harris, C. R. S., *Duns Scotus*, 2 vols., 1927.
Harris, Victor, *All Cohaerence Gone*, 1949.
Harvey, Gabriel, *Marginalia*, ed. G. C. Moore Smith, 1913.
Henson, H. Hensley, *Studies in English Religion in the Seventeenth Century*, 1903.
Herbert, Edward, first Baron Herbert of Cherbury, *De veritate*, trans. Meyrick H. Carré, 1937.
Herbert, George, *The Works*, ed. Robert Aris Willmott, 1857.
Hobbes, Thomas, *The English Works*, ed. Sir William Molesworth, 11 vols., 1839-1845.
———, *Leviathan*, Everyman's Library, 1943.
Hooker, Richard, *Of the Laws of Ecclesiastical Polity*, 2 vols., Everyman's Library, n.d.
Hoopes, Robert, 'Voluntarism in Jeremy Taylor and the Platonic Tradition', *The Huntington Library Quarterly*. XIII (1950), 341-354.
Huizinga, J., *The Waning of the Middle Ages*, 1927.
Huygens, Christiaan, *Oeuvres Complètes*, 21 vols., 1888-1944.
Hyde, Edward, first Earl of Clarendon, *The History of the Rebellion and Civil Wars in England*, 3 vols. in 6, 1819.

James I of England, see McIlwain, Charles Howard.
James, Thomas, *The Strange and Dangerous Voyage of Captaine Thomas James, in his intended Discovery of the Northwest Passage into the South Sea*, 1633.
Jewel, John, *The Works*, ed. John Ayre, 4 vols., 1845-1850.

Johnson, Francis R. and Sanford V. Larkey, 'Thomas Digges, the Copernican System, and the Idea of the Infinity of the Universe in 1576', *The Huntington Library Bulletin*, no. 5 (1934), 69-117.

Jones, Richard F., *Ancients and Moderns: A Study of the Background of the 'Battle of the Books'*, 1936.

Jonson, Ben, *Discoveries 1641 Conversations with William Drummond of Hawthornden 1619*, ed. G. B. Harrison, 1923.

———, *The Complete Plays*, 2 vols., Everyman's Library, 1934.

Jonston, John, *An History of the Constancy of Nature, Wherein By comparing the latter Age with the former, it is maintained that the World doth not decay universally*, 1657.

Jordani Bruni Nolani, *Opera Latine conscripta*, ed. F. Fiorentino, 3 vols. in 8 parts, 1884-1891.

Kepler, Johann, *Opera omnia*, ed. Ch. Frisch, 8 vols., 1859-1871.

Knappen, M. M. (ed.), *Two Elizabethan Puritan Diaries by Richard Rogers and Samuel Ward*, 1933.

Knollys, Hanserd, *A Moderate Answer unto Dr. Bastwicks Book; Called, Independency not Gods Ordinance*, 1645.

Kurtz, Benjamin P., 'Gifer the Worm: An Essay toward the History of an Idea', *University of California Publications in English*, II (1928-1929), 235-261.

Lactantius Firmianus, Lucius Caelius, *The Works*, trans. William Fletcher, The Ante-Nicene Fathers, 2 vols., 1886.

La Primaudaye, Pierre, *The French Academie. Fully discoursed and finished in foure bookes*, 1618.

Laud, William, *The Works*, 7 vols., 1847-1860.

Laurentius Andreas, *A Discourse of the Preservation of the Sight: of Melancholike Diseases; or Rheumes, and of Old Age* (1599), trans. Thomas Surphlet, with an introduction by Sanford V. Larkey, Shakespeare Association Facsimiles, no. 15, 1938.

Leighton, Alexander, *An Appeal to the Parliament, or Sions Plea against the Prelacy*, 2d ed., [1628].

Le Roy, Louis, *Of the Interchangeable Course, or Variety of Things in the Whole World*, trans. R[obert] A[shley], 1594.

Lewis, C. S., *The Allegory of Love: A Study in Medieval Traditions*, 1936.

Lipsius, Justus, *Two Bookes of Constancie*, trans. Sir John Stradling, edited with an introduction by Rudolf Kirk, with notes by Clayton Morris Hall, 1939.

Locke, John, *An Essay Concerning Human Understanding*, ed. Alexander Campbell Fraser, 2 vols., 1894.

———, *The Works*, 10 vols., 1812.

Lord Herbert of Cherbury, see Herbert, Edward.

Luther, Martin, *Tischreden*, 6 vols., 1912-1921.

Macaulay, Thomas Babbington, *The History of England from the Accession of James the Second*, ed. C. H. Firth, 6 vols., 1913 ff.

BIBLIOGRAPHY

Machiavelli, Niccoló, *Discourses on the First Decade of Titus Livius*, trans. Ninian Hill Thomson, 1883.
Mâle, Emile, *L'Art religieux de la fin du moyen âge en France*, 2d ed., 1922.
Marston, John, *Works*, ed. A. H. Bullen, 3 vols., 1887.
Masson, David, *The Life of John Milton: Narrated in Connexion with the Political, Ecclesiastical, and Literary History of His Time*, 7 vols., 1859-1894.
McColley, Grant, 'The Seventeenth Century Doctrine of a Plurality of Worlds', *Annals of Science*, I (1936), 385-430.
———, see Campanella, Thomas.
McGiffert, Arthur Cushman, *A History of Christian Thought*. Vol. II: *The West from Tertullian to Erasmus*, 1933.
McIlwain, Charles Howard (ed.), *The Political Works of James I*, 1918.
Mexio, Pedro, *Treasurie of Auncient and Moderne Times. Containing the Learned Collections, Judicious Readings, and Memorable observations*, [trans. Thomas Milles], 1613.
Middleton, Thomas, *Thomas Middleton*, ed. Havelock Ellis, The Mermaid Series, n.d.
Migne, Jacques Paul (ed.), *Patrilogiae cursus completus, series Graeca*, 161 vols., 1857-1866.
——— (ed.), *Patriologiae cursus completus, series Latina prior*, 291 vols., 1879-.
Miller, Perry, *The New England Mind: The Seventeenth Century*, 1939.
———, 'The Marrow of Puritan Divinity', *Transactions 1933-37* of The Colonial Society of Massachusetts (1937), pp. 247-300.
——— and Thomas H. Johnson (edd.), *The Puritans*, 1938.
Milton, John, *Paradise Regained The Minor Poems and Samson Agonistes*, ed. Merritt Y. Hughes, 1937.
———, *Paradise Lost*, ed. Merritt Y. Hughes, 1935.
———, *The Prose Works*, Bohn's Standard Library, 5 vols., 1883.
A Mirror for Magistrates, ed. Lily B. Campbell, 1938.
Montaigne, Michel Eyquem, *The Essays*, trans. E. J. Trechmann, 2 vols., 1927.
More, Henry, *An Antidote against Atheisme*, 1652.
———, *Conjectura Cabbalistica. Or, A Conjectural Essay of Interpreting the minde of Moses, according to a threefold Cabbala*, 1653.
———, *Divine Dialogues, Containing sundry Disquisitions & Instructions Concerning the Attributes of God And his Providence in the World*, 2d ed., 1713.
———, *Enchiridion Ethicum, The English Translation of 1690 Reproduced from the First Edition*, The Facsimile Text Society, 1930.
———, *The Immortality of the Soul*, 1659.
———, *Philosophical Writings*, ed. Flora Isabel MacKinnon, 1925.

Nashe, Thomas, *Works*, ed. R. B. McKerrow, 5 vols., 1904-1910.
Newton, Sir Isaac, *Mathematical Principles of Natural Philosophy and his System of the World* [i.e. *Principia mathematica*], trans. Andrew Motte, rev. and ed. Florian Cajori, 1934.
Nicholson, Marjorie, 'Milton and the Telescope', *ELH*, II (1935), 1-32.
———, 'The "New Astronomy" and English Literary Imagination', *SP*, XXXII (1935), 428-462.
———, 'The Telescope and Imagination', *MP*, XXXII (1934-1935), 233-260.

Norden, John, *Vicissitudo Rerum* (*1600*), Shakespeare Association Facsimiles, no. 4, 1931.

Ockham, William of, *Studies and Selections*, ed. Stephen Chak Tornay, 1938.

The Paradise of Dainty Devices, ed. Hyder Edward Rollins, 1927.
Parentalia; or Memoirs of the Family of Wrens, 1750.
Parker, Samuel, *A Free and Impartial Censure of the Platonick Philosophie*, 1666.
Pascal, Blaise, *Oeuvres*, ed. Jacques Chevalier, 1936.
Perkins, William, *A Golden Chaine, or, The Description of Theologie*, trans. Robert Hill, 1621.
———, *The Whole Treatise of the Cases of Conscience*, 1651.
Petty, William, *The Advice of W. P. to Mr. Samuel Hartlib. For the Advancement of some particular Parts of Learning*, 1647.
Pollock, Sir Frederick, *Essays in the Law*, 1922.
Power, Henry, *Experimental Philosophy, in Three Books: Containing New Experiments Microscopical, Mercurial, Magnetical*, 1664.

Rabelais, François, *The Urquhart-Le Motteaux Translation of the Works*, ed. Albert Jay Nock and Catherine Rose Wilson, 2 vols., 1931.
Ralegh, Sir Walter, *The Works*, 8 vols., 1829.
Ramus, Peter, *Dialecticae libri duo . . . cum commentariis Georgii Dounami*, 1669.
Randall, John Herman Jr., 'The Development of Scientific Method in the School of Padua', *JHI*, I (1940), 177-206.
———, see Cassirer, Ernst *et al*.
Richardson, Alexander, *The Logicians School-Master: or, A Comment upon Ramus Logick*, 1657.
Rogers, Richard, see Knappen, M. M.
Rosen, Edward (trans. and ed.), *Three Copernican Treatises* (Copernicus' *Commentariolus* and *Letter against Werner*, and Rheticus' *Narratio prima*), 1939.
Ross, Alexander, *Leviathan drawn out with a Hook. Or Animadversions upon Mr. Hobbs Leviathan*, 1653.
———, *The Philosophical Touch-stone: or Observations upon Sir Kenelm Digby's Discourses of the Nature of Bodies, and of the reasonable Soule*. 1645.
Roth, Leon (ed), *Correspondence of Descartes and Constantine Huygens, 1635-1647*, 1926.
Ruskin, John, *The Works*, ed. E. T. Cook and Alexander Wedderburn, 39 vols., 1903-1912.

S[adler], J[ohn], *Flagellum Flagelli: or Doctor Bastwicks Quarters Beaten up in two or three Pomeridian Exercises*, 1645.
Saltmarsh, John, *The Smoke in the Temple. Wherein is a Designe for Peace and Reconciliation of Believers of the several Opinions of these Times about Ordinances*, 1646.
———, *Sparkles of Glory, or, Some Beams of the Morning-Star*, 1647.
Salusbury, Thomas, *Mathematical Collections and Translations*, vol. I, 1661.
Selden, John, *Table Talk*, ed. Sir Frederick Pollock, 1927.

BIBLIOGRAPHY

Shirley, James, *James Shirley*, ed. Edmund Gosse, The Mermaid Series, n.d.
Sibbes, Richard, *The Complete Works*, ed. Alexander B. Grosart, 7 vols., 1862-1864.
Skelton, John, *The Poetical Works . . . Principally according to the Edition of the Rev. Alexander Dyce*, 3 vols., 1856.
Smith, Preserved, *The Age of the Reformation*, 1920.
———, *A History of Modern Culture*. Vol. I: *The Great Renewal, 1547-1687*, 1930.
Spencer, Theodore, *Death and Elizabethan Tragedy*, 1936.
Spenser, Edmund, *The Complete Poetical Works*, ed. R. E. Neil Dodge, 1908.
Spinoza, Baruch, *Selections*, ed. John Wild, 1930.
Sprat, Thomas, *The History of the Royal-Society of London, for the Improving of Natural Knowledge*, 2d ed., 1702.
Strowski, Fortunat, *Montaigne*, 2d ed., 1931.
Stubbe, Henry, *Campanella Revived, Or an Enquiry into the History of the Royal Society, Whether the Virtuosi there do not pursue the Projects of Campanella for the reducing England unto Popery*, 1670.
———, *A Censure upon Certaine Passages Contained in the History of the Royal Society, As being Destructive to the Established Religion and Church of England*, 1670.
———, *Legends no Histories; Or, A Specimen of some Animadversions Upon the History of the Royal Society*, [1670].
———, *The Plus Ultra reduced to a Non Plus: or, A Specimen of some Animadversions upon the Plus Ultra of Mr. Glanvill*, 1670.
———, *A Reply to a letter of Dr. Henry More*, 1671.
Swan, John, *Speculum Mundi: Or A Glasse Representing the Face of the World*, 2d ed., 1643.

Tawney, R. H., *Religion and the Rise of Capitalism*, 1926.
———, see Wilson, Thomas.
Taylor, Jeremy, *The Golden Grove: Selected Passages from the Sermons and Writings*, ed. Logan Pearsall Smith, 1930.
———, *The Rule and Exercises of Holy Dying*, [1864].
———, *The Rule and Exercises of Holy Living*, [1864].
———, *The Sermons*, 1864.
———, *The Whole Works*, ed. Reginald Heber and Charles Page Eden, 10 vols., 1847-1854.
Tornay, Stephen Chak, see Ockham, William of.
Tourneur, Cyril, *The Plays and Poems*, ed. John Churton Collins, 2 vols., 1878.
Troeltsch, Ernst, *The Social Teachings of the Christian Churches*, trans. Olive Wyon, 2 vols., 1931.
Tulloch, John, *Rational Theology and Christian Philosophy in England in the Seventeenth Century*, rev. ed., 2 vols., 1874.

Villey, Pierre, *Les Sources & l'évolution des essais de Montaigne*, 2 vols., 1908.
Vindiciae contra tyrannos: *A Defence of Liberty against Tyrants. . . Being a Treatise written in Latin and French by Junius Brutus, and Translated out of both into English*, 1689.

DD*

BIBLIOGRAPHY

Walton, Izaak, *Lives of John Donne, Henry Wotton, Richd. Hooker, George Herbert,* &c., The Temple Classics, 2 vols., 1898.
Ward, Samuel, see Knappen, M. M.
[Ward, Seth], *Vindiciae Academiarum containing Some briefe Animadversions upon Mr Websters Book, Stiled, The Examination of Academies,* 1654.
Webster & Tourneur, ed. John Addington Symonds, The Mermaid Series, n.d.
Webster, John, *Academiarum Examen, or the Examination of Academies,* 1654.
———, *The Saints Guide, or, Christ the Rule, and Ruler of Saints,* 1654.
Whichcote, Benjamin, *Moral and Religious Aphorisms,* with an introduction by W. R. Inge, n.d.
———, *Select Sermons,* 1742.
Whitehead, Alfred North, *Science and the Modern World,* 1931.
Wilkins, John, *The First Book. The Discovery of a New World or, A Discourse tending to prove that 'tis probable there may be another habitable World in the Moon,* 1640.
———, *Sermons Preached on Several Occasions,* 1682.
Willey, Basil, *The Seventeenth Century Background,* 1934.
Wilson, Thomas, *The Arte of Rhetorique 1560,* ed. G. H. Mair, 1909.
———, *A Discourse upon Usury* [1572], with an historical introduction by R. H. Tawney, 1925.
———, *The Rule of Reason, conteinyng the Arte of Logique,* 1553.
Wolf, A., *A History of Science Technology, and Philosophy in the 16th & 17th Centuries,* 1935.
Woodhouse, A. S. P., 'Milton, Puritanism, and Liberty', *The University of Toronto Quarterly,* IV (1934-1935), 483-513.
———, 'Nature and Grace in the Faerie Queene', *ELH,* XVI (1949), 194-228.
——— (ed.), *Puritanism and Liberty: Being the Army Debates (1647-9) from the Clarke Manuscripts with Supplementary Documents,* 1938.
———, 'Puritanism and Liberty', *The University of Toronto Quarterly,* IV (1934-1935), 395-404 [a review of William Haller (ed.), *Tracts on Liberty in the Puritan Revolution*].

INDEX

Dates of birth and death, where known, have been included for all persons except contemporary scholars mentioned in the notes. The notes themselves are indexed for factual material not included in the text, but not for mere citations of titles. No effort has been made to record every casual occurrence of proper names. The letter f means 'the page following'; ff, 'the two pages following'. Where page numbers are followed by references to footnotes they are indicated thus: (n + number of footnote).

Abbott, George, Archbishop of Canterbury (1562-1633), 258
Academiarum Examen (Webster), 108, 165, 178, 341
Acontius, Jacobus (Giacomo Aconio, 1500?-1566?), 227
Addison, Joseph (1672-1719), 366; on Puritanism, 214
Address of the Lost Soul to the Body, The, 44
Advancement of Learning, The (Bacon), 81f, 144, 159, 246, 305
'Agreement of the People, The', 287
Agrippa, Henry Cornelius (Cornelius Heinrich, 1486-1535), as skeptic, 2f, 148f; Nashe on, 155; see Obscurantism, Skepticism
Albright, Evelyn May, on Spenser, 70 (n94)
Allen, M. S., on Marston, 52
Althusius, Johannes (1557-1638), 269
Ames, William (1576-1633), 194; as casuist, 189; as Calvinist, 293
Anabaptists, the, Taylor on, 233 (n156)
Anatomy of Melancholy, The (Burton), 153f
Andrewes, Lancelot (1555-1626), 28; on God's attributes, 10 (n15); on providence, 23; on natural religion, 96f; and deism, 117; and the Bible, 189; as casuist, 190 (n10); on monarchy, 247
Anglican Church, the, and deism, 117f; and the Bible, 191; and tradition, 215-20; see Sir Thomas Browne, John Donne, George Herbert, Thomas Hobbes, Richard Hooker, William Laud, 'The *via media*' (V.ii), 'Anglican Rationalism' (V.v)
Anniversaries, The (Donne), 75
Annus Mirabilis (Dryden), 178
Anselm, St (1033-1109), 137, 138
Anthropomorphism, in Renaissance theology, 7-12, 144f
Antidote against Atheism (More), 129, 159
Aphorisms (Whichcote), 125, 126, 131
Apologetical Narration, 280f
Apology for Raymond Sebond (Montaigne), 149ff, 332f
Apology for Smectymnuus, An (Milton), 273

Apology . . . of the Power of God, An (Hakewill), 9, 82ff
Apostles Creed, the, 223
Appeal to the German Nobility (Luther), 249
Aquinas, St Thomas (1225?-1274), 9, 66; rationalism of, 4f, 91f; on human knowledge, 6; on providence, 13; on human misery, 43; and Taylor, 65; on law, 94; and deism, 116, 117; and transubstantiation, 135; and scholastic realism, 136ff; on the intellectual soul, 141; on pre-existing ideas, 141 (n18); on astronomy, 167; and Bacon, 173; epistemology of, 309; see Rationalism, Scholasticism
Areopagitica (Milton), 273, 280
Argyle, Earl of, see Campbell, Archibald
Ariosto, Ludovico (1474-1533), 2
Aristotle (384-322 B.C.), 163; and Ramus, 98; and Ockham, 138; in the Renaissance, 146, 310 (n20), 312; logic of, 165; Selden on, 166 (n111); Webster on, 179; Hobbes on, 240, 244, 339; and Galileo, 315ff; Spinoza on, 324f; Ross on, 355; see Rationalism, Scholasticism
Arminianism, and Cambridge Platonists, 126; and Milton, 131f, 221 (n104); and Taylor, 254
Arminius, Jacobus (Jacobus Härmensen, 1560-1609), 221 (n104)
Army debates, the, see Putney debates, the
Arraignment of Mr Persecution, The (Overton), 106, 285
Ascham, Roger (1515-1568), on goodness, 30; on mathematics, 321
Ashley, Robert (1565-1641), translator of Louis le Roy, 70 (n95)
Athanasian Creed, the, 224
Attributes, the doctrine of, 9-12
Aubrey, John (1626-1697), on Andrewes, 190 (n10)
Augustine, St (354-430), 66ff; and Luther, 2; on providence, 13; on the Fall, 32f; on election, 35; dualism of, 43, 297; on sex, 53; on knowledge, 91
Averroists, the, naturalism of, 3, 167; and Petrarch, 93, 147

Bacon, Sir Francis, first Baron Verulam and Viscount St Albans (1561–1626), 4, 21, 78ff, 162, 164, 165, 303, 304; *Instauratio magna*, 4; on God, 10; skepticism of, 44, 154, 155; on progress, 81f; Glanvill on, 89; and Fulke Greville, 153; on Roman Catholics, 158; and Descartes, 161; empiricism of, 167; on religion, 119, 168, 169, 172; methodology of, 169, 305, 316, 326–31; on scholasticism, 170f; on Telesio, 171 (n126); on natural knowledge, 171ff, 325; on logic, 176; and Puritanism, 179; and Locke, 186; on Elizabethan conformity, 197; and Robert Greville, 227; on the law of nature, 241; political theory of, 246f; on final cause, 306f; and Galileo, 314f; on authority, 324; on the doctrine of form, 325f, 330; on induction, 329; style of, 341; and Boyle, 350, 352; and Ross, 356

Baillie, Robert (1599–1662), 257 (n38), 281

Baldwin, William (fl. 1547), 47

Bancroft, Richard, Archbishop of Canterbury (1544–1610), 196

Baptists, the, 261

Barclay, Alexander (1475?–1552), 50

Barker, Arthur, 277

Barksted, William (fl. 1611), 50 (n22)

Barneveldt, Jan van Olden (1547?–1619), 221 (n104)

Baronius (or Baronio), Cesare (1538–1607), 320

Barrow, Henry (d. 1593), 260

Barrow, Isaac (1630–1677), 322

Barth, Karl, 309

Bastard, Thomas (1566–1618), 51 (n24)

Bastwick, John (1593–1654), trial of, 256, 257 (n38); and the Independents, 280

Baxter, Richard (1615–1691), on providence, 17, 19, 20; and human misery, 46; on human knowledge, 93 (n11), 102 (n42); on piety, 175; as casuist, 189; on salvation, 207f, 209; on sin, 209f; on the ministry, 212 (n69); on heaven, 214; on the law of nature, 241; on sects, 261 (n51); on Charles I, 267; on the Westminster Assembly, 275; on Cromwell, 336; style of, 342; on sensation, 350 (n163); see Presbyterians

Beard, Thomas (d. 1632), 49

Beaumont, Sir John (1583–1627), 50 (n22)

Behemoth (Hobbes), 219

Bellarmine (or Bellarmino), Roberto (1542–1621), political theory of, 251, 269

Bentley, Richard (1662–1742), on Galileo, 321; and Newton, 353

Bérenger of Tours (998–1088), 135

Berkeley, George (1685–1753), 366

Bernard of Cluny, St (fl. 1150), 44, 45

Bible, the, authority of, in the seventeenth century, 187–94

Birch, Thomas (1705–1766), on Boyle, 350

Bloody Tenent, The (Williams), 280, 300ff

Bodin, Jean (1530–1596), political theory of, 1; on progress, 68, 78, 80f

Boethius, Anicius Manilius Severinus (475?–524?), on providence, 13, 110; and Spenser, 70 (n94)

Boileau-Despréaux, Nicholas (1636–1711), and Descartes, 332

Bolingbroke, first Viscount (Henry Saint-John, 1678–1751), 366

Boniface III, Pope (fl. seventh century), 192

Book of Common Prayer, the, 196, 275

Book of Discipline, The (Cartwright), 259

Book of Sports, The, 256 (n37)

Boorde, Andrew (1490?–1549), 3

Bosco, Johannes de Sacro (fl. 1230), 73f

Bossuet, Jacques Bénigne (1627–1704), on providence, 14

Bound (or Bownde), Nicholas (d. 1613), 256 (n37)

Boyle, Robert (1627–1691), on Descartes, 12; and More, 130; and Hobbes, 347; positivism of, 350ff; theology of, 351ff; on materialism, 354 (n176)

Bradford, William (1590–1657), 18f; on sects, 265 (n60)

Brahe, Tycho (1546–1601), 72, 73, 89; and Kepler, 313; and Copernicus, 318

Bramhall, John (1594–1663), and Hobbes, 346

Brandenburg, the House of, and Calvinism, 37

Brant, Sebastian (1457–1521), 50

Briggs, Henry (1561–1630), 83

Bright, Timothy (1551?–1615), 338

Bristol, the fall of, 286

Brooke, first and second Barons, see Greville, Fulke and Robert

Browne, Robert (1550?–1633?), 197 (n21), 260

Browne, Sir Thomas (1605–1682), 30, 45, 98; on God, 10; on providence, 12, 13, 17, 18; on man's dignity, 26, 28; on the Fall, 31; on human misery, 48; on change, 56–9, 66, 74, 75; on authority, 81; on natural religion, 119f; as skeptic, 154; and Roman Catholics, 157; on truth, 158f; on error, 160; on the Schoolmen, 177; on the Anglican Church, 201; on sensation, 335; and Ross, 356

Bruised Reed and Smoking Flax, The (Sibbes), 46, 212

INDEX 379

Bruno, Giordano (1548?-1600), 21, 312; and Spenser, 70 (*n*94); and astronomy, 73, 318
Buchanan, George (1506-1582), political theory of, 268f
Bunyan, John (1628-1688), 212; on learning, 106, 107; and Roman Catholics, 158 (*n*81); and the Bible, 189; on salvation, 208f; on sin, 210; style of, 343
Burckhardt, Jakob (1818-1897), 7, 310
Burnet, Thomas (1635?-1715), and Newton, 353
Burton, Henry (1578-1648), 256, 257 (*n*38)
Burton, Robert (1577-1640), 53 (*n*31); on the Fall, 31, 32; on human misery, 48; and Donne, 62; on time, 65; and science, 76f; and natural religion, 120; skepticism of, 147, 153f; on Roman Catholics, 158; on the Schoolmen, 176; on Sectarians, 216; on the Anglican Church, 255 (*n*31); on Galileo, 321; see Skepticism
Burtt, E. A., on Neo-Platonism, 309; on seventeenth-century science, 334
Butler, Samuel (1612-1680), on Sectarians, 104 (*n*49); on religious individualism, 217; on Presbyterians, 251; on the Royal Society, 331; on experimental philosophy, 363 (*n*199)

Cabala, the, and More, 130
Calvin, Jean (1509-1564), 9, 25, 28, 79, 90; on providence, 13, 14, 16 (*n*29); on the Fall, 31-6; and Thomistic rationalism, 36; on individualism, 36; psychology of, 40 (*n*110); on human misery, 45f; on decay, 67; and Hooker, 93; on deism, 117; on truth, 168; and Montaigne, 168; and Augustine, 168; on natural truth, 168f; and the Bible, 173, 188; and Webster, 179; on the spirit, 205f, 259; on evil, 209; political theory of, 262; in the seventeenth century, 291-302; on Christian liberty, 3, 292; dualism of, 297; see St Augustine, Richard Baxter, Martin Luther, Presbyterians
Cambridge Platonists, the, 22, 124-31; and right reason, 97f; and Lord Herbert, 121; and mathematics, 128f; see Natural religion, Rationalism
Cambridge University, and Ramean logic, 98 (*n*33); and Calvinism, 211f
Campanella, Tommaso (1568-1639), 81; on nature, 320; Huygens on, 324 (*n*79)
Campanella Revived (Stubbe), 362
Campbell, Archibald, Marquis of Argyle and eighth Earl (1598-1661), 266

Campion, Edmund (1540-1581), 157, 197
Campo Santo, the (Pisa), 47
Capel, Arthur, Earl of Essex (1631-1683), 286
Carbery, Lady (Frances Altham Vaughan, d. 1650), Taylor's sermon on, 75
Carbery, Lord, see Vaughan, Richard
Cardan (or Cardano), Girolamo (1501-1576), 81; on truth, 313 (*n*29)
Carpenter, Nathanael (1589-1628?), on Aristotle, 177
Cartwright, Thomas (1535-1603), 28, 195, 203, 250, 259, 260, 261; and Hooker, 93; and Whitgift, 198; on church discipline, 206, 212 (*n*68); see Presbyterians
Cary, Lucius, second Viscount Falkland (1610?-1643), on the Anglican Church, 225, 226; and Presbyterians, 267
Casaubon, Méric (1599-1671), 111 (*n*69), 355; conservatism of, 357f
Cases of Conscience (Perkins), 211
Cassirer, Ernst, on Cusanus, 310 (*n*18)
Castellio (or Castalion or Châteillon), Sébastien (1515-1563), 227
Castiglione, Baldassare (1478-1529), 309
Casuistry, 189f
Cellini, Benvenuto (1500-1571), 310
Celsus, Aulus Cornelius (first century), 3
Censure upon . . . the History of the Royal Society, A (Stubbe), 262
Centilogium (Ockham), 143
Chaderton, Laurence (1536?-1640), 211
Changeling, The (Middleton), 56
Chapman, George (1559?-1634), 30, 50 (*n*22), 53 (*n*31), 155; on human misery, 47; on human reason, 96, 97 (*n*26); and Neo-Stoicism, 111ff, 116
Charles I of England (1600-1649), and the Presbyterians, 264f, 266, 286; and the Independents, 284, 297
Chaucer, Geoffrey (1340?-1400), 50, 145
Cheynell, Francis (1608-1665), and Chillingworth, 226
Chillingworth, William (1602-1644), 156, 157; and Calvinism, 42; and the Cambridge Platonists, 125f; as skeptic, 154; and scholasticism, 174; on the Bible, 188, 222ff; on reason, 194; on toleration, 202; on truth, 226
Christian Liberty, Luther on, 291f; Calvin on, 292; Milton on, 296; Webster on, 297f; Dell on, 297; see Covenantal theology
Christian Virtuoso, The (Boyle), 352
Chubb, Thomas (1679-1747), 309
Cicero, Marcus Tullius (106-43 B.C.), on Stoicism, 111; on natural law, 241 (*n*176)
City of God, The (Augustine), 43, 54, 67
Clarendon, first Earl of, see Hyde, Edward

INDEX

Cochrane, Charles Norris, 91 (*n*3)
Coke, Sir Edward (1552-1634), political theory of, 247f; and Laud, 256
Coleridge, Samuel Taylor (1772-1834), on Chapman's Homer, 112 (*n*72); on Laud, 258; on Newton's theology, 354
Colet, John (1467?-1519), 148
Collier, Thomas (fl. 1645-1691), 205
Comenius, Johann Amos (1592-1670), 179
Common notions, the, of Lord Herbert, 121f; see Deism, Rationalism
Confirmatio Thesium (Erastus), 248 (*n*10)
Congregationalists, the, 259f, 261
Congreve, William (1670-1729), and Tillotson, 343 (*n*144)
Contemptus mundi, the tradition of, 43-50
Copernicus, Nikolaus (1473-1543), 2; influence in the seventeenth century, 65f, 72-5; on astronomy, 311f; and Bacon, 324
Coriolanus (Shakespeare), 249
Cornwallis, Sir William (d. 1631?), on man, 29; on time, 75; as skeptic, 153
Correspondence, the theory of in Renaissance cosmology, 26ff
Cotton, John (1584-1652), 212; political theory of, 251
Council of Trent, the, and Thomism, 1, 144; Hooker and Browne on, 157; Donne on, 158
Covenant, the, 266, 268
Covenantal theology, 291-302
Cowley, Abraham (1618-1667), on Bacon, 170; Stubbe on, 364
Craig, Hardin, 53 (*n*31), 98 (*n*33)
Crane, R. S., 66 (*n*83)
Crashaw, Richard (1613?-1649), on God, 10
Croll, Morris, on seventeenth-century prose style, 341
Cromwell, Oliver (1599-1658), on providence, 20; and Beard, 49; and the Presbyterians, 277; as general, 286; and Parliament, 287; and the Independents, 288; and the Diggers, 290 (*n*129); at the Putney debates, 288ff
Cromwell, Thomas (1485?-1540), 256
Cudworth, Ralph (1617-1688), 125, 126, 127, 128, 131; on providence, 22; on scholasticism, 178; on atheism, 241f; political theory of, 252 (*n*20); and Hobbes, 346; on Boyle, 352 (*n*169)
Culverwel, Nathanael (d. 1651?), 125
Cumming, W. P., on Spenser, 70 (*n*94)
Cusanus, Nicholas (Nicolaus de Cusa, 1401-1464), 149, 310 (*n*18)
Cyprian (Thascius Caecilius Cyprianus, d. 258), on time, 68

Dante Alighieri (1265-1321), 28; rationalism of, 4; and Aquinas, 136
Davies, Godfrey, on Arminianism, 221 (*n*104)
Davies, Sir John (1569-1626), as skeptic, 152; on sensation, 333f
Da Vinci, Leonardo (1452-1519), modernism of, 310, 311; on Copernicus, 324
De docta ignorantia (Cusanus), 149
De doctrina Christiana (Milton), 39, 132
Defensio regia (Salmasius), 260
Degeneration, the theory of, 65-78
De incertitudine et vanitate scientiarum et artium (Agrippa), 148f, 155
Deism, 116-24; see Edward Herbert, Natural religion, Rationalism, 'Natural Theology' (III. iv)
Dekker, Thomas (1570?-1641?), 166; on human misery, 48f; as dramatist, 54
Dell, William (d. 1664), anti-rationalism of, 104-8; on Christian liberty, 297; see Obscurantism
Deloney, Thomas (1543?-1607?), and Roman Catholics, 157; style of, 342
De magnete (Gilbert), 73, 155
Democritus Platonissans (More), 129
De occulta philosophia (Agrippa), 148
Descartes, René (1596-1650), 4, 80, 162, 164, 165, 235f, 303; on God, 12; on providence, 13, 22; dualism of, 21f, 163, 332; and Calvin, 36; as skeptic, 44, 154; Glanvill on, 89, 180; on reason, 98 (*n*32), 332f; and religion, 119; and Lord Herbert, 121; rationalism of, 122ff; on authority, 161; methodology of, 305; on final cause, 307f; on sensation, 317; on mathematics, 321f, 334; on the body-soul relationship, 337 (*n*121); on free will, 337 (*n*122); on Hobbes, 346; reputation in the Restoration, 354 (*n*176); see Rationalism, Spinoza
De veritate (Herbert), 121f
Devotions upon Emergent Occasions (Donne), 60
Dewey, John, on Hobbes, 336f
De Wulf, Maurice, on scholasticism, 163
Dialecticae libri duo (Ramus), 100
Dialogues Concerning Two New Sciences (Galileo), 315
Digby, Sir Kenelm (1603-1665), 180; Glanvill on, 89; and Ross, 165, 356f
Diggers, the, 261, 290 (*n*129)
Digges, Thomas (d. 1595), 73, 164
Dilthey, Wilhelm, 314
Dioscorides, Pedacius (first or second century), 3
Directory, The, 268, 275, 276 (*n*89)
Discourse of the Light of Nature (Culverwel), 125

INDEX

Discourse of Things above Reason, A (Boyle), 352
Discours de la Methode (Descartes), 122f, 240, 305, 356
Dit de trois morts et des trois vifs, 46
Divine right, the theory of, 238, 247f, 250f; see the House of Stuart, William Laud, John Milton, the Social contract
Dod, John (1549?–1645), 212
Donne, John (1573–1631), 30, 53 (n31); as satirist, 4, 51; on God, 10; on miracles, 24; on human dignity, 27; on the Anglican Church, 28, 253 (n24); on the Fall, 32; on death and time, 56f, 59–62; on change, 75f; and natural religion, 117, 118; as skeptic, 147; and Roman Catholics, 158, 191; on truth, 159; on human reason, 160, 194, 221; on the religious life, 174; on the Bible, 189; on the Puritans, 216; on Copernicus, 319; see the Anglican Church
Downame, George (d. 1634), on Ramean logic, 98 (n33), 101
Drayton, Michael (1563–1631), 47, 155
Dryden, John (1631–1700), on providence, 17, 87; on literary authority, 69 (n90); on latitudinarian theology, 131; on experimental philosophy, 178; on Biblical interpretation, 219 (n97); style of, 343; and the Royal Society, 361
Du Bartas, Guillaume de Salluste (1544–1590), on mathematics, 318
Doctor Dubitantium (Taylor), 62, 97, 194, 230, 233–38
Duns Scotus, Joannes (1265?–1308), 135ff, 138, 142
Dürer, Albrecht (1471–1528), 47
Durie, John (1596–1680), 179
Dutch Courtesan, The (Marston), 54

Earle, John (1601?–1665), on logic, 166; on the Anglican Church, 202; on the Puritans, 218
Edgehill, battle of, 275
Edict of Nantes, the, 37
Edwards, Jonathan (1703–1758), 110, 308f
Edwards, Richard (1523?–1566), 48
Edwards, Thomas (1599–1647), 196, 261 (n51), 276, 280 (n97), 281, 282
Eikon Basilikon, 202, 258 (n42), 274; see John Gauden
Eikonoklastes (Milton), 274
Eius qui immobilis (Paul III), 196
Election, the doctrine of, 34ff, 206; see St Augustine, John Calvin
Elements, the four, 26
Elizabeth I of England (1533–1603), and Roman Catholics, 196; and the *via media*, 197; see the Anglican Church

Elizabethan Settlement, the, 37, 195, 196
Elyot, Sir Thomas (1490?–1546), 1, 3, 98, 338
Emmanuel College, Cambridge, and the Cambridge Platonists, 125; and Puritanism, 211
Empiricism, and natural religion, 119f; and science, 303f
Entretien avec M. Saci (Pascal), 151
Epictetus (60?–120?), 111
Epistles (Hall), 114
Erasmus, Disiderius (1465?–1536), 98; conservatism of, 1, 2, 3,; on progress, 79; anti-clericalism in, 156; and scholasticism, 173f
Erastianism, 195, 238; and Hobbes, 245; and the House of Stuart, 248f
Erastus, Thomas (1524–1583), 248 (n10)
Erigena, Johannes Scotus (800?–891?), 162
Esdras, books of, 68
Essays in Divinity (Donne), 118
Essay towards a Real Character and a Philosophical Language (Wilkins), 343
Essex, Earl of, see Capel, Arthur
Ethics (Spinoza), 307f
Evelyn, John (1620–1706), on providence, 20
Examen vanitatis doctrinae gentium (Pico della Mirandola), 149
Experimental philosophy, see Chapter VII, *passim*

Faerie Queene, The (Spenser), 38f, 74
Fahie, J. J., on Galileo, 315 (n34)
Fairfax, Thomas, third Baron Fairfax of Cameron (1612–1671), 105, 286
Falkland, second Viscount, see Cary, Lucius
Fall, the doctrine of the, 30–6; see St Augustine, John Calvin, John Milton
Fall of Man, The (Goodman), 66, 77
Fenn, William H., on Calvinism, 35 (n100)
Ferne, Henry (1602–1662), 248 (n6)
Ficino, Marsilio (1433–1499), as Neo-Platonist, 3, 309; on human dignity, 45; and the Cambridge Platonists, 127
Fideism, 146f; see Skepticism
Fifth Monarchy Men, the, 85, 203, 261
Filmer, Sir Robert (d. 1653), and the law of nature, 284
Final cause, disesteem in the seventeenth century, 306ff; see Empiricism, Methodology, Positivism, Rationalism
Fischer, Kuno, on scholastic realism, 138
Fisher, John (i.e. John Percy, 1569–1641), 157
Flores doctorum (Thomas Hibernicus), 166
Fludd, Robert (1574–1637), 179

Fontenelle, Bernard le Bovier de (1657–1757), 82
Ford, John (fl. 1639), on sex, 53 (*n*31)
Formula of Concord, the, 36f
Francis of Assisi, St (1182–1226), 45
Franco-Gallia (Hotman), 263
François I of France (1494–1547), and Calvin, 36, 67
Frank, Sebastian (1499?–1542?), 227
Fraunce, Abraham (fl. 1587–1633), on Ramean logic, 98 (*n*33), 101, 103; on sensation, 333
Free and Impartial Censure of the Platonick Philosophie, A (Parker), 178
Fuller, Thomas (1608–1661), on providence, 22; and Aquinas, 156; on Selden, 276 (*n*90); on Perkins' style, 342
Further Discovery of M. Stubbe, A (Glanvill), 362

Galen (Claudius Galenus; b. 130?), 3
Galileo Galilei (1564–1642), 6, 13, 80, 155, 164, 167, 303; astronomical discoveries of, 7, 72; Glanvill on, 89; methodology of, 314ff; and Copernicus, 315; metaphysics of, 316f, 334; theology of, 317, 319f; letter to the Duchess of Tuscany, 319f
Gangraena (Edwards), 276
Gascoigne, George (1525?–1577), 51
Gassendi, Pierre (1592–1655), 21f; Glanvill on, 89; and Descartes, 21f; on mathematics, 354
Gauden, John (1605–1662), and *Eikon Basilikon*, 274
Gentle Craft, The (Deloney), 342
Gilbert, William (1540–1603), 73; on authority, 155; Huygens on, 324 (*n*79)
Glanvill, Joseph (1636–1680), on progress, 88f; and More, 130; and Stubbe, 162, 362–5; on scholasticism, 180ff; on Galileo, 321; on mathematics, 322f; and Hobbes, 347; positivism of, 348ff; on experimental philosophy, 358–62; and Descartes, 361 (*n*196)
Golden Chain, A (Perkins), 211
Gonville and Caius College, Cambridge, 105
Gooch, G. P., on the Anglican Church, 255
Goodman, Godfrey (1583–1656), 66; and skepticism, 44; on time, 68, 78; *The Fall of Man*, 77; on Ramean logic, 103
Goodwin, John (1594–1665), on second causes, 24; on Royalists, 283, 284; on natural rights, 288; on persecution, 289
Goodwin, Thomas (1600–1680), 212, 277; and the Presbyterians, 280, 281
Gorboduc (Sackville-Norton), 249
Gorgeous Gallery of Gallant Inventions, A, 48

Gorgias (485?–380? B.C.), 163
Gouge, William (1578–1653), 212
Grace Abounding (Bunyan), 208
Grand Remonstrance, the, 267
Gratian(us) (fl. 1150), 94
Graves, Frank P., on Ramean logic, 98 (*n*33)
Greene, Robert (1560?–1592), 2
Greene, Robert, and Thomas Lodge, *Looking-Glass for London and England, A*, 15, 49, 97 (*n*26)
Greenlaw, Edwin A., on Spenser, 70 (*n*94)
Greville, Fulke, first Baron Brooke (1554–1628), as skeptic, 149, 152f
Greville, Robert, second Baron Brooke (1608–1643), on progress, 85; and the Cambridge Platonists, 125f; on prelacy, 213; on truth, 226–9
Grimald, Nicholas (1519–1562), 111 (*n*69)
Grotius, Hugo (1583–1645), political theory of, 269ff; see the Law of nature, the Social contract
Guilpin, Edward (or Everard, fl. 1598), 51 (*n*24)

Hake, Edward (fl. 1579), 51
Hakewill, George (1578–1649), on time, 66, 68, 77; on progress, 82ff; and Jonston, 85; and Glanvill, 88; see the idea of Progress
Hales, John (1584–1656), on truth, 160f, 226; on piety, 175; on Biblical interpretation, 218; on the Synod of Dort, 221 (*n*104); sermons of, 224f
Hall, John (1627–1656), 179; on progress, 86
Hall, Joseph (1574–1656), as satirist, 51, 52 (*n*25); and Neo-Stoicism, 114, 116; as casuist, 189; as an Anglican apologist, 257 (*n*38)
Haller, William, 285f
Hampden, John (1594–1643), 267
Hampton Court Conference, the, 250, 255
Harington, Sir John (1561–1612), 49; on Agrippa, 148 (*n*31); on the Puritans, 213; on James I, 248; on the Hampton Court Conference, 250
Harris, Victor, 77 (*n*123)
Hartlib, Samuel (d. 1670?), 179
Harvey, Gabriel (1545?–1630), on change, 2, 68; on human reason, 97 (*n*26); on Stoicism, 113; on Wilson, 165; on religious controversy, 193; on sensation, 333
Hawkins, Sir John (1532–1595), 2
Hazlitt, William (1778–1830), on Taylor, 64 (*n*78)
Headlong Hall (Peacock), 89
'Heads of the Proposals, The', 287

INDEX 383

Helwys, Thomas (1550?-1616?), 260 (*n*47)
Henderson, Alexander (1583?-1646), 257 (*n*38)
Henry VI (Shakespeare), 157
Henry VIII of England (1491-1547), and Paul III, 196
Henson, H. Hensley, on Erastianism, 248 (*n*10), 254; on the Westminster Assembly, 275
Herbert, Edward, first Baron Herbert of Cherbury (1583-1648), and natural reason, 97, 119; and deism, 120ff; and the Cambridge Platonists, 125f; see René Descartes, Rationalism
Herbert, George (1593-1633), 28, 30; on providence, 23 (*n*61), 25; and Donne, 61; on the Anglican Church, 105, 201; and tradition, 215
Heresiography (Pagitt), 276
Heywood, Jasper (1535-1598), 48
Heywood, John (1497?-1580?), 50
Hildersham, Arthur (1563-1632), 212
Hippocrates (460?-377? B.C.), 3
History of Henry VII (Bacon), 362
History of the Royal Society, The (Sprat), 87, 358, 360, 362, 364
History of the World, The (Ralegh), 152, 249
History of Tithes, The (Selden), 276 (*n*90)
Hobbes, Thomas (1588-1679), 4, 21, 41, 80, 159, 162, 165, 226, 303; on God, 10, 12 (*n*22); and the law of nature, 120, 241; and the Cambridge Platonists, 129; on Roman Catholics, 157, 177; on piety, 175; on the Bible, 188, 189; on religious individualism, 217; on Biblical interpretation, 219; and Taylor, 236, 239, 240; materialism of, 241, 336-40; absolutism of, 243ff; on religion, 245; on Sectarians, 260; on mathematics, 318, 323; on sensation, 334; epistemology of, 338ff, 343f; psychology of, 339f; on language, 340; ethics of, 344f; and Calvin, 345; influence of, 354f; and Ross, 356; and Digby, 356; see the Law of nature, Nominalism, Positivism, the Social contract
Holmby House, 287
Holyday, Barten (1593-1661), 50 (*n*22)
Holy Dying (Taylor), 62f, 64, 115
Holy Living (Taylor), 115
Honest Whore, The (Dekker), 54
Hooke, Robert (1635-1703), on progress, 87; positivism of, 348
Hooker, Richard (1554?-1600), 79, 98, 115, 119, 194, 195, 196; conservatism of, 3; on providence, 17; on the Incarnation, 27, 28; on truth, 29, 220f; on the Fall, 32; and Calvinism, 42; and Taylor, 65, 238f; on change, 74f; on human reason, 90, 199; and Aquinas, 93, 167; rationalism of, 93ff; and law, 93ff, 269; and Bacon, 95; on the limits of reason, 96; on Ramean logic, 103; and deism, 117f; and the Cambridge Platonists, 127; and Milton, 131, 132; and Petrarch, 147; on Roman Catholics, 157; on tradition, 166, 199ff, 215; and Whitgift, 198; on religious individualism, 216; on the Bible, 218f; political theory of, 252; style of, 342 (*n*139); on atheism, 355; see the Anglican Church, Rationalism
Hoopes, Robert, on Taylor's voluntarism, 238 (*n*173)
Horace (Quintus Horatius Flaccus, 65-8 B.C.), in the Renaissance, 50
Hotman, François (1524-1590), political theory of, 263
House of Stuart, the, political theory of, 246ff, 250f, 255f
Huguenots, the, political theory of, 262ff
Huizinga, J., 45 (*n*6)
Hulme, T. E., 162
Hume, David (1711-1776), 80, 178, 366
Hutchinson, Mrs Anne (1590?-1643), 106
Huygens, Christiaan (1629-1695), on Bacon, 324 (*n*79)
Hyde, Edward, first Earl of Clarendon (1609-1674), on providence, 19; on Lucius Cary, 226; on Hobbes, 244 (*n*190); on Laud, 258; and the Presbyterians, 267; on the Westminster Assembly, 275; on Lilburne, 279
Hydriotaphia (Browne), 59
'Hymne of Heavenly Love, An' (Spenser), 38

Incarnation, the doctrine of the, in Hooker, 27, 28; in St Anselm, 137
Independents, the, 259f; and the Presbyterians, 264; political activities, 277-91
Individualism, in the Renaissance, 144f; and covenantal theology, 295f
Innocent III, Pope (1161-1216), *De contemptu mundi*, 44f, 52
Institutes (Calvin), 168, 195, 262, 292, 293
Ireton, Henry (1611-1651), and the Heads of the Proposals, 287; and the Putney debates, 288ff

James I of England (1566-1625), on prelacy, 197, 198; on Hooker, 201; political theory of, 248f, 255f; and Buchanan, 268; and Kepler, 314
James, Thomas (1593?-1635?), 57 (*n*46), 177
Jean de Meung (Jean Chopinel, 1240?-1305?), 145
Jenkinson, Anthony (d. 1611), 2

Jesuits, the, as English missionaries, 196f, 198
Jewel, John (1522–1571), 194, 195, 196, 254; and the Bible, 190; *Apology*, 198 (*n*24)
John XXII, Pope (1244?–1334), 143
John of Jandun (Joannes de Janduno, fl. 1325), 144
Johnson, Francis R., on Renaissance science, 72 (*n*103), 73 (*n*106)
Johnson, Samuel (1709–1784), 69 (*n*90)
Johnson, Samuel (1696–1772), on Ramean logic, 98 (*n*33)
Jonson, Benjamin (1573?–1637), 47; as satirist, 51; on nature, 81
Jonston, John (Joannes Jonstonus, 1603–1675), on progress, 84, 85f
Justification, the doctrine of, 34
Juvenal (Decimus Junius Juvenalis, 60?–140?), 51

Kant, Immanuel (1724–1804), 178
Kepler, Johann (1571–1630), 73, 334; astronomical discoveries of, 312ff
King and No King, A (Beaumont-Fletcher), 53 (*n*31)
Kinwelmersh, Francis (d. 1580?), 48
Knollys, Hanserd (1599?–1691), on progress, 85, 267; on the Independents, 291
Knott, Edward (i.e. Matthew Wilson, 1582–1656), 157; and Chillingworth, 222 (*n*105), 224
Knox, John (1505–1572), and Mary Stuart, 37; and Calvin, 262
Kurtz, Benjamin F., on *contemptus mundi*, 44 (*n*2)
Kyd, Thomas (1557?–1595?), on God, 10, 164

Lactantius Firmianus, Lucius Caelius (fl. 310), on natural law, 241 (*n*176)
Lambeth Articles, the, 197
Langland, William (1330?–1400?), 50
Langport, 286
Languet, Hubert (1518–1581), 263
La Primaudaye, Pierre (fl. 1545), on human misery, 49f
Large Petition, the, 277
Larkey, Sanford V., on Renaissance astronomy, 73 (*n*106)
Lateran Council, the fourth, 135
Laud, William, Archbishop of Canterbury (1573–1645), 28, 105, 157, 166, 195, 201, 202, 219f, 266, 267, 281; on God, 12; and Calvinism, 42; and natural religion, 117; and Taylor, 158; and Fisher the Jesuit, 190; on prelacy, 215; and Chillingworth, 223; political theory of, 253–8; and Hooker, 254; see the Anglican Church, Erastianism, Richard Hooker, the House of Stuart
Laurentius, Andreas (André du Laurens, 1558–1609), 74 (*n*113)
Law, in antiquity and the Middle Ages, 94; see the Law of nature, the Social contract
Law of nature, the, 94, 120, 240f; Milton on, 132, 283; Wilson on, 132 (*n*152); Taylor on, 235–8, 241; Hooker on, 241; Hobbes on, 242f, 284; Prynne on, 266; Grotius on, 270f; the Independents on, 278, 283; John Goodwin on, 283; Lilburne on, 283; John Cook on, 283f; and the Putney debates, 288ff; see Deism, Natural religion, Rationalism
Legends no Histories (Stubbe), 362
Leibnitz, Gottfried Wilhelm von (1646–1714), 323, 366
Leighton, Alexander (1568–1649), 258, 265, 271
Leo X, Pope (1475–1521), 79
Le Roy, Louis (1510–1577), on progress, 68, 70f, 72, 78, 81
Leslie, Alexander (1580?–1661), 266
Letter to a Friend (Browne), 59
Levelers, the, 261; and the Putney debates, 287–90
Leviathan, The (Hobbes), 159, 337f, 345
Levinson, Ronald B., on Spenser, 70 (*n*94)
Liberty of conscience, Independents on, 280ff; and Christian liberty, 298–302
Liberty of Conscience (Robinson), 280, 284f
Liberty of Prophesying, The (Taylor), 64, 117, 233, 239, 254
Lilburne, John (1614?–1657), 108, 194, 195, 203, 219, 284; and the law of nature, 120, 283; and Bastwick, 257 (*n*38); political aims of, 261; and the Presbyterians, 277, 278; early career of, 279; and the Levelers, 287–90; and Ireton, 289; on Christian liberty, 299; see Covenantal theology, the Independents, the Social contract
Linacre, Thomas (1460?–1524), 3
Lipsius, Justus (1547–1606), as Neo-Stoic, 3, 111; on time, 68, 74; style of, 341
Litany, The (Donne), 60
Locke, John (1632–1704), 6, 178, 303, 312, 328, 365; and Ramean logic, 100; and religion, 119, 184f; and Roman Catholics, 158; and scholasticism, 175, 182–6; on Sectarians, 216; on language, 343; see Deism, Empiricism, Natural religion, Positivism
Lodge, Thomas (1558?–1625), 51; and Seneca, 111 (*n*69); see Robert Greene
Logic, Ockham's, 138f; scholastic, 164ff; Locke on, 183; see Ramean logic, Rationalism

INDEX

Lombard, Peter (1100?-1160), 5
Long Parliament, the, 250, 262, 276 (*n*89); Macaulay on, 356 (*n*37); and Charles I, 266f
Lord Herbert of Cherbury, see Herbert, Edward
Louis of Bavaria (1286-1347), 143f
Lucretius (Titus Lucretius Carus, 96?-55 B.C.), on time, 68; and Spenser, 70 (*n*94)
Luther, Martin (1483-1546), conservatism of, 2, 3; on the Fall, 31; on human misery, 45; and the Bible, 173; Glanvill on, 182; political theory of, 192f, 248f, 262; on Christian liberty, 291f; and Copernicus, 318

Macaulay, Thomas Babbington (1800-1859), on Bacon, 78; on Puritanism, 256 (*n*37)
Machiavelli, Niccoló (1469-1527), 270; and Hobbes, 336
Magdalen College, Oxford, 212
Mainwaring (or Manwaring), Roger (1590-1653), 201
Mâle, Emile, on medieval religious art, 45
Malebrance, Nicholas (1638-1715), 89
Manchester, second Earl of (Edward Montagu, 1602-1671), 286
Mandeville, Bernard (1670?-1733), 366
Manetti, Gionnozzo (1396-1459), 45
Marcus Aurelius Antonius (121-180), 111
Marlowe, Christopher (1564-1593), *Tamburlaine*, 16; and Neo-Stoicism, 111, 113
Marsiglio (or Marsilius) of Padua (Marsiglio Mainardino, 1270-1342), 144
Marston, John (1575?-1634), 62, 78; as satirist, 51ff; as dramatist, 54ff; and Neo-Stoicism, 111ff
Martial (Marcus Valerius Martialis, 43-104?), 50
Mary Stuart of Scotland, 37, 198
Materialism, in the Restoration, 354-66
Mathematics, Glanvill on, 181f; Kepler on, 313f; Galileo on, 315f, 354; Hobbes on, 318, 323, 336f, 354; Descartes on, 323f, 354; and English utilitarianism, 322f; Spinoza on, 323; Bacon on, 324; Huygens on, 324 (*n*79), 354; in the seventeenth century, 334; in the Restoration, 354; see Empiricism, Methodology, Positivism
Mather, Cotton (1663-1728), on providence, 20
Maurice of Nassau (1567-1625), 221 (*n*104)
McColley, Grant, on seventeenth-century astronomy, 72 (*n*103)
Meditations (Descartes), 348
Meditations and Vows Divine and Moral (Hall), 114

Mersenne, Marin (1588-1648), and Descartes, 322
Metaphor, 341ff
Methodology, in the seventeenth century, 304-9; Bacon on, 326-31; see Thomas Hobbes, Mathematics, Positivism
Mexio (or Mexia), Pedro (1496?-1552?), 75 (*n*119)
Micrographia (Hooke), 348
Middleton, Thomas (1570?-1627), 55, 56; on logic, 176
Millenarians, the, 261
Millenary Petition, the, 250
Miller, Perry, on Ramean logic, 98 (*n*33); on Puritan piety, 204, 205; on covenantal theology, 292 (*n*135), 294f
Milton, John (1608-1674), 30, 43, 44, 98, 194, 195, 260, 365; on God, 10, 29; on providence, 16, 18, 24f; on miracles, 22; on cosmology, 26; on human dignity, 27, 39-42; on the Fall, 32, 33 (*n*90); on election, 35 (*n*95); on sin, 35 (*n*100); and Calvinism, 42, 131; on decay, 67; on progress, 84f; on the limits of reason, 96, 295; on the moral sense, 97; on Ramean logic, 98 (*n*33); on regeneration, 90, 204; on natural religion, 119; as a Christian humanist, 131-4; and Petrarch, 147; as skeptic, 154; on truth, 156; on prelacy, 156, 203, 206f, 220; and Roman Catholics, 158; on custom and error, 159, 161f; on the Schoolmen, 175, 176f; on the Bible, 188f, 190f; on conscience, 192; on Elizabeth, 197; on the Anglican Church, 210; on works, 210f; on Puritan piety, 214; on the Sabbatarian controversy, 256 (*n*37); and Joseph Hall, 257 (*n*38); on sects, 261; political theory of, 273f; as Independent, 280ff; on liberty, 296; on Galileo, 321
Mirandola, Pico della, see Pico della Mirandola
Mirror for Magistrates, A, 47, 69
Montaigne, Michel Eyquem de (1533-1592), as skeptic, 3, 44, 149ff, 154; and Fulke Greville, 153; on sensation, 332f; style of, 341; see Skepticism
Montrose, fifth Earl and first Marquis (James Graham, 1612-1650), 286
More, Henry (1614-1687), on God's attributes, 12; on providence, 17; Glanvill on, 89, 180; as a Cambridge Platonist, 125-31; and Descartes, 125, 126, 129f; and Calvinism, 126; and science, 129f, 156; and superstition, 159; on reason, 161; and Hobbes, 346, 347; on Stubbe, 364f; see the Cambridge Platonists; Chapter III, *passim*

More, Sir Thomas (1478-1535), *The Four Last Things*, 46f
Moulin, Pierre du (1568-1658), on election, 211 (*n*67); on Boyle, 352 (*n*169)
Muggletonians, the, 260
Mutability, the theme of, 44-50; see the theory of Degeneration

Naseby, battle of, 277, 286
Nashe, Thomas (1567-1601), prose style of, 2; *Christ's Tears over Jerusalem*, 49; defense of plays, 55 (*n*39); on Agrippa, 155; and Roman Catholics, 157f; on Puritans, 342; on atheists, 355 (*n*177)
Natural religion, in the Restoration, 360ff; see Deism, Edward Herbert, John Locke, Positivism, Rationalism
Neo-Platonism, 119
Neo-Stoicism, 110-16; and deism, 118
Newbury, battles of, 275, 286
New Model Army, the, 278, 286, 287
Newton, Sir Isaac (1642-1727), 6, 13, 41, 178, 365; on God, 12; on providence, 14; and Hobbes, 347; positivism of, 352ff; and Bentley, 353; and Burnet, 353; see Mathematics, Methodology, Positivism
Nicholson, Marjorie, on seventeenth-century astronomy, 72 (*n*103); on More, 129 (*n*142)
Niebuhr, Reinhold, 309
Nominalism, and Ockham, 137-40; in the Renaissance, 144f; see Thomas Hobbes, John Locke, Positivism, Jeremy Taylor, 'The Flight from Reason' (V. vi)
Norden, John (1548-1625?), on decay, 68f, 74
Nosce Teipsum (Davies), 152
Novum Organum (Bacon), 159f, 169

Oakes, Urian (1631?-1681), on providence, 15
Obscurantism, in the Renaissance, 147ff; and the Sectarians, 104-8; see Christian liberty, William Dell, John Webster
Observations upon Some of His Majesty's Late Answers and Expresses (Parker), 272f
Ockham, William of (1270?-1349?), 79, 92, 135, 137-44, 162; and the Cambridge Platonists, 126; and Calvin, 167; and Locke, 186; and Taylor, 229, 238; see Nominalism, Scholasticism
Of the Laws of Ecclesiastical Polity (Hooker), 117, 194, 198, 252
Organon (Aristotle), 166
Overton, Richard (fl. 1642-1663), 106, 203, 219, 277, 278, 282; and the Presbyterians, 284f; on Parliament, 286f; and the Levelers, 287f; on Christian liberty, 299

Ovid (Publius Ovidius Naso, 43-17? B.C.), on time, 68; and Spenser, 70 (*n*94)
Oxford, capitulation of, 286

Padua, University of, and naturalism, 310f
Pagitt, Ephraim (1575?-1647), 261 (*n*51), 276
Paracelsus, Phillipus Aureolus (1493-1541), 3
Paradise Lost (Milton), 39ff, 133f
Paradise of Dainty Devices, The, 47f
Paradise Regained (Milton), 133, 274
Parker, Henry (1604-1652), political theory of, 272f
Parker, Matthew, Archbishop of Canterbury (1504-1575), 165f, 194, 196, 254
Parker, Samuel (1640-1688), on scholasticism, 178; positivism of, 347
Parmenides (fl. 450 B.C.), 66
Parsons (or Persons), Robert (1546-1610), 157, 197
Pascal, Blaise (1623-1662), 58, 80 (*n*126); on Descartes, 21; on providence, 24; and Donne, 61f; and Montaigne, 151; on truth, 160; on mathematics, 354
Paschasius Radbertus (Robert, Abbot of Corbie, d. 860?), 135
Paul III, Pope (1468-1549), 196, 311
Paul V, Pope (1552-1621), 196
Paul, St (d. 67?), on sex, 53; and Seneca, 110
Peacock, Thomas Love (1785-1866), on progress, 89
Perkins, William (1558-1602), 22, 28, 194, 211; on evil, 16; on second causes, 22; on the Fall, 31; on election, 35; as casuist, 189; on the Bible, 189; on salvation, 208, 209; as a Calvinist, 293
Persius (Aulus Persius Flaccus, 34-62), 50, 51
Petrarch, Francesco (1304-1374), conservatism of, 3, 43; as a Christian humanist, 92f; as skeptic, 147; *Secretum*, 310
Petrus Hispanus (Petrus Juliani, later Pope Joannes XXI, d. 1277), and Ockham, 138
Petty (or Pettus), Maximilian (fl. 1648), and the Putney debates, 288ff
Petty, Sir William (1623-1686), 179
Philosophical Touchstone, The (Ross), 356
Pico della Mirandola, Giovanni (1463-1494), on human dignity, 26, 45; and the Cambridge Platonists, 127; as skeptic, 149; as Neo-Platonist, 309
Plato (429?-347 B.C.), 312; and Calvin, 36; the *Timaeus*, 66; and Ramus, 99; and Ockham, 138; dualism of, 297; and Bacon, 323, 325 (*n*84)
Pliny the Elder (Caius Plinius Secundus, 23-79), 3

INDEX 387

Plus Ultra (Glanvill), 88f, 357, 362
Plus Ultra Reduced to a Non Plus, The (Stubbe), 362, 363
Politica methodice digesta (Althusius), 269
Pollock, Sir Frederick, on law, 94 (*n*15)
Pomponazzi, Pietro (1462–1525), and Aristotle, 2, 146; on decay, 67; psychology of, 79, 310; and the double truth, 167
Pope, Alexander (1688–1744), 366
Positivism, Locke on, 183f; in the Restoration, 347–54; see Mathematics, Methodology
Potter, Christopher (1591–1646), and Chillingworth, 222 (*n*105)
Power, Henry (1623–1668), on progress, 86; on the Schoolmen, 175
Predestination, the doctrine of, Calvin on, 34ff; Ockham on, 142; see St Augustine, Presbyterians
Prefatory Answer, A (Glanvill), 362
Presbyterians, 104; political theory of, 249ff, 259, 260–7; at the Westminster Assembly, 275f; and the Independents, 280–90; and Charles I, 287; see St Augustine, Richard Baxter, John Calvin, William Perkins, Chapter VI, *passim*
Preston, John (1587–1628), 211, 293; on covenantal theology, 294
Principia mathematica (Newton), 315, 354
Progress, the idea of, 78–89
Protagoras of Abdera (481?–411? B.C.), 163
Providence, the doctrine of, 12–25; and the Fall, 30f; and the idea of progress, 84f; and natural religion, 119; Bacon on, 172
Prynne, William (1600–1669), 194, 196, 214, 256, 257 (*n*38), 276, 280 (*n*97), 281; political theory of, 266; and Lilburne, 284
Pseudodoxia Epidemica (Browne), 58, 160, 336
Pseudo-Martyr (Donne), 118
Pseudo-St Bernard, the, 44
Ptolemaic cosmology, 9, 72, 73f, 318 (*n*46); Copernicus on, 311 (*n*23)
Puritans, the, on providence, 15, 18f; obscurantism of, 103–8; subjectivism of, 105ff; and utilitarianism, 107f; rationalism of, 109f; on the Bible, 188, 218; piety of, 204; intensity of, 206–10; reformist zeal of, 211; and holy communities, 212; individualism of, 259; see John Calvin, the Independents, the Presbyterians
Putney debates, the, 268, 278, 287–90
Puttenham, [George?] (d. 1590), 141 (*n*18)
Pym, John (1584–1643), 267
Pythagoras (582?–500? B.C.), and Kepler, 313f, 315

Quakers, the, 260, 261
Quod nihil scitur (Suarez), 149

Rabelais, François (1495?–1553), 1; as skeptic, 149
Rainborough, William (fl. 1650), at the Putney debates, 288ff
Ralegh, Sir Walter (1552?–1618), 45, 48, 78; on God, 9; on providence, 17f, 23; on causality, 18 (*n*38); as skeptic, 44, 151f; on death and time, 57f; on change, 68f; on reason, 97; and deism, 119; on divine right, 248 (*n*6); political theory of, 250
Ramean logic, 42, 98–110; and Calvinism, 101ff; and covenantal theology, 295
Ramée, Pierre de la, see Ramus, Peter
Ramus, Peter (or Petrus, 1515–1572), 98f, 165; on progress, 86
Randall, John Herman, Jr., on Renaissance naturalism, 310 (*n*20)
Ranters, the, 260
Raphael, Sanzio (1483–1520), 145
Rationalism, in the Renaissance, 4ff, 90–8, 103f; and Puritanism, 104–10; Ockham's attack on, 135–44; varieties of, 162; and the Anglican Church, 220–6; see St Thomas Aquinas, René Descartes, Richard Hooker, Baruch Spinoza, Chapter III, *passim*
Ready and Easy Way, The (Milton), 274
Realism, Ockham's attack on, 137–44; see Nominalism, Scholasticism
Reason of Church Government, The (Milton), 273
Recta ratio, see Right reason
Regnans in excelsis (Paul V), 196
Regeneration, the doctrine of, 204f; see John Calvin, Presbyterians
Relation of the Conference, A (Laud), 117, 253f
Religio Medici (Browne), 160
Religion of Protestants, The (Chillingworth), 117, 194, 222ff, 226
Remonstrance of Many Thousand, A (Overton), 286f
Remonstrance of the Army, The, 274
Reprobation, the doctrine of, 34, 205; see John Calvin, Presbyterians
Reuchlin, Johann (1455–1522), 309
Revenger's Tragedy, The (Tourneur), 54
Rheticus (or Rhaticus), Georg Joachim (1514–1576), 311 (*n*23); see Nikolaus Copernicus
Richardson, Alexander (fl. 1650), on Ramean logic, 98 (*n*33), 102f
Right reason, 92, 95, 97f, 120, 132, 156; Greville on, 228f; Taylor on, 235–8

388 INDEX

Robinson, Henry (1605?-1664), 280, 284f, 299
Robinson, John (1576?-1625), 260 (n47)
Rogers, Richard (1550?-1618), and Roman Catholics, 46, 157 (n74); on his sins, 207, 209
Rogers, Thomas (d. 1616), 256 (n37)
Roman Catholic Church, the, antagonism to, 157f; Stubbe on, 364; see William Chillingworth, John Donne, Thomas Hobbes, John Milton
Root and Branch Bill, the, 267
Roscelinus (or Roscellinus, 1050?-1122?), and St Anselm, 137
Ross, Alexander (1590-1654), on logic, 165; on Hobbes, 243 (n183); as Aristotelian, 355ff
Royal Society, the, 73, 86; and Bacon, 329, 331; and Sprat, 360; and Dryden, 361; and Stubbe, 362-5; see John Glanvill, Mathematics, Positivism, Thomas Sprat
Rule of Reason, The (Wilson), 165, 333
Rupert, Prince of the Palatinate (1619-1682), 286
Ruskin, John (1819-1900), 145
Rutherford, Samuel (1600-1661), 266, 271, 281, 292

Sabbatarian Controversy, the, 256 (n37)
Sacheverell, Henry (1674?-1724), on Hobbes and Spinoza, 21
Sackville, Thomas, first Earl of and Baron Buckhurst (1536-1608), on change, 69
Saint-Pierre, Bernardin de (1737-1814), 82
Saint's Guide, The (Webster), 336
St Bartholomew's Eve, 99, 262
Salmasius, Claudius (Claude de Saumaise, 1588-1653), 260
Saltmarsh, John (d. 1647), on sects, 261 (n51); on Christian liberty, 298
Samson Agonistes (Milton), 39, 41
Sanctification, the doctrine of, 205
Sanderson, Robert (1587-1663), 195; as casuist, 189; on the Anglican Church, 201
Satire, in the Renaissance, 50-3
Savoy Conference, the, 85
Scepsis Scientifica (Glanvill), 361 (n196)
Sceptic, The (Ralegh), 151
Schneider, Herbert and Carol, on Ramean logic, 98 (n33)
Scholasticism, the *summae*, 5; and human dignity, 5f; reaction to, in the Renaissance, 145f, 166-9, 173-86; logic, 164ff; Bacon on, 326f; see St Thomas Aquinas, William of Ockham, Rationalism, 'Custom and Error' (IV. iii)
Scire scepticos et scepticorum a jure disputationis exclusio (White), 362

Scottish Kirk, the, and Charles I, 266
Scourge of Villainy, The (Marston), 51ff, 148
Sebond, Raymond, Donne on, 118 (n96); Montaigne on, 149
Second causes, 13, 21, 22ff
Second Defense, The (Milton), 260
Secretum (Petrarch), 310
Sectarians, the, 203, 259, 260f
Secunda pastorum, 145
Seekers, the, 260
Selden, John (1584-1654), erudition of, 4; on providence, 23; and right reason, 120; on logic, 166; on Puritan prayers, 213 (n72); on religious individualism, 217; on Biblical interpretation, 218, 219; on Roman Catholics, 249; political theory of, 276 (n90)
Select Discourses (Smith), 125
Seneca, Lucius Annaeus (4? B.C.-A.D. 65), on time, 67f; and St Paul, 110; and Hall, 114
Sensabaugh, G. F., on Ford, 53 (n31)
Separatists, the, 106
Sewall, Samuel (1652-1730), 209; on providence, 20
Sexby, Edward (d. 1658), and the Putney debates, 289
Sextus Empiricus (fl. 200), and Montaigne, 149, 150; see Skepticism
Shadwell, Thomas (1642?-1692), on the Royal Society, 331
Shakespeare, William (1564-1616), on providence, 15; *Venus and Adonis*, 49; on human misery, 49; on sex, 53; and Neo-Stoicism, 113; on nature, 313
Shepard, Thomas (1604-1649), 265 (n60)
Shirley, James (1596-1666), 56 (n40)
Short Parliament, the, 266
Sibbes, Richard (1577-1635), 28, 46, 212; on God, 12; and the Bible, 189, 190; on salvation, 207; on sin, 210; on religious striving, 213f; as a Calvinist, 293; on style, 341f
Siderius nuncius (Galileo), 72
Sidney, Sir Philip (1554-1586), on goodness, 30
Skelton, John (1460?-1529), 50; funerary verse of, 46 (n12)
Skepticism, in the Renaissance, 144-54; Glanvill's, 180f; see Sir Francis Bacon, René Descartes, John Milton; Chapter IV, *passim*
'Smectymnuus', 257 (n38)
Smith, John (1618-1652), 125, 127
Smyth, John (d. 1612), 260 (n47)
Social contract, the, Hobbes on, 241-5; in the *Vindiciae contra tyrannos*, 263f; Althusius on, 269; Grotius on, 269f; Parker on, 272f; Milton on, 273f

INDEX 389

Socrates (470?–399 B.C.), and Hooker, 95; and Bacon, 326
Some Observations and Annotations (Steuart), 280
Songs and Sonnets (Donne), 147
Speculum Mundi (Swan), 72f
Spencer, Theodore, 45 (*n*6)
Spenser, Edmund (1552?–1599), 2, 30, 98, 155; conservatism of, 3; on human dignity, 37ff; and Calvinism, 42; *The Ruins of Time*, 47; as satirist, 51; on fertility, 53; on time, 68, 69f, 72 (*n*104), 74; on decay, 82; on suicide, 113; and Roman Catholics, 157
Spinoza, Baruch (or Benedict, 1632–1677), on the order of nature, 7; on God, 12; on providence, 22; on nature, 80; on reason, 98 (*n*32), 122, 124, 303; on authority, 161; methodology of, 305; on final cause, 307f; on mathematics, 323; on experience, 331; see René Descartes, Rationalism
Sprat, Thomas (1635–1713), on providence, 22; on progress, 87; on the Schoolmen, 166; and Bacon, 170, 305; on Galileo, 321; on style, 343; positivism of, 350; and experimental philosophy, 359f; see the Royal Society
Stanhope, George (1660–1728), 111 (*n*69), 114
Sterry, Peter (d. 1672), 125
Steuart, Adam (fl. 1640), 280
Stillingfleet, Edward (1635–1699), on Boyle, 352 (*n*169)
Stirling, Brents, on Spenser, 70 (*n*94)
Stoicism, 66, 235
Stradling, Sir John (1563–1637), 111 (*n*69)
Strange and Dangerous Voyage, The (James), 177
Strong, E. W., 309
Strowski, Fortunat, 146f
Style, development of, in the seventeenth century, 341ff
Stubbe(s), Henry (1632–1676), as conservative, 355; and Glanvill, 362–5
Suarez, Francisco (1548–1617), 149, 269
Summa theologica (Aquinas), 91f, 135
Summulae logicales (Petrus Hispanus), 138
Swan, John (fl. 1635), on second causes, 23f; on human dignity, 26f; on nature, 313
Swift, Jonathan (1667–1745), 52, 53, 216, 366
Symonds, John Addington (1840–1893), 310
Synod of Dort, the, 157, 221 (*n*104)

Tale of a Tub, A (Swift), 216
Taylor, A. E., 328
Taylor, Jeremy (1613–1667), 45, 162, 271; on God, 10f; on salvation, 11; on social inequality, 16; on providence, 16, 19, 23; on man, 25; on the Fall, 32; on death and time, 56f, 58, 62–5; on time, 75; and right reason, 97; and Neo-Stoicism, 115f; and Roman Catholics, 158; on the Schoolmen, 174f; and the Bible, 189; as casuist, 189; on reason, 194; on the Anglican Church, 201f; on the Puritans, 213; and tradition, 215; on religious individualism, 217; on truth, 219; on the Athanasian Creed, 224 (*n*109); anti-rationalism of, 229–38; on free will, 229f; on toleration, 231ff; political theory of, 253; on nature, 313; on sensation, 335; see the Anglican Church, the House of Stuart, William Laud, Nominalism, William of Ockham
Telesio, Bernardino (1509–1588), 79, 310; Bacon on, 171 (*n*126); Huygens on, 324 (*n*79)
Temple, Sir William (1555–1627), on Ramean logic, 98 (*n*33)
Tenure of Kings and Magistrates, The (Milton), 273f, 276
Tertullian (Quintus Septimus Florens Tertullianus, 150?–230?), 66
Theses (Erastus), 248 (*n*10)
Things indifferent, in Anglican theology, 199f, 221f; Greville on, 227f
Thirty-Nine Articles, the, 28, 220, 224; and the Westminster Assembly, 196, 275; see the Anglican Church
St Thomas Aquinas, see Aquinas, St Thomas
Thomas Hibernicus (Thomas Palmer), 166
Thomason, George (d. 1666), collection of Commonwealth pamphlets, 268
Tillotson, John, Archbishop of Canterbury (1630–1694), and Roman Catholics, 158; and Congreve, 343 (*n*144)
Tindal, Matthew (1657–1733), 309, 366
Toland, John (1670–1722), 366
Toleration Act, the (1689), 255
Tornay, Stephen Chak, on Ockham, 138 (*n*9)
Tourneur, Cyril (1575?–1626), 53 (*n*31), 62, 78; *The Atheist's Tragedy*, 15f; on sex, 54ff; and Neo-Platonism, 113
Transubstantiation, the doctrine of, 135
Travers, Walker (1548?–1635), and Hooker, 93, 195, 198 (*n*24), 203
Treatie of Humane Learning, A (Greville), 149, 152f
Treatise Concerning Eternal and Immutable Morality (Cudworth), 129
Troeltsch, Ernst, on Luther, 262 (*n*52)
Troilus and Cressida (Shakespeare), 249

True Intellectual System of the Universe, The (Cudworth), 125
Tuckney, Anthony (1599–1670), and the Cambridge Platonists, 126, 127f
Turvervil(l)e, George (1540?–1610), 51
Turnham Green, 284
Two Treatises (Digby), 356
Tyndale, William (d. 1536), and the Bible, 173; on the Schoolmen, 174

Unum Necessarium (Taylor), 65

Vanity of Dogmatizing, The (Glanvill), 88, 348, 361 (*n*196)
Vaughan, Richard, second Earl of Carbery (1600?–1686), and Taylor, 115, 234
Vestiarian controversy, the, 195, 198; see Thomas Cartwright, Presbyterians
Villey, Pierre, on Montaigne, 151
Villon, François (1431–1484?), 46, 145
Vindiciae contra tyrannos, 263f, 268
Voltaire (François Marie Arouet, 1694–1778), 366
Voluntarism, in Duns Scotus, 135; in Ockham, 142ff; in the Reformation, 145f; in Taylor, 234–8; see Nominalism

Waddington, Charles, on Ramean logic, 98 (*n*33)
Wallis, John (1616–1703), and Hobbes, 354
Walton, Izaak (1593–1683), on Hooker, 19f; on the Puritans, 219
Walwyn, William (fl. 1649), 277; on a learned ministry, 106f; on the Schoolmen, 175; political theory of, 261, 299; on the Presbyterians, 282f
Ward, Samuel (1577–1640), on sin, 210
Ward, Seth (1617–1689), 108; and Webster, 165; on mathematics, 354
Watts, William (1590?–1649), on Aristotle, 177f
Webster, John (1580?–1625), 53 (*n*31), 54ff, 58
Webster, John (1610–1682), as antirationalist, 104–8; on scholasticism, 178ff; and Glanvill, 181; on Christian liberty, 297; and Bacon, 297 (*n*143); on mathematics, 322; on sensation, 335; style of, 341; see Christian liberty, Obscurantism, the Puritans

Wentworth, Thomas, first Earl of Strafford (1593–1641), 266, 267
Wesley, John (1703–1791), 309
Westminster Assembly, the, 104, 212, 250, 262, 264, 268, 275, 276 (*n*90), 280
Westminster Confession, the, 28, 220
Whichcote, Benjamin (1609–1683), 125, 127, 131, 156, 174
White, Thomas (1593–1676), 362
White Devil, The (Webster), 54
Whitehead, A. N., on seventeenth-century science, 6, 163, 164, 332
Whitgift, John, Archbishop of Canterbury (1530?–1604), 51, 196, 197; and Cartwright, 198
Wildman, Sir John (1621?–1693), and the Putney debates, 288ff
Wilkins, John (1614–1672), on the infinite universe, 73; on style, 343; and Ross, 356
Willard, Rudolf, 44 (*n*3)
Willey, Basil, on Hobbes, 12; on seventeenth-century thought, 162f; on Glanvill, 180; on Descartes, 332
Williams, Roger (1604?–1683), 261, 277; on Christian liberty, 299–302
Williamson, George, 77 (*n*123)
Wilson, Thomas (1525?–1581), on usury, 1; on human dignity, 9; on the law of nature, 132 (*n*152); logic of, 165; on sensation, 333
Winstanley, Gerrard (fl. 1648–1652), 261; and the Diggers, 290 (*n*129)
Winthrop, John (1588–1649), on liberty, 265; on the covenant, 294
Woodhouse, A. S. P., on Spenser, 39 (*n*103) on Puritanism, 169
Work of the Beast, A (Lilburne), 279
Worthington, John (1618–1671), 125
Worthy Communicant, The (Taylor), 62
Wotton, Sir Henry (1568–1639), and the Bible, 190; on religious controversy, 216
Wren, Sir Christopher (1632–1723), on Galileo, 321
Wright, Edward (1558?–1615), on astronomy, 73, 319 (*n*54)
Wyatt, Sir Thomas (1503?–1542), 50f

Yeats, W. B., 68
Young, Edward (1683–1765), 69 (*n*90)

Zabarella, Giacomo (1533–1589), 146, 167

www.ingramcontent.com/pod-product-compliance
Lightning Source LLC
Chambersburg PA
CBHW052139300426
44115CB00011B/1443